NUASHA

OL. 56

Shonen Sunday Edition

STORY AND ART BY
UMIKO TAKAHASHI

CONTENTS

Long ago, in the "Warring States" era of Japan's Muromachi period, dog-like half demon Inuyasha attempted to steal the Shikon Jewel—or "Jewel of Four Souls"—from a village. The village priestess, Kikyo, put a stop to his thievery with an enchanted arrow. Pinned to a tree, Inuyasha fell into a deep sleep, while mortally wounded Kikyo took the jewel with her into her funeral pyre. Years passed...

In the present day, Kagome, a Japanese high school girl, is pulled down into a well and transported into the past. There she discovers trapped Inuyasha—and frees him.

When the Shikon Jewel mysteriously reappears, demons attack. In the ensuing battle, the jewel *shatters*!

Now Inuyasha is bound to Kagome with a powerful spell, and the grudging companions must battle to reclaim the shattered shards of the Shikon Jewel to keep them out of evil hands...

LAST VOLUME Sesshomaru cuts Magatsuhi down, restoring Kagome's full priestess powers and returning purifying light to the Shikon Jewel. But now Naraku is attempting to merge himself completely with the Jewel! The dog-demon brothers set upon Naraku in earnest. Naraku claims that even if he perishes, the Shikon Jewel, and thus their troubles, will go on forever. Just as the battle reaches its climax, Byakuya appears and slashes Kagome with a blade imbued with the demon power of the Meido Zangetsuha...

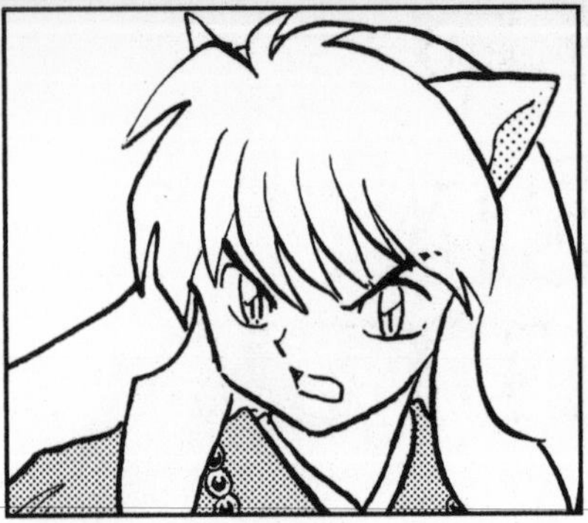

INUYASHA
Half-demon hybrid, son of a human mother and demon father. His necklace is enchanted, allowing Kagome to control him with a word.

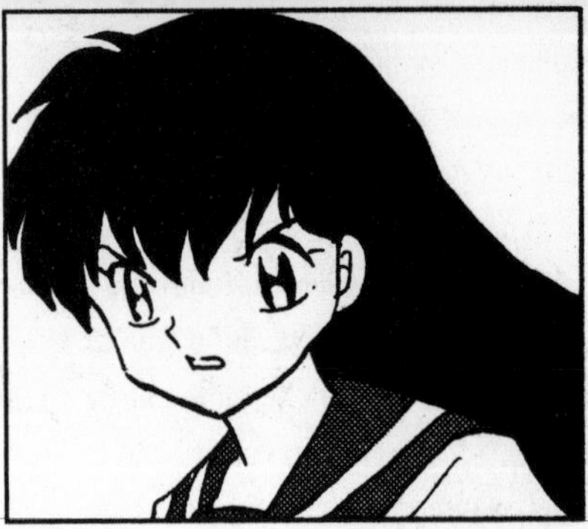

KAGOME
Modern-day Japanese schoolgirl who can travel back and forth between the past and present through an enchanted well.

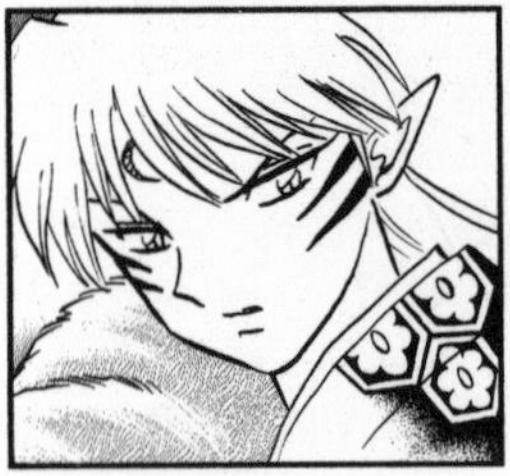

SESSHOMARU
Inuyasha's pureblood-demon half brother. They have the same demon father. Sesshomaru has a soft spot for the little human girl Rin.

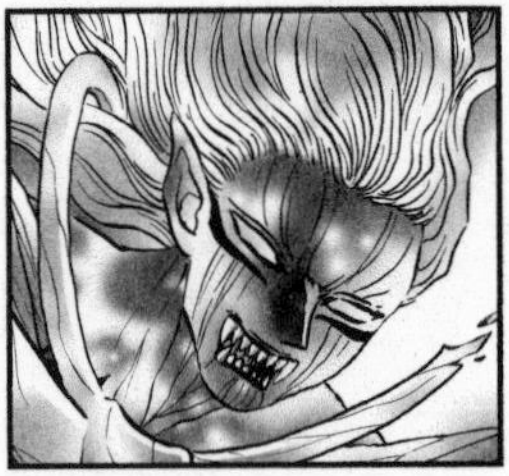

NARAKU
Enigmatic demon mastermind behind the miseries of nearly everyone in the story. He has the power to create illusions to confound his enemies.

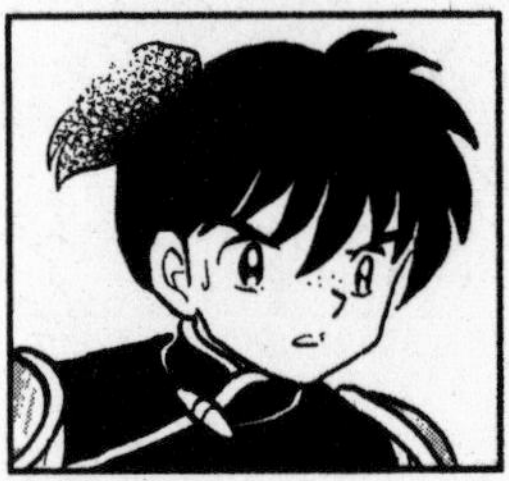

KOHAKU
Naraku controlled Kohaku with a Shikon shard and used him as a puppet. Kohaku regained his memories and is trying to redeem himself.

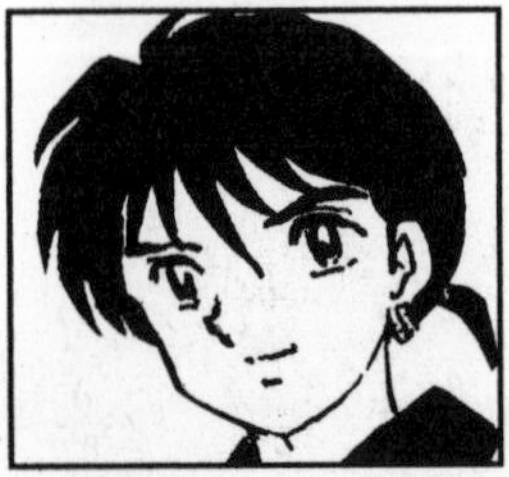

MIROKU
A Buddhist monk cursed with a mystical "Wind Tunnel" imbedded in his hand that is both a weapon and is slowly killing him.

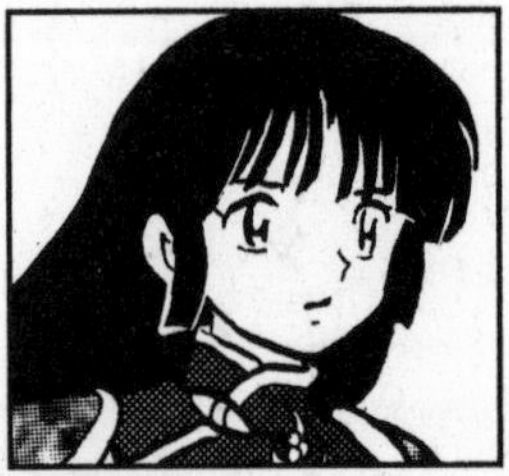

SANGO
A demon slayer from the village where the Shikon Jewel originated.

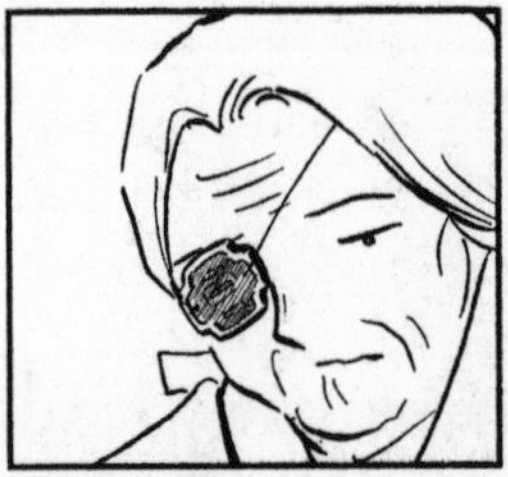

LADY KAEDE
Kikyo's little sister, now an old woman and leader of the village. She is the one who cast the spell on the necklace that allows Kagome to control Inuyasha.

SCROLL 1

AMASSING FOR BATTLE

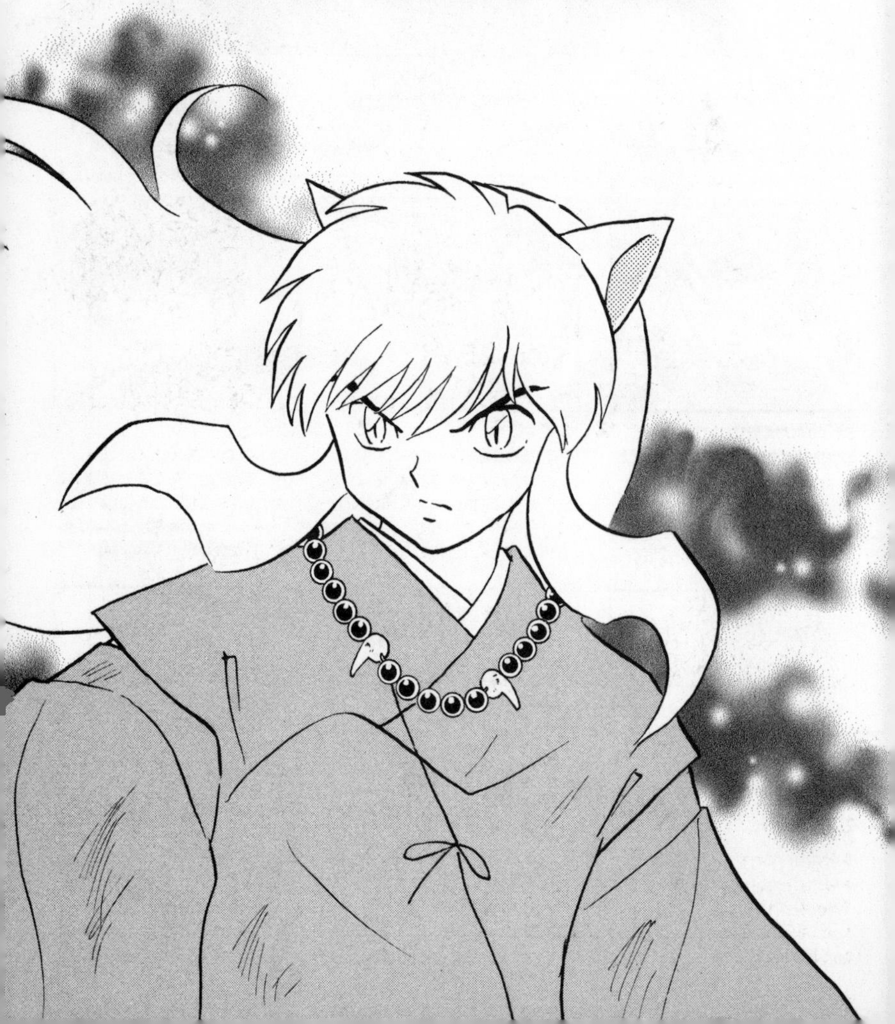

HOOO

K K K K

NARAKU
STILL LIVES...

INUYASHA!
WHAT'S TAKING
YOU SO LONG?!

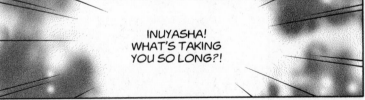

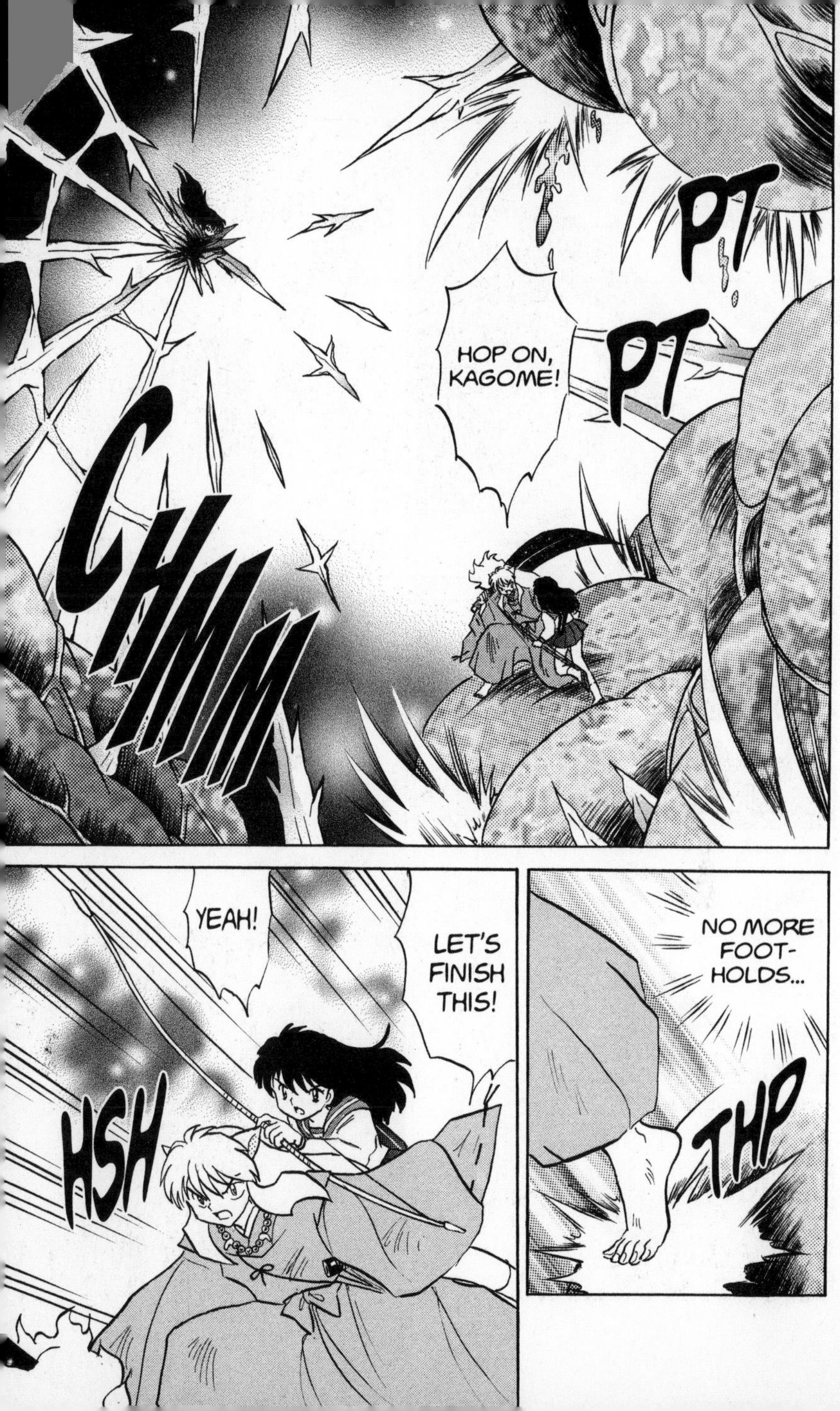
PT
PT
HOP ON, KAGOME!
CHMM
NO MORE FOOT-HOLDS...
THP
YEAH!
LET'S FINISH THIS!
HSH

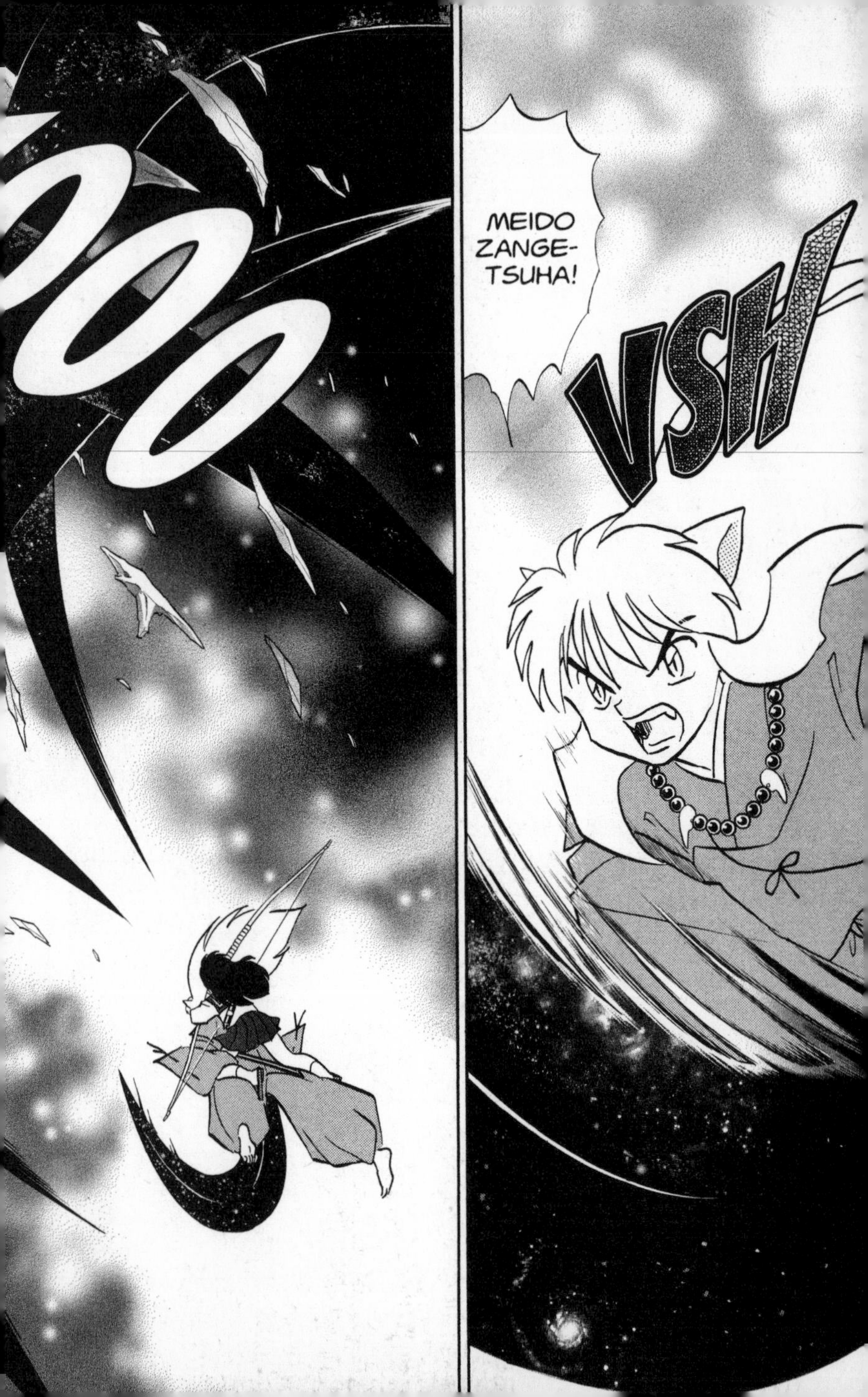
MEIDO ZANGE-TSUHA!
VSH
OOOO

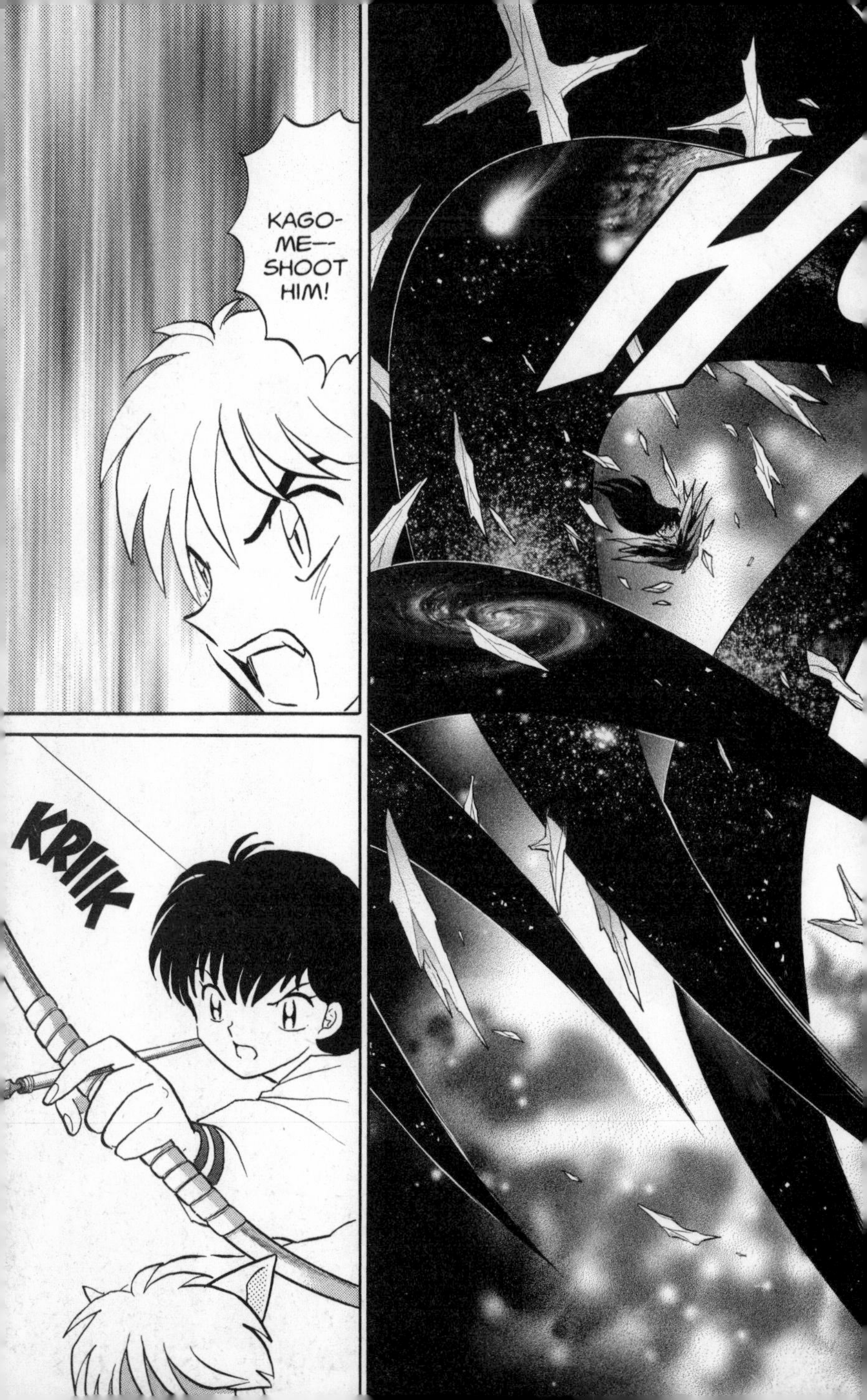
KAGO-
ME--
SHOOT
HIM!
KRIIK

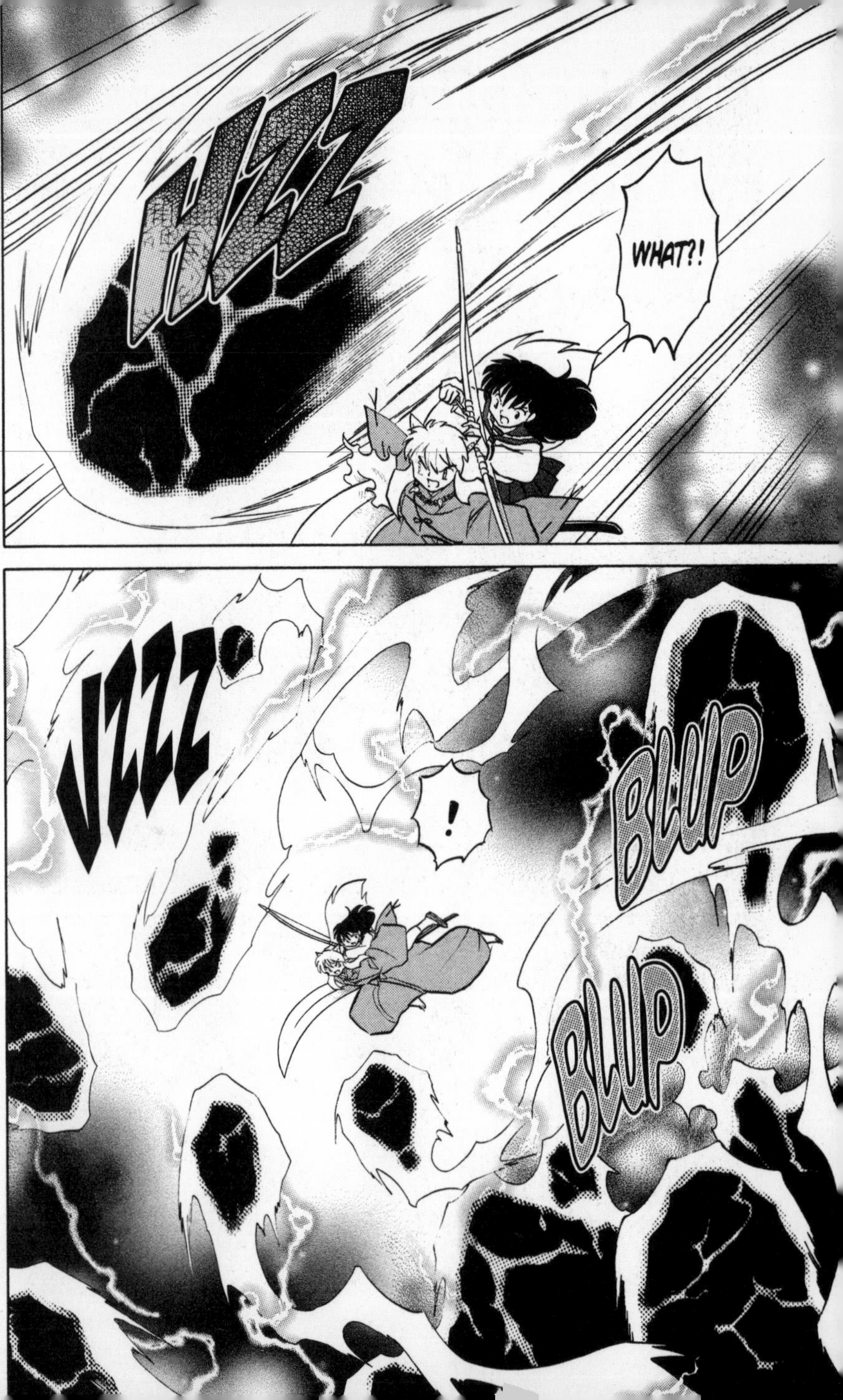
WHAT?!
HZZ
BLUP
BLUP
!
JZZZ

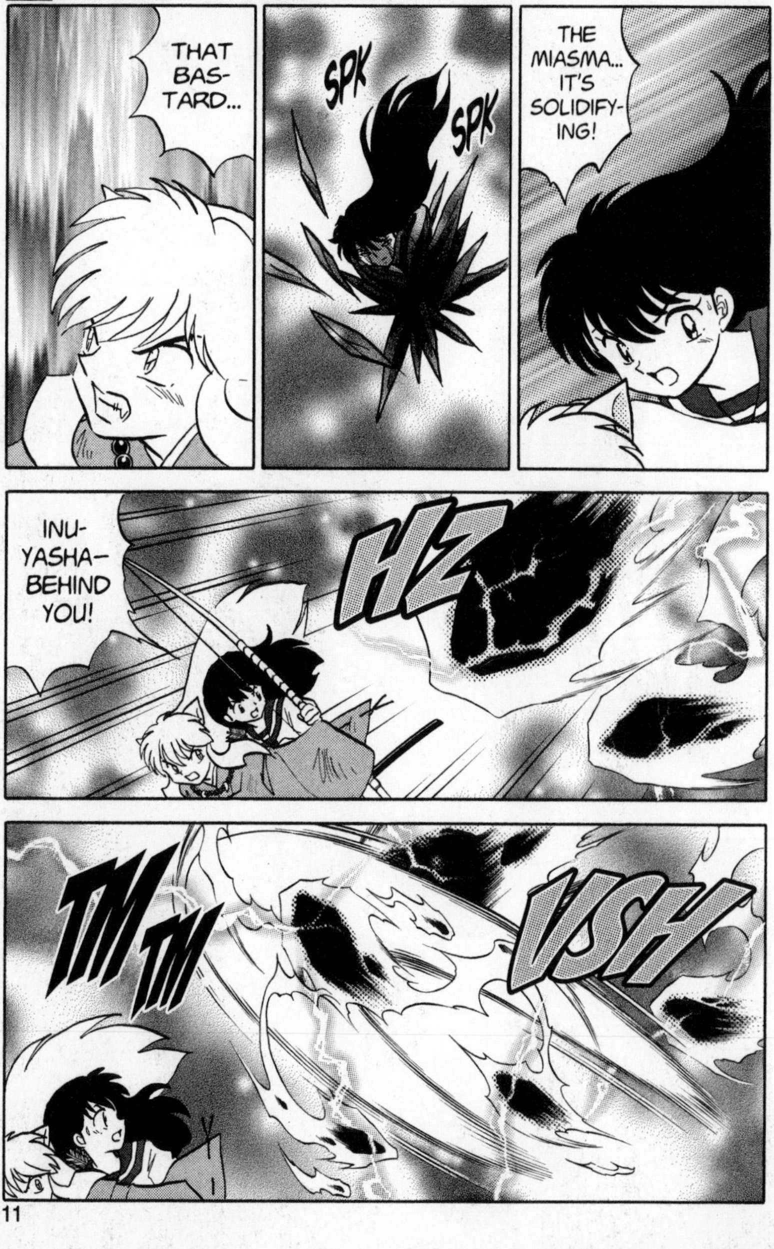
THE MIASMA... IT'S SOLIDIFY-ING!
SPK
SPK
THAT BAS-TARD...
HZ
INU-YASHA-BEHIND YOU!
VSH
TM
TM

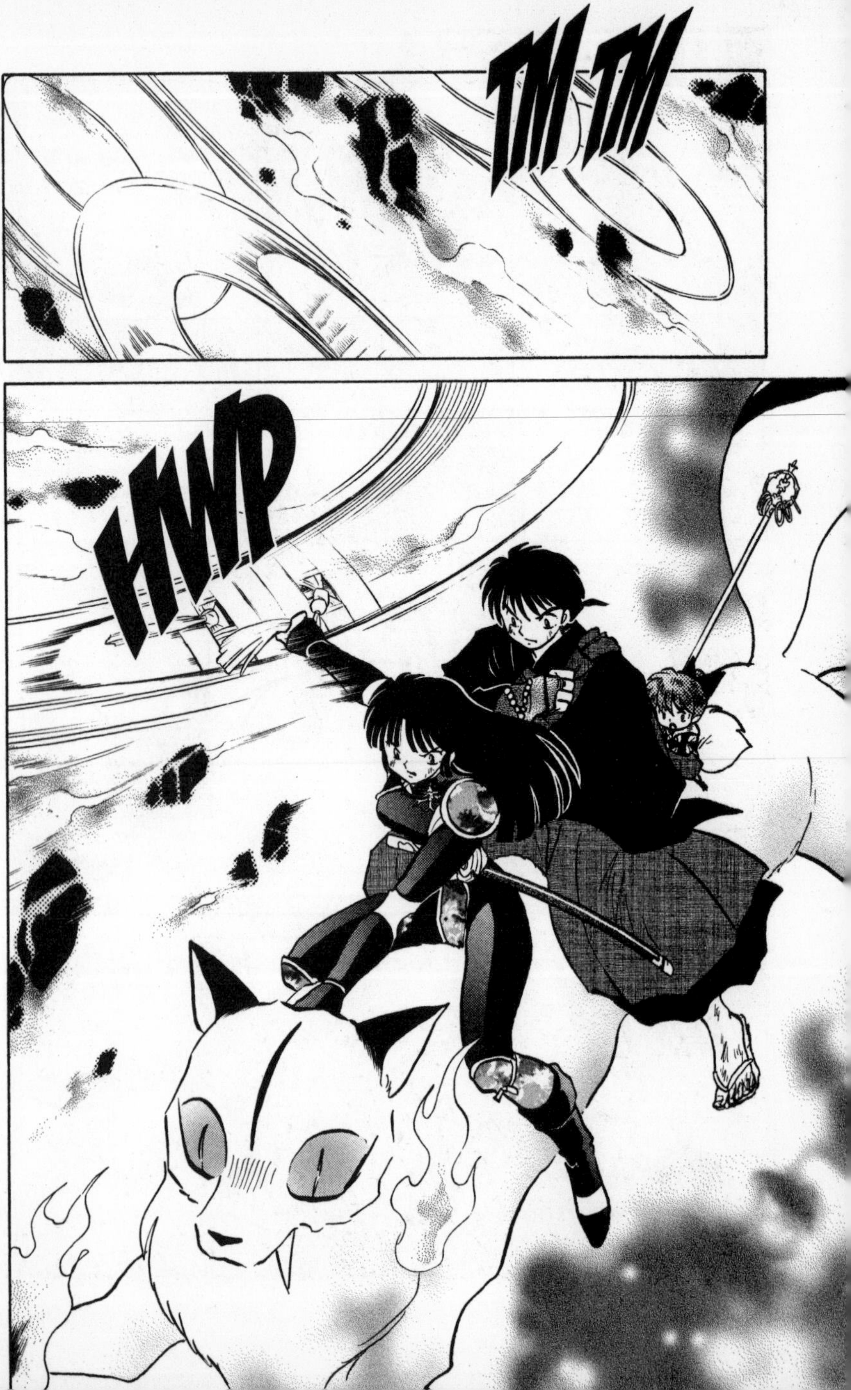
TM TM
HWP

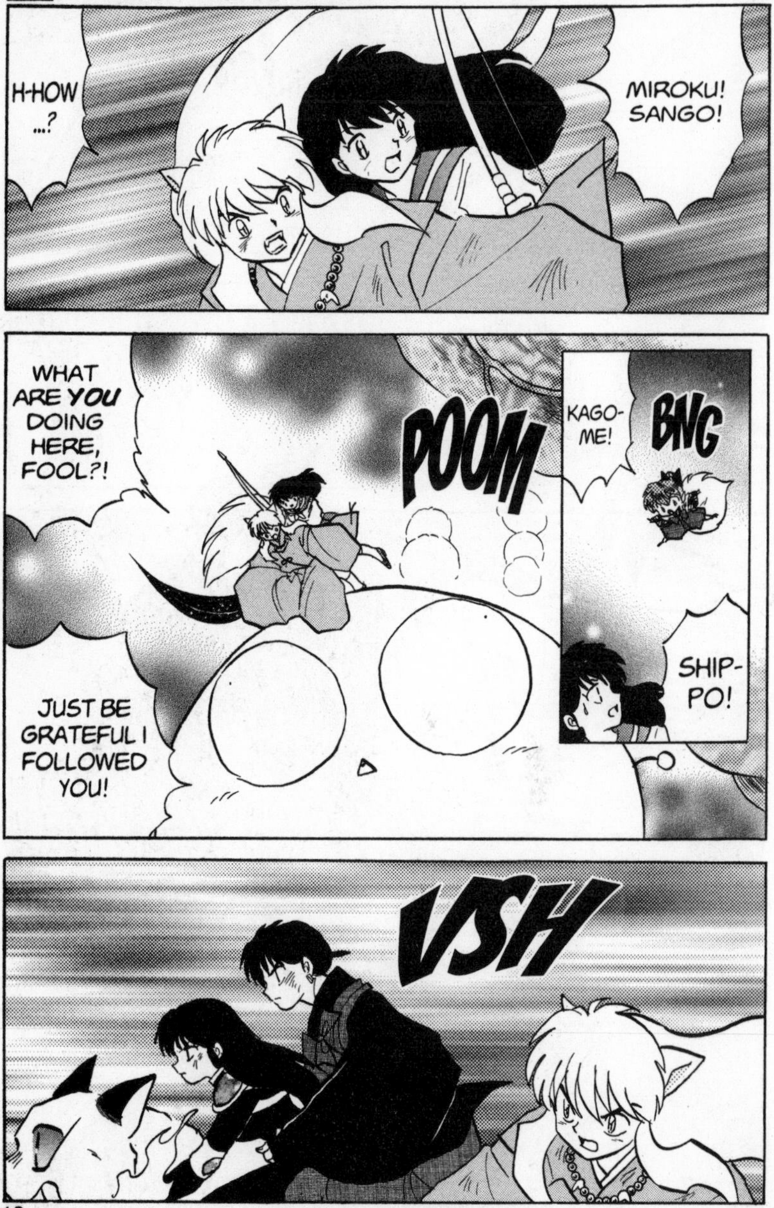
MIROKU! SANGO!
H-HOW ...?
KAGO-ME!
BNG
SHIP-PO!
POOM
WHAT ARE YOU DOING HERE, FOOL?!
JUST BE GRATEFUL I FOLLOWED YOU!
VSH

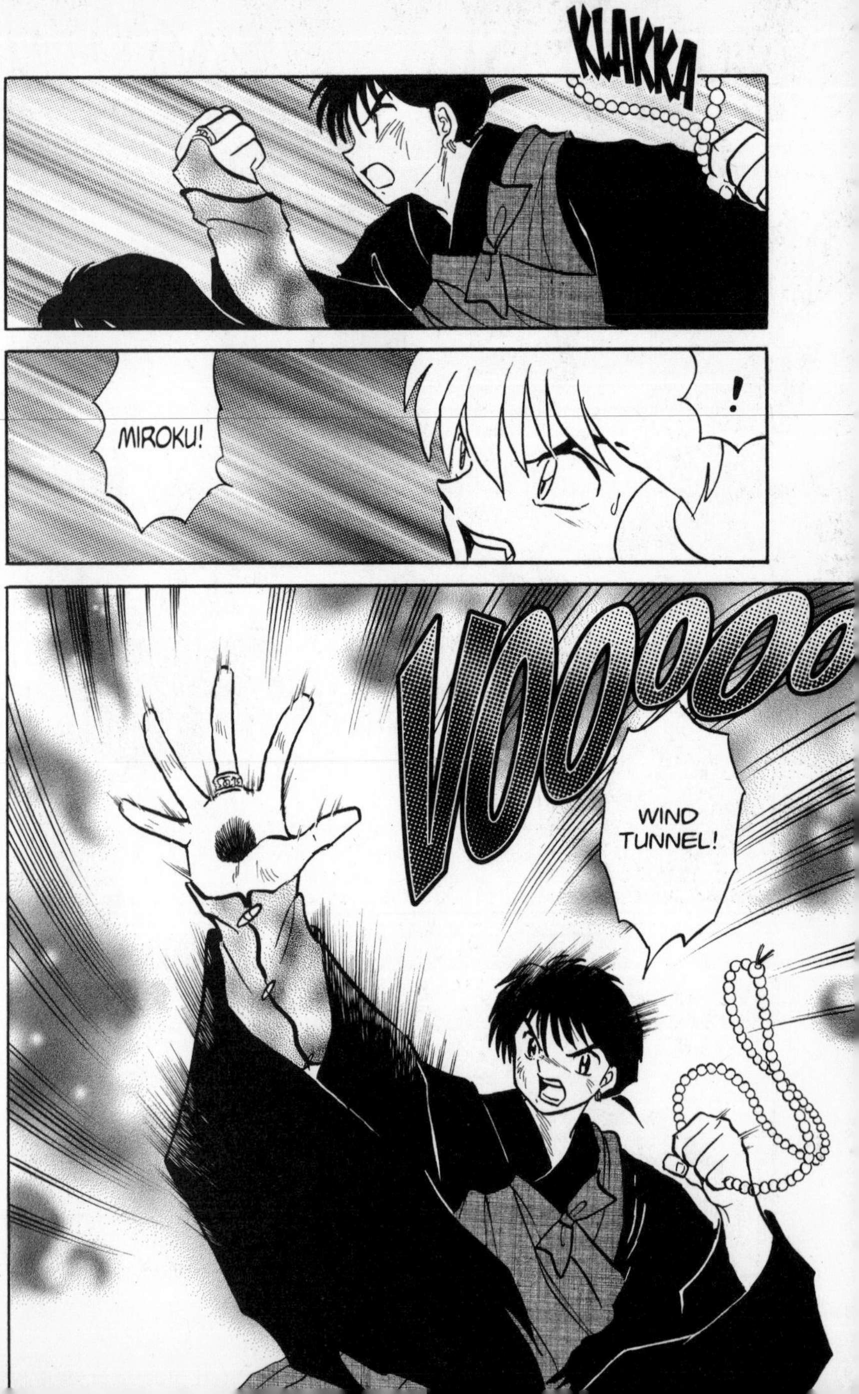
KLAKKA
!
MIROKU!
VOOOOOO
WIND TUNNEL!

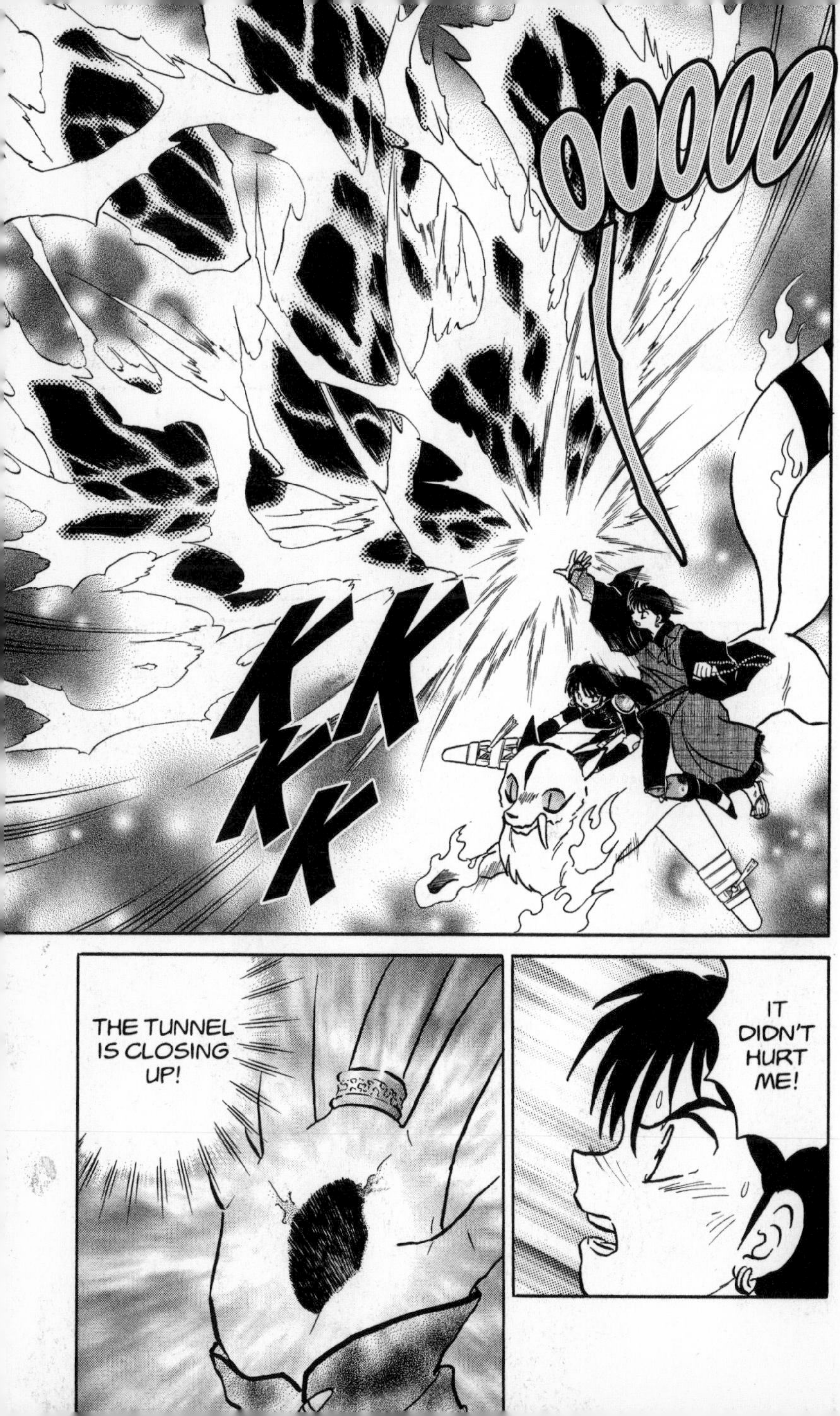
OOOOO
KKKK
IT DIDN'T HURT ME!
THE TUNNEL IS CLOSING UP!

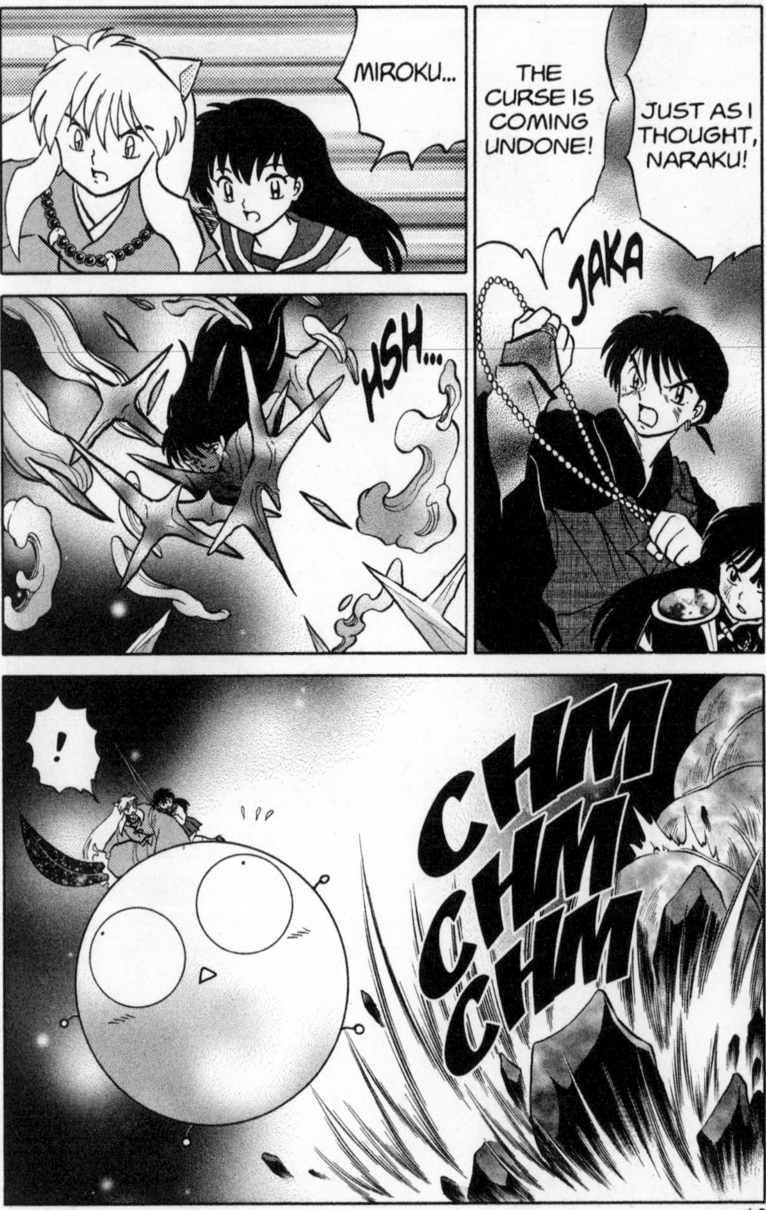
JUST AS I THOUGHT, NARAKU!
THE CURSE IS COMING UNDONE!
JAKA
MIROKU...
HSH...
CHM CHM CHM
!

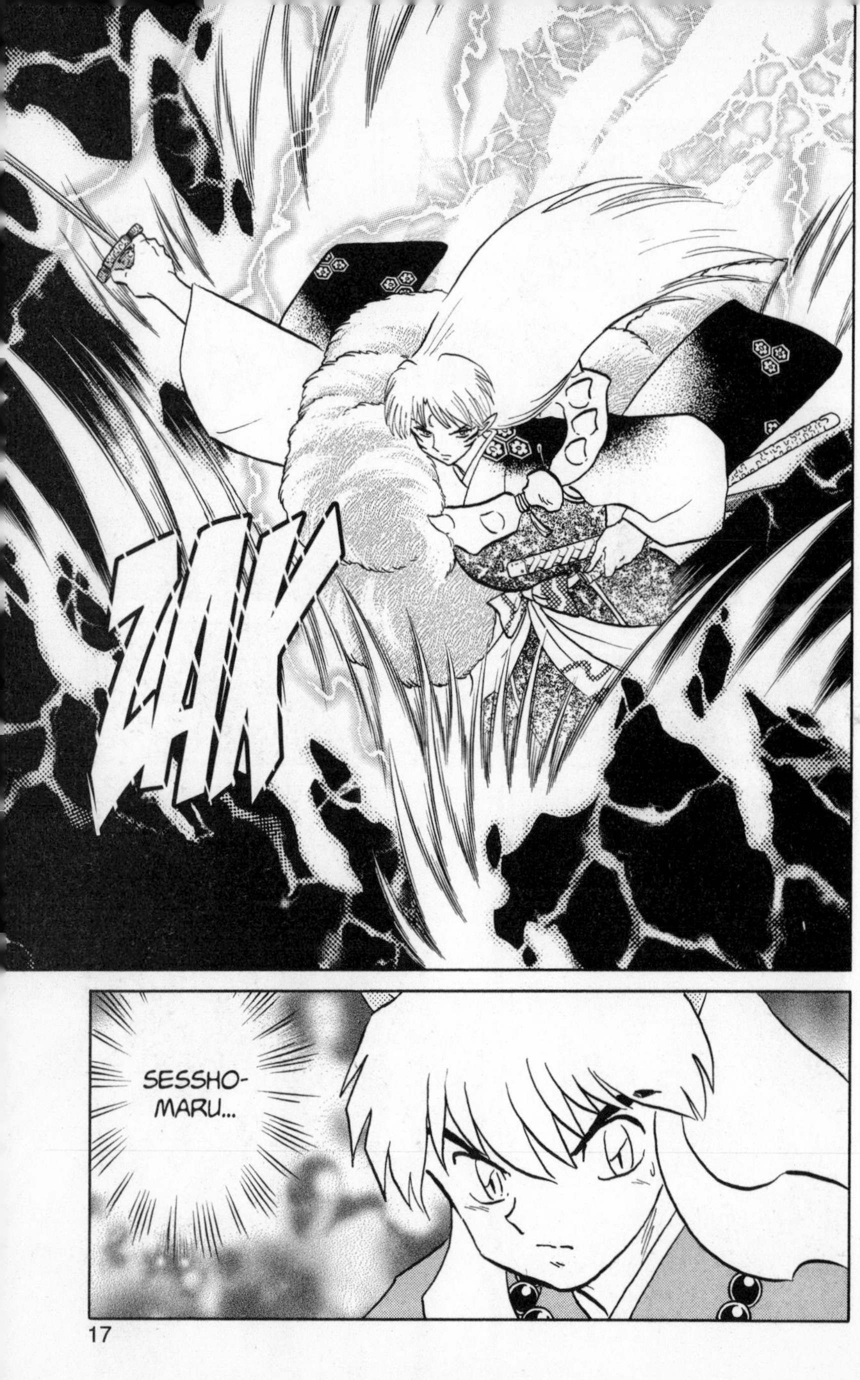
ZAK
SESSHO-
MARU...

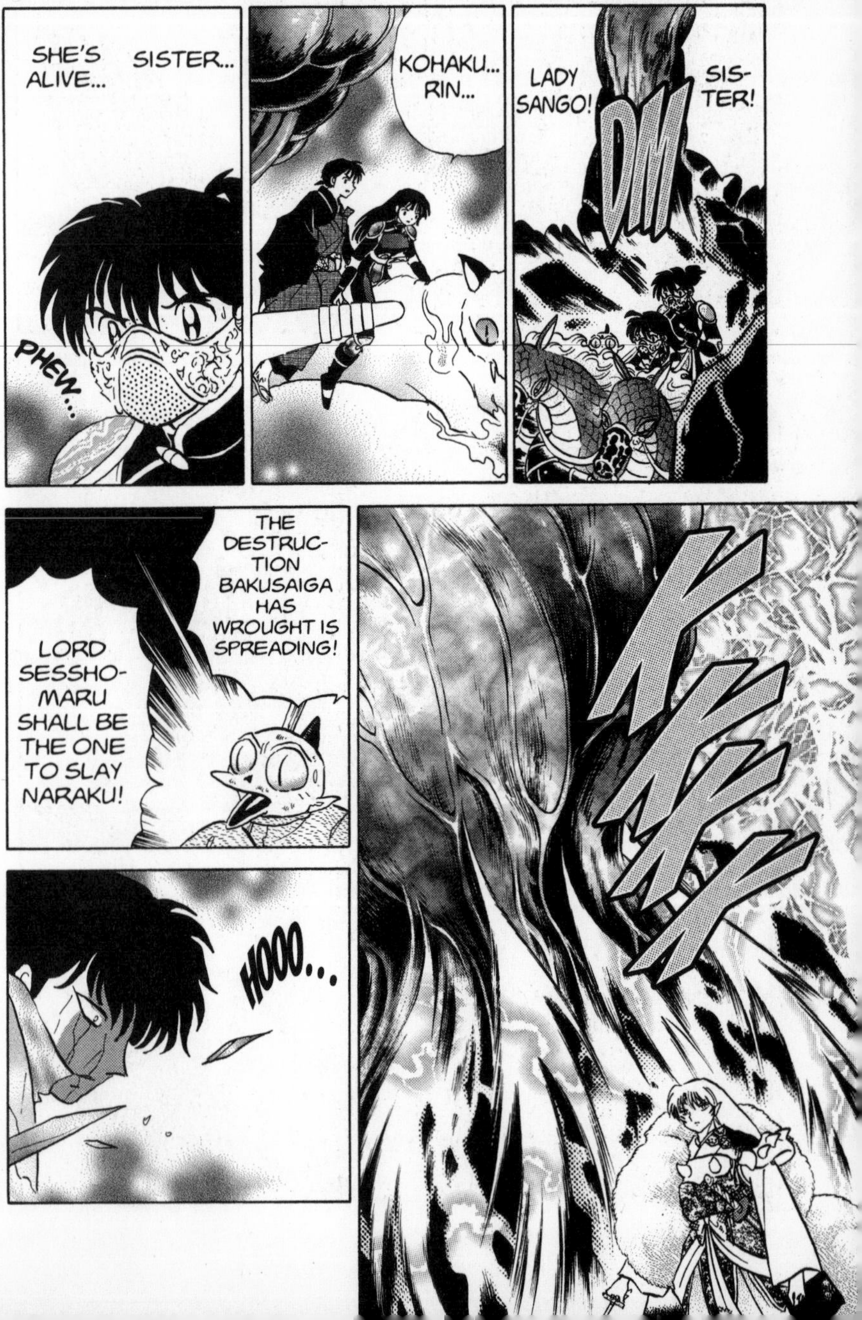
SIS-TER!
LADY SANGO!
DM
KOHAKU... RIN...
SISTER...
SHE'S ALIVE...
PHEW...
THE DESTRUCTION BAKUSAIGA HAS WROUGHT IS SPREADING!
LORD SESSHOMARU SHALL BE THE ONE TO SLAY NARAKU!
HOOO...

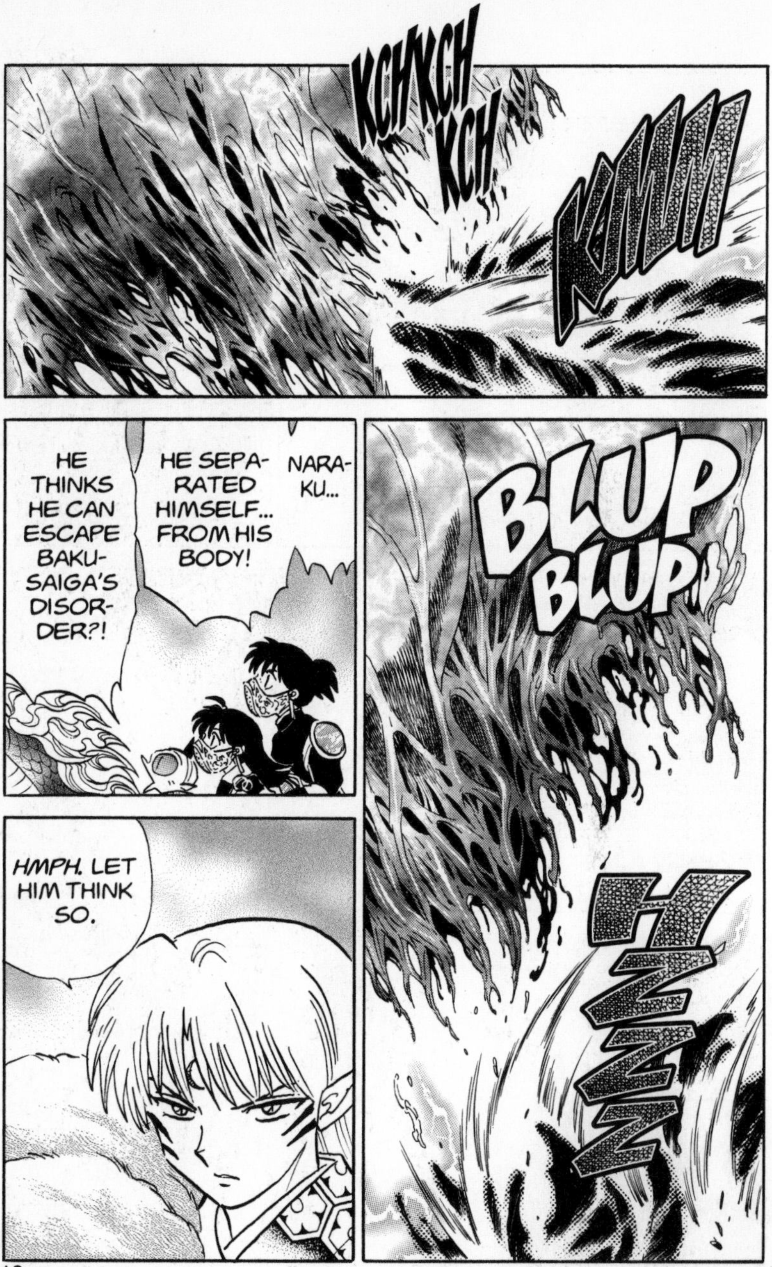
KCHKCH KCH
KMMM
BLUP BLUP!
NARAKU...
HE SEPARATED HIMSELF... FROM HIS BODY!
HE THINKS HE CAN ESCAPE BAKUSAIGA'S DISORDER?!
HMPH. LET HIM THINK SO.

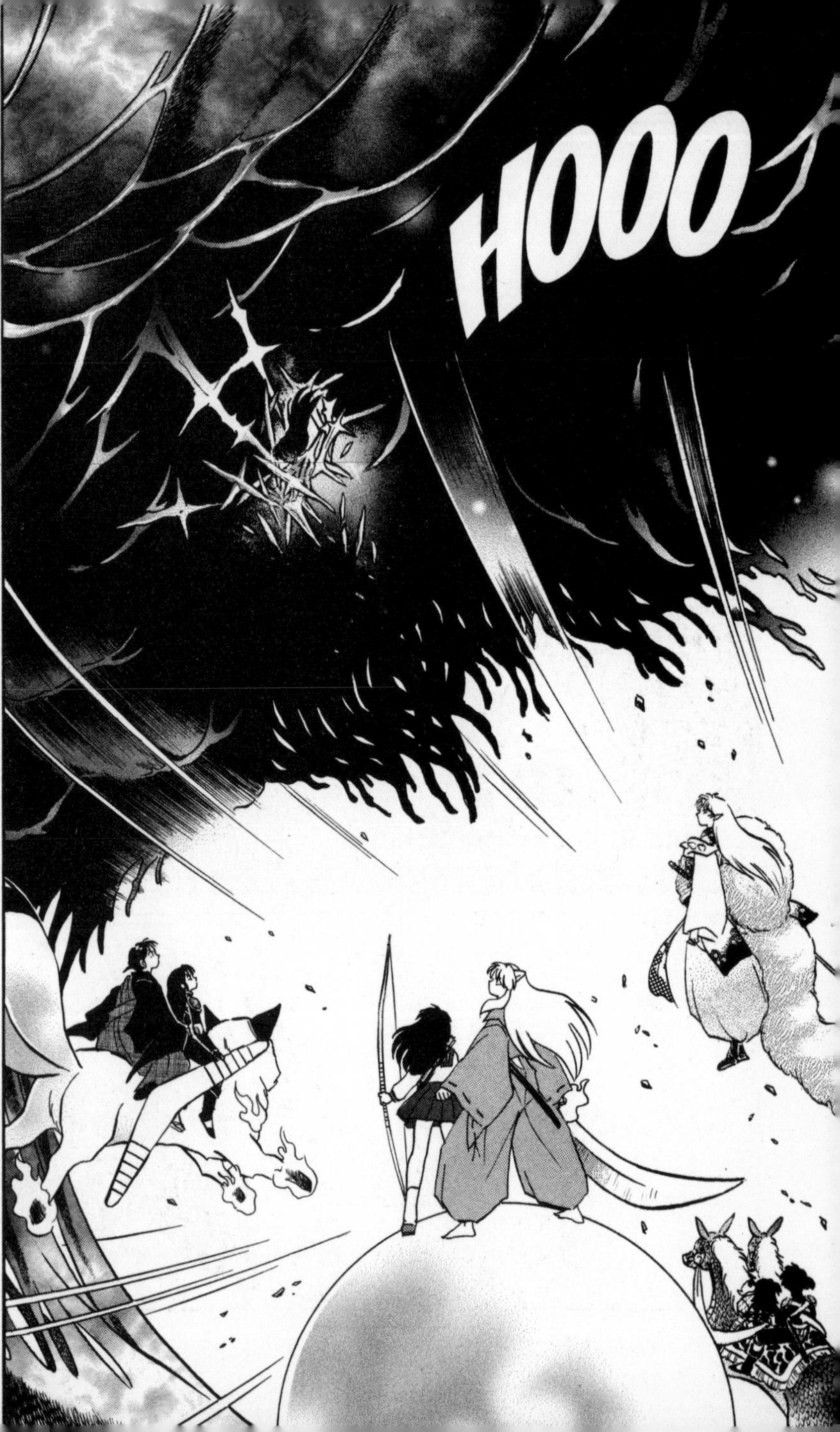
HOOO

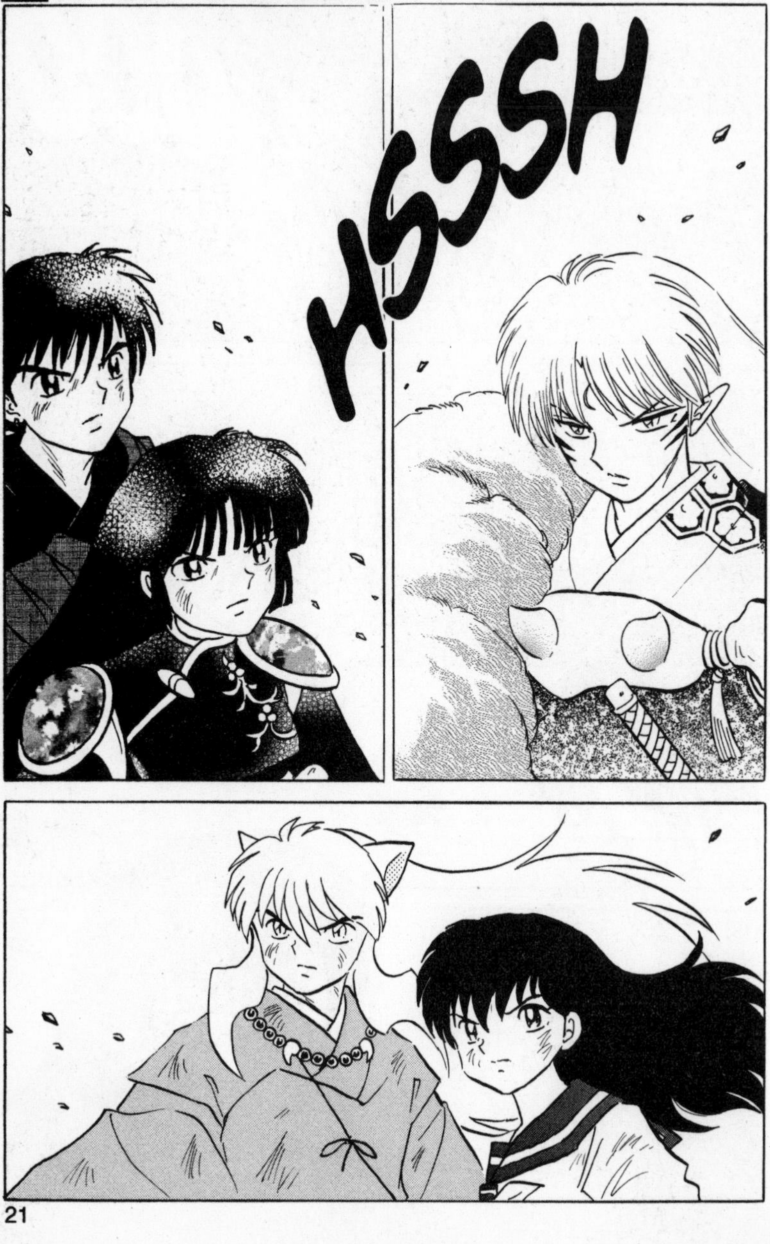
HSSSH

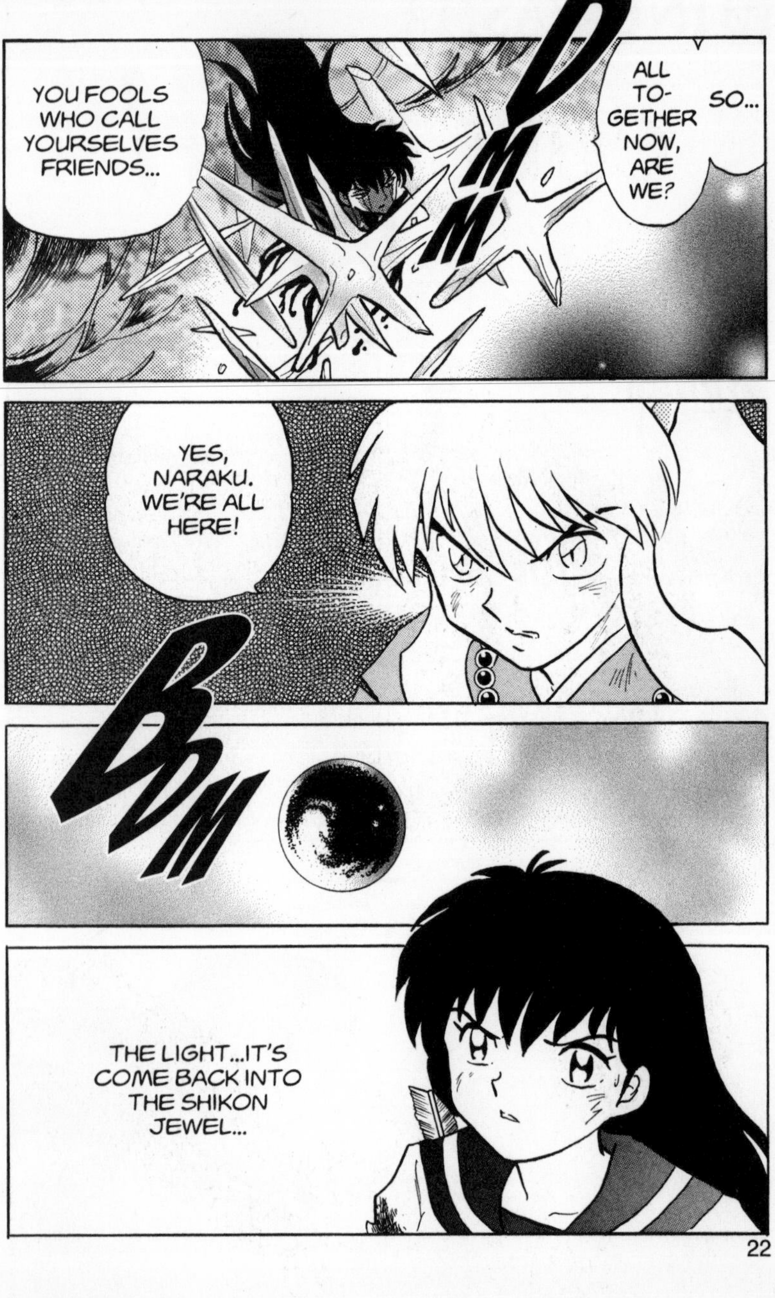
SO...
ALL TO-GETHER NOW, ARE WE?
YOU FOOLS WHO CALL YOURSELVES FRIENDS...
YES, NARAKU. WE'RE ALL HERE!
THE LIGHT...IT'S COME BACK INTO THE SHIKON JEWEL...

SCROLL 2

COLLAPSE

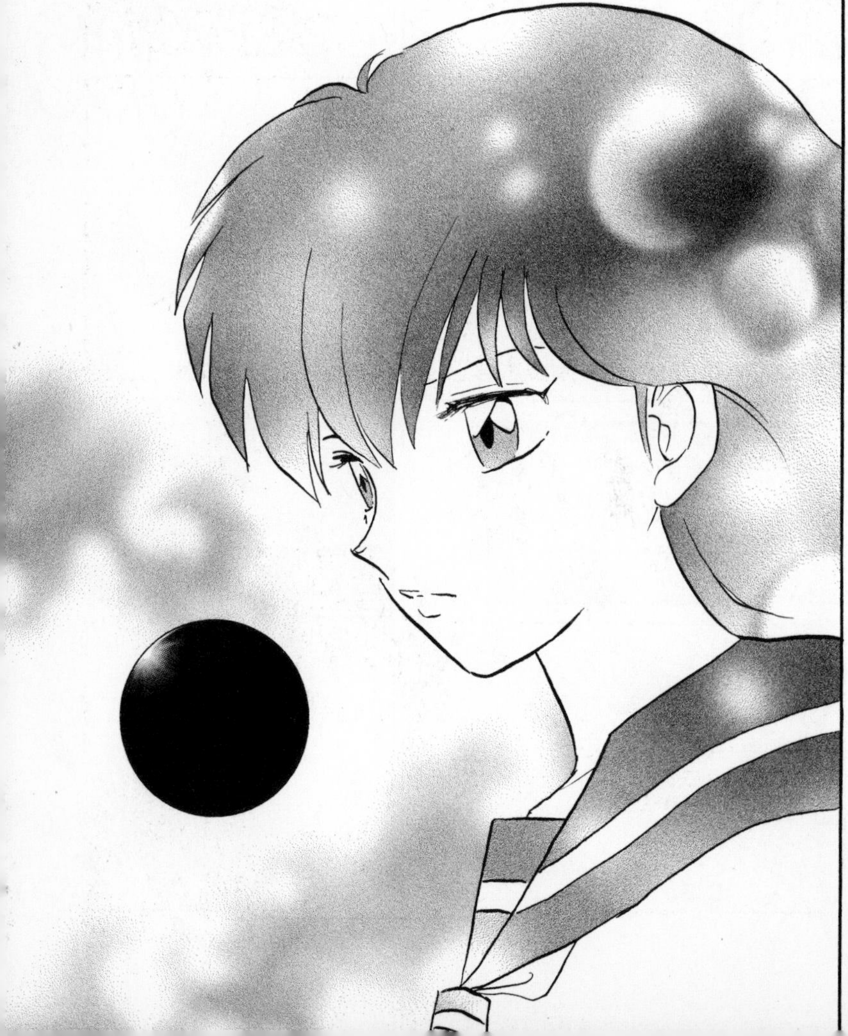

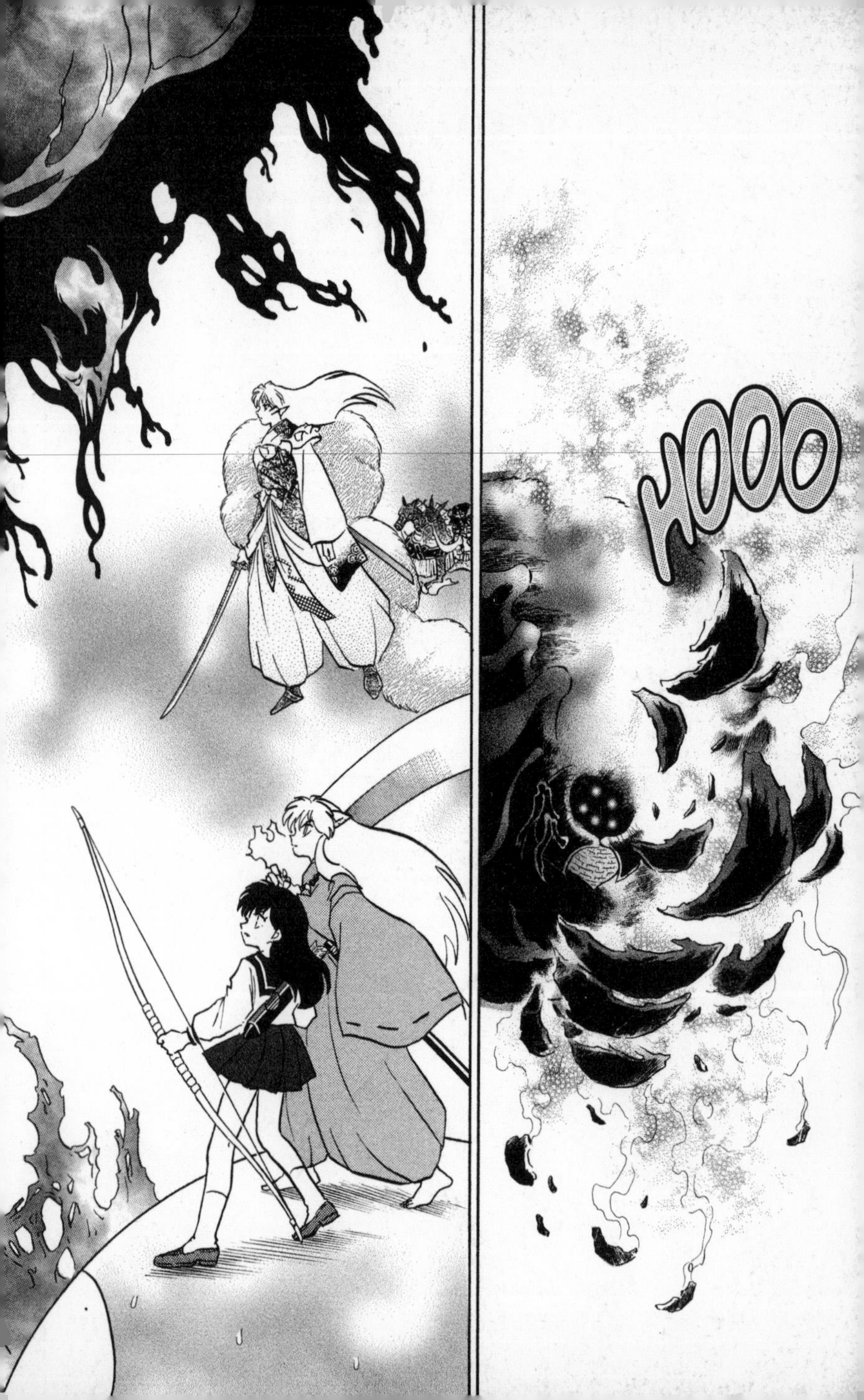
HOOO

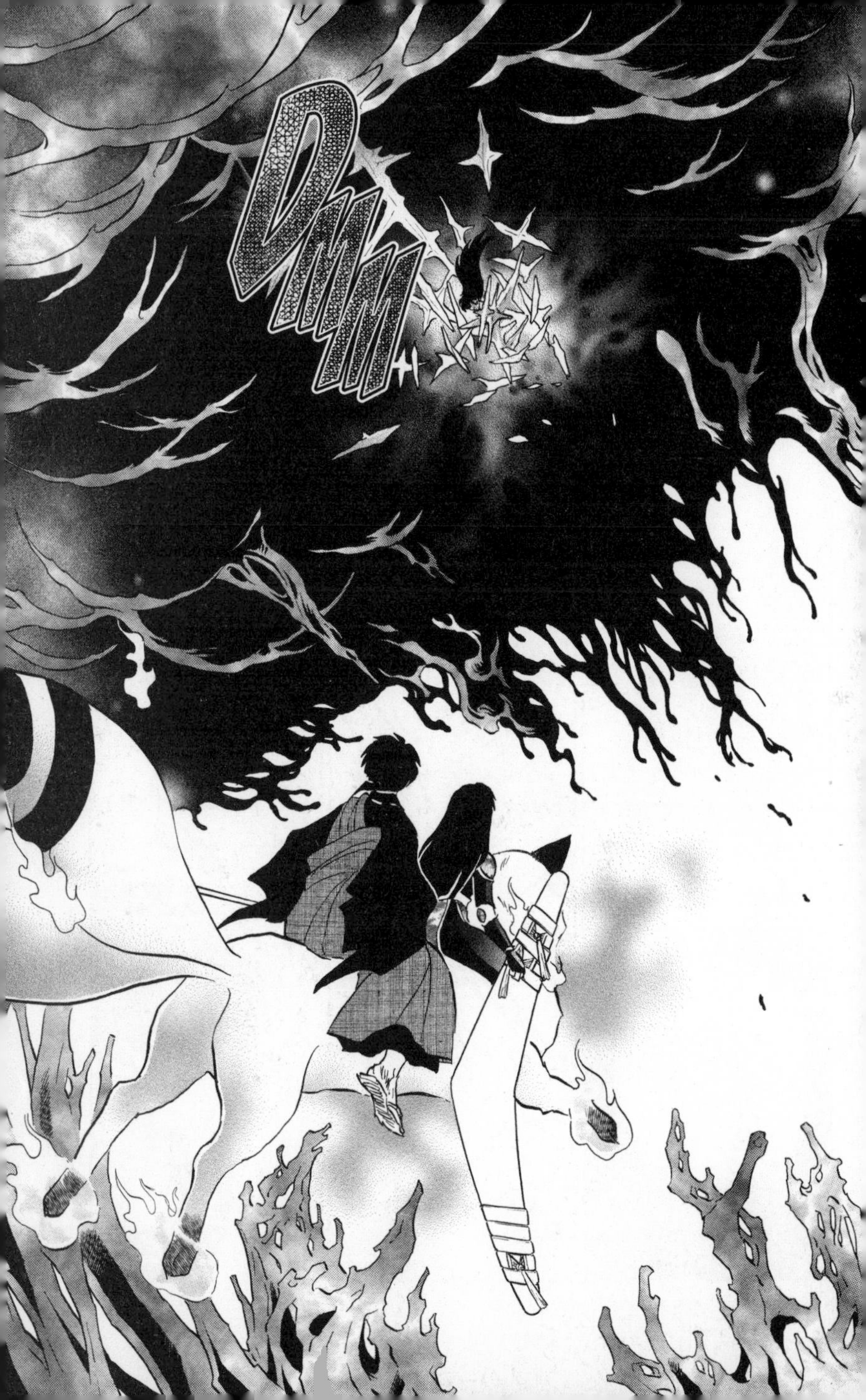
DMMM

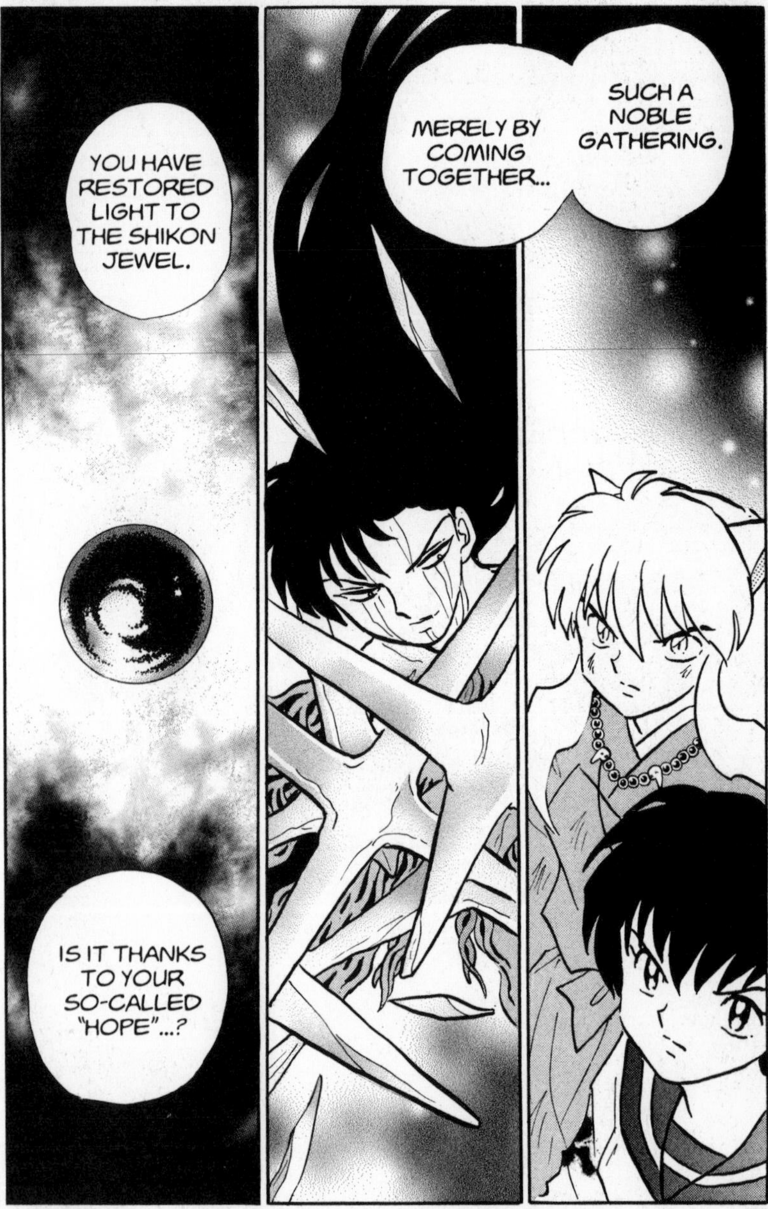
SUCH A NOBLE GATHERING.
MERELY BY COMING TOGETHER...
YOU HAVE RESTORED LIGHT TO THE SHIKON JEWEL.
IS IT THANKS TO YOUR SO-CALLED "HOPE"...?

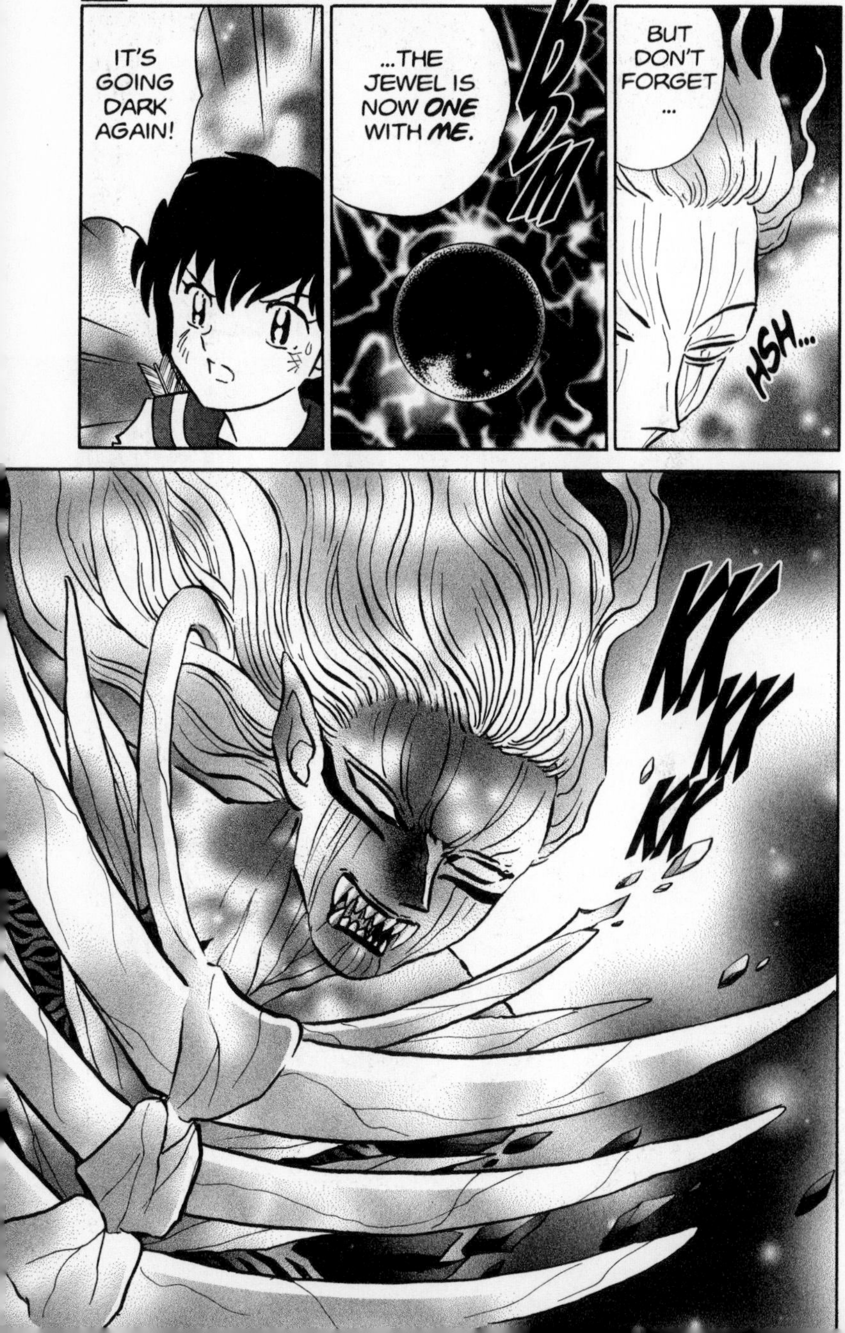
BUT DON'T FORGET ...
HSH...
...THE JEWEL IS NOW ONE WITH ME.
BDM
IT'S GOING DARK AGAIN!
KKKKKK

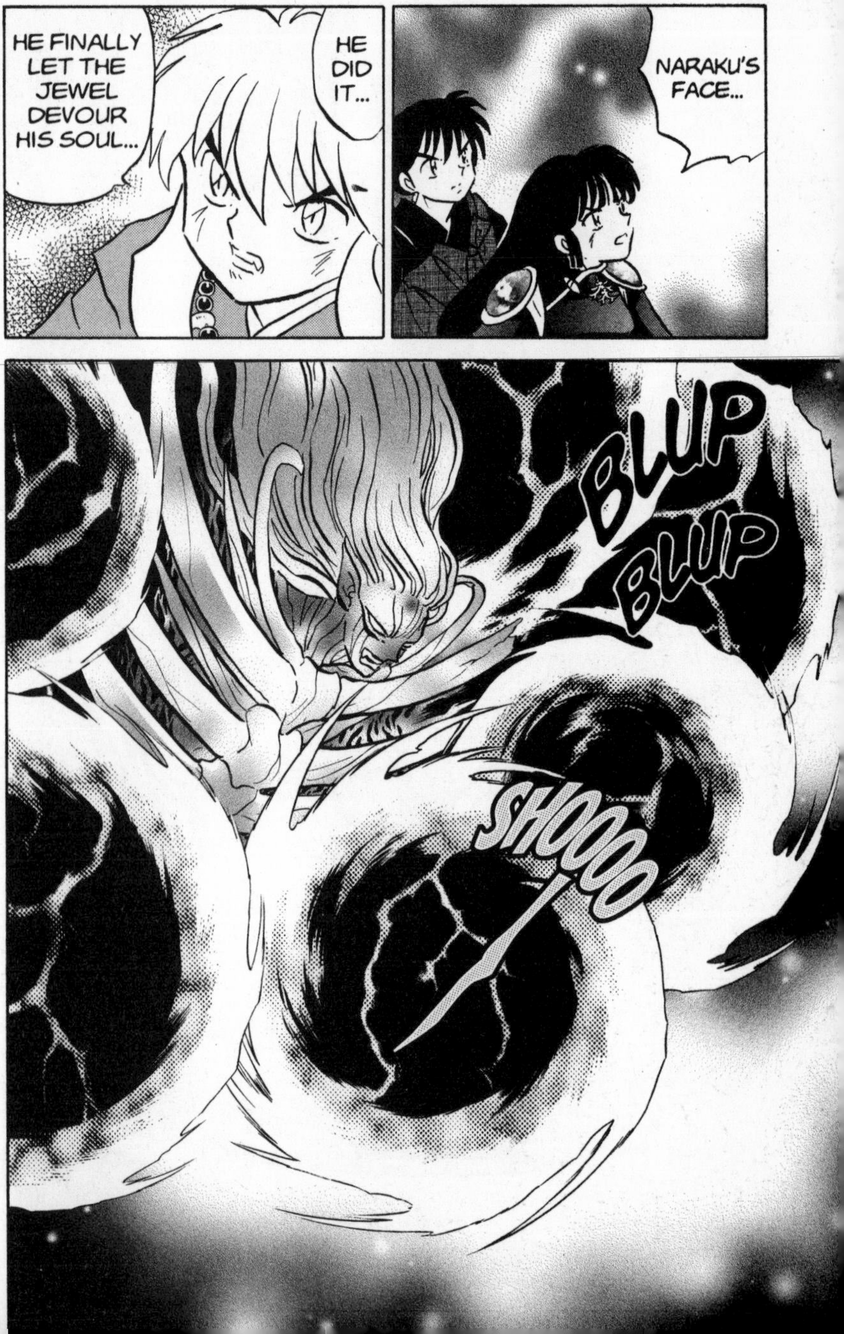
NARAKU'S FACE...
HE DID IT...
HE FINALLY LET THE JEWEL DEVOUR HIS SOUL...
BLUP BLUP
SHOOOO

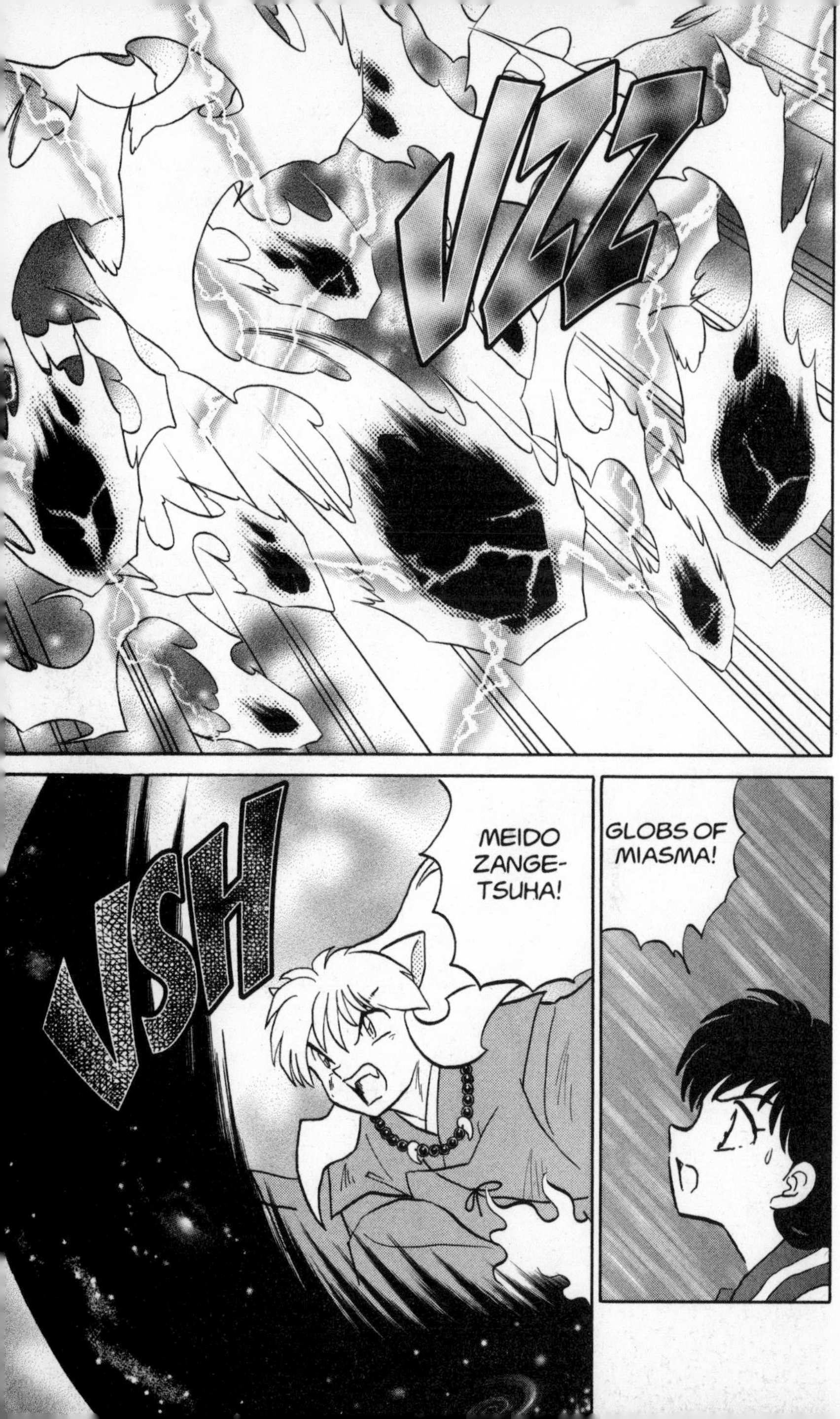
VZZ
GLOBS OF MIASMA!
MEIDO ZANGE-TSUHA!
VSH

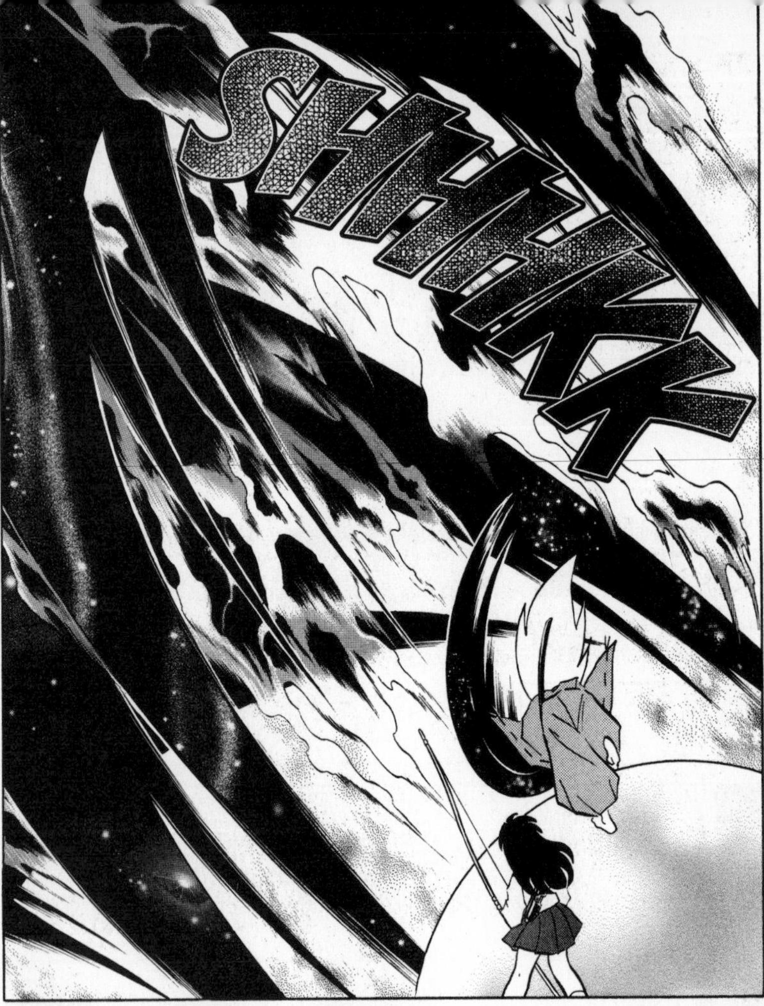
SHHHKK

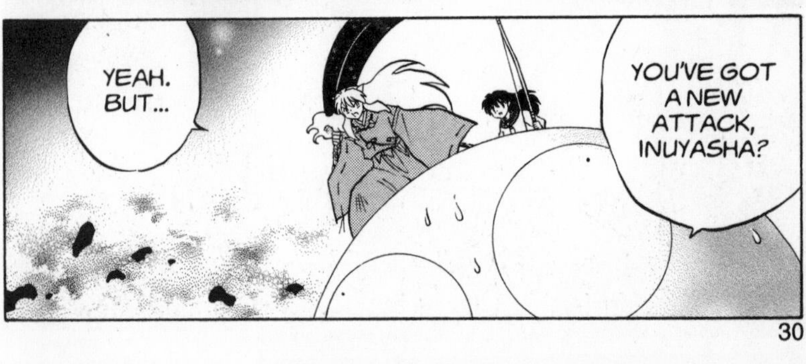
YOU'VE GOT A NEW ATTACK, INUYASHA?
YEAH. BUT...

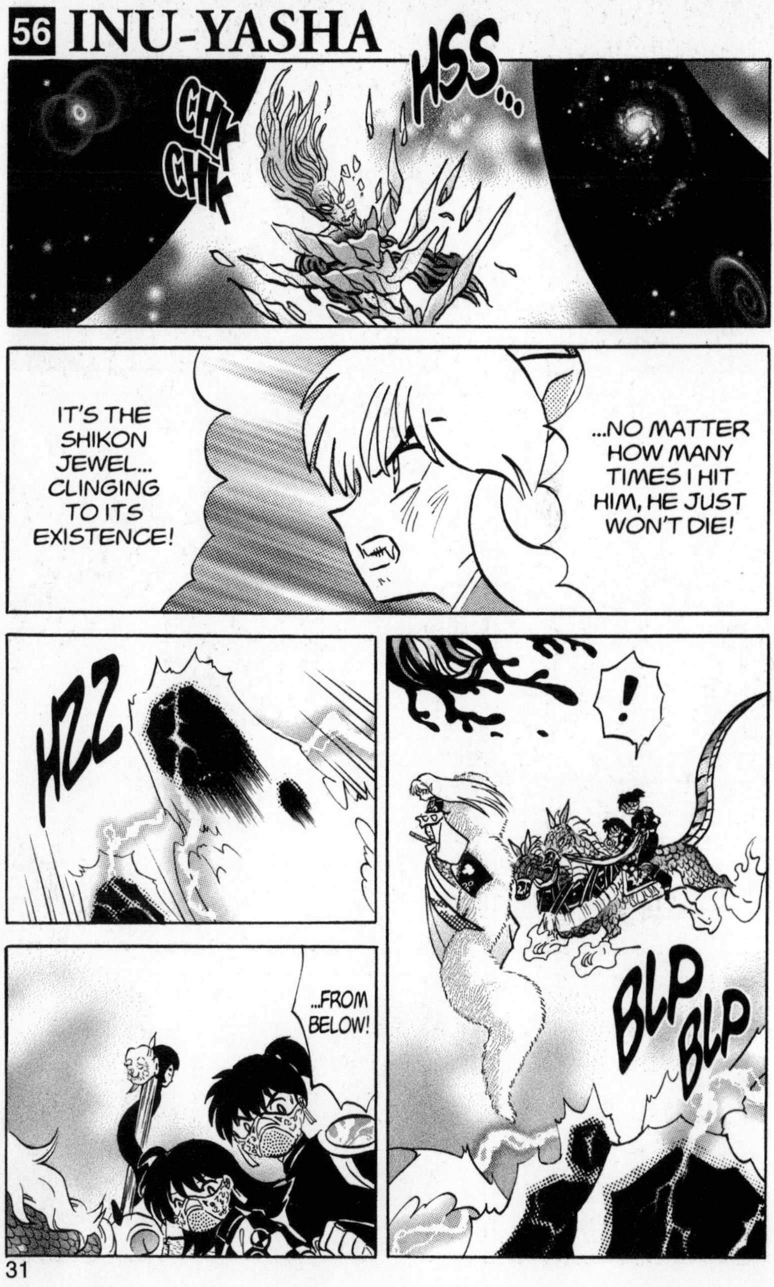
HSS...
CHK CHK
...NO MATTER HOW MANY TIMES I HIT HIM, HE JUST WON'T DIE!
IT'S THE SHIKON JEWEL... CLINGING TO ITS EXISTENCE!
!
BLP BLP
HZZ
...FROM BELOW!

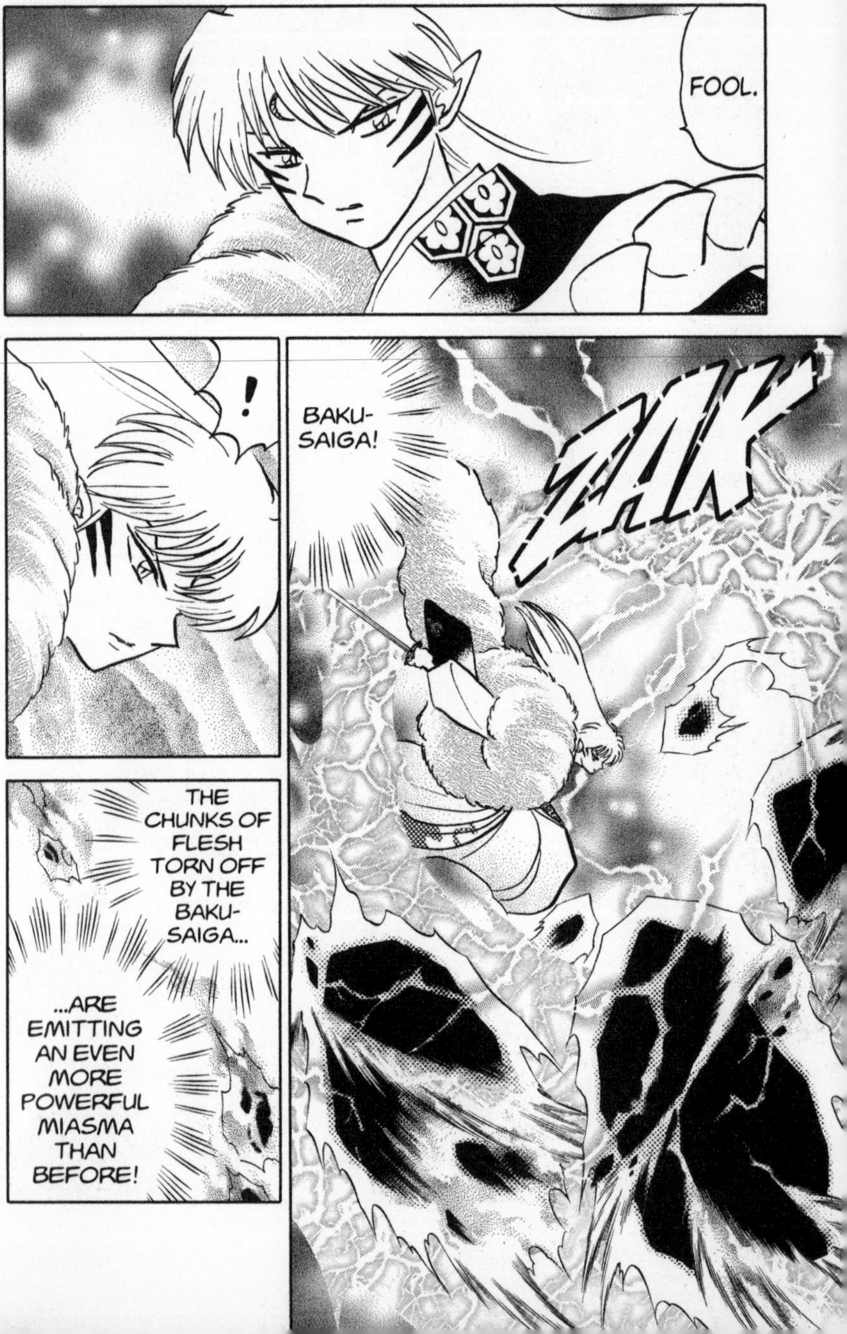
FOOL.
ZAK
BAKU-SAIGA!
!
THE CHUNKS OF FLESH TORN OFF BY THE BAKU-SAIGA...
...ARE EMITTING AN EVEN MORE POWERFUL MIASMA THAN BEFORE!

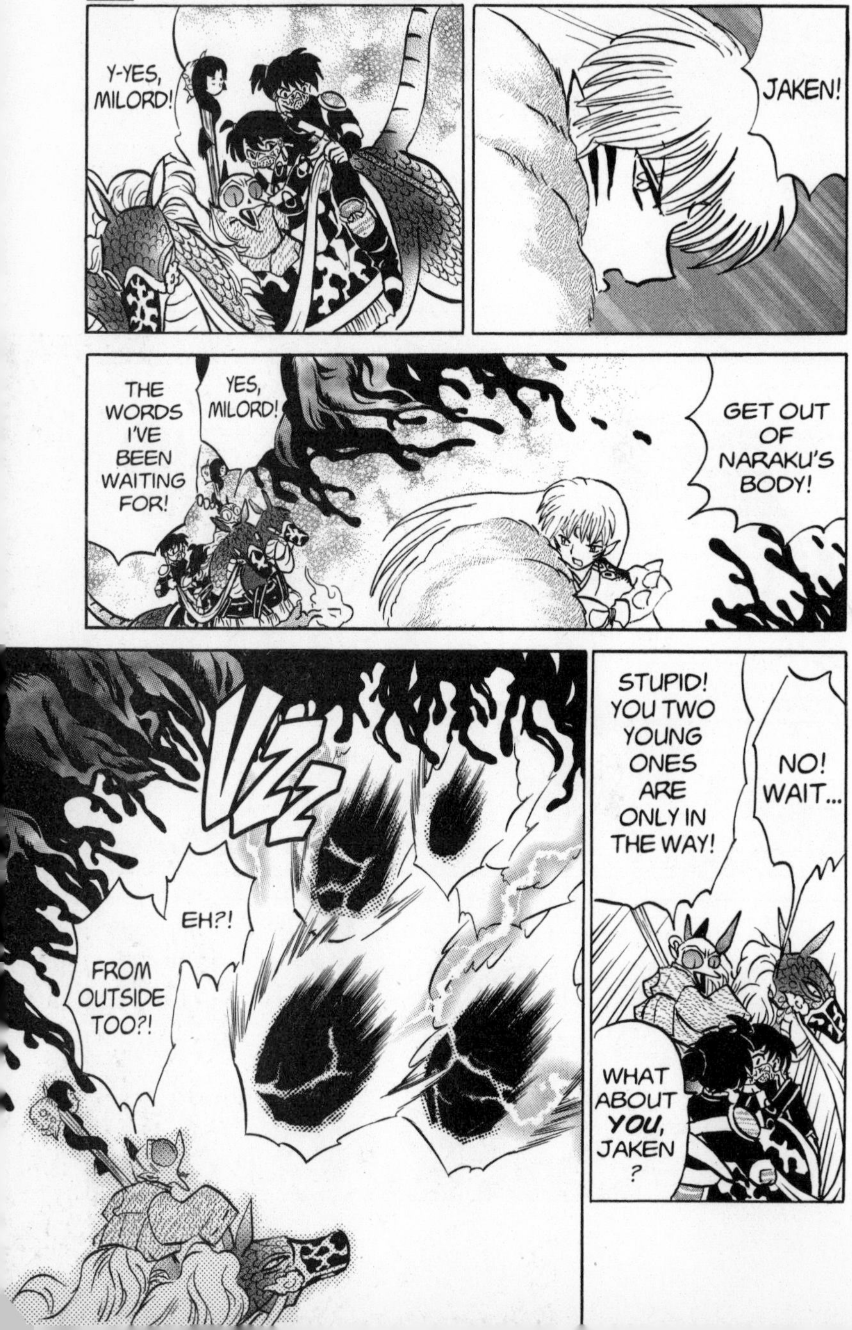
JAKEN!
Y-YES, MILORD!
GET OUT OF NARAKU'S BODY!
YES, MILORD!
THE WORDS I'VE BEEN WAITING FOR!
NO! WAIT...
STUPID! YOU TWO YOUNG ONES ARE ONLY IN THE WAY!
WHAT ABOUT *YOU*, JAKEN?
VZZ
EH?!
FROM OUTSIDE TOO?!

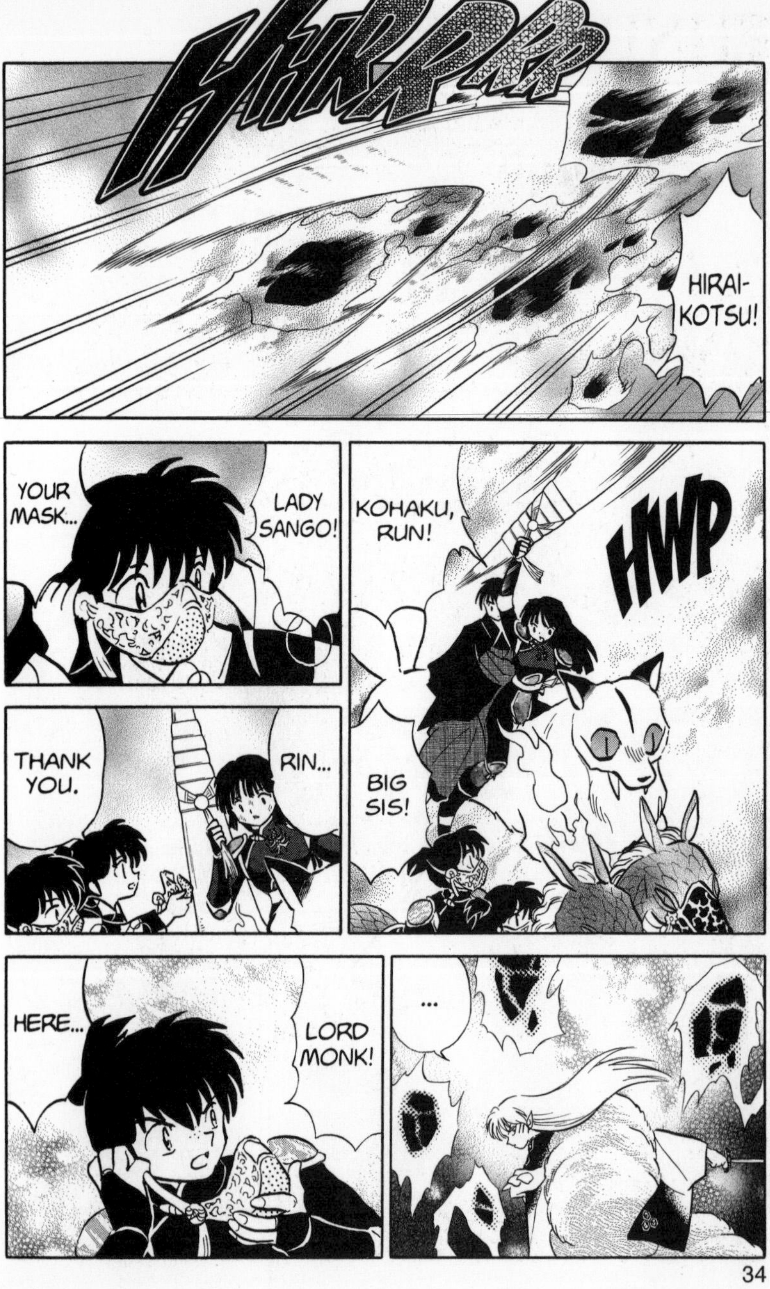
WHIRRRR
HIRAI-KOTSU!
KOHAKU, RUN!
HWP
BIG SIS!
LADY SANGO!
YOUR MASK...
RIN...
THANK YOU.
...
LORD MONK!
HERE...

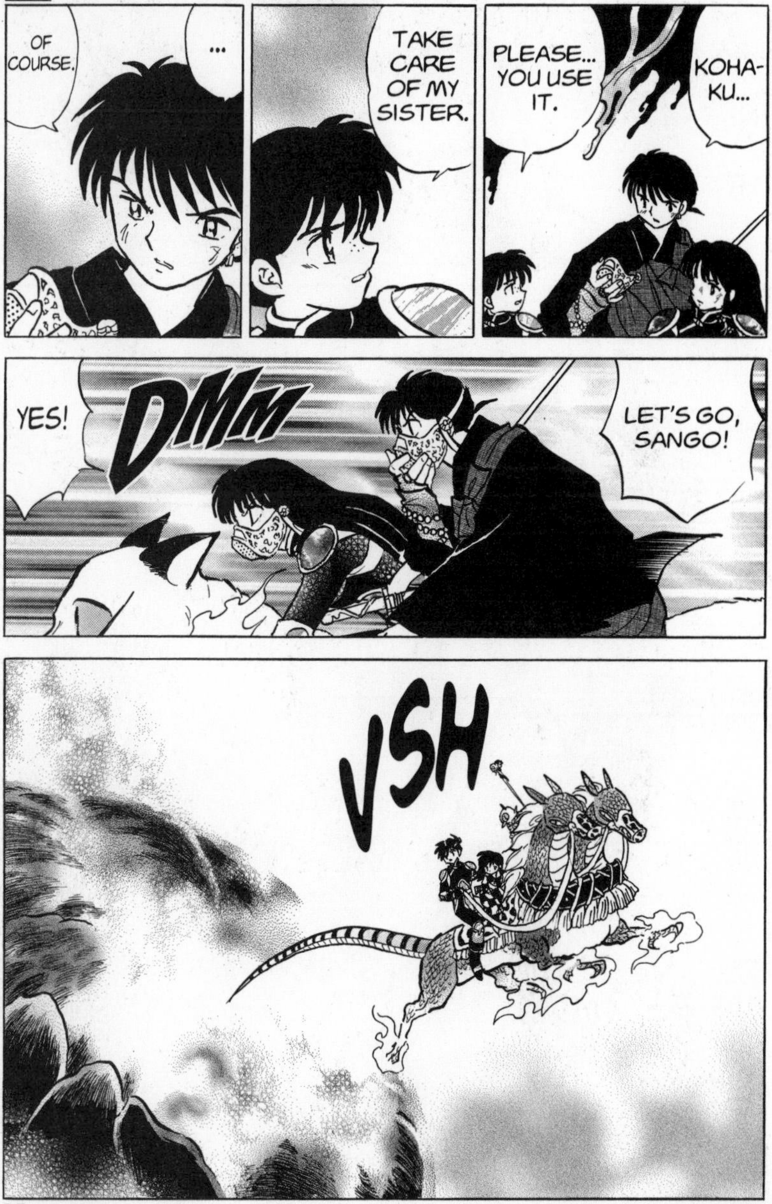
KOHAKU...
PLEASE... YOU USE IT.
TAKE CARE OF MY SISTER.
...
OF COURSE.
LET'S GO, SANGO!
DMM
YES!
VSH

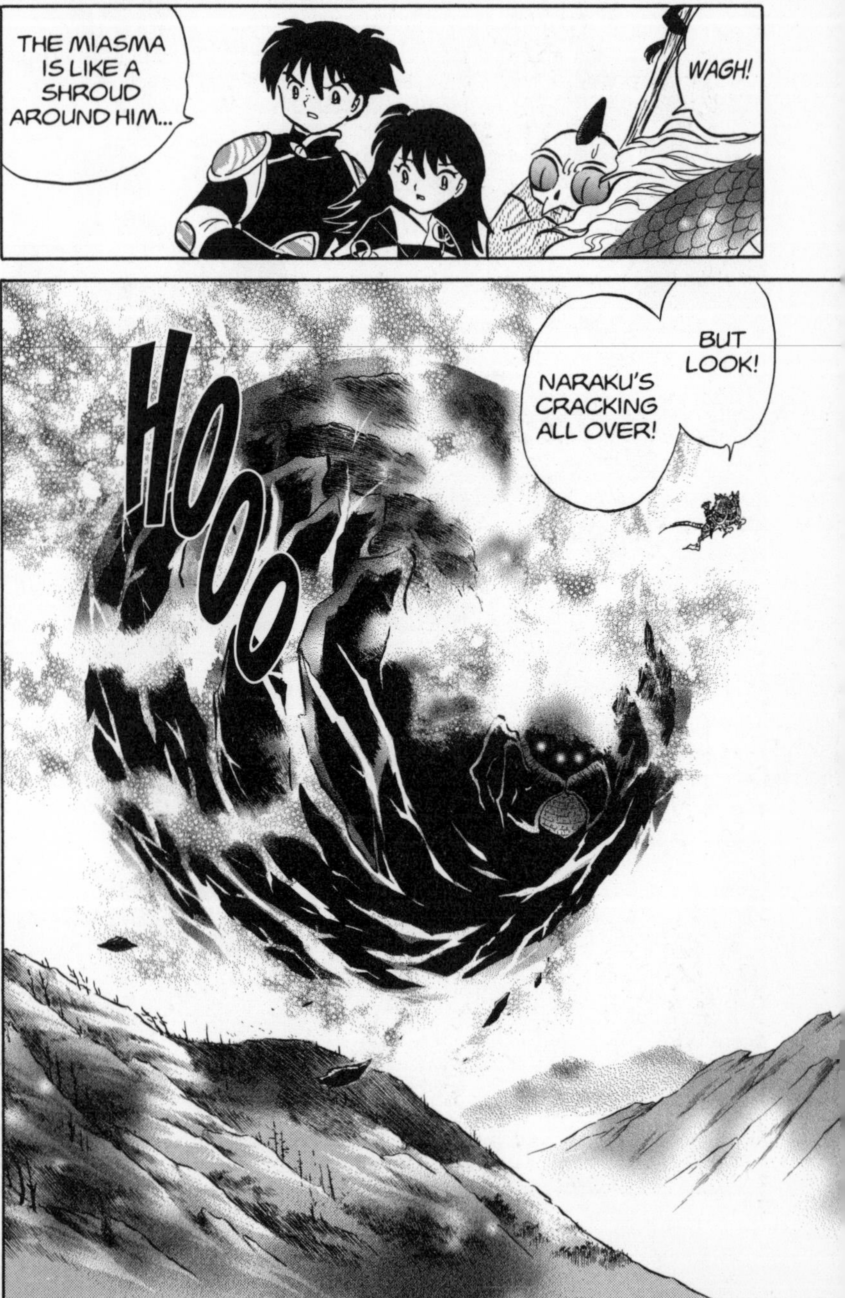
WAGH!
THE MIASMA IS LIKE A SHROUD AROUND HIM...
BUT LOOK! NARAKU'S CRACKING ALL OVER!
HOOOO

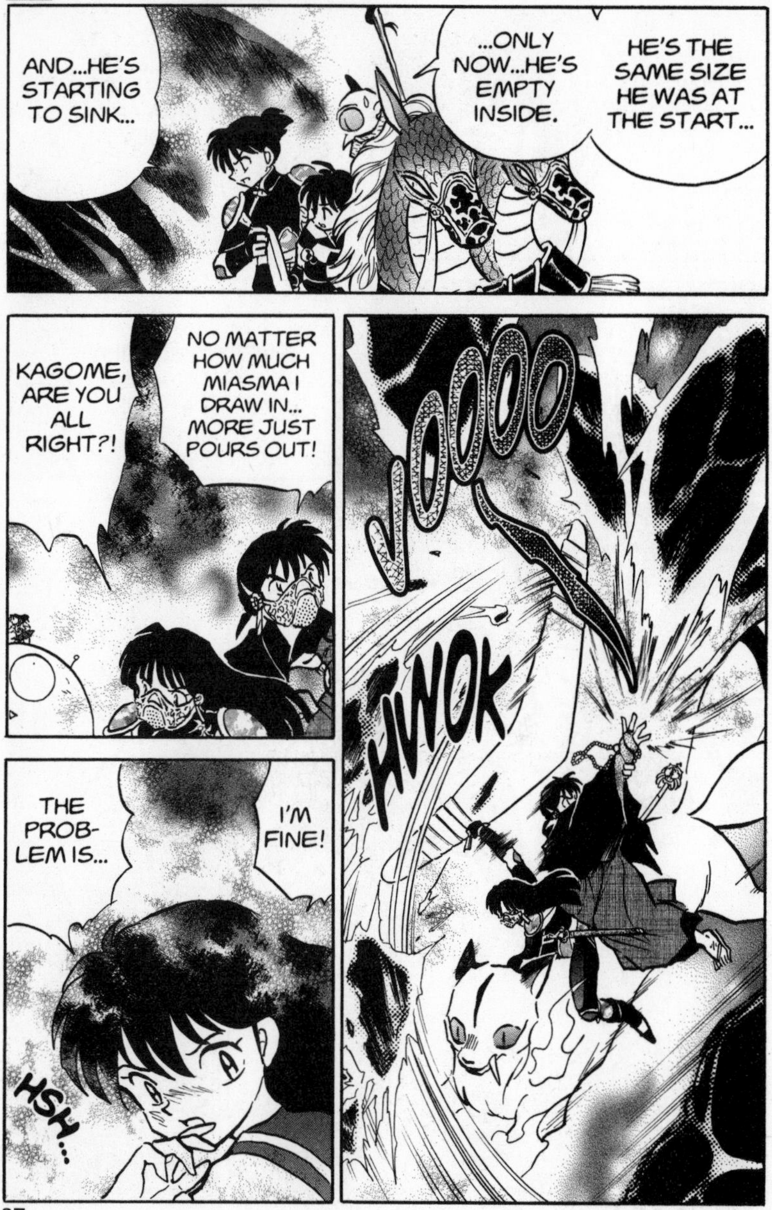
HE'S THE SAME SIZE HE WAS AT THE START...
...ONLY NOW...HE'S EMPTY INSIDE.
AND...HE'S STARTING TO SINK...
VOOOOO
HWOK
NO MATTER HOW MUCH MIASMA I DRAW IN... MORE JUST POURS OUT!
KAGOME, ARE YOU ALL RIGHT?!
I'M FINE!
THE PROB-LEM IS...
HSH...

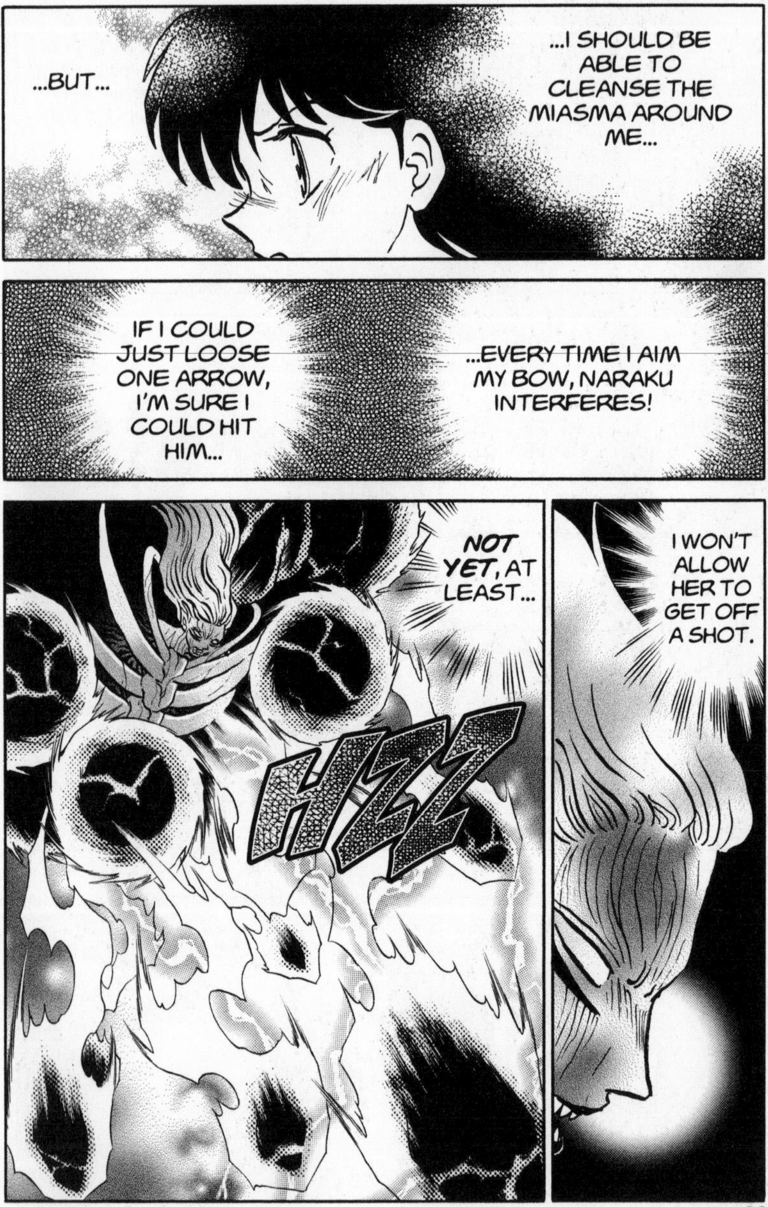
...I SHOULD BE ABLE TO CLEANSE THE MIASMA AROUND ME...
...BUT...
...EVERY TIME I AIM MY BOW, NARAKU INTERFERES!
IF I COULD JUST LOOSE ONE ARROW, I'M SURE I COULD HIT HIM...
I WON'T ALLOW HER TO GET OFF A SHOT.
NOT YET, AT LEAST...
HZZ

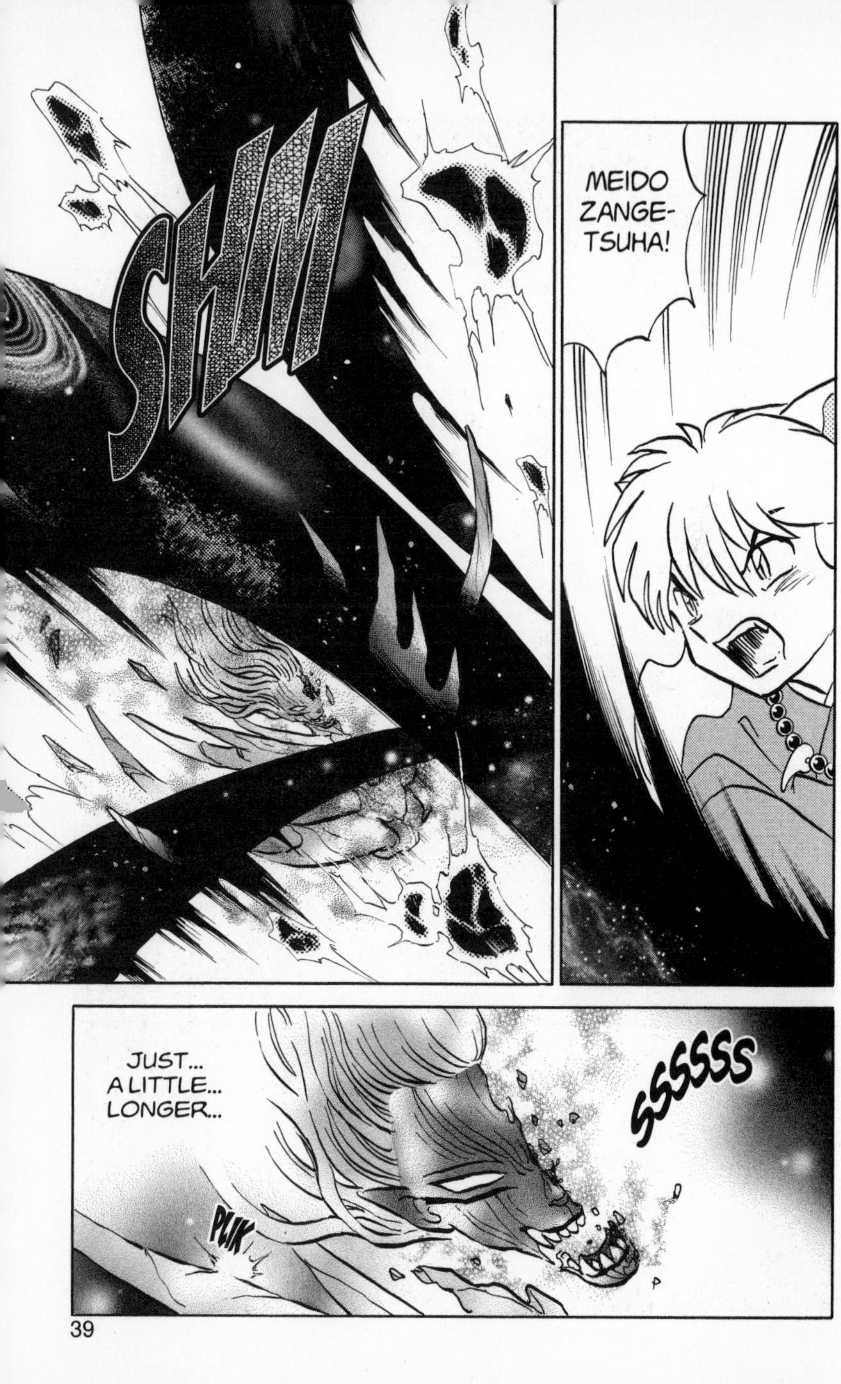
MEIDO ZANGE-TSUHA!
SHIM
SSSSSS
JUST... A LITTLE... LONGER...
PLIK

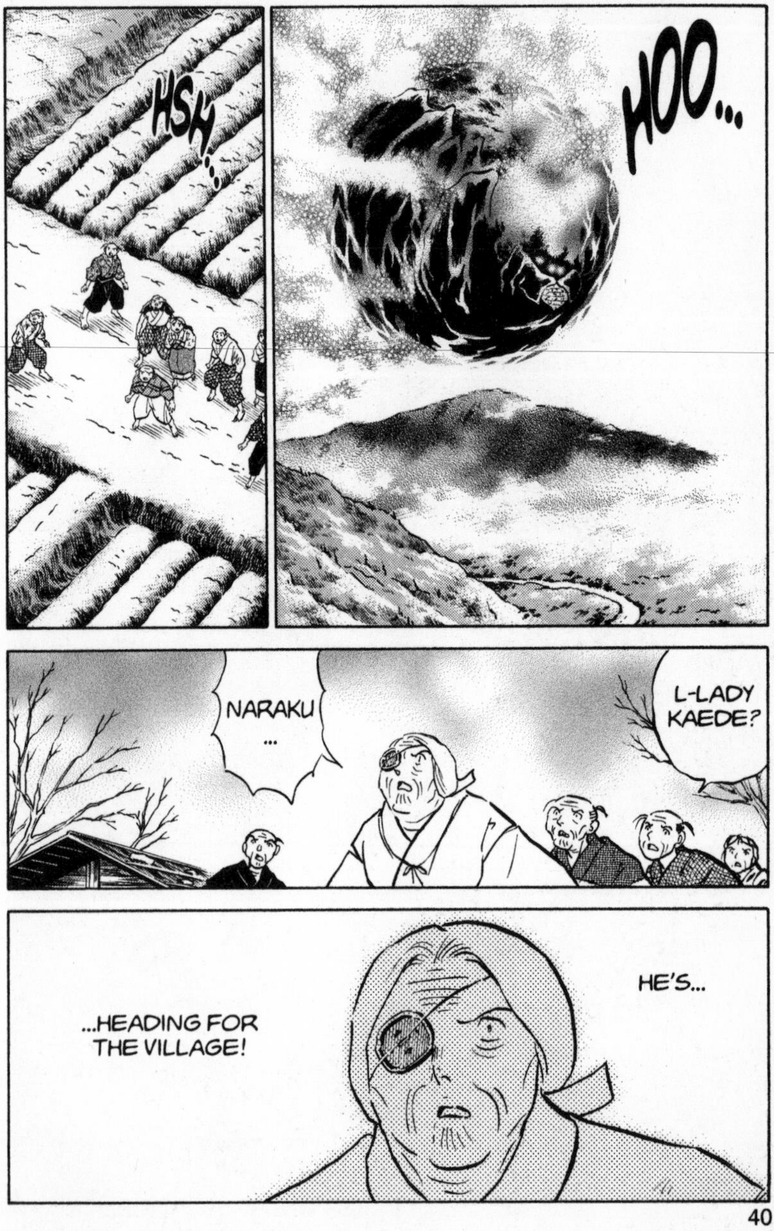
HOO...
HSH...
L-LADY KAEDE?
NARAKU ...
HE'S...
...HEADING FOR THE VILLAGE!

SCROLL 3

THE PLUNGE

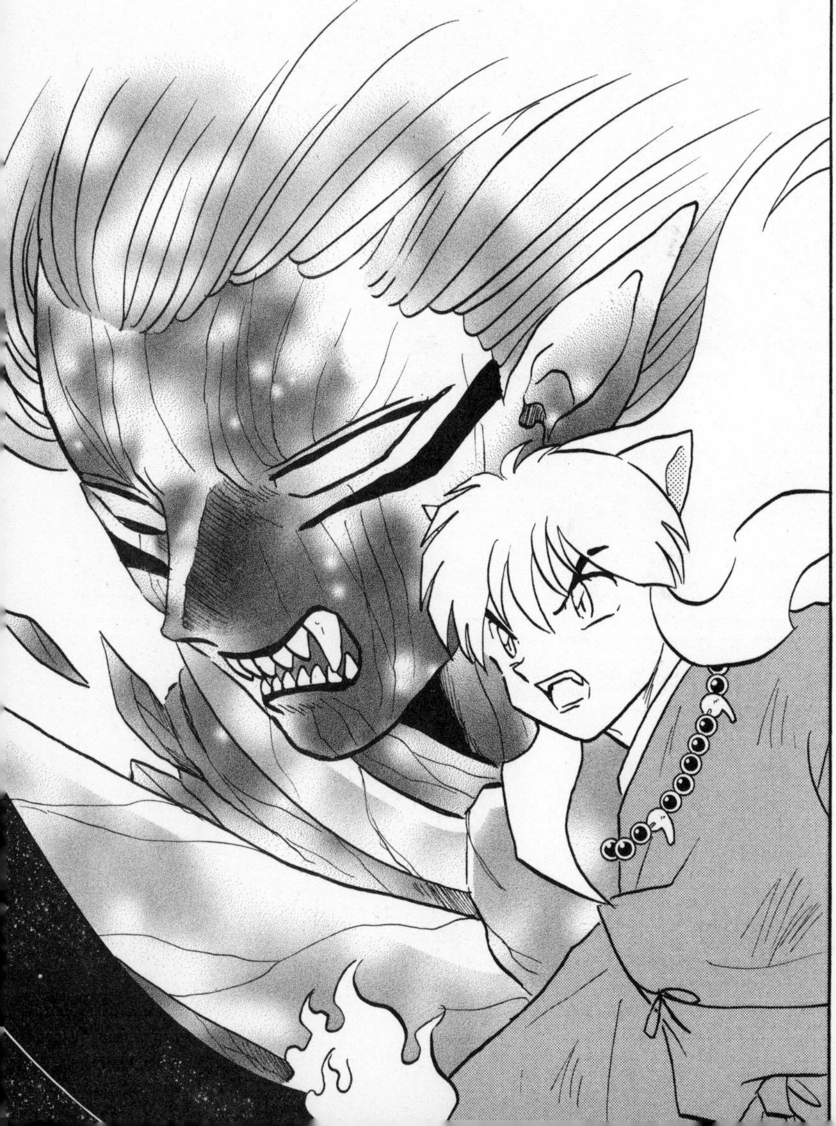

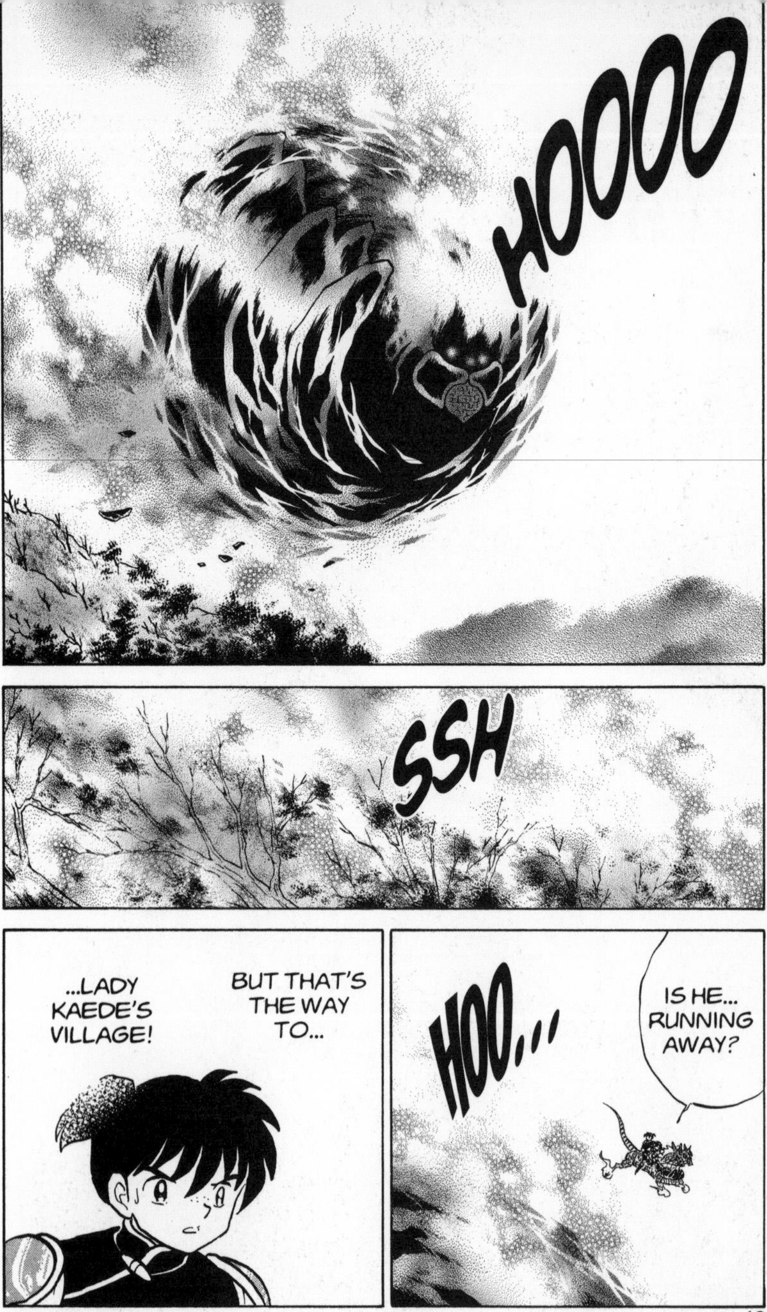
HOOOO
SSH
HOO...
IS HE... RUNNING AWAY?
BUT THAT'S THE WAY TO...
...LADY KAEDE'S VILLAGE!

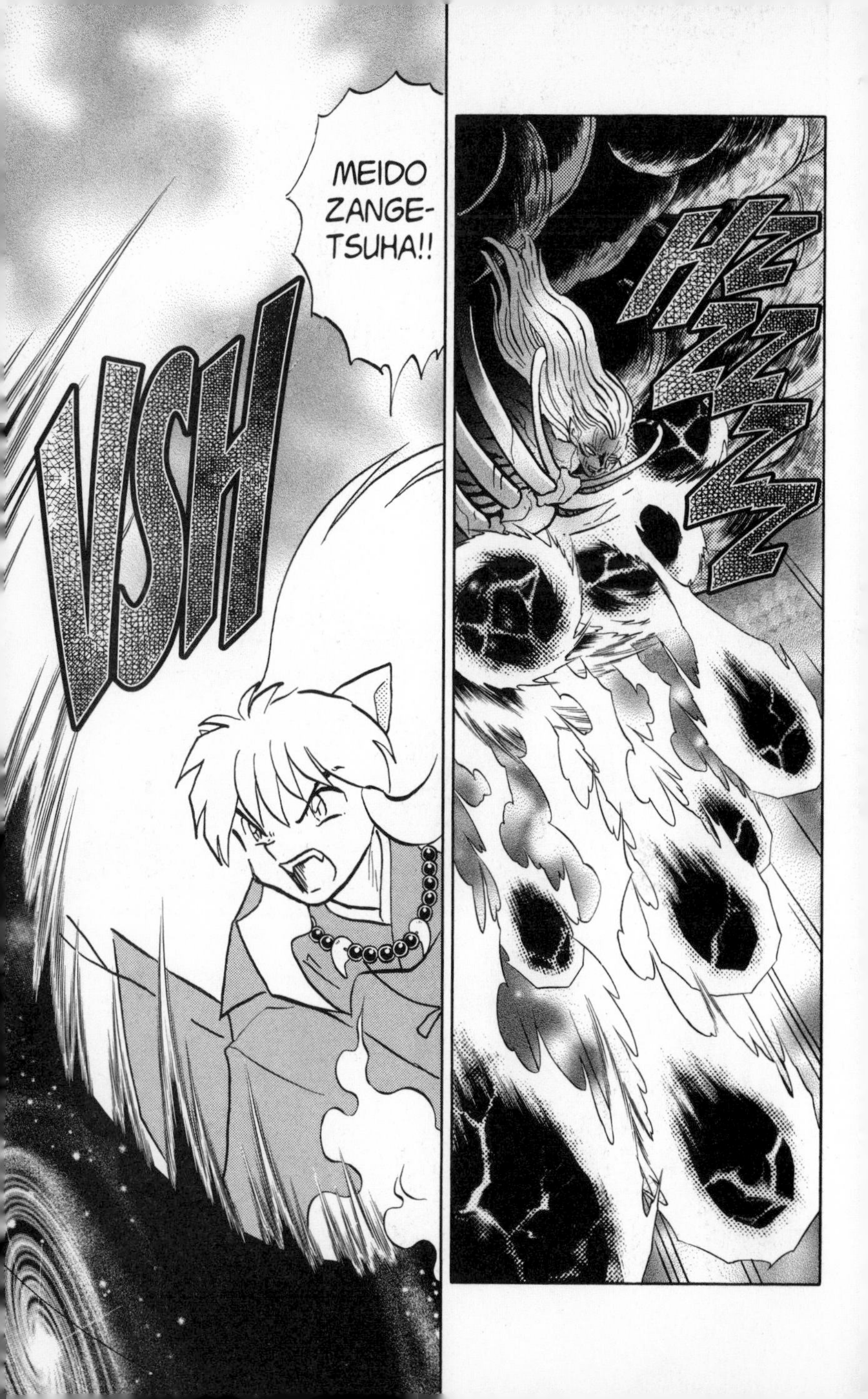
MEIDO ZANGE-TSUHA!!
VSH

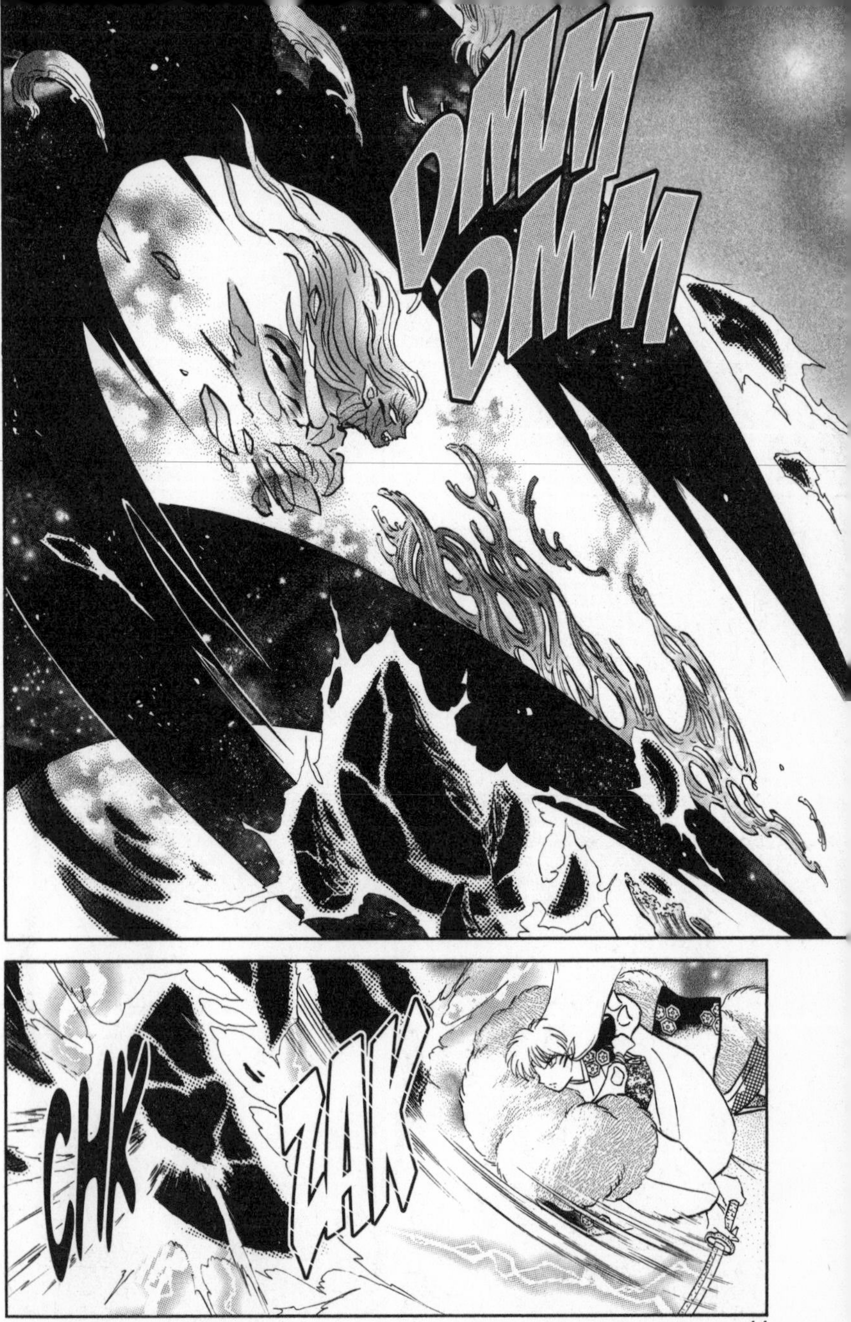
DMM
DMM
ZAK
CHK

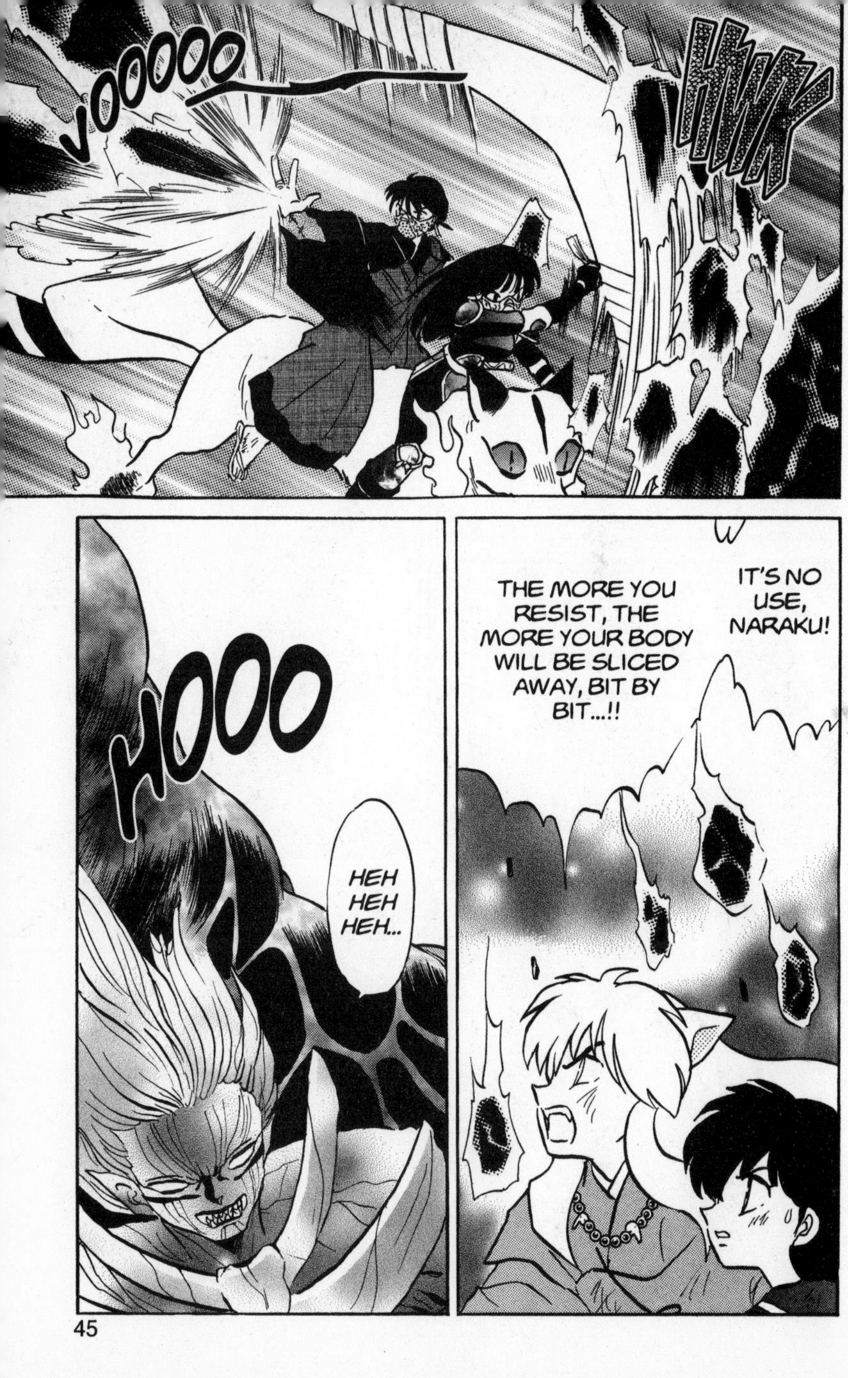
HWK
VOOOO
IT'S NO USE, NARAKU!
THE MORE YOU RESIST, THE MORE YOUR BODY WILL BE SLICED AWAY, BIT BY BIT...!!
HOOO
HEH HEH HEH...

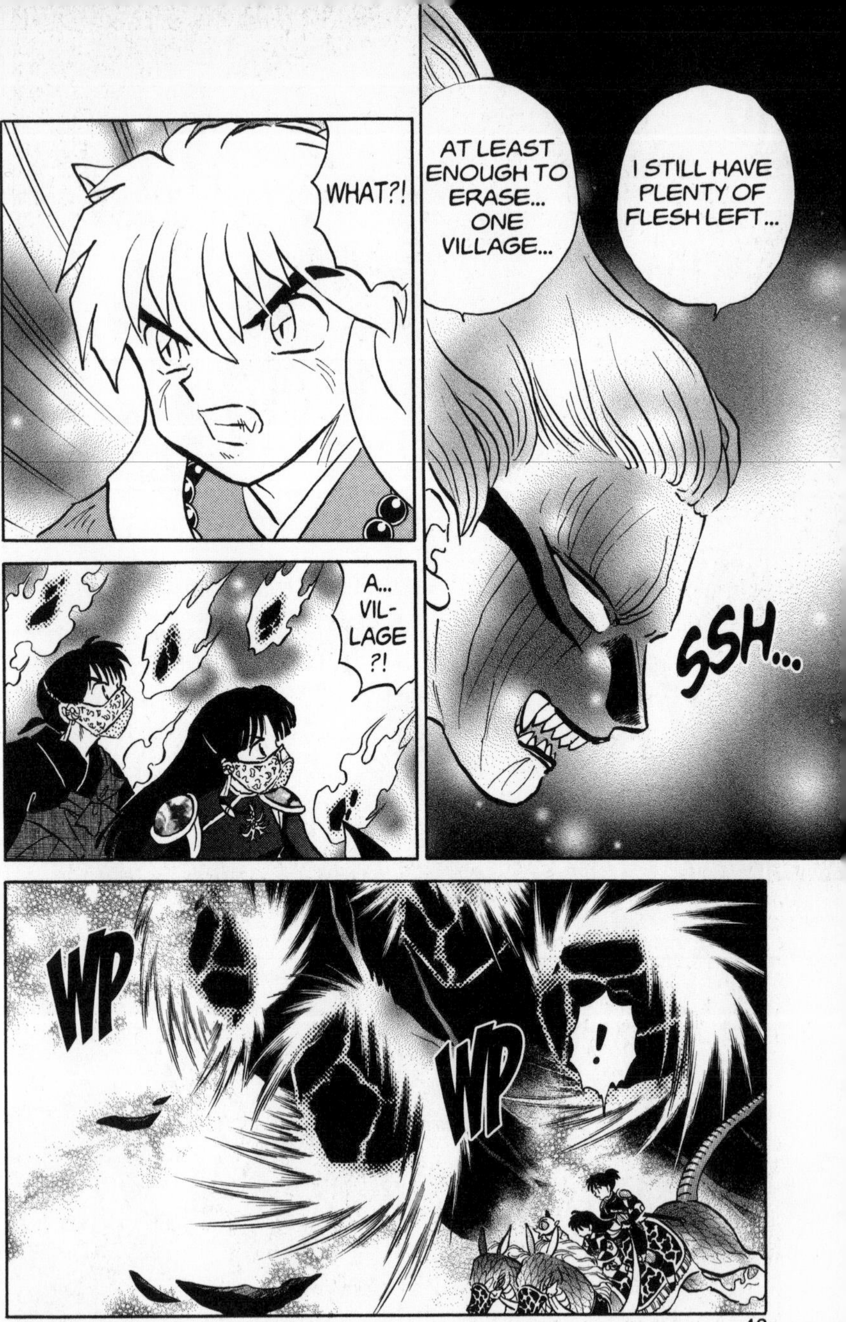
I STILL HAVE PLENTY OF FLESH LEFT...
AT LEAST ENOUGH TO ERASE... ONE VILLAGE...
SSH...
WHAT?!
A... VIL-LAGE?!
!
WP
WP

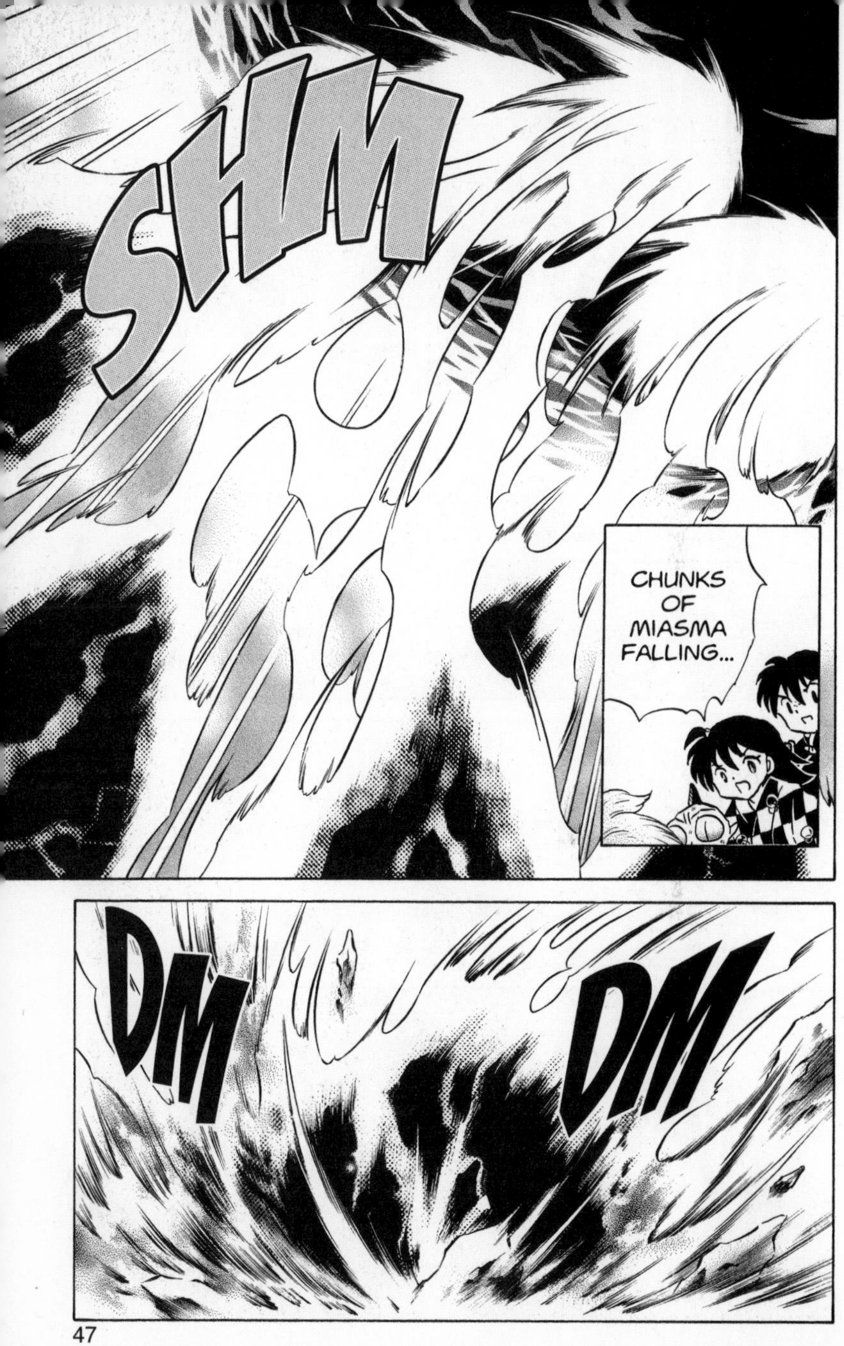
SHM
CHUNKS OF MIASMA FALLING...
DM
DM

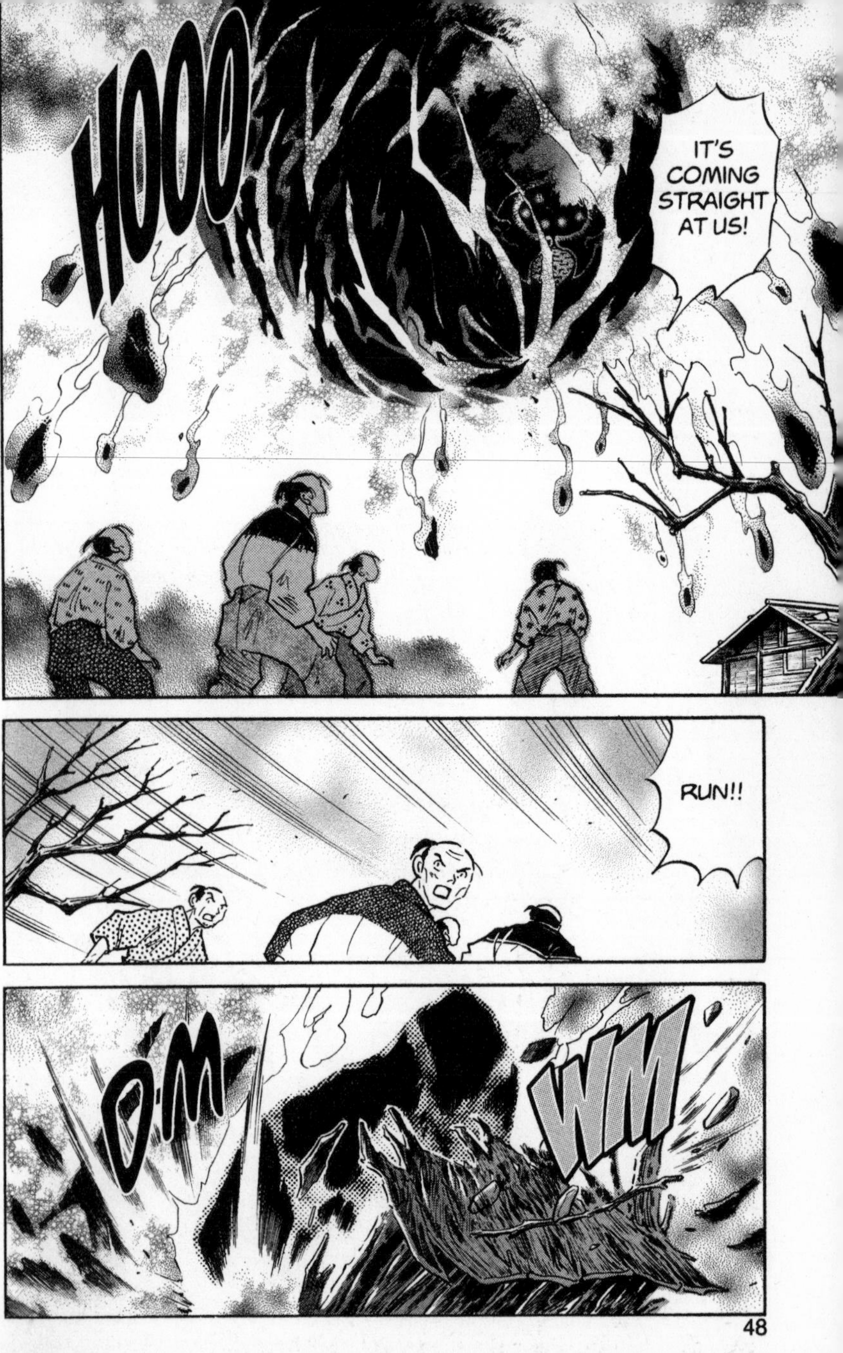
IT'S COMING STRAIGHT AT US!
HOOO
RUN!!
WM
DOM

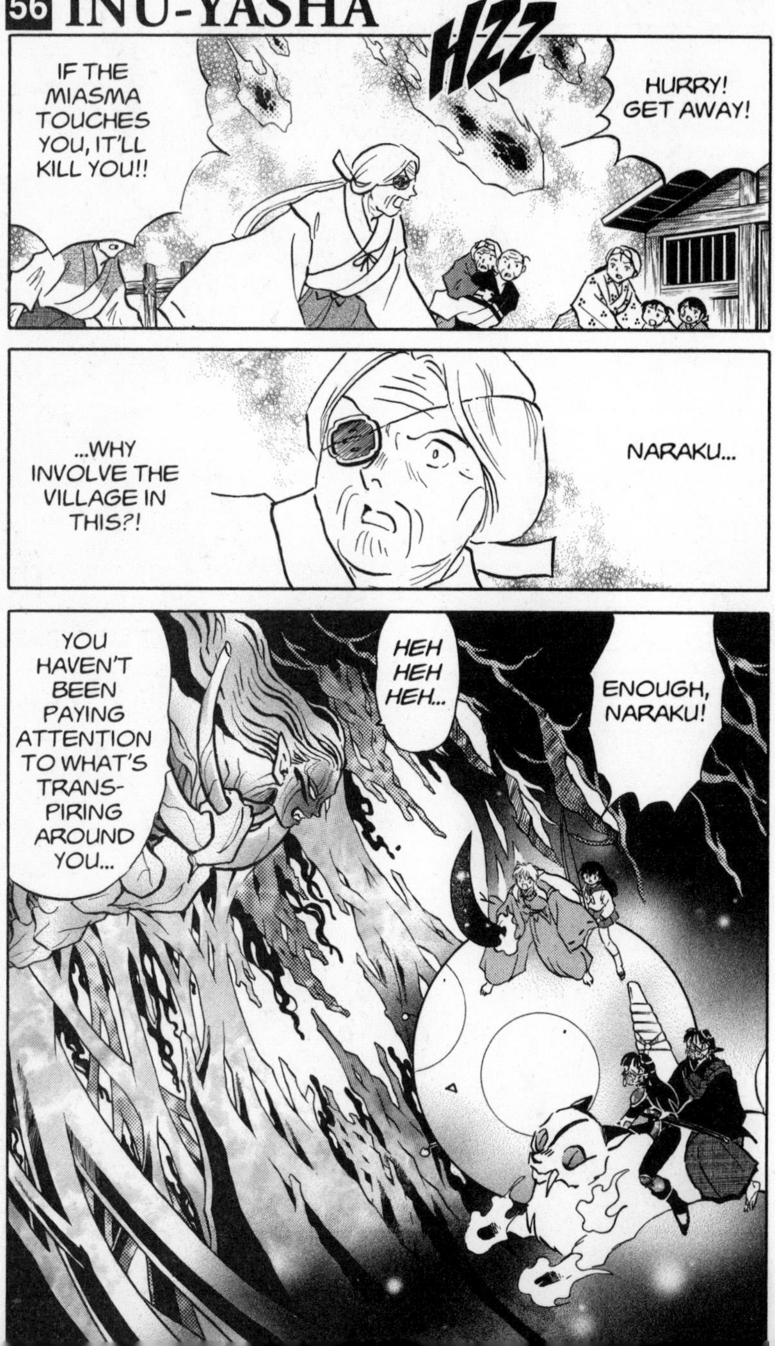
HZZ
HURRY! GET AWAY!
IF THE MIASMA TOUCHES YOU, IT'LL KILL YOU!!
NARAKU...
...WHY INVOLVE THE VILLAGE IN THIS?!
ENOUGH, NARAKU!
HEH HEH HEH...
YOU HAVEN'T BEEN PAYING ATTENTION TO WHAT'S TRANS-PIRING AROUND YOU...

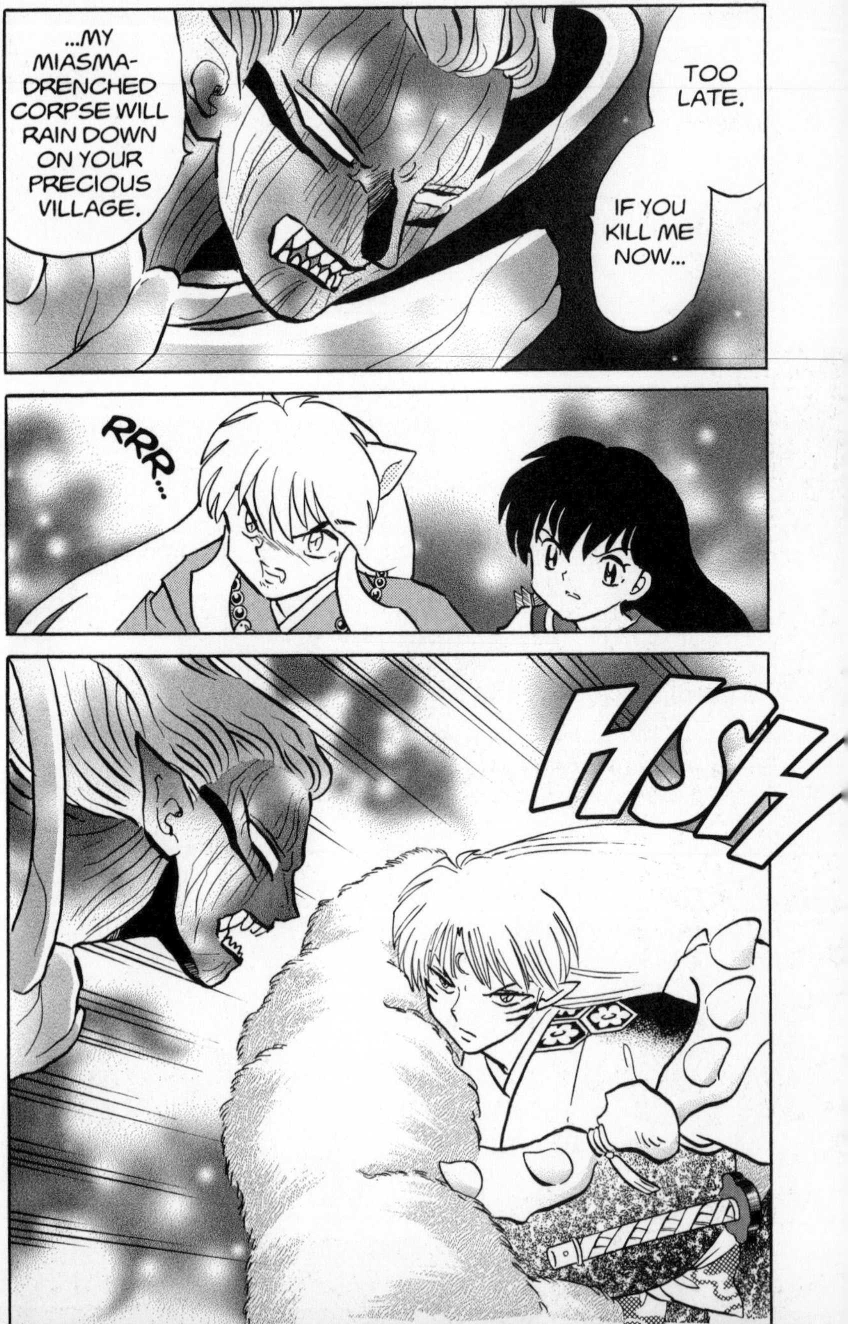
TOO LATE.
IF YOU KILL ME NOW...
...MY MIASMA-DRENCHED CORPSE WILL RAIN DOWN ON YOUR PRECIOUS VILLAGE.
RRR...
HSH

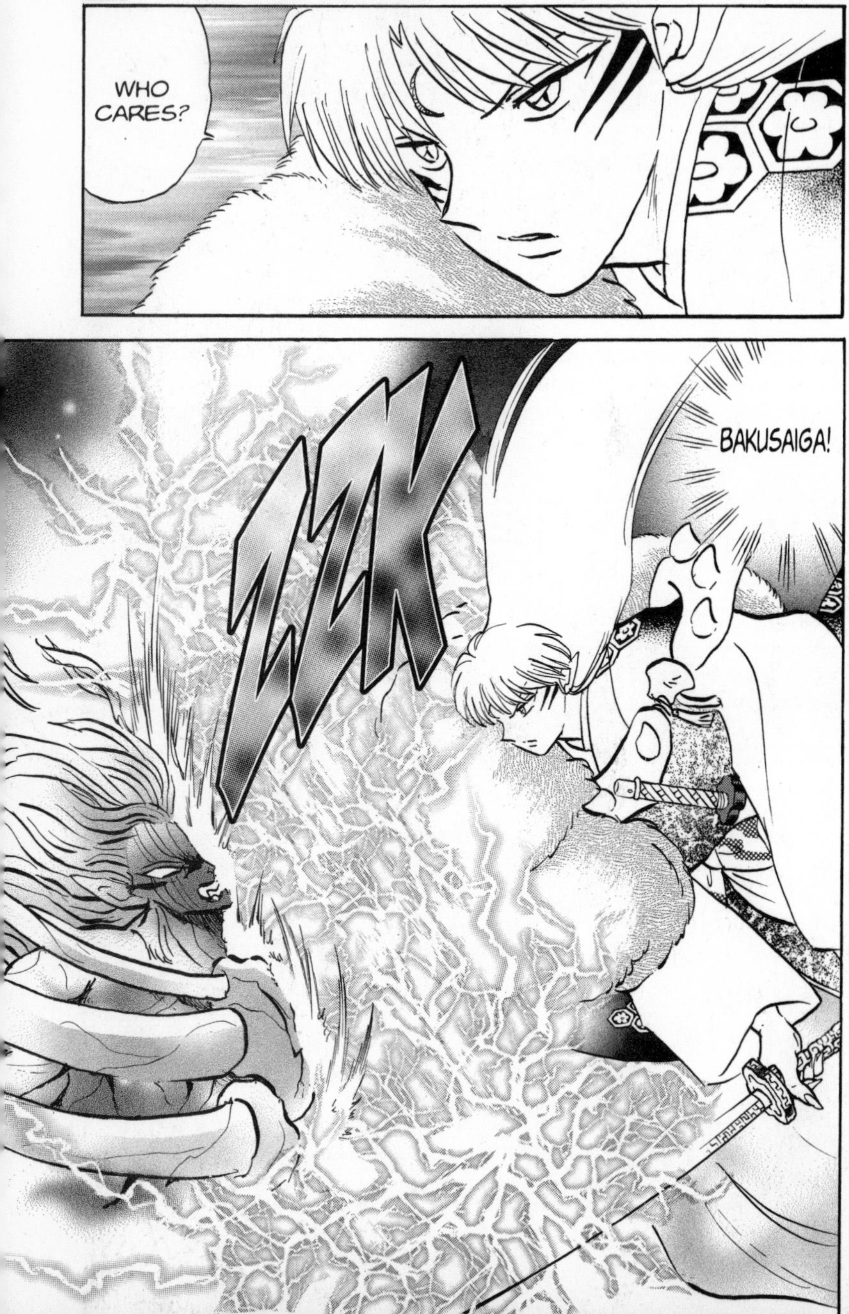
WHO CARES?
BAKUSAIGA!
ZZK

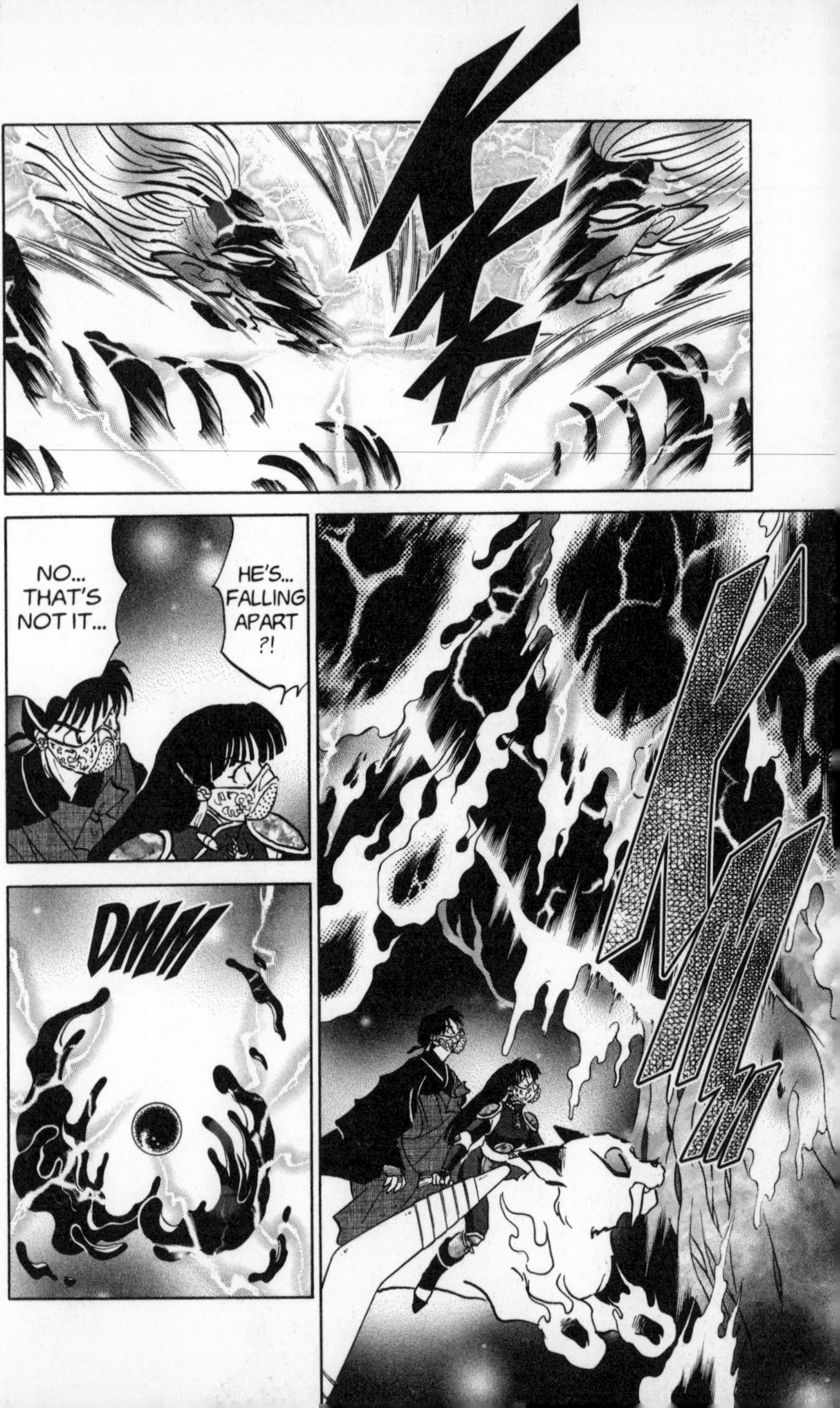
HE'S... FALLING APART ?!
NO... THAT'S NOT IT...
DMM

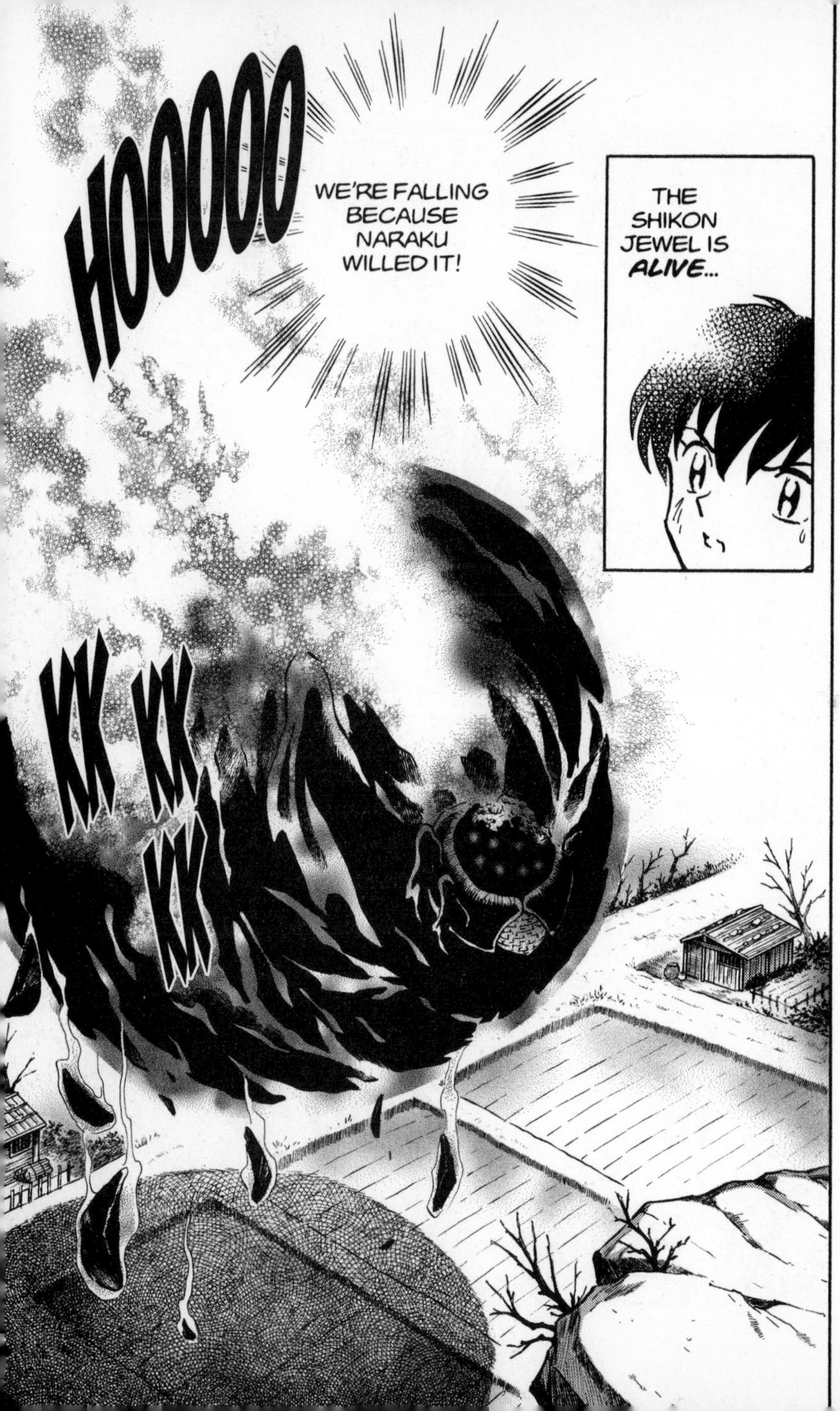
THE SHIKON JEWEL IS ALIVE...
WE'RE FALLING BECAUSE NARAKU WILLED IT!
HOOOOO
KK KK KK

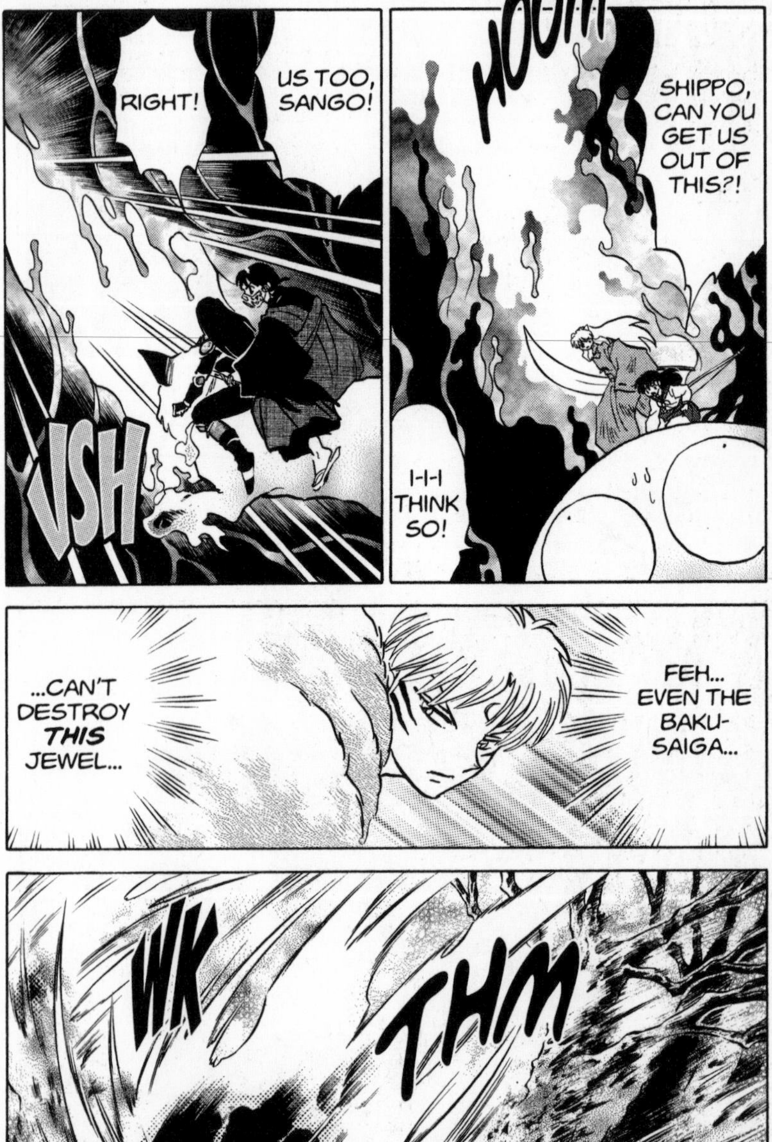
HOOM
SHIPPO, CAN YOU GET US OUT OF THIS?!
I-I-I THINK SO!
US TOO, SANGO!
RIGHT!
JSH
FEH... EVEN THE BAKU-SAIGA...
...CAN'T DESTROY *THIS* JEWEL...
THM
WK

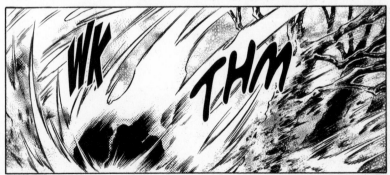

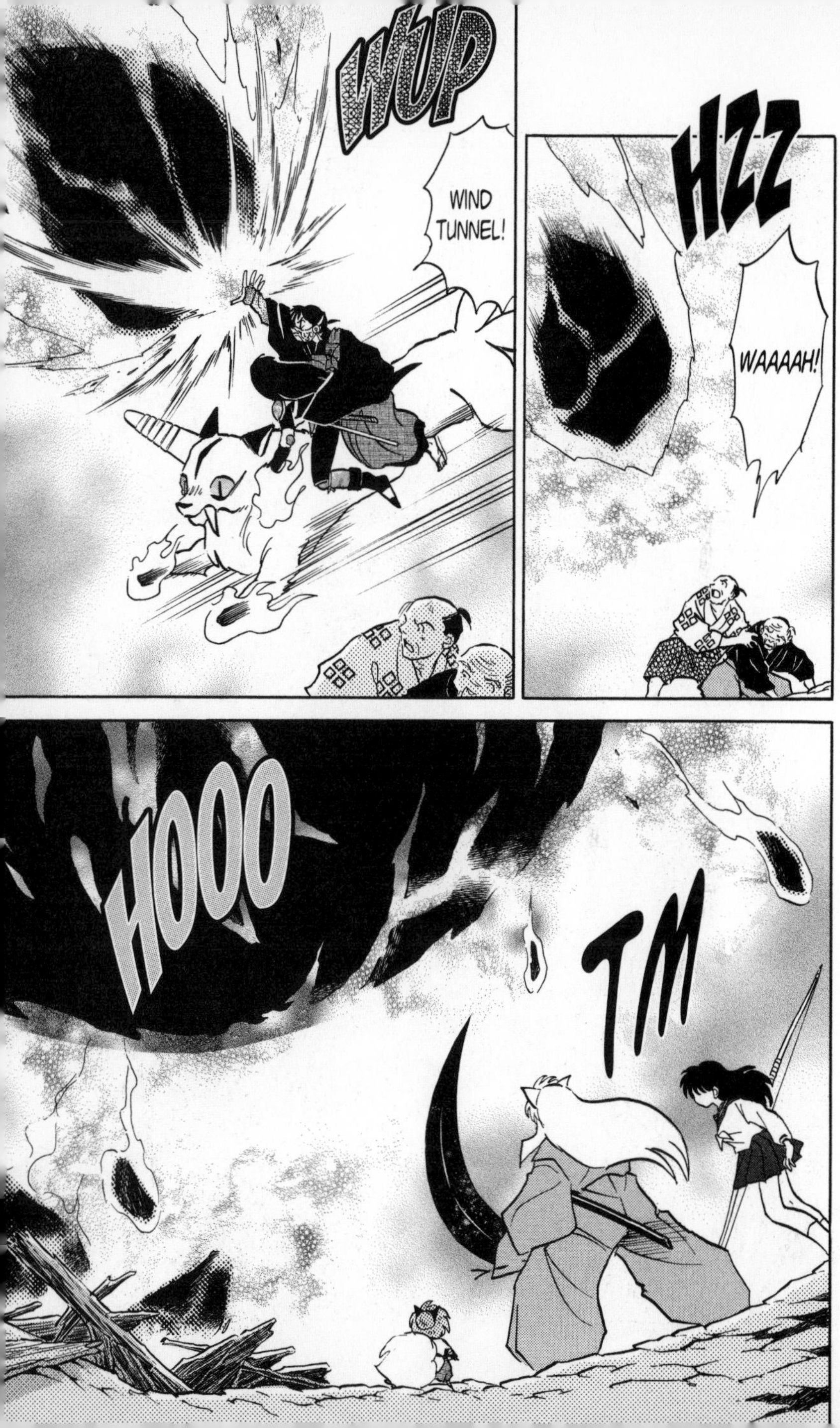
HZZ
WAAAAH!
WUP
WIND TUNNEL!
TM
HOOO

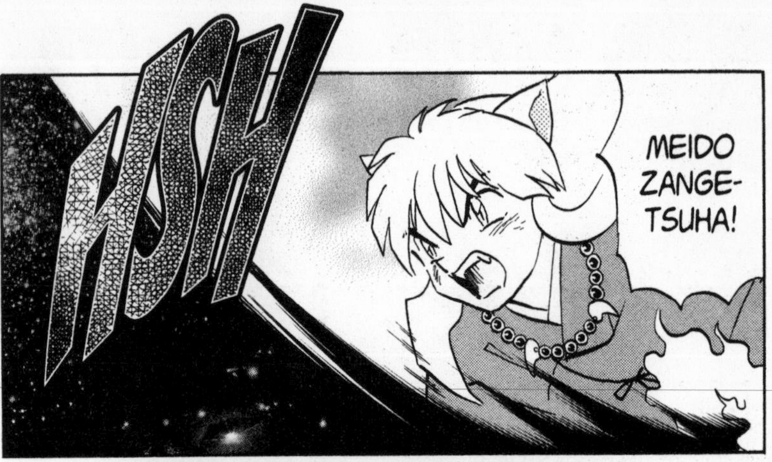
HSH
MEIDO ZANGE-TSUHA!
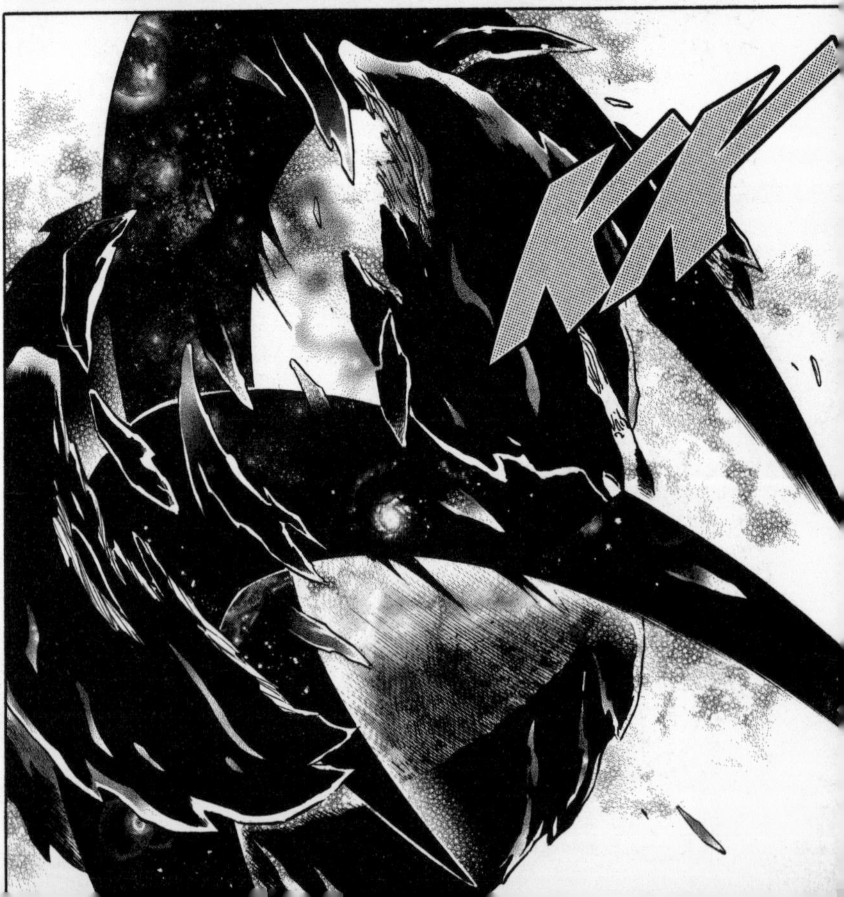

HOOO

W... HZZ ZZ OOO...

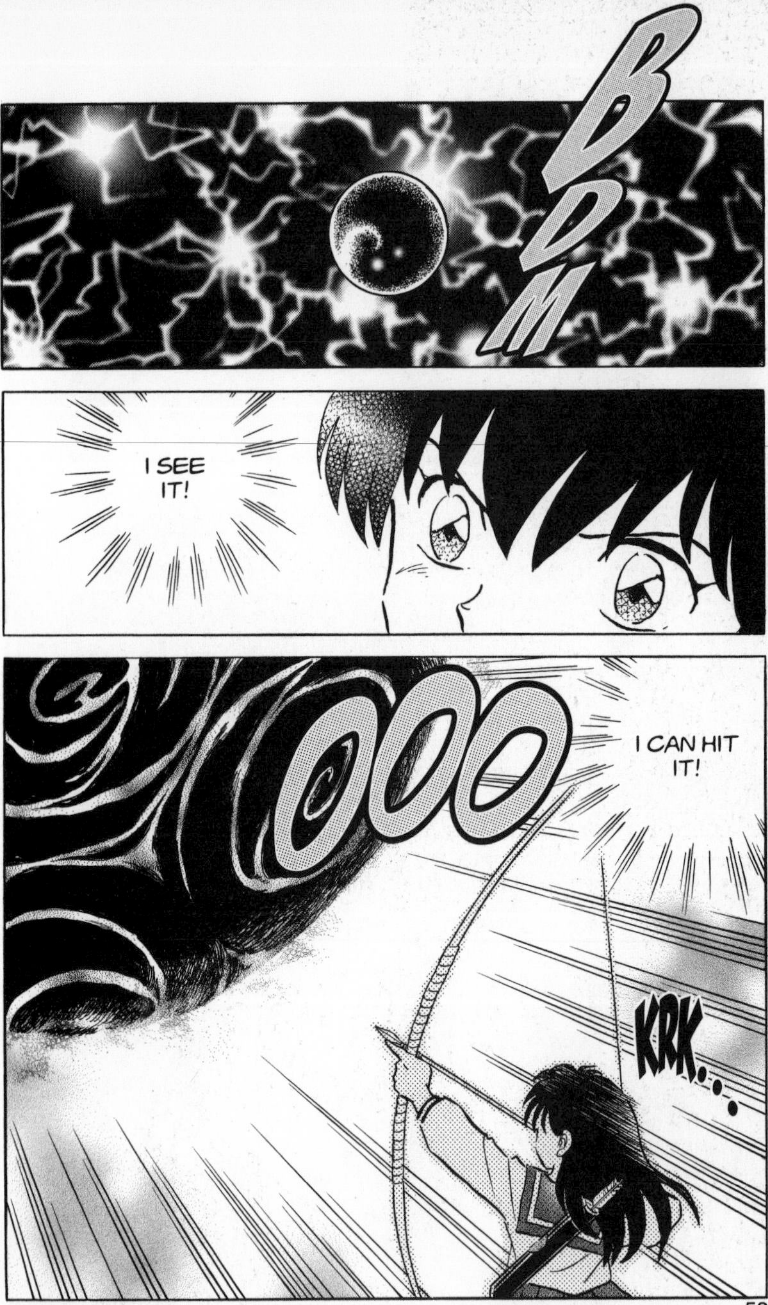
BDM
I SEE IT!
OOO
I CAN HIT IT!
KRK...

SCROLL 4
THE DEATH OF NARAKU

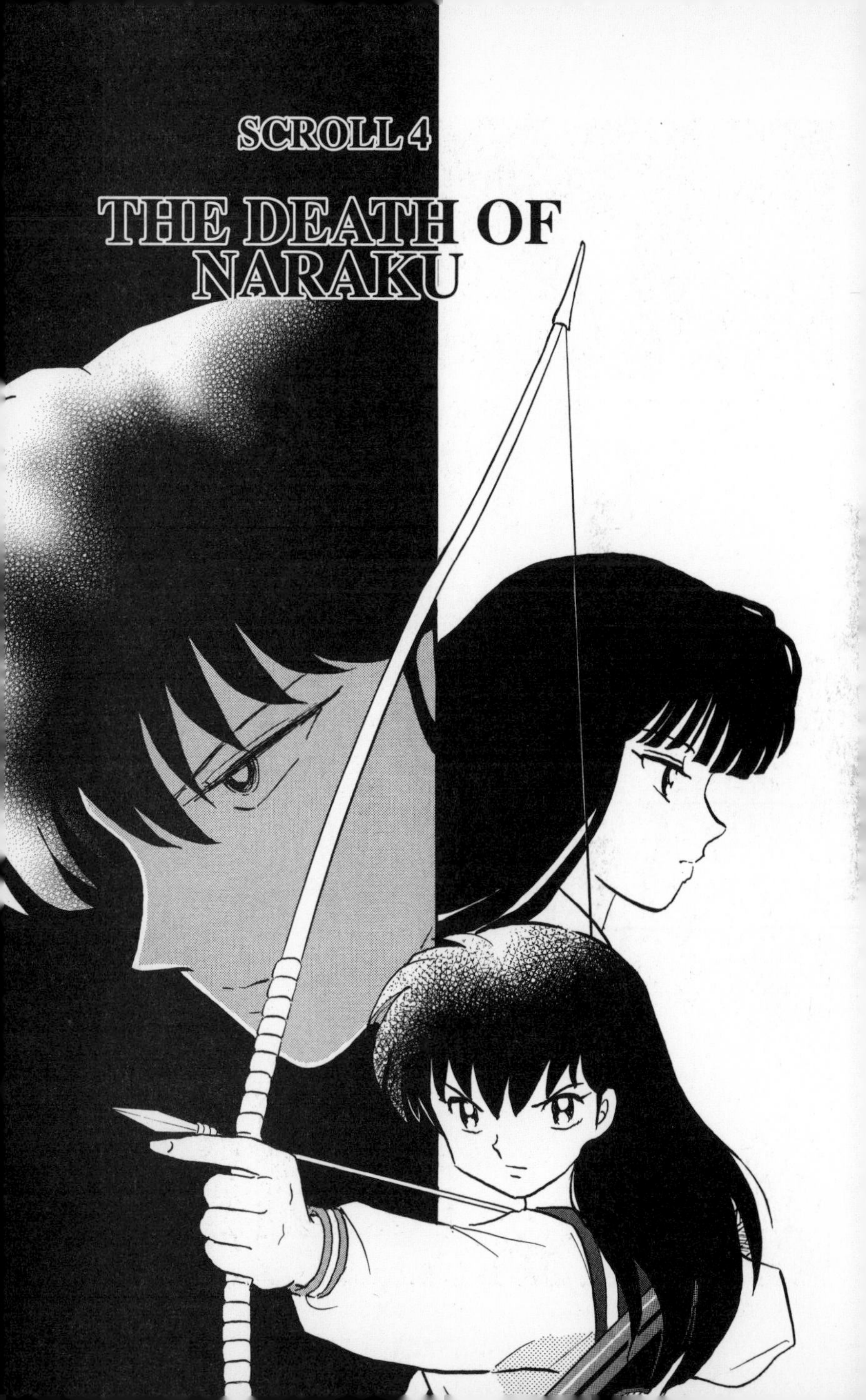

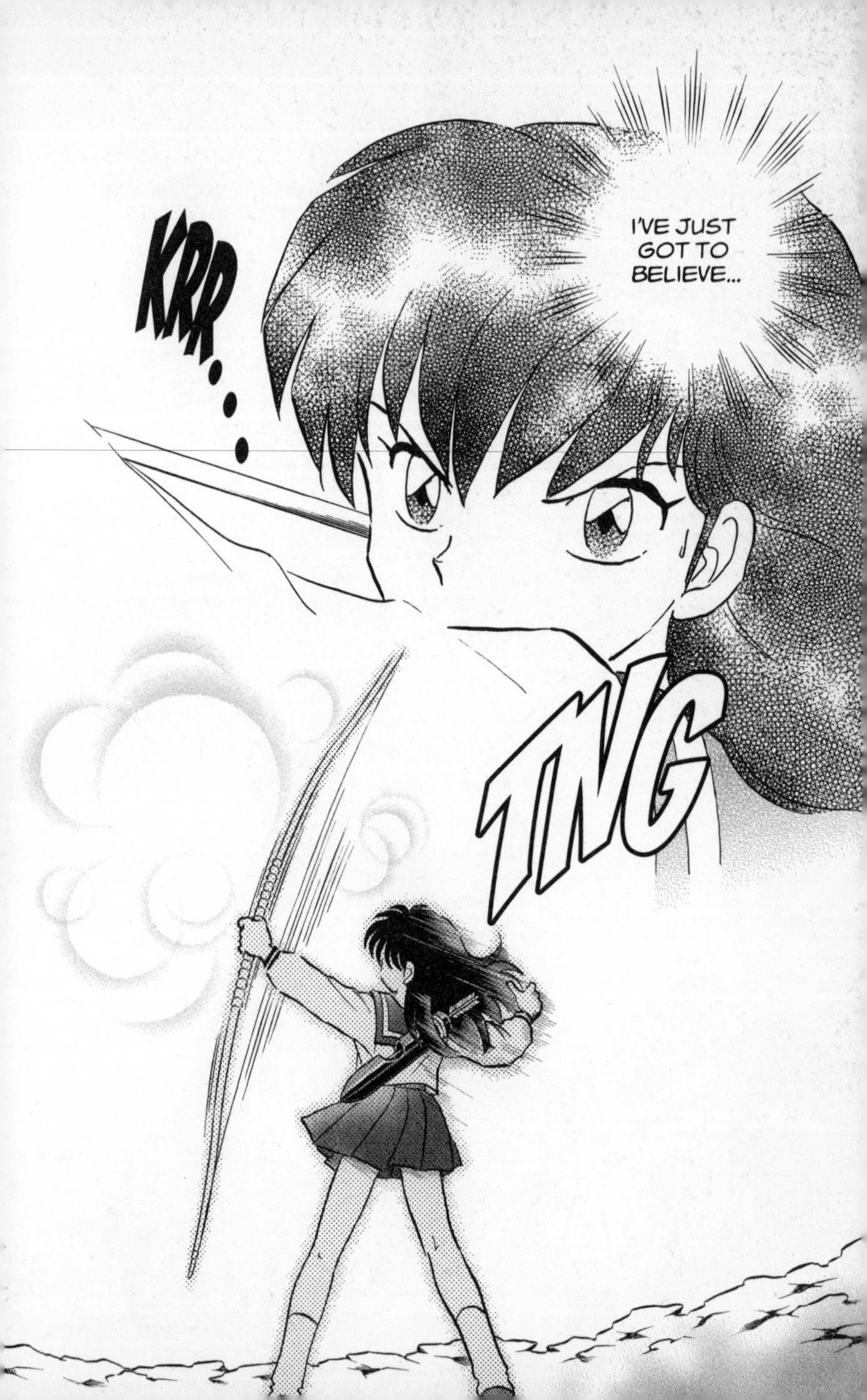
I'VE JUST GOT TO BELIEVE...
KRR...
TNG

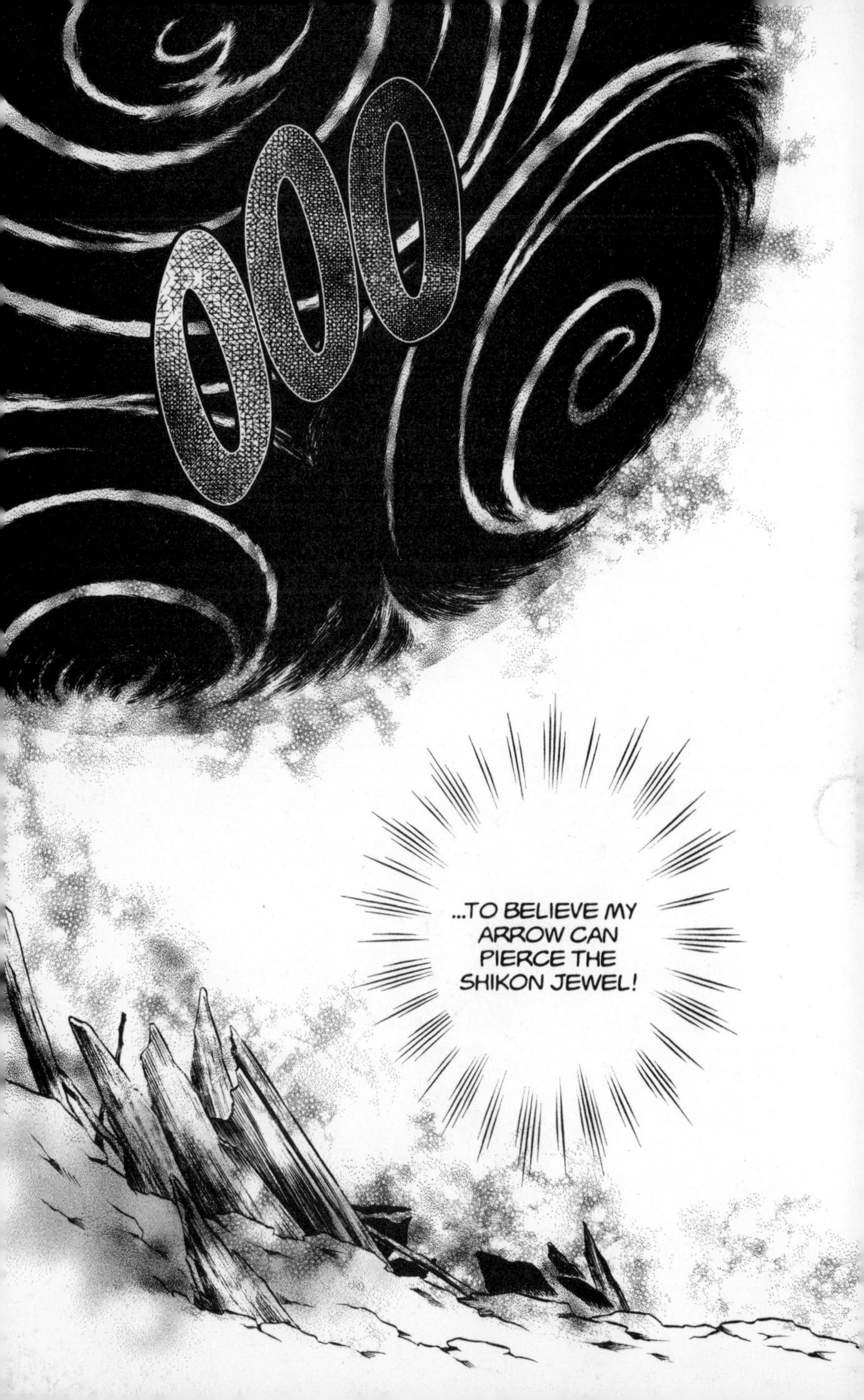
...TO BELIEVE MY ARROW CAN PIERCE THE SHIKON JEWEL!

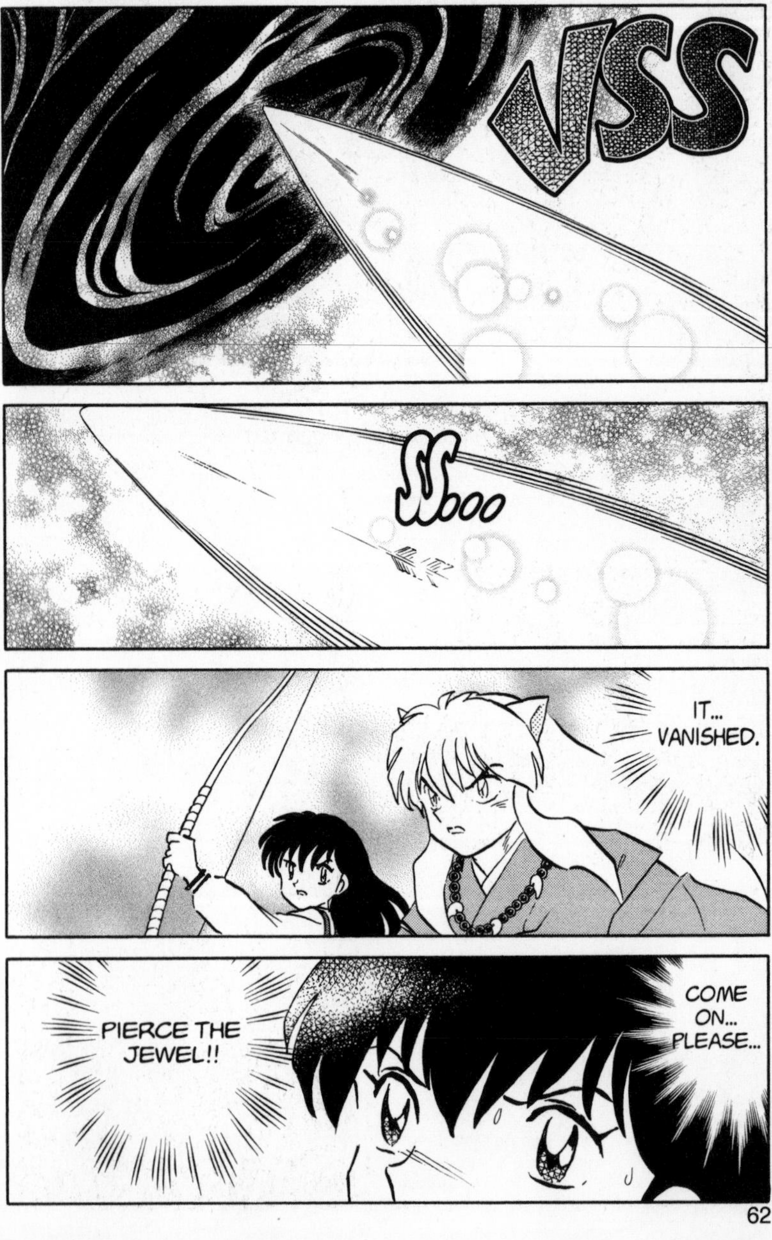
VSS
SSooo
IT... VANISHED.
COME ON... PLEASE...
PIERCE THE JEWEL!!

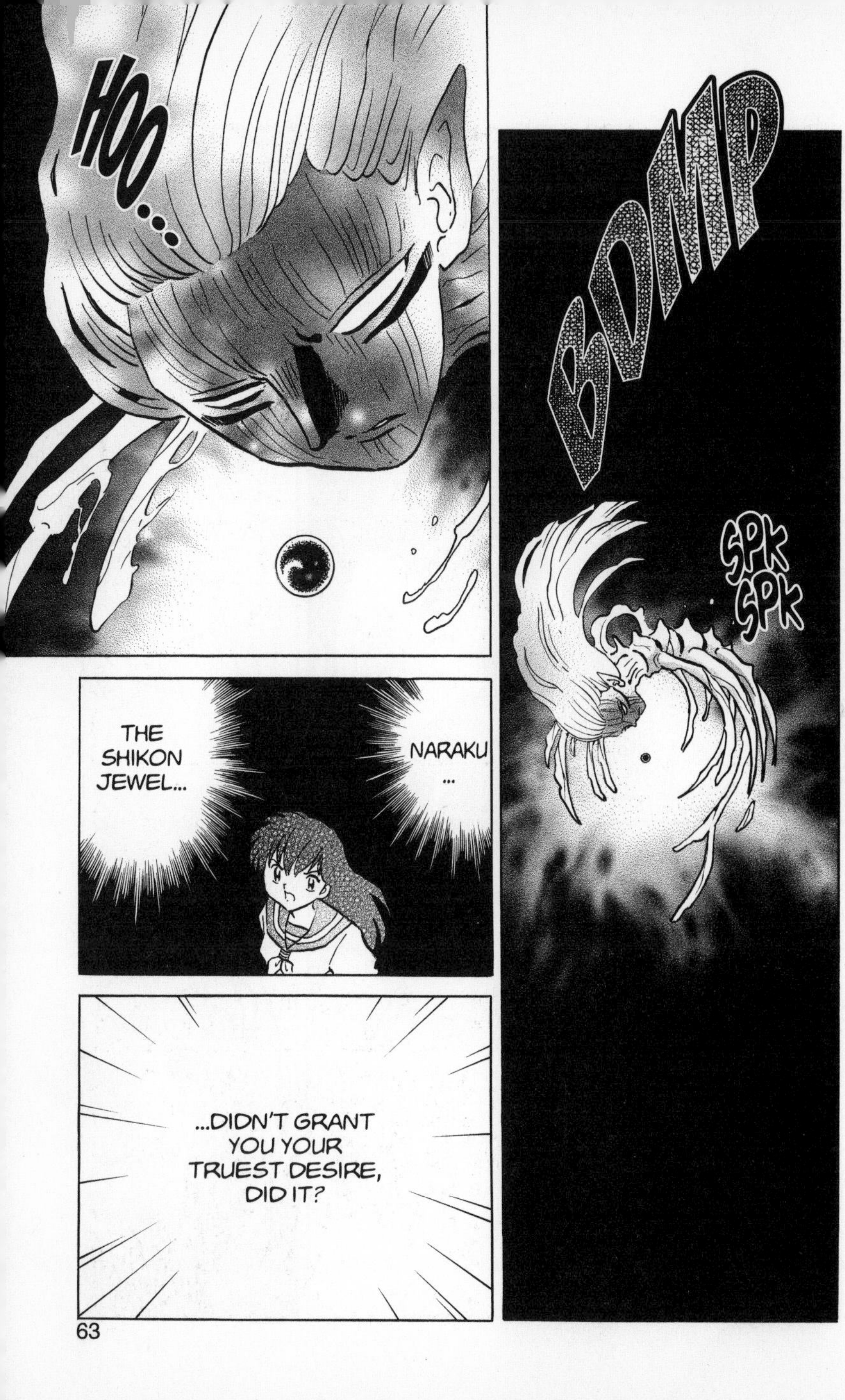
BOMP
SPK SPK
HOO....
NARAKU ...
THE SHIKON JEWEL...
...DIDN'T GRANT YOU YOUR TRUEST DESIRE, DID IT?

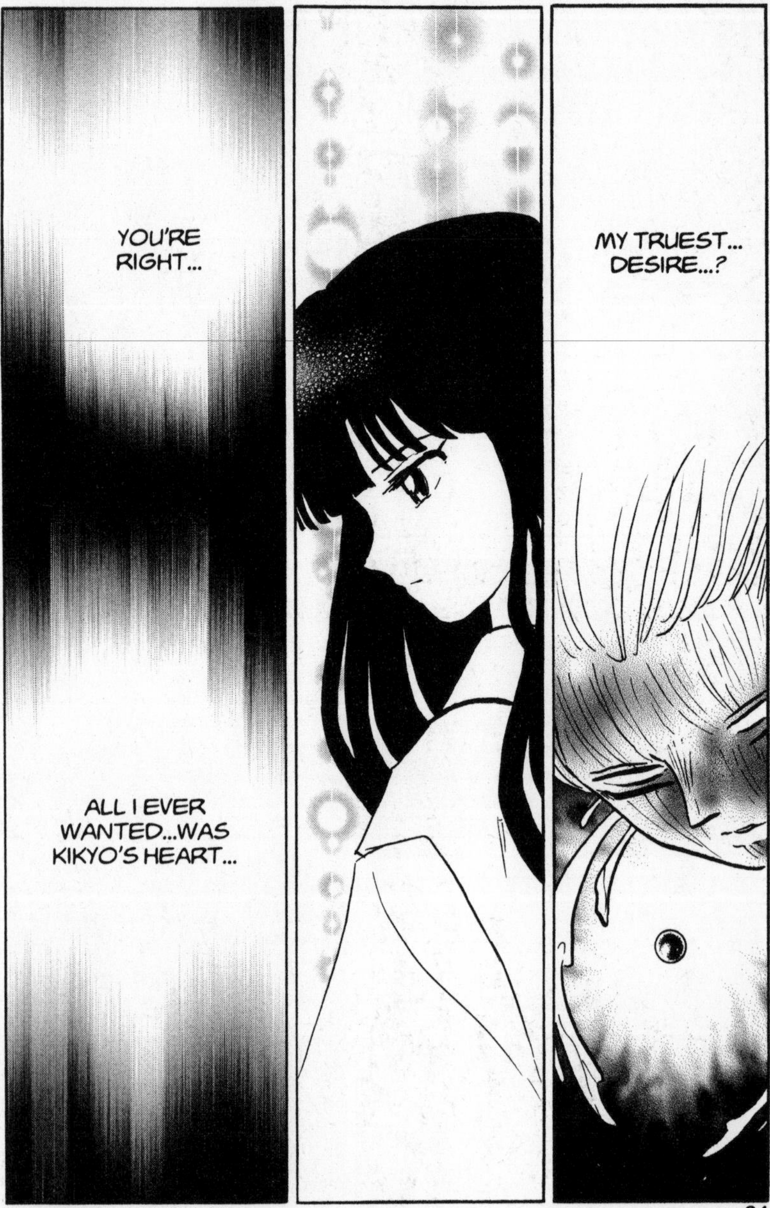
MY TRUEST... DESIRE...?
YOU'RE RIGHT...
ALL I EVER WANTED...WAS KIKYO'S HEART...

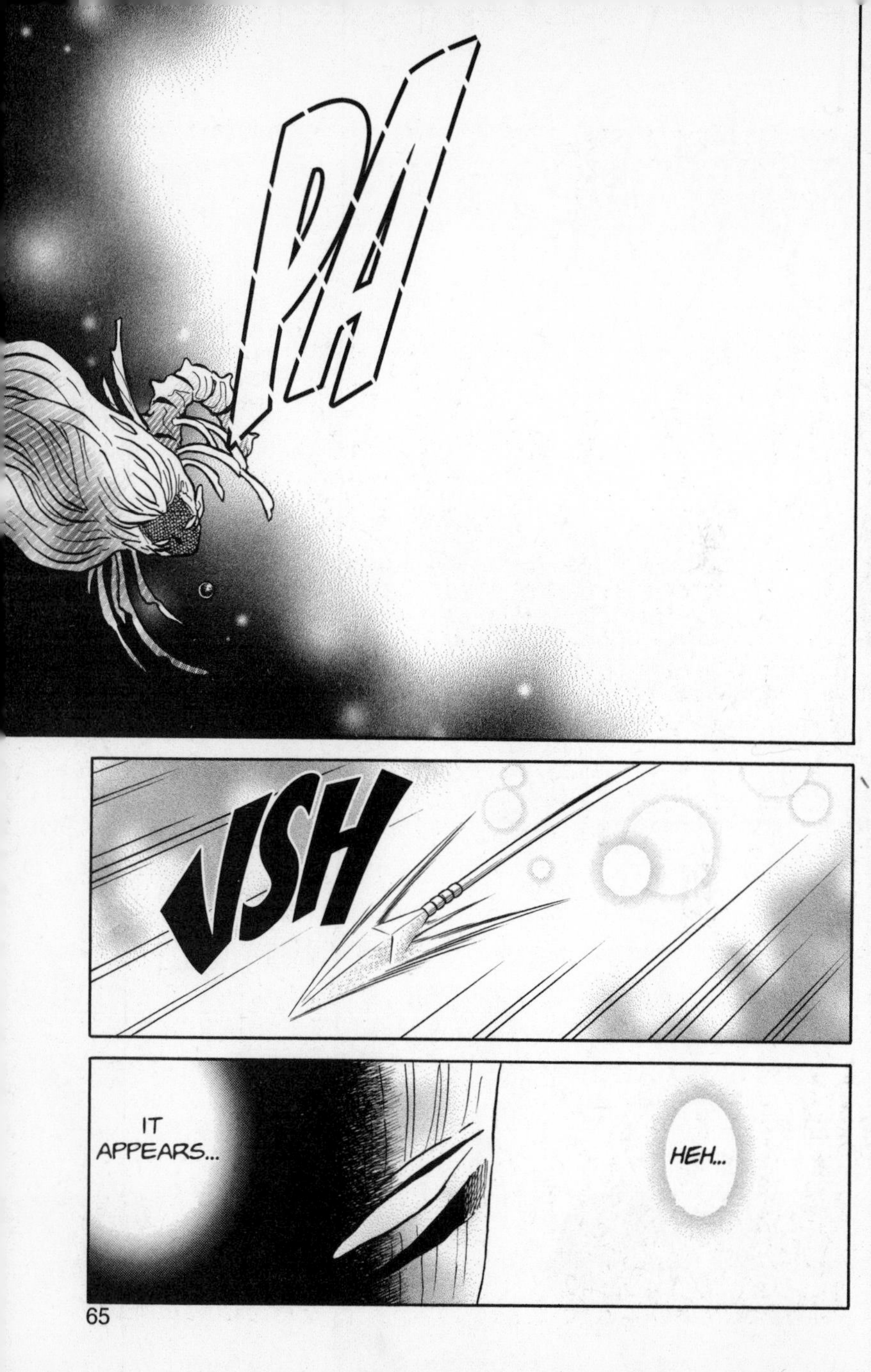
PA
VSH
HEH...
IT APPEARS...

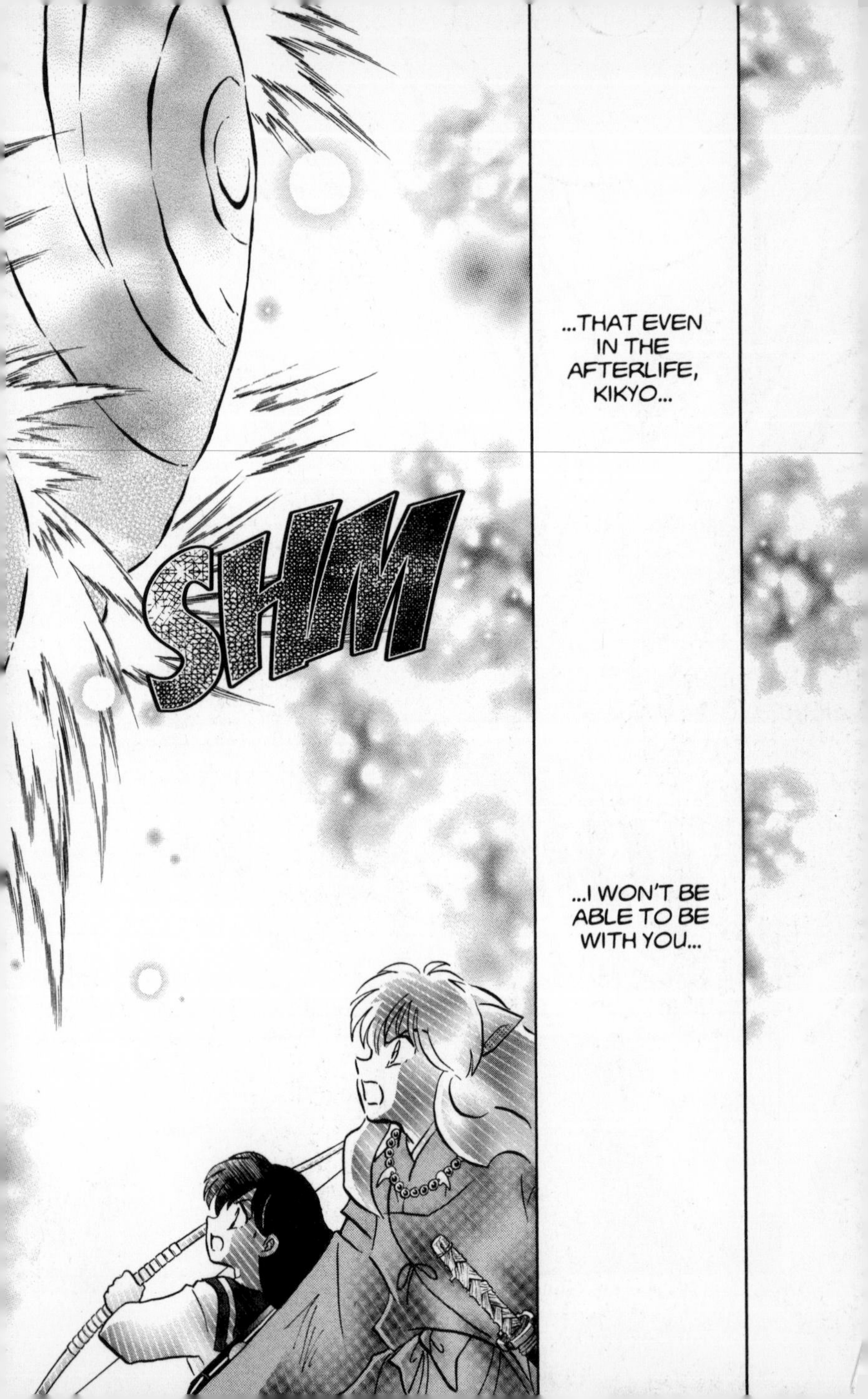
...THAT EVEN IN THE AFTERLIFE, KIKYO...
...I WON'T BE ABLE TO BE WITH YOU...
SHM

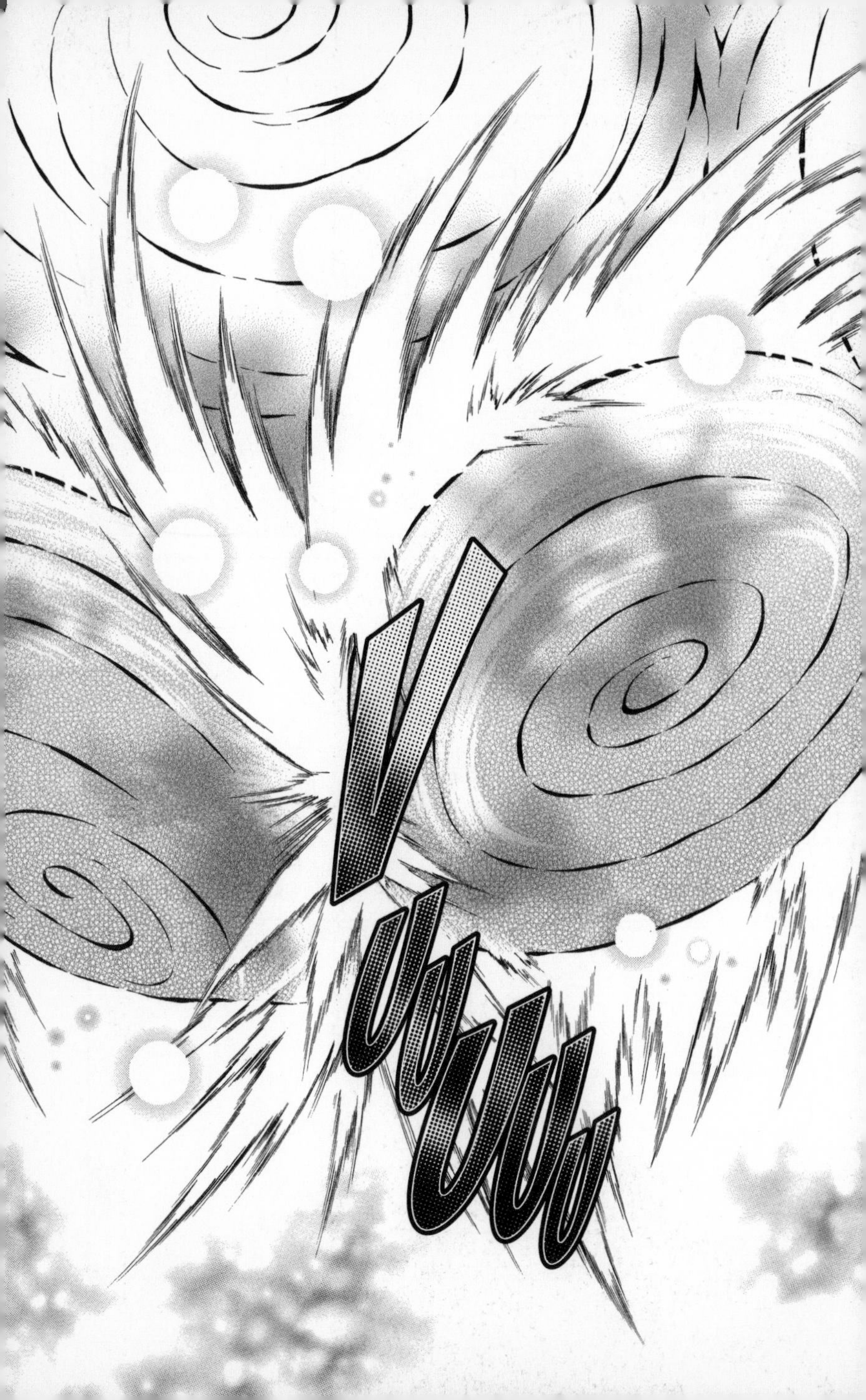
VUUUUU

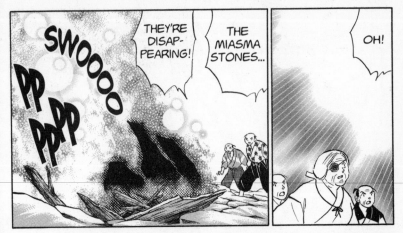

OH!
THE MIASMA STONES...
THEY'RE DISAP-PEARING!
SWOOOOPPPPPP
THE MIASMA IS BEING PURIFIED!
SSH...
SO...LADY KAGOME'S ARROW MUST HAVE...?

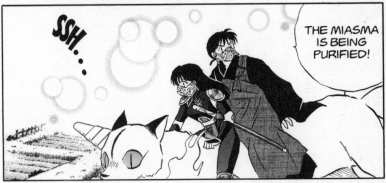

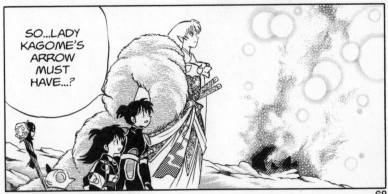

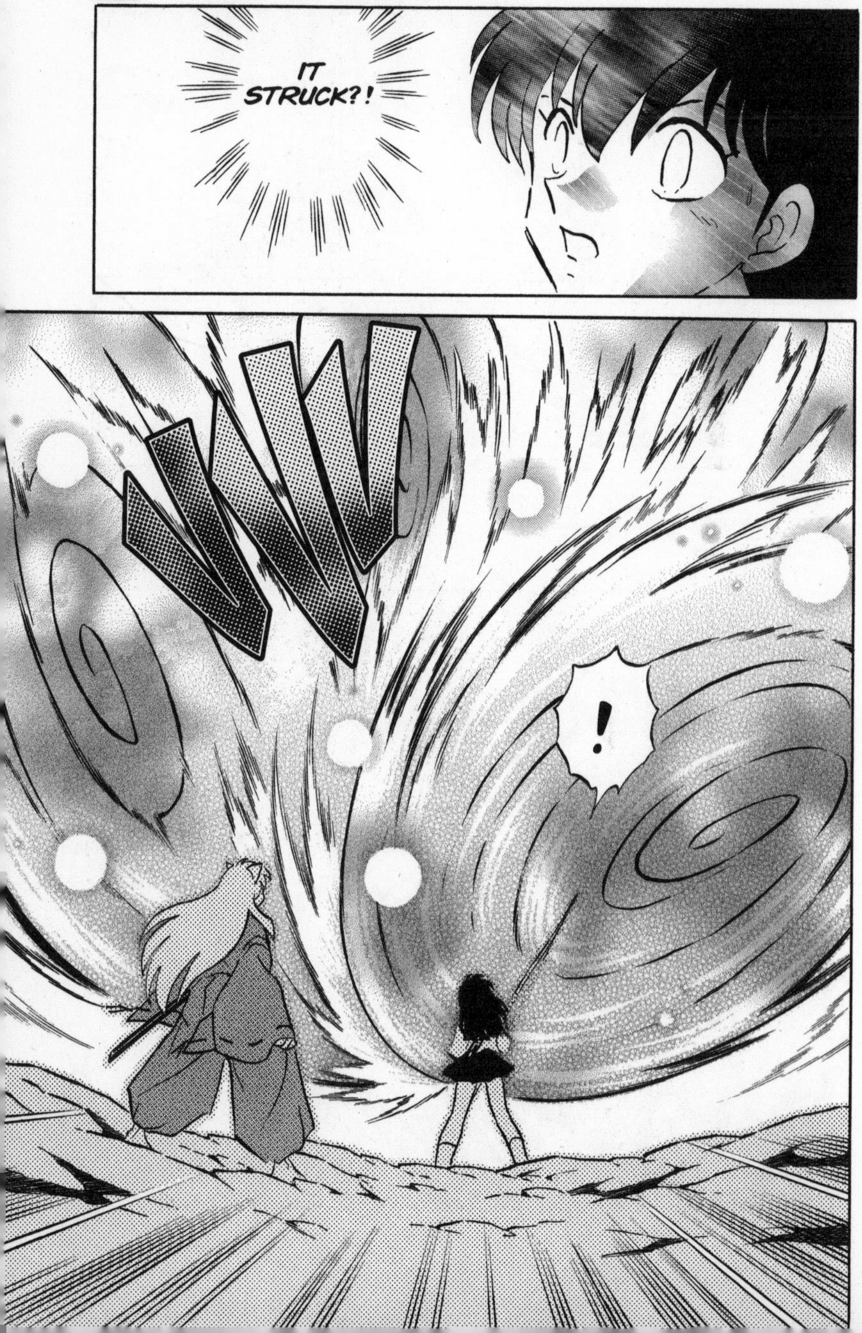
IT STRUCK?!
!

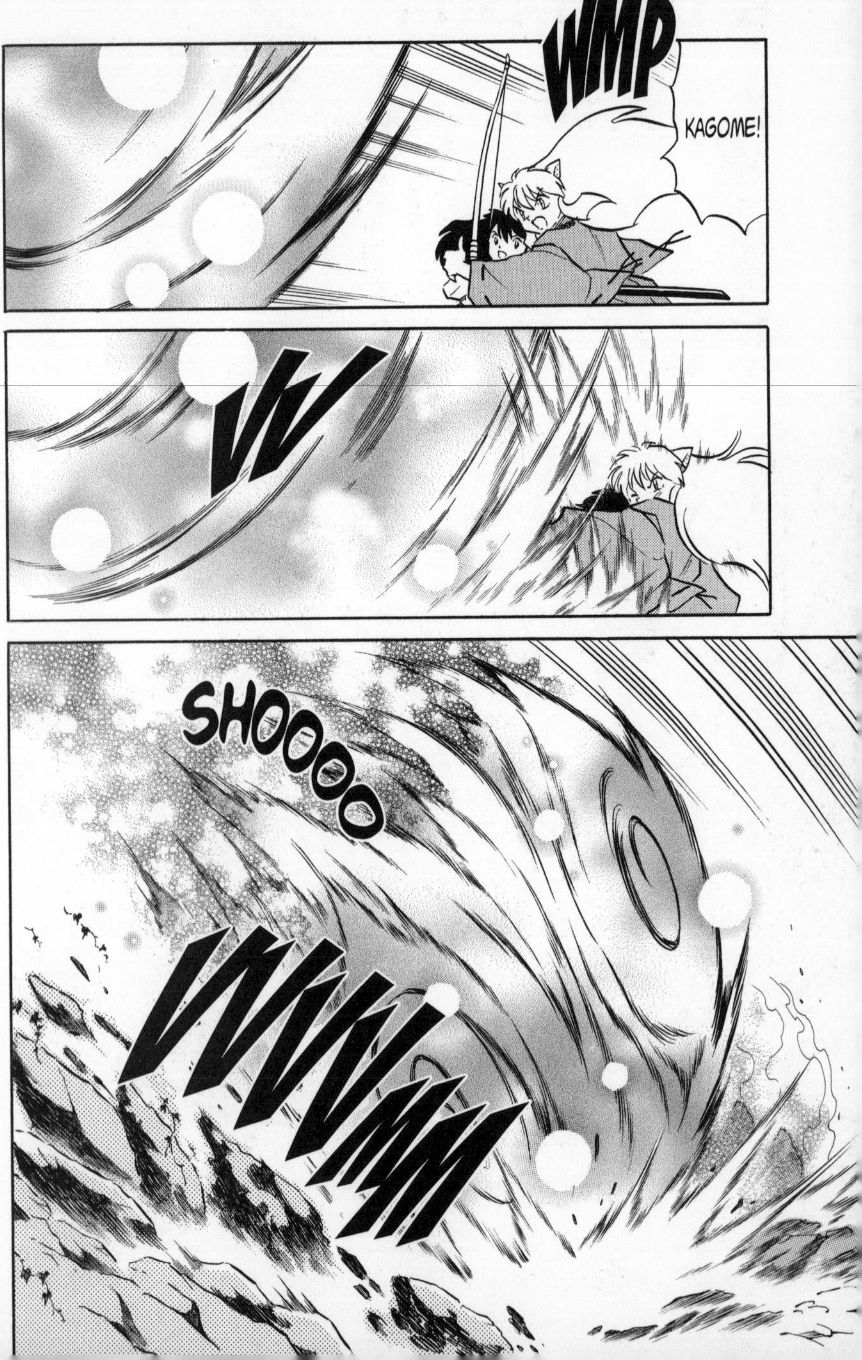
WMP
KAGOME!
SHOOOOO

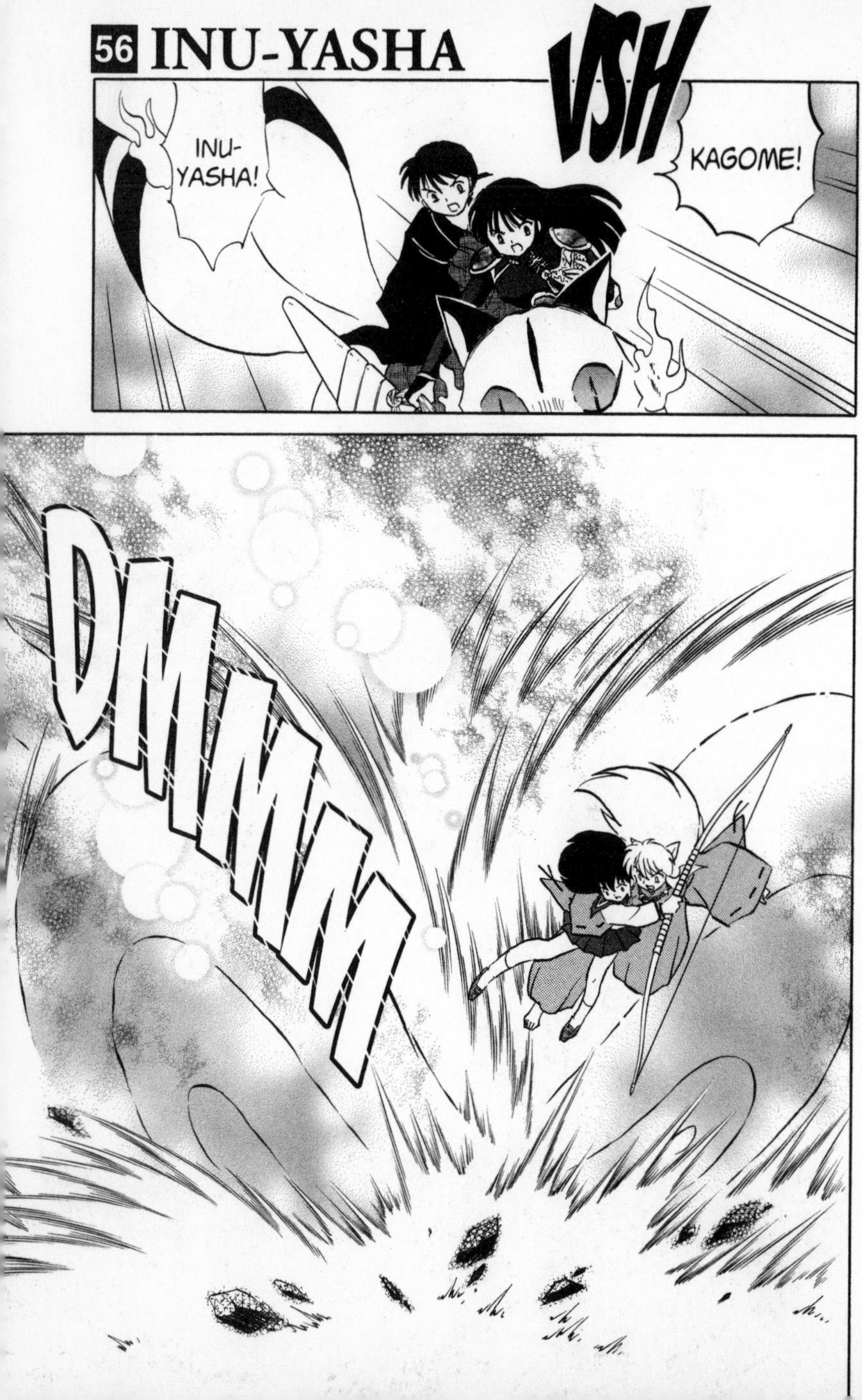
KAGOME!
VSH
INU-YASHA!
DMMMM

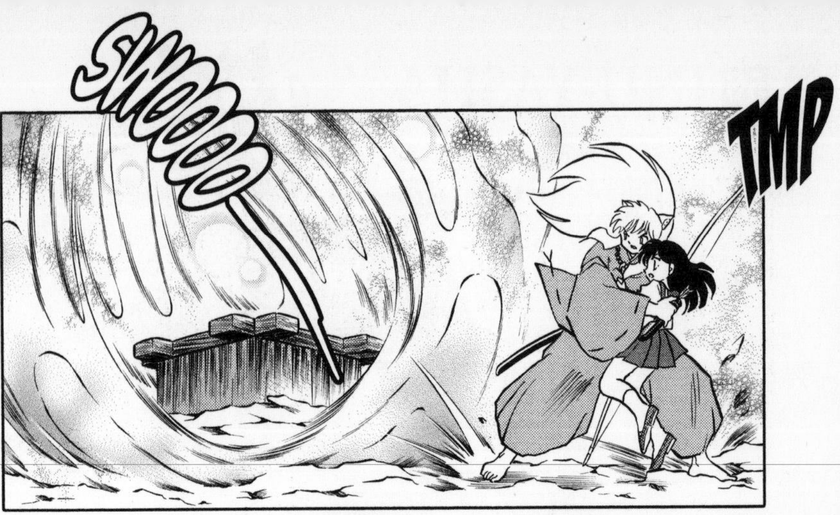
TMP
SHOOOOO
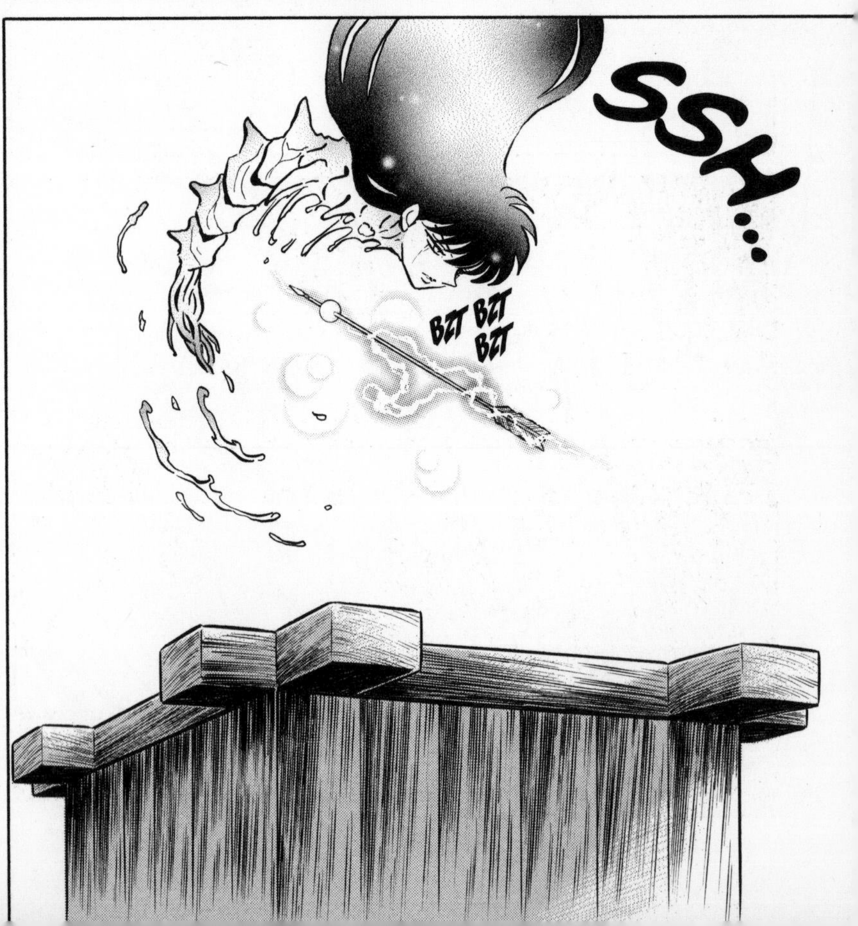
SSH...
BZT BZT BZT

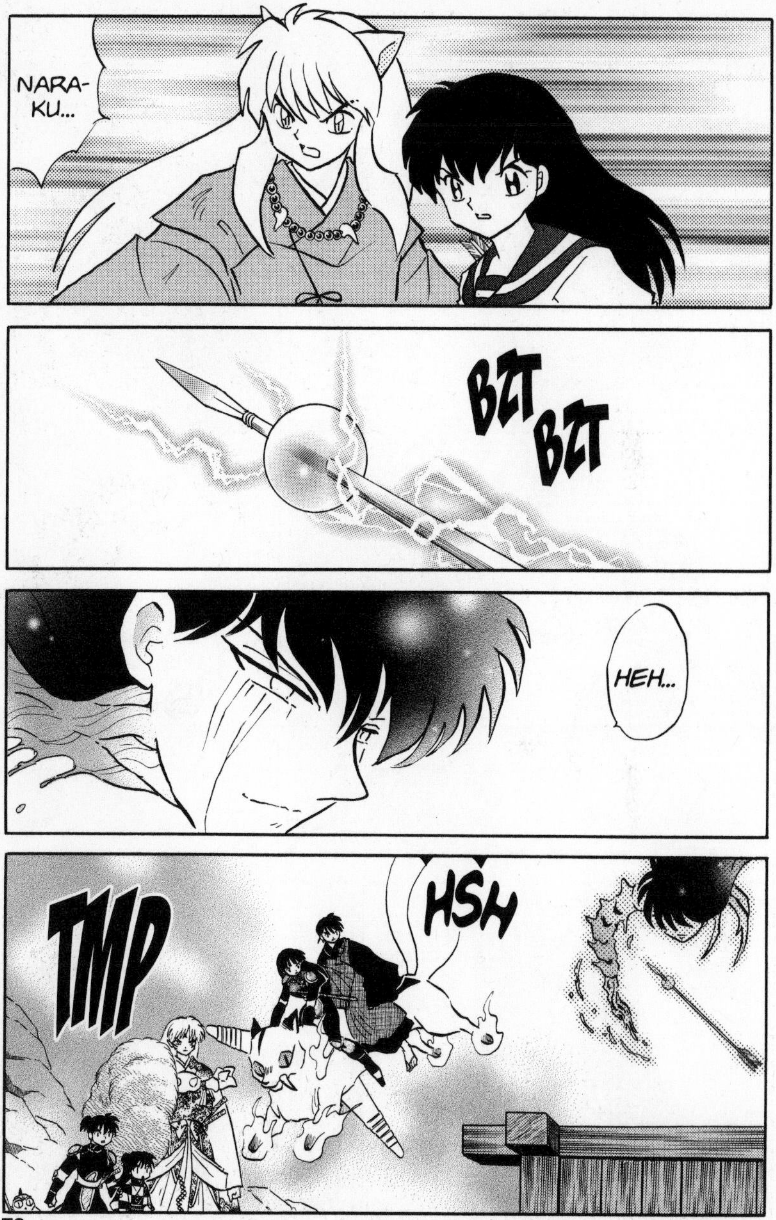
NARA-
KU...
BZT BZT
HEH...
HSH
TMP

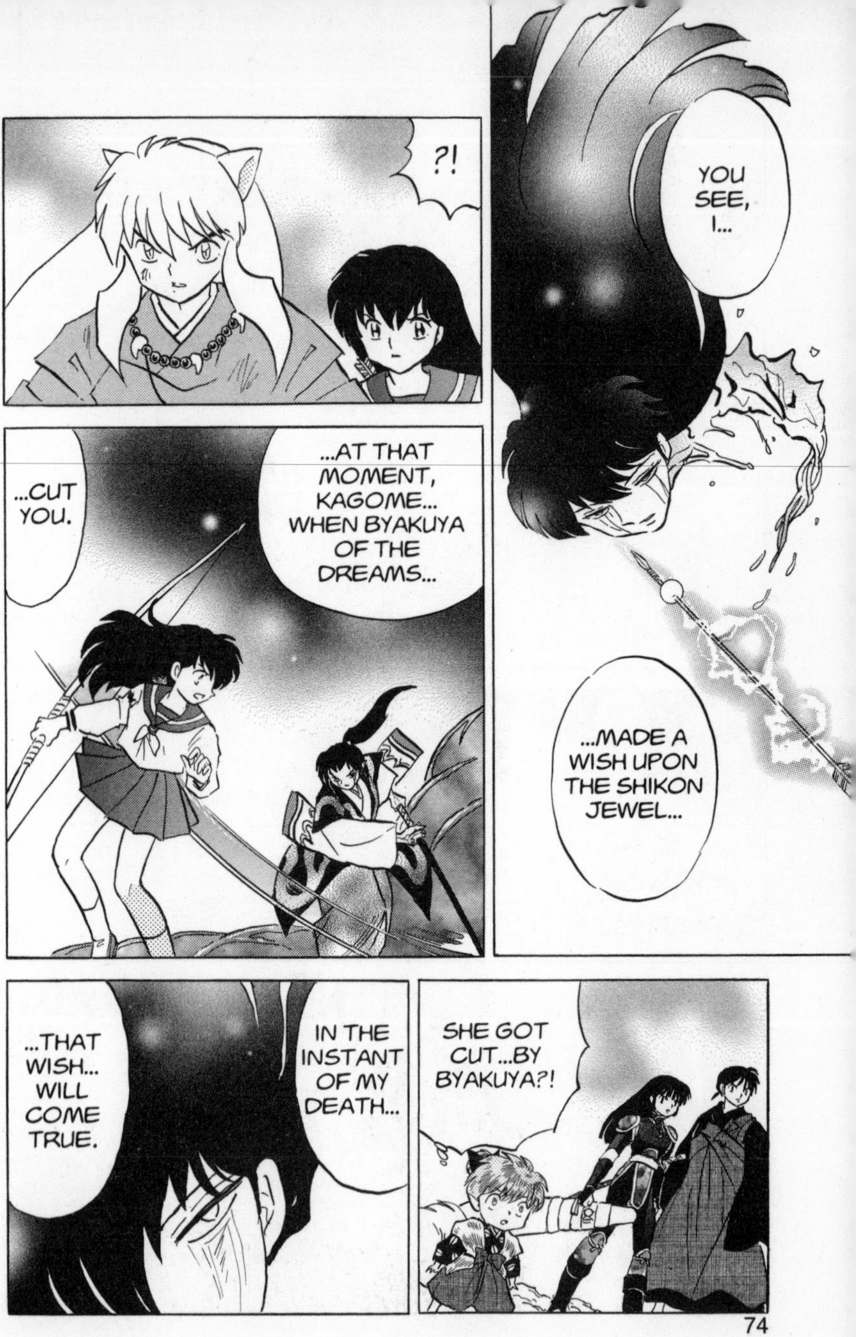
YOU SEE, I...
...MADE A WISH UPON THE SHIKON JEWEL...
?!
...AT THAT MOMENT, KAGOME... WHEN BYAKUYA OF THE DREAMS...
...CUT YOU.
SHE GOT CUT...BY BYAKUYA?!
IN THE INSTANT OF MY DEATH...
...THAT WISH... WILL COME TRUE.

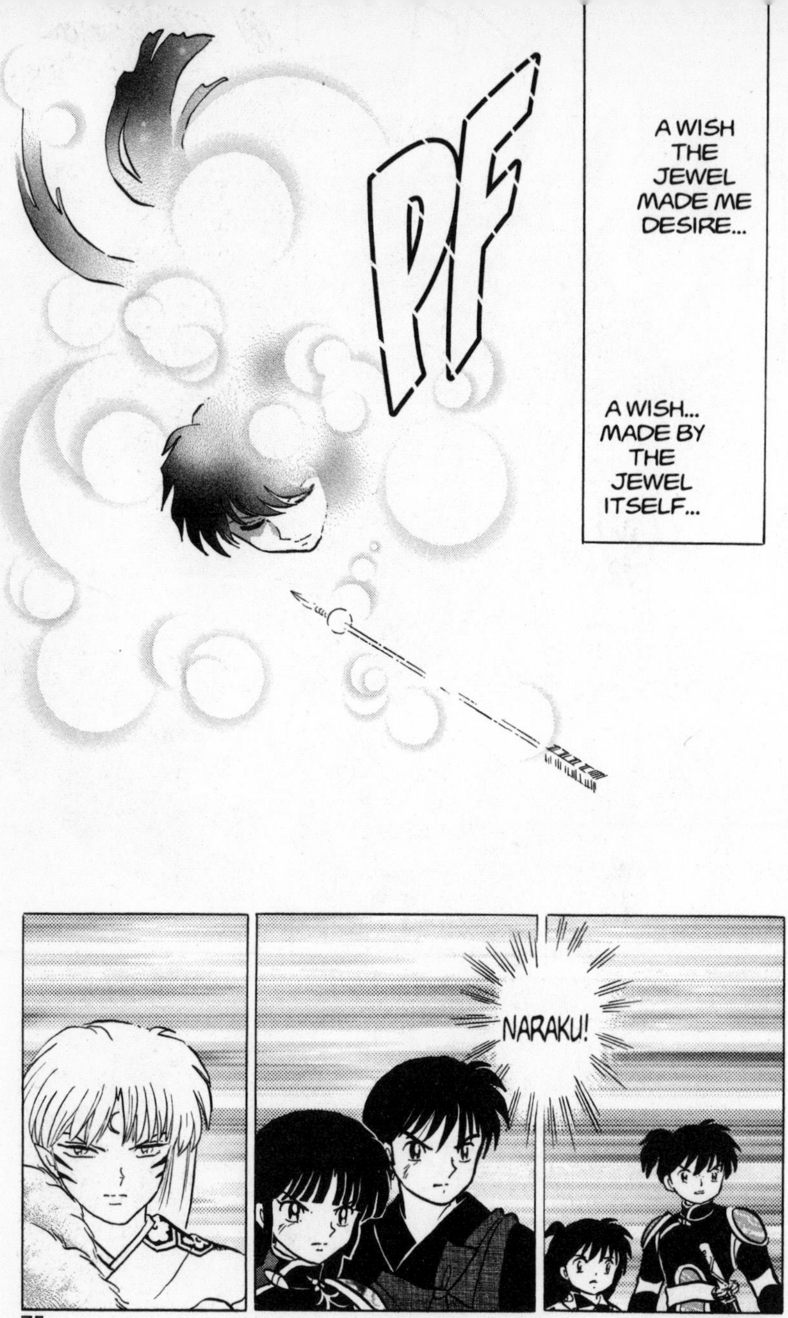
A WISH THE JEWEL MADE ME DESIRE...
A WISH... MADE BY THE JEWEL ITSELF...
PF
NARAKU!

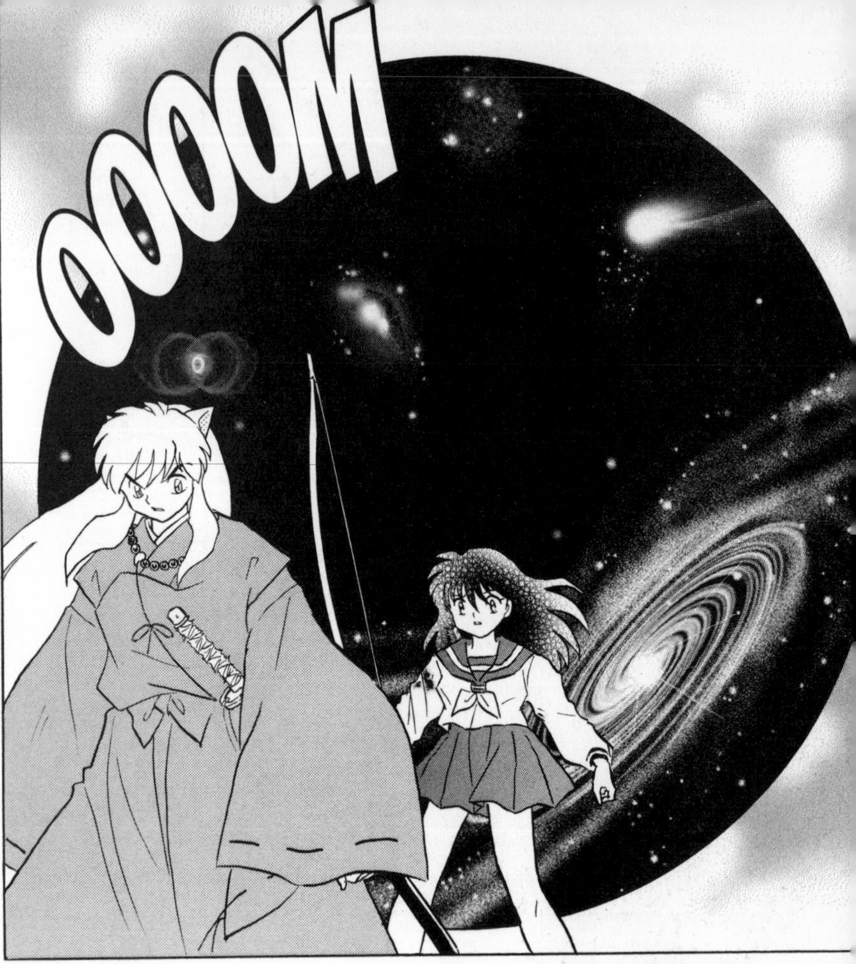
OOOOM

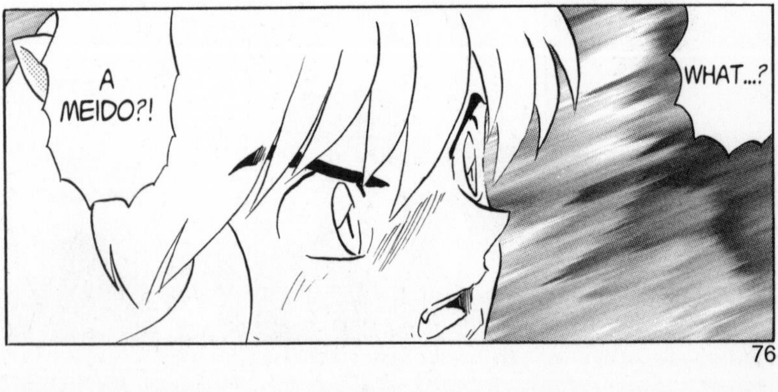
WHAT...?
A MEIDO?!

SCROLL 5

THE WELL TRANSFORMED

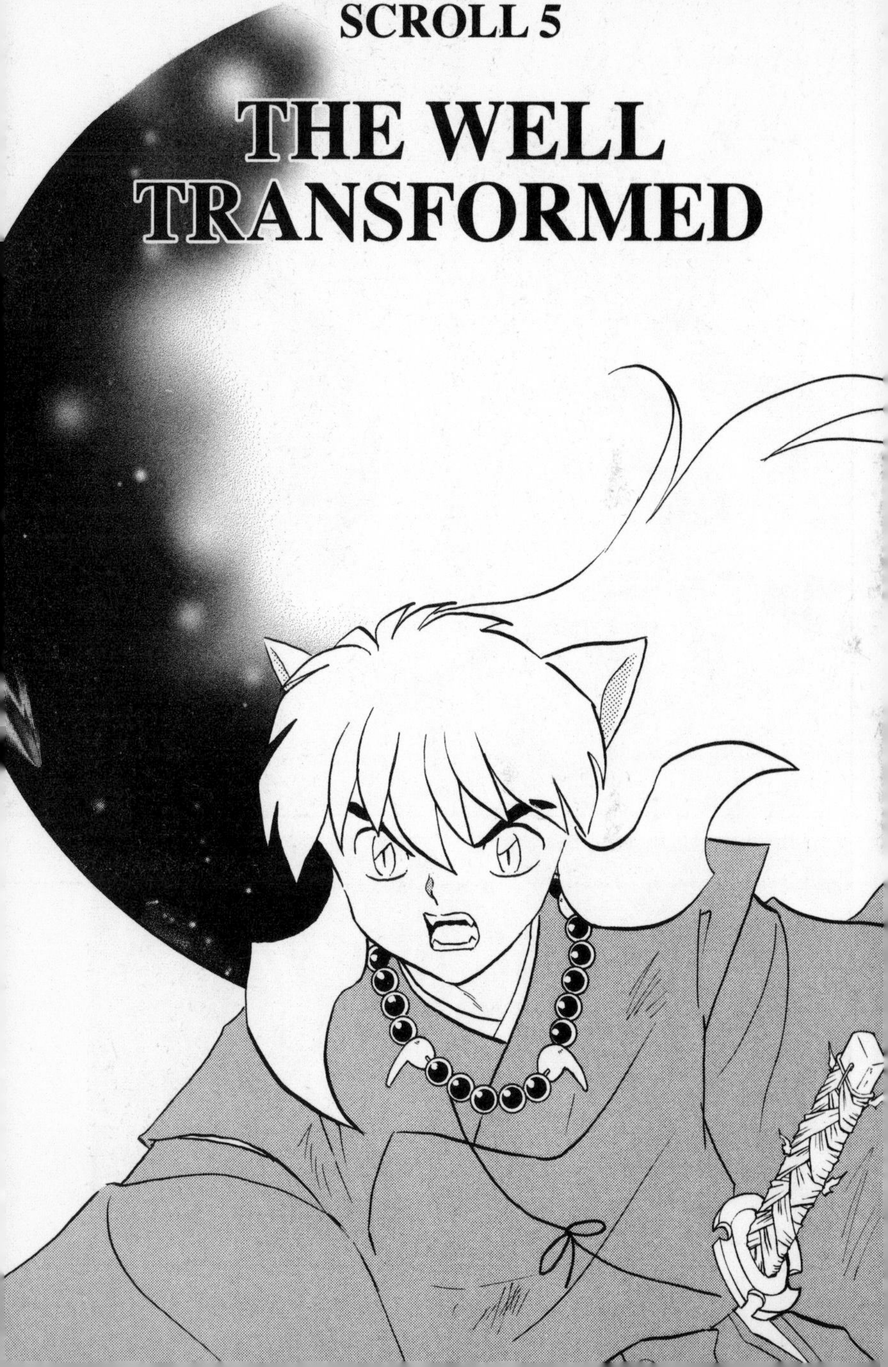

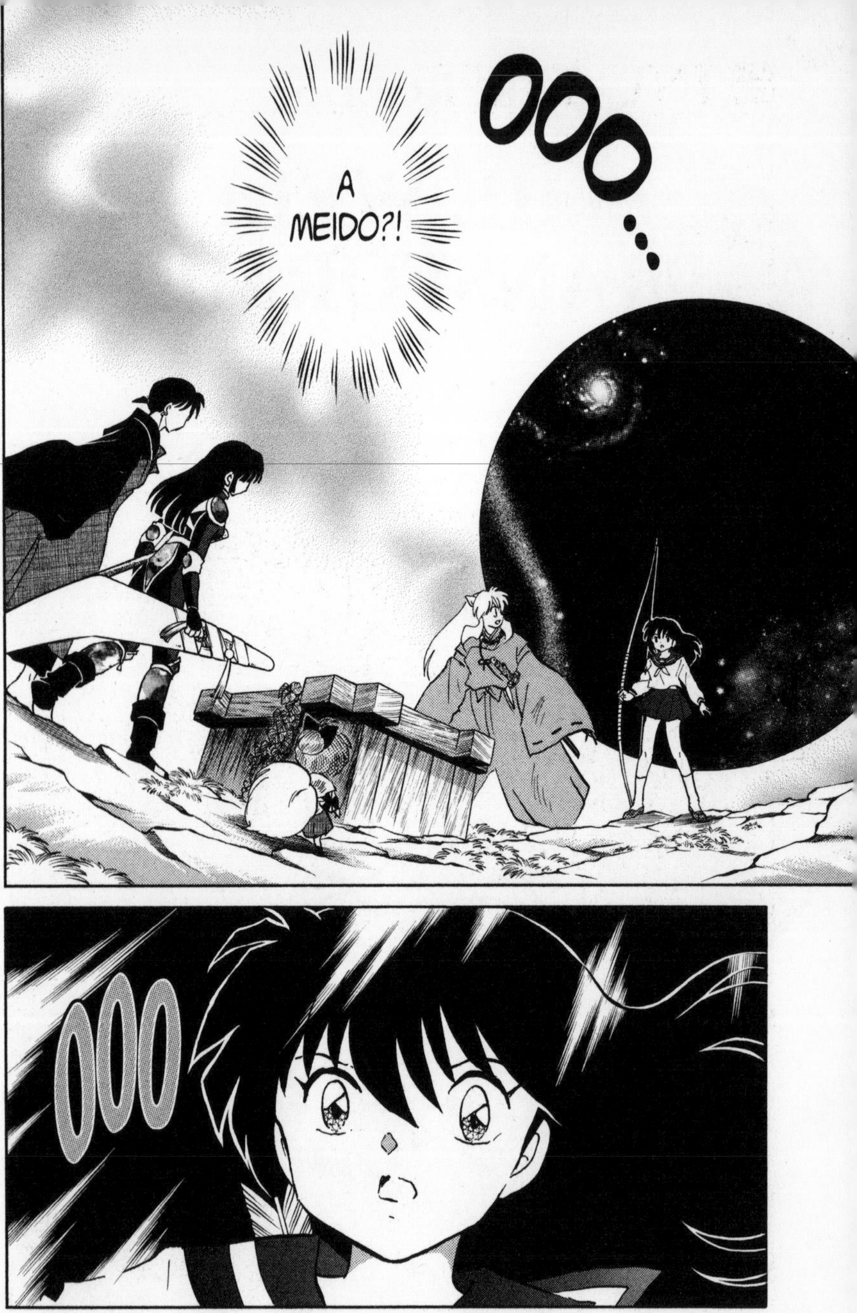
OOO...
A MEIDO?!
OOO

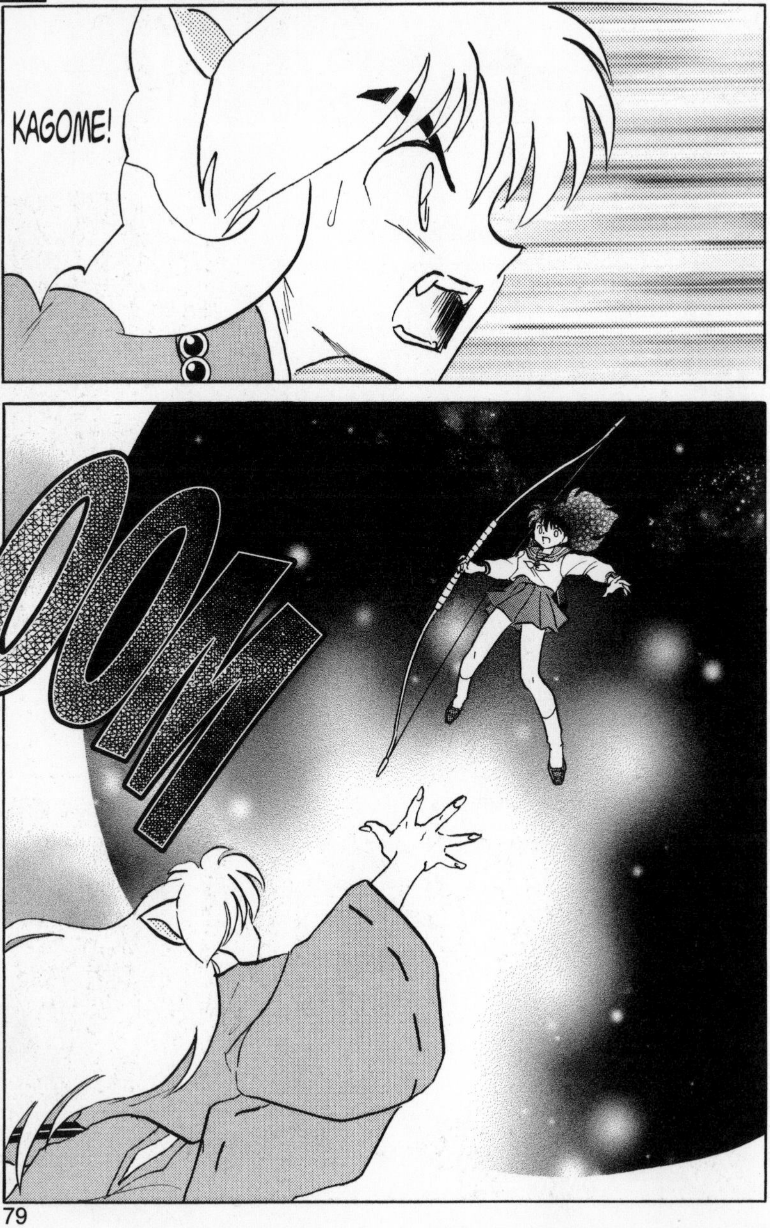
KAGOME!
OOM

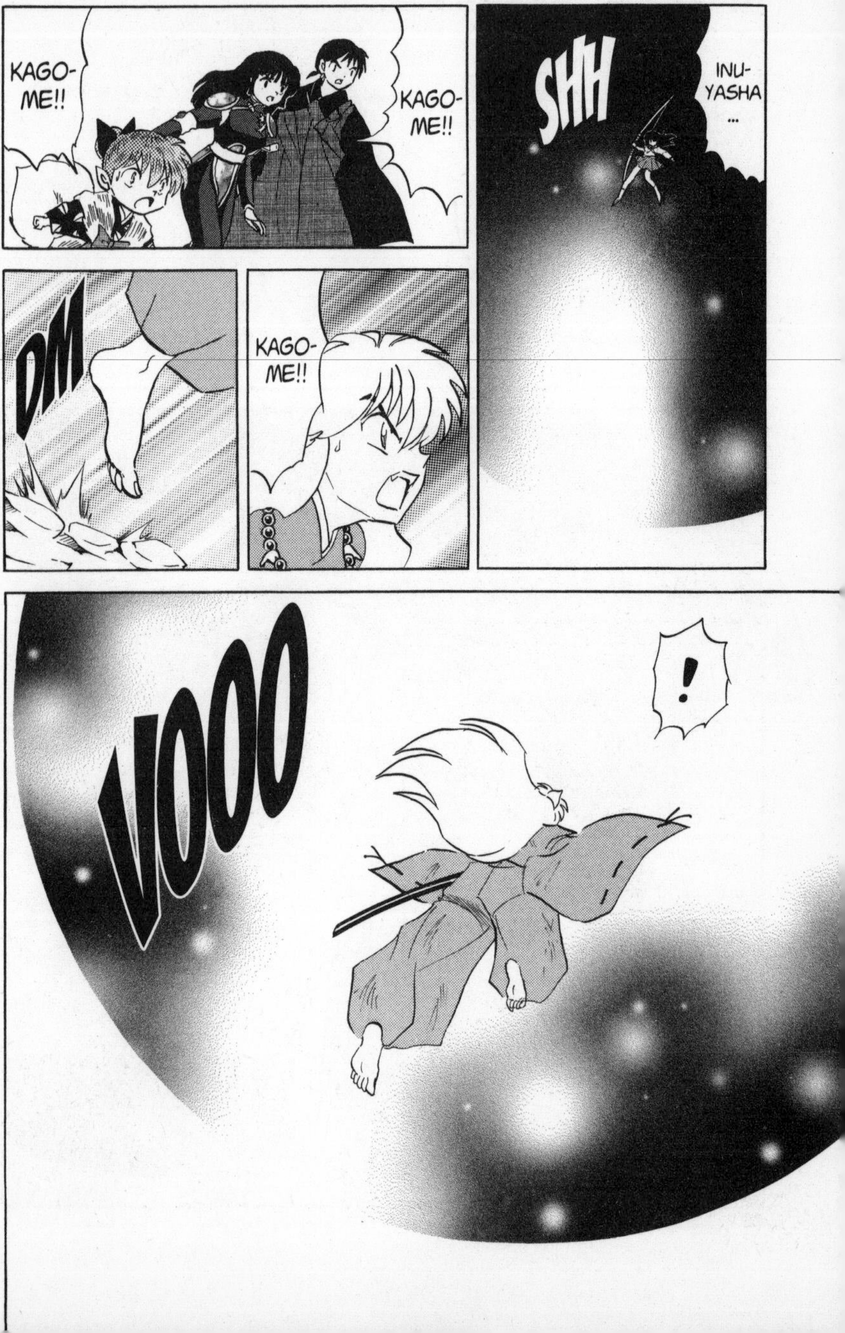
SHH
INU-YASHA...
KAGO-ME!!
KAGO-ME!!
KAGO-ME!!
DM
!
VOOO

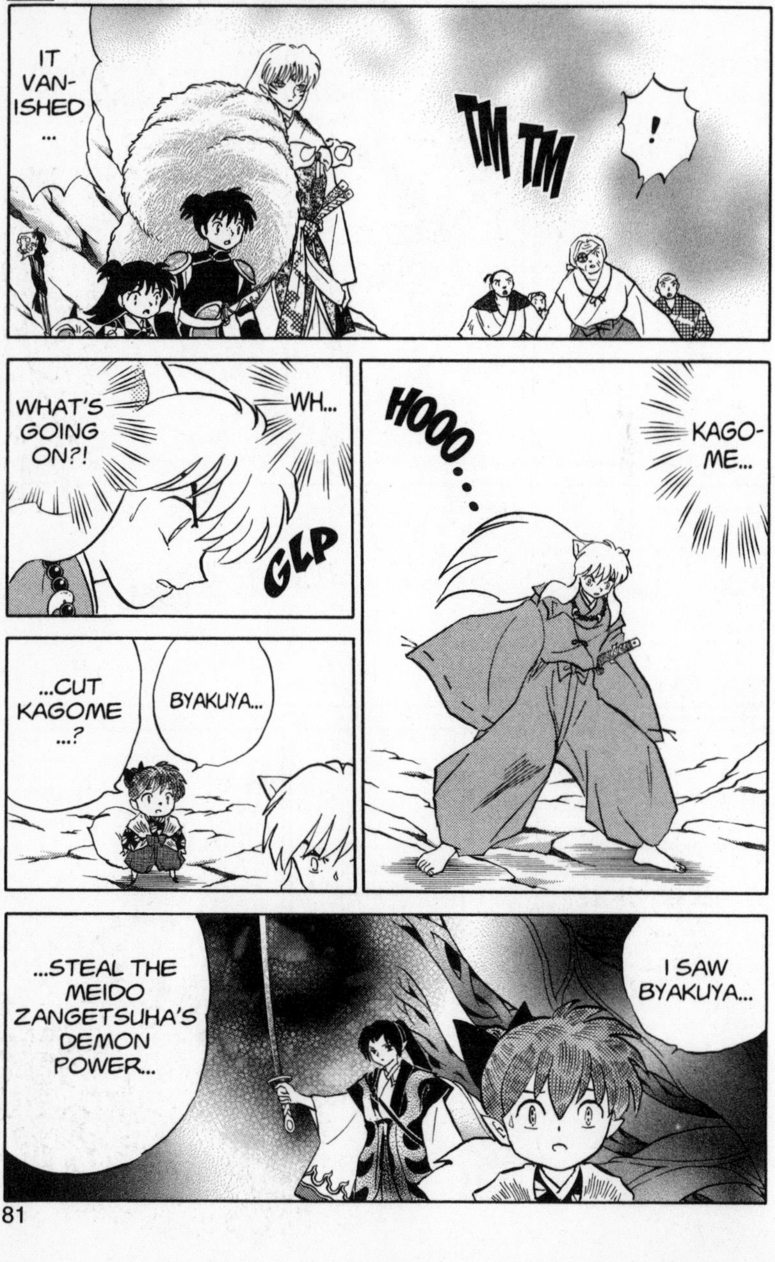
!
TM TM
IT VAN-ISHED ...
KAGO-ME...
HOOO...
WH...
GLP
WHAT'S GOING ON?!
BYAKUYA...
...CUT KAGOME ...?
I SAW BYAKUYA...
...STEAL THE MEIDO ZANGETSUHA'S DEMON POWER...

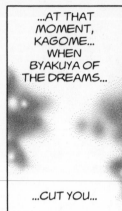

STEAL ITS POWER...?
YOU SEE, I...
...MADE A WISH UPON THE SHIKON JEWEL...
...AT THAT MOMENT, KAGOME... WHEN BYAKUYA OF THE DREAMS...
...CUT YOU...
IN THE INSTANT OF MY DEATH...
...THAT WISH... WILL COME TRUE...
KAGO-ME...
WHERE ARE YOU...?
THE WELL...
LADY KAEDE!
WHAT'S HAPPENED TO THE BONE EATER'S WELL?!

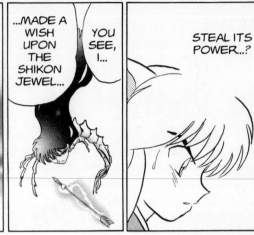

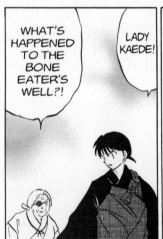

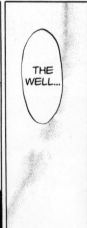

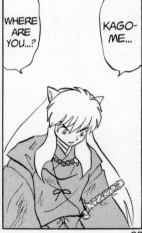

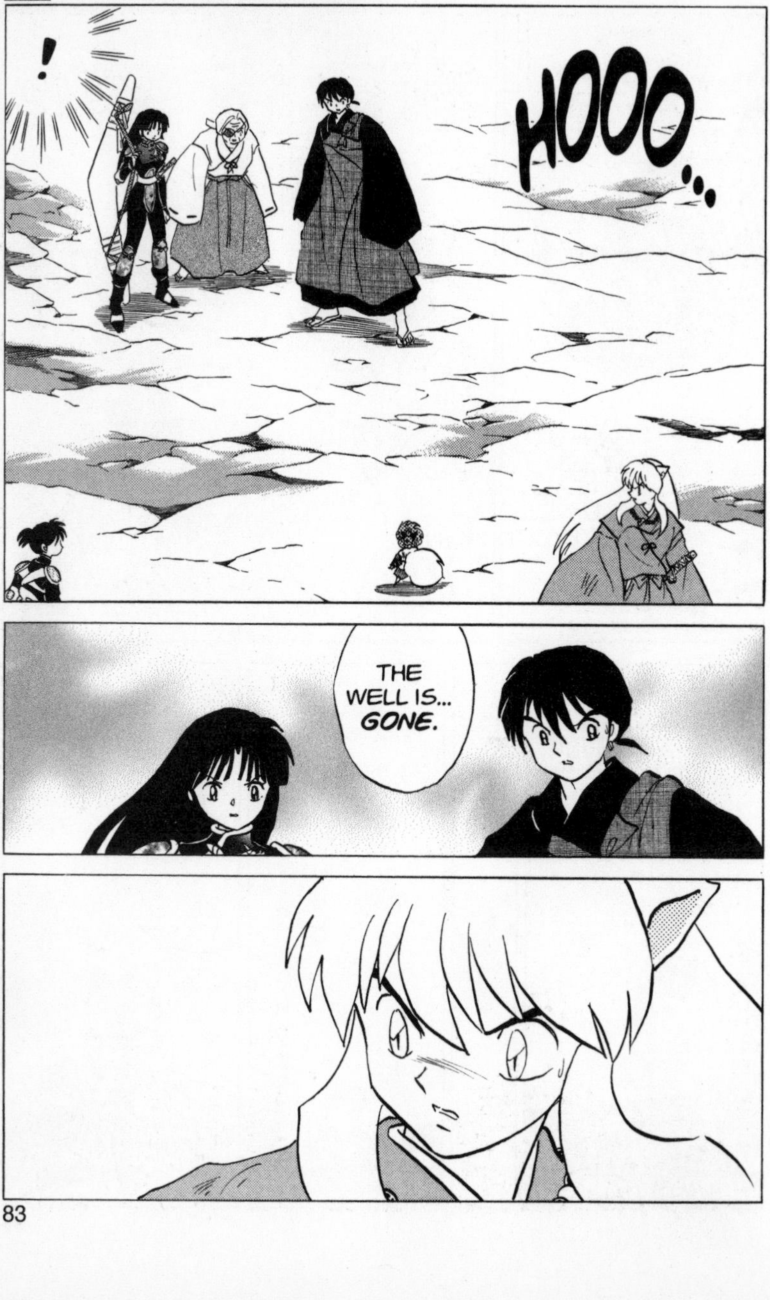
HOOO...
!
THE WELL IS... GONE.

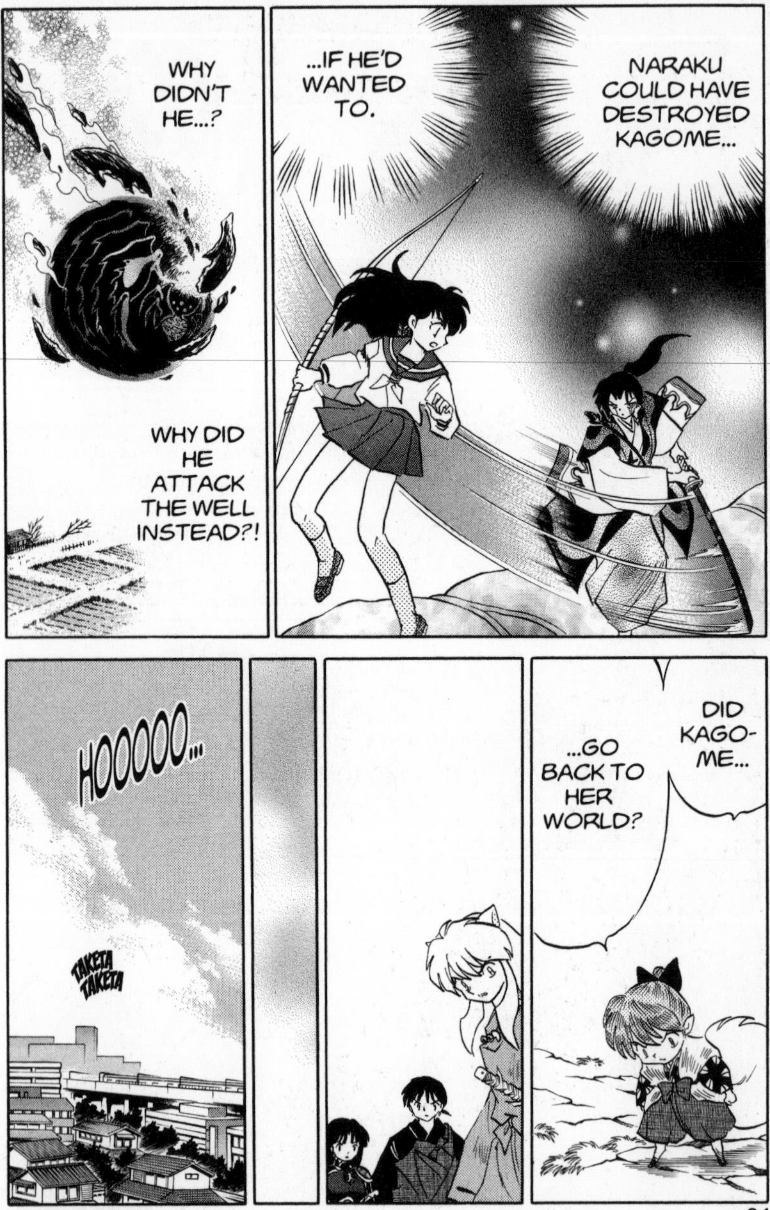
NARAKU COULD HAVE DESTROYED KAGOME...
...IF HE'D WANTED TO.
WHY DIDN'T HE...?
WHY DID HE ATTACK THE WELL INSTEAD?!
DID KAGO-ME...
...GO BACK TO HER WORLD?
HOOOOO...
TAKETA TAKETA

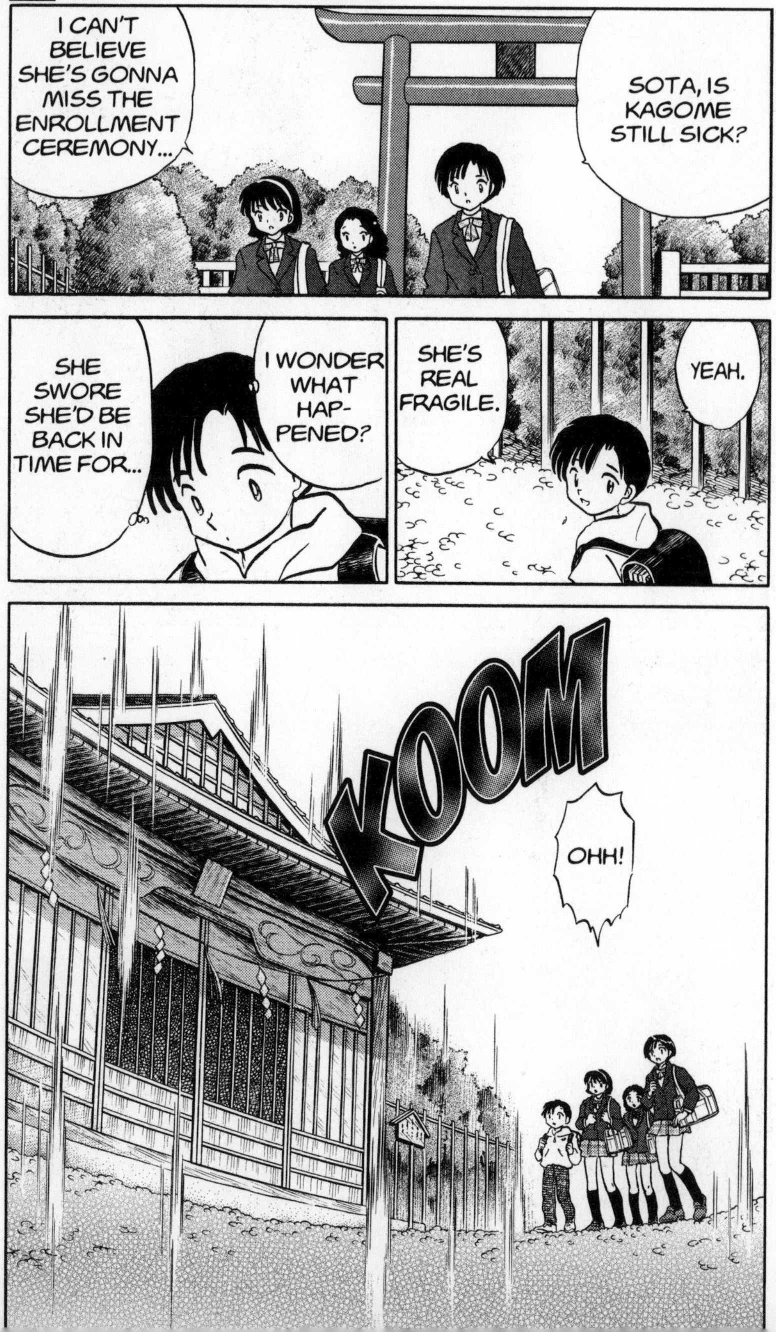
SOTA, IS KAGOME STILL SICK?
I CAN'T BELIEVE SHE'S GONNA MISS THE ENROLLMENT CEREMONY...
YEAH.
SHE'S REAL FRAGILE.
I WONDER WHAT HAP-PENED?
SHE SWORE SHE'D BE BACK IN TIME FOR...
KOOM
OHH!

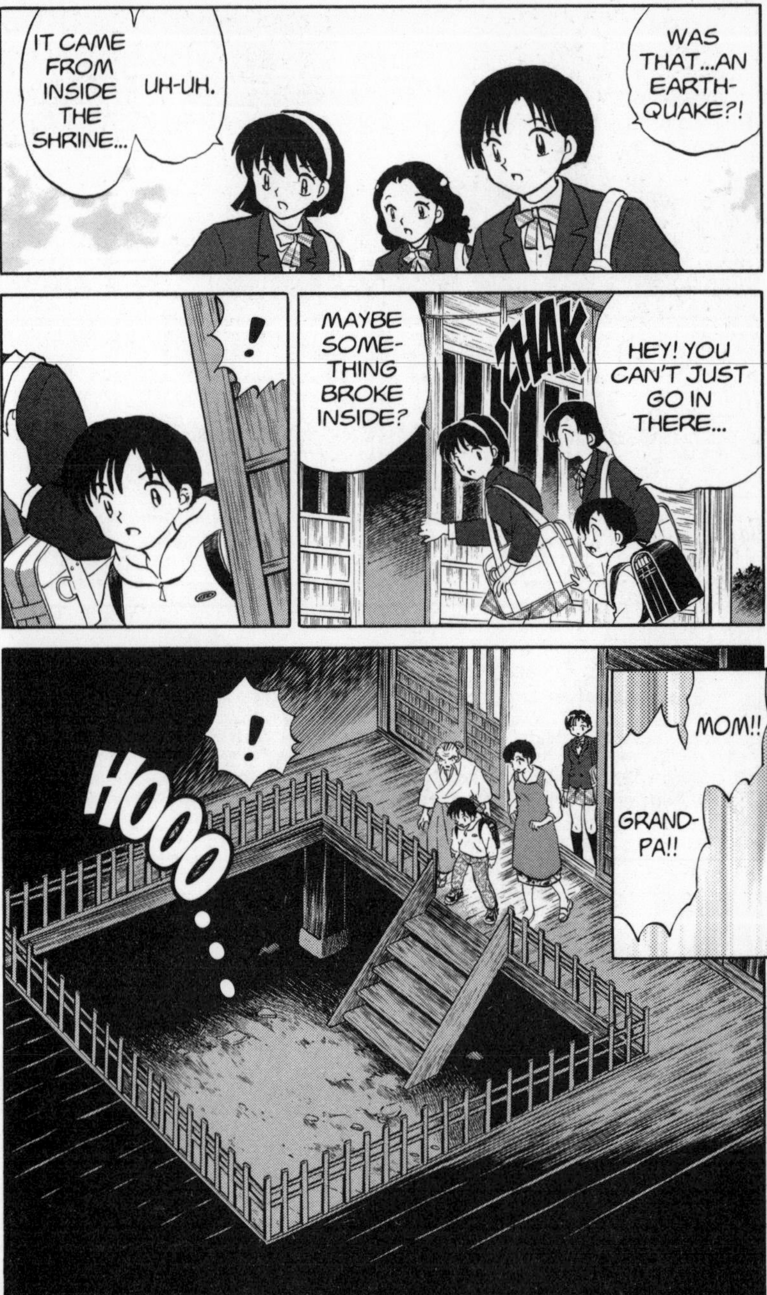
WAS THAT...AN EARTH-QUAKE?!
UH-UH.
IT CAME FROM INSIDE THE SHRINE...
HEY! YOU CAN'T JUST GO IN THERE...
ZHAK
MAYBE SOME-THING BROKE INSIDE?
!
MOM!!
GRAND-PA!!
!
HOOO...

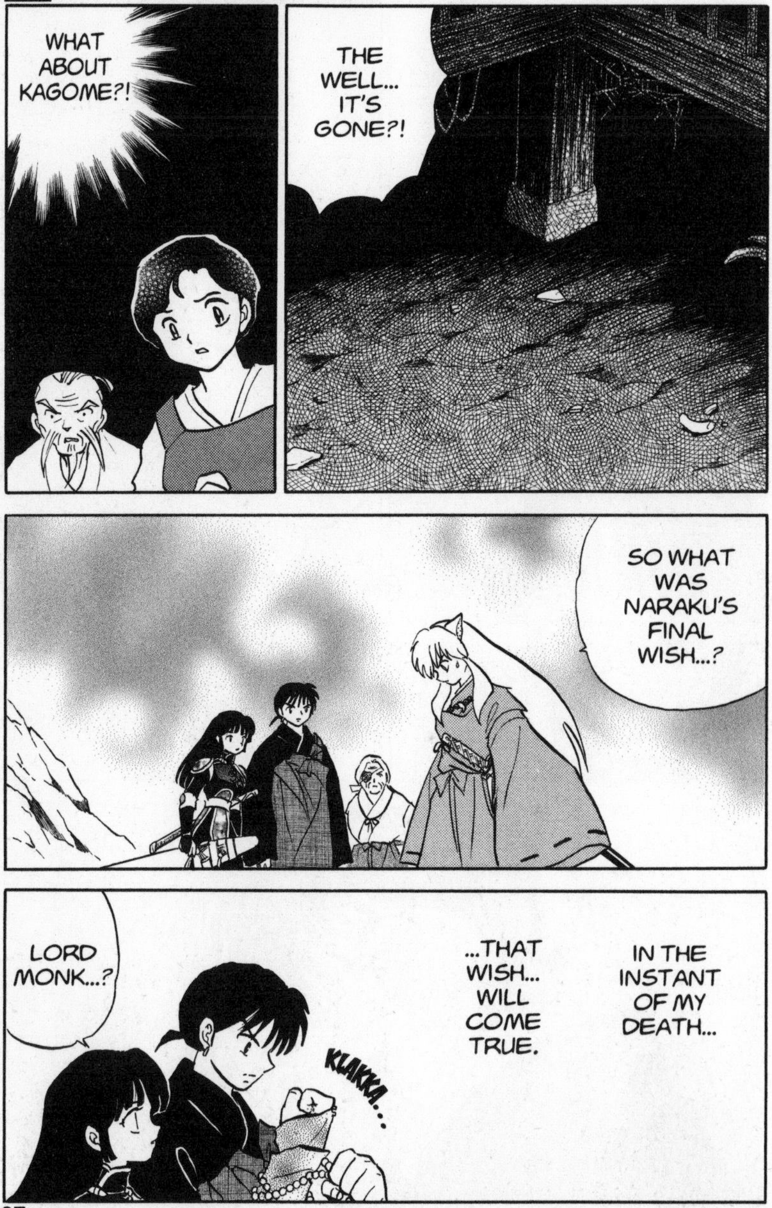
THE WELL... IT'S GONE?!
WHAT ABOUT KAGOME?!
SO WHAT WAS NARAKU'S FINAL WISH...?
IN THE INSTANT OF MY DEATH...
...THAT WISH... WILL COME TRUE.
KLAKKA...
LORD MONK...?

YOU MEAN...

THE WIND TUNNEL ...IT'S GONE!

THE CURSE... HAS BEEN UNDONE ...?

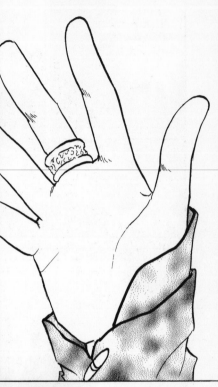

THERE'S NO MISTAKE THEN...

NARAKU IS NO MORE.

BUT...

88

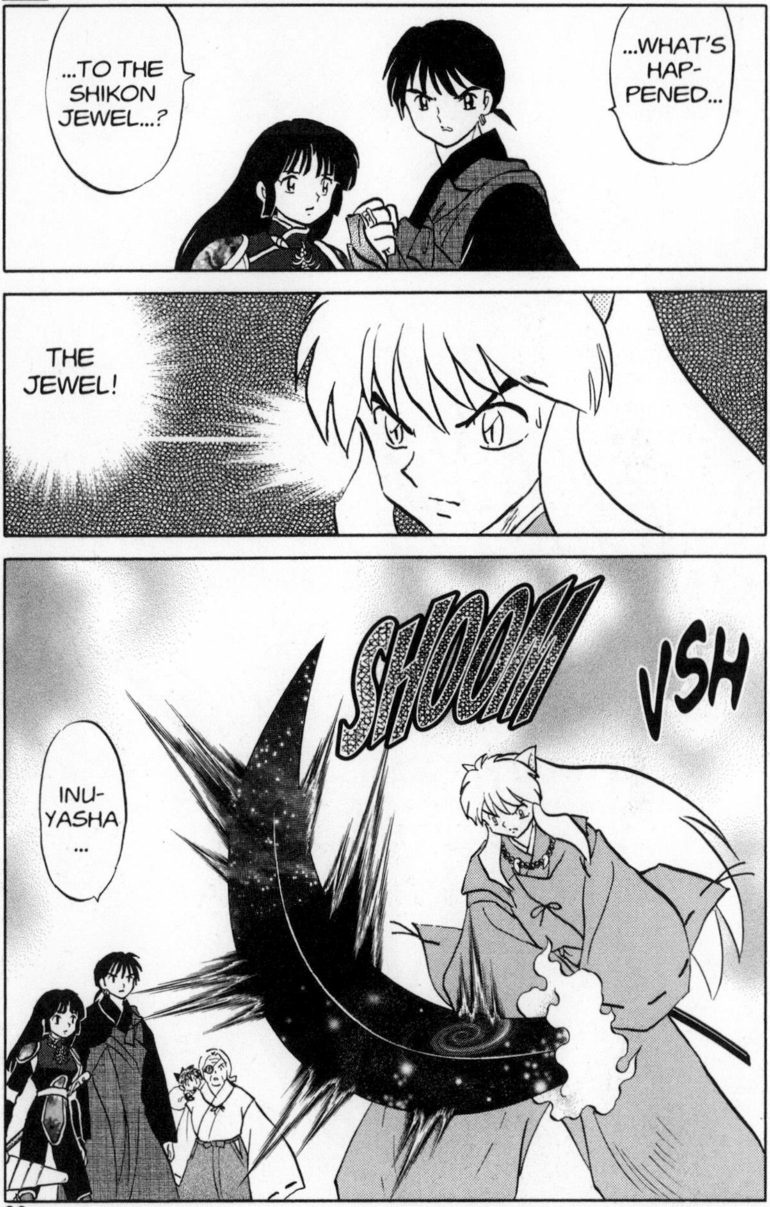
...WHAT'S HAP-PENED...
...TO THE SHIKON JEWEL...?
THE JEWEL!
VSH
SHOOM
INU-YASHA...

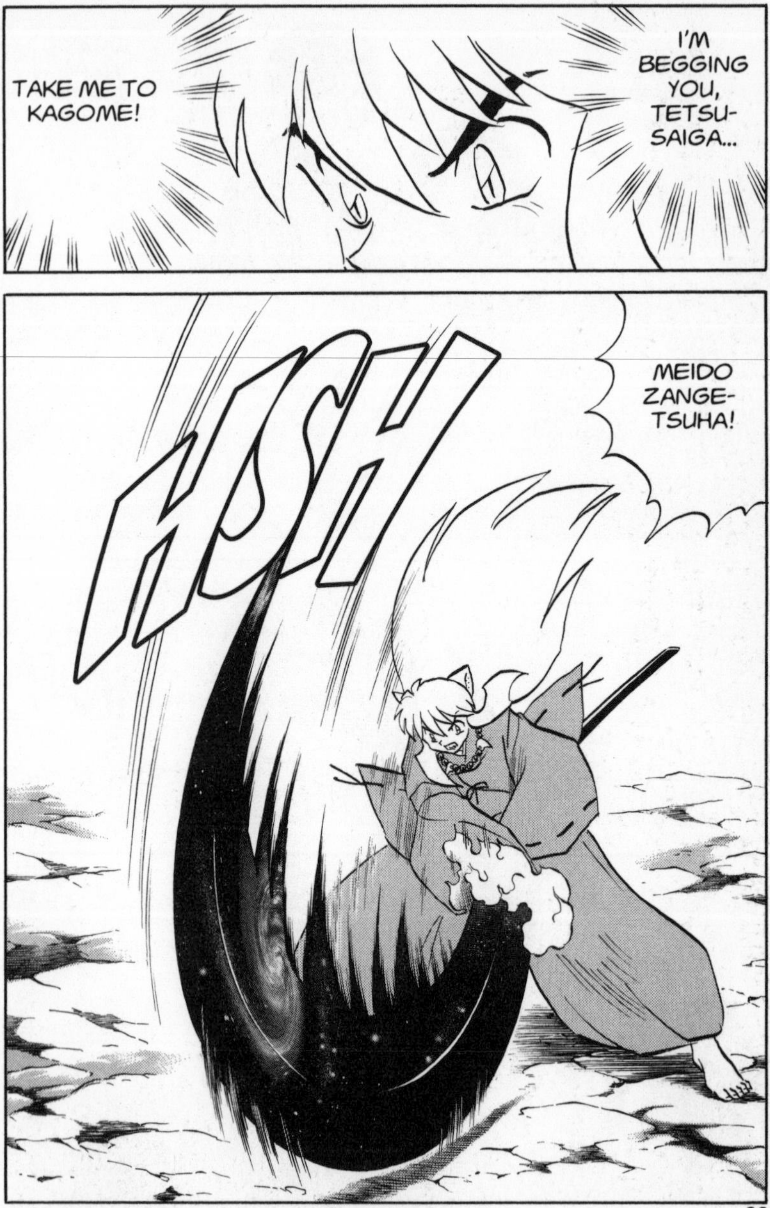
I'M BEGGING YOU, TETSU-SAIGA...
TAKE ME TO KAGOME!
MEIDO ZANGE-TSUHA!
HSH

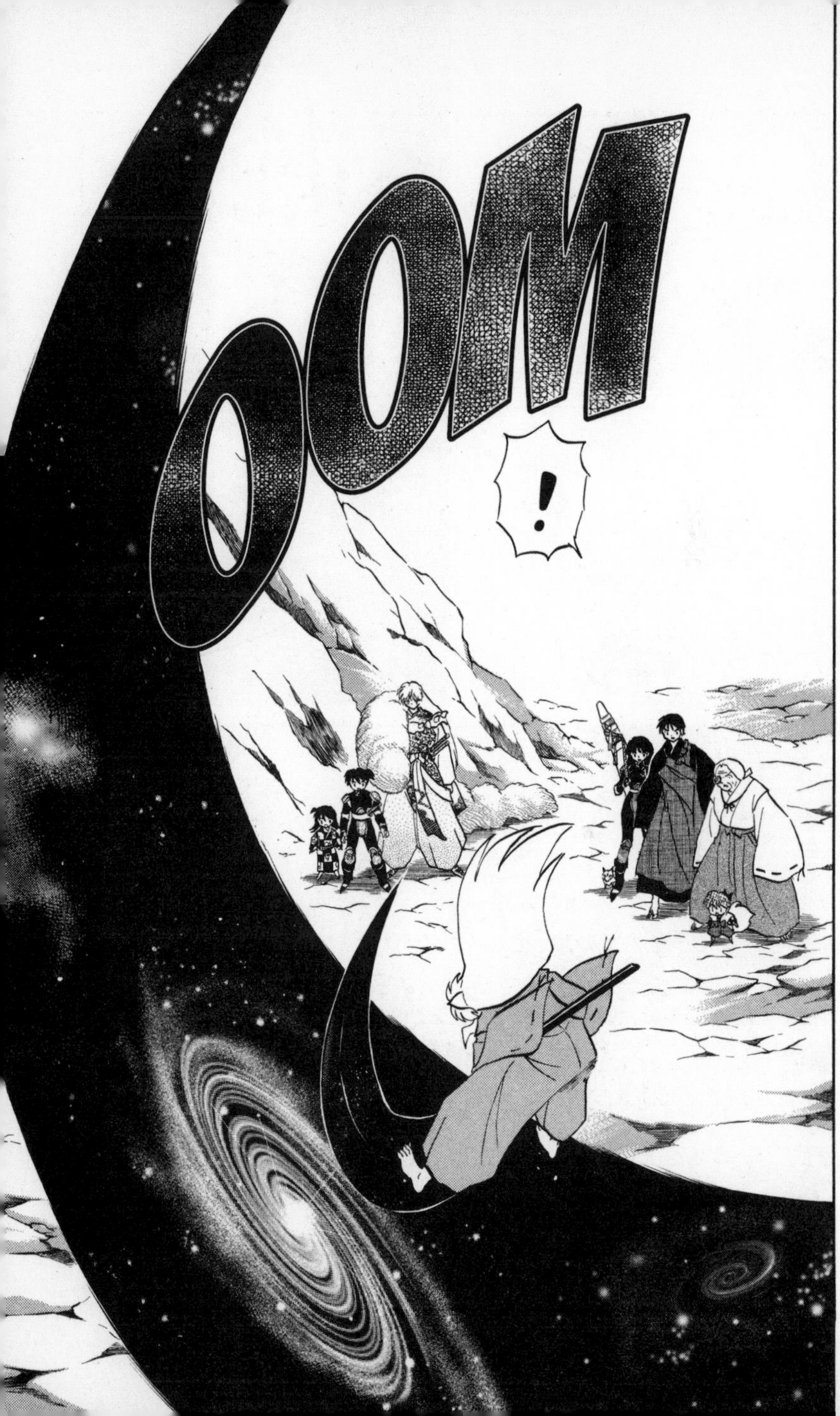

OOM
!

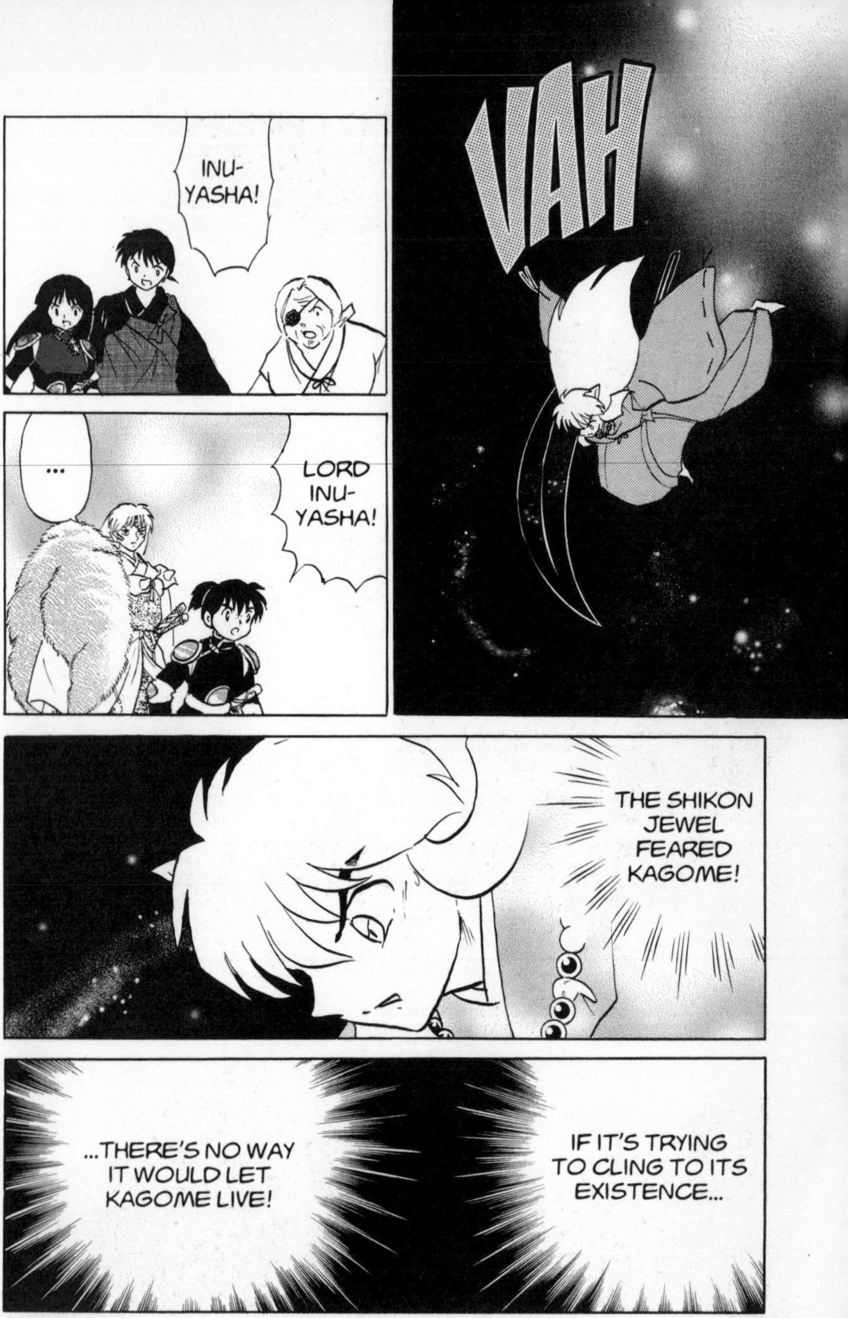
VAH
INU-
YASHA!
LORD
INU-
YASHA!
...
THE SHIKON
JEWEL
FEARED
KAGOME!
IF IT'S TRYING
TO CLING TO ITS
EXISTENCE...
...THERE'S NO WAY
IT WOULD LET
KAGOME LIVE!

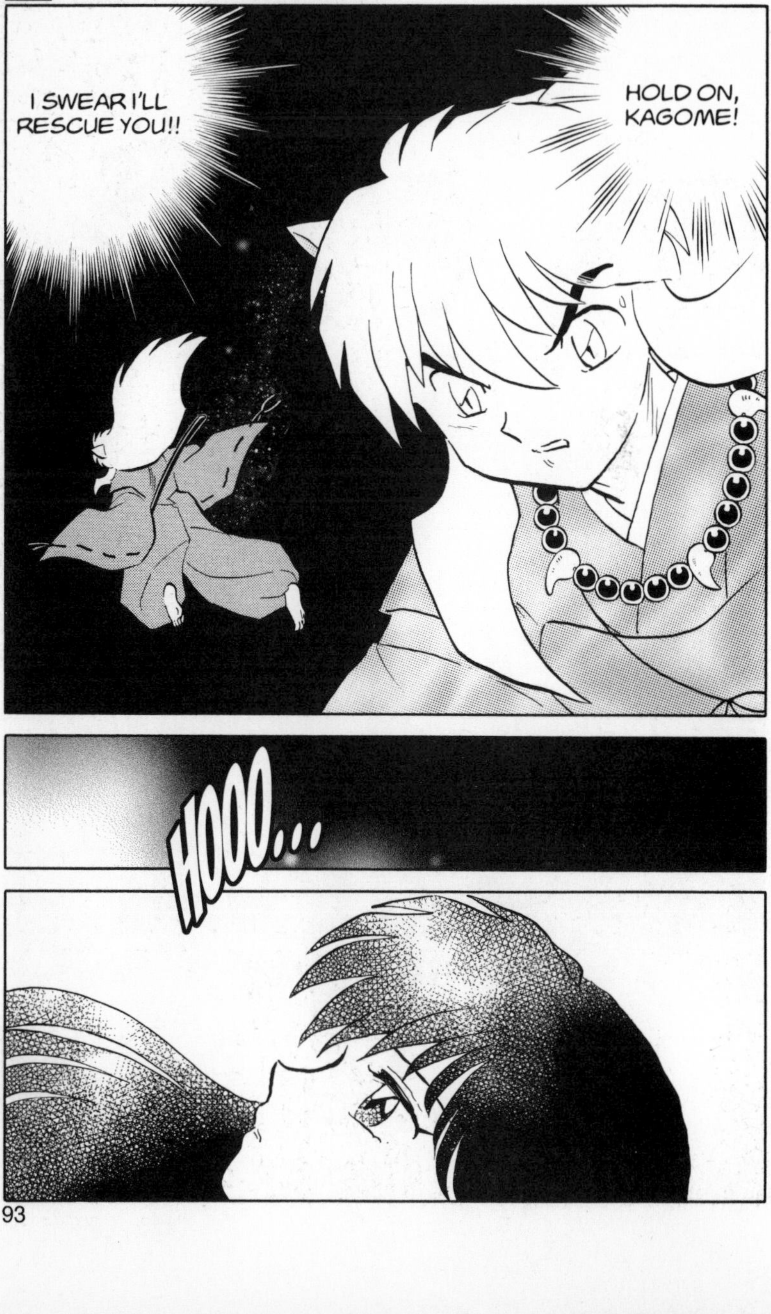
HOLD ON, KAGOME!
I SWEAR I'LL RESCUE YOU!!
HOOO...

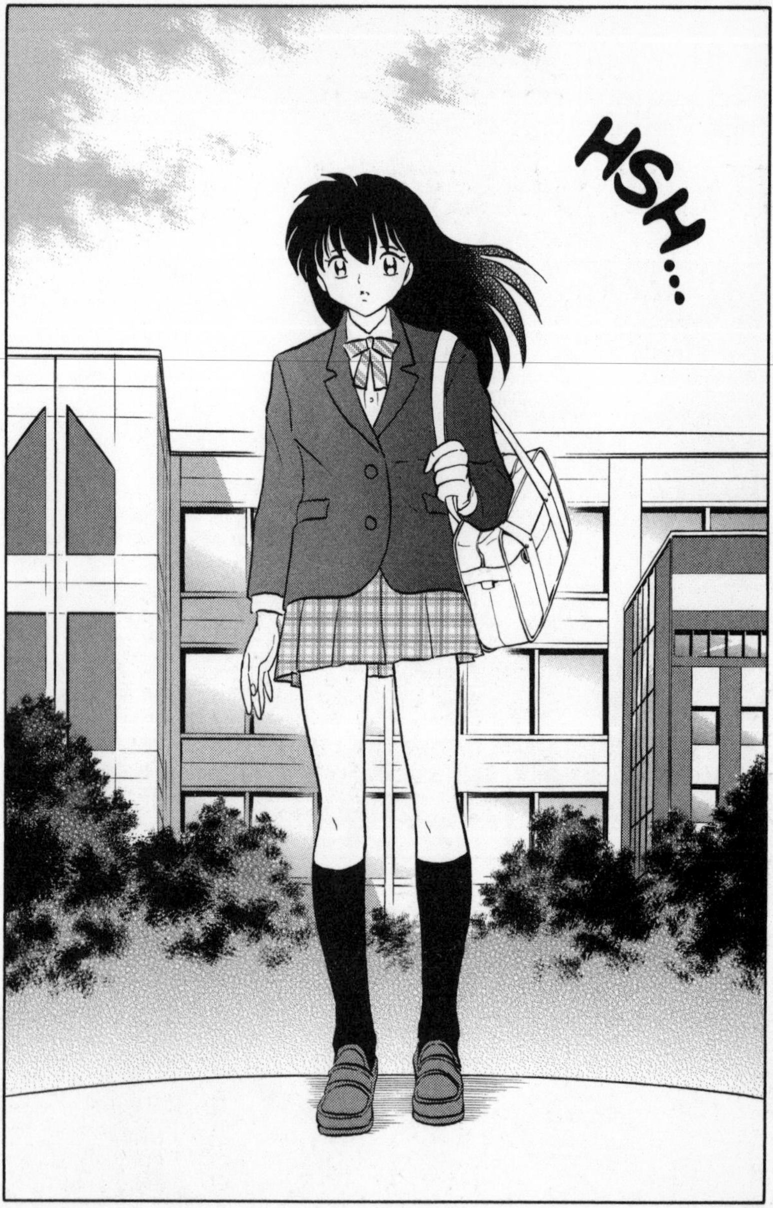
HSH...

SCROLL 6
HIGH SCHOOL LIFE

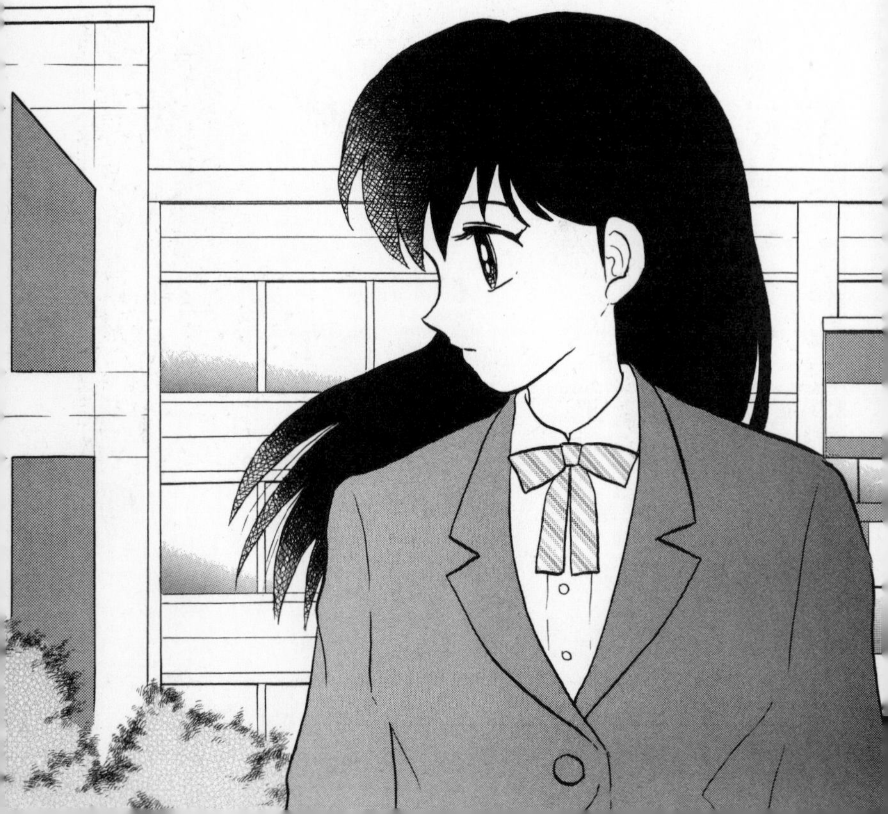

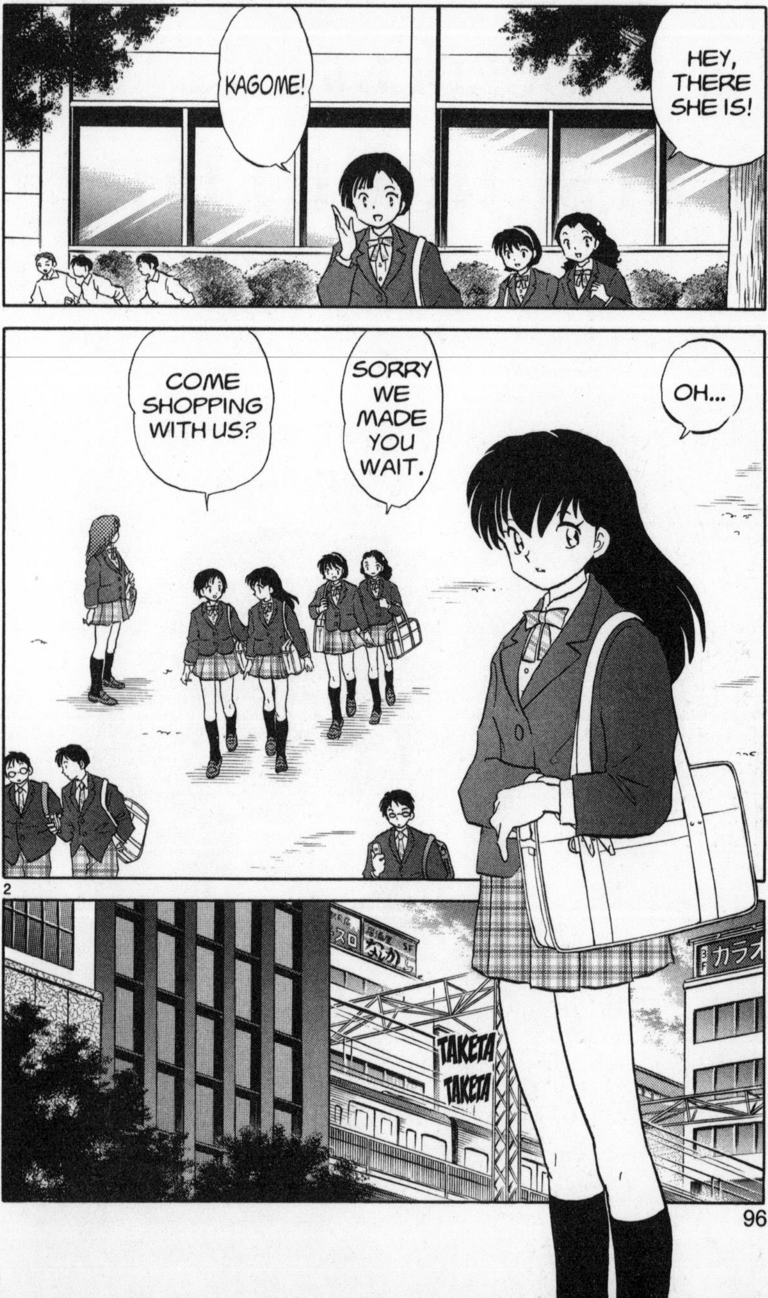
HEY, THERE SHE IS!
KAGOME!
OH...
SORRY WE MADE YOU WAIT.
COME SHOPPING WITH US?
TAKETA
TAKETA

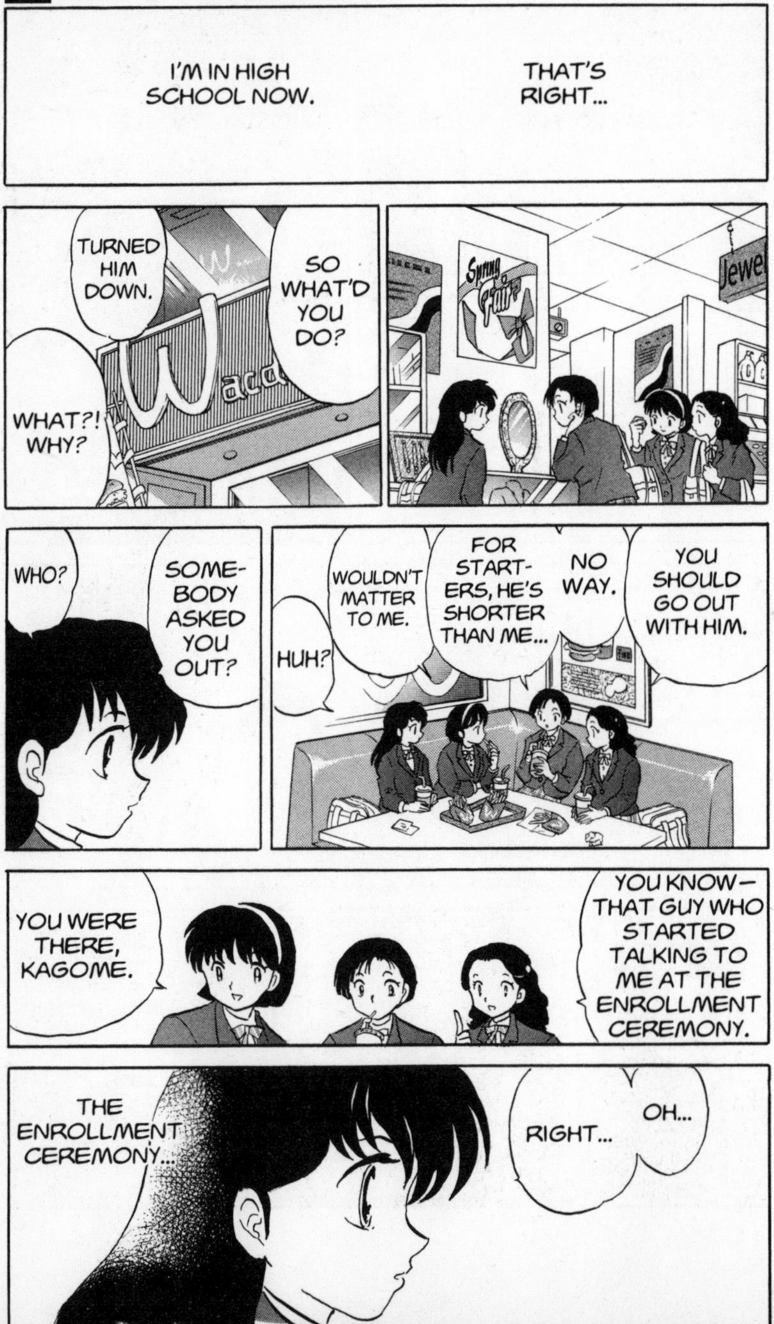
THAT'S RIGHT...
I'M IN HIGH SCHOOL NOW.
SO WHAT'D YOU DO?
TURNED HIM DOWN.
WHAT?! WHY?
YOU SHOULD GO OUT WITH HIM.
NO WAY.
FOR START-ERS, HE'S SHORTER THAN ME...
WOULDN'T MATTER TO ME.
HUH?
SOME-BODY ASKED YOU OUT?
WHO?
YOU KNOW— THAT GUY WHO STARTED TALKING TO ME AT THE ENROLLMENT CEREMONY.
YOU WERE THERE, KAGOME.
OH...
RIGHT...
THE ENROLLMENT CEREMONY...

KAGOME, CAN YOU HELP ME IN THE KITCHEN?
HAVE YOU DECIDED WHICH CLUBS TO JOIN?
YUP.
THE TENNIS CLUB.
THAT REMINDS ME, GRAND-PA.
YOU STILL OWE ME A GRADUA-TION GIFT!
EH?
I ALREADY GAVE YOU GRADUA-TION GIFTS.

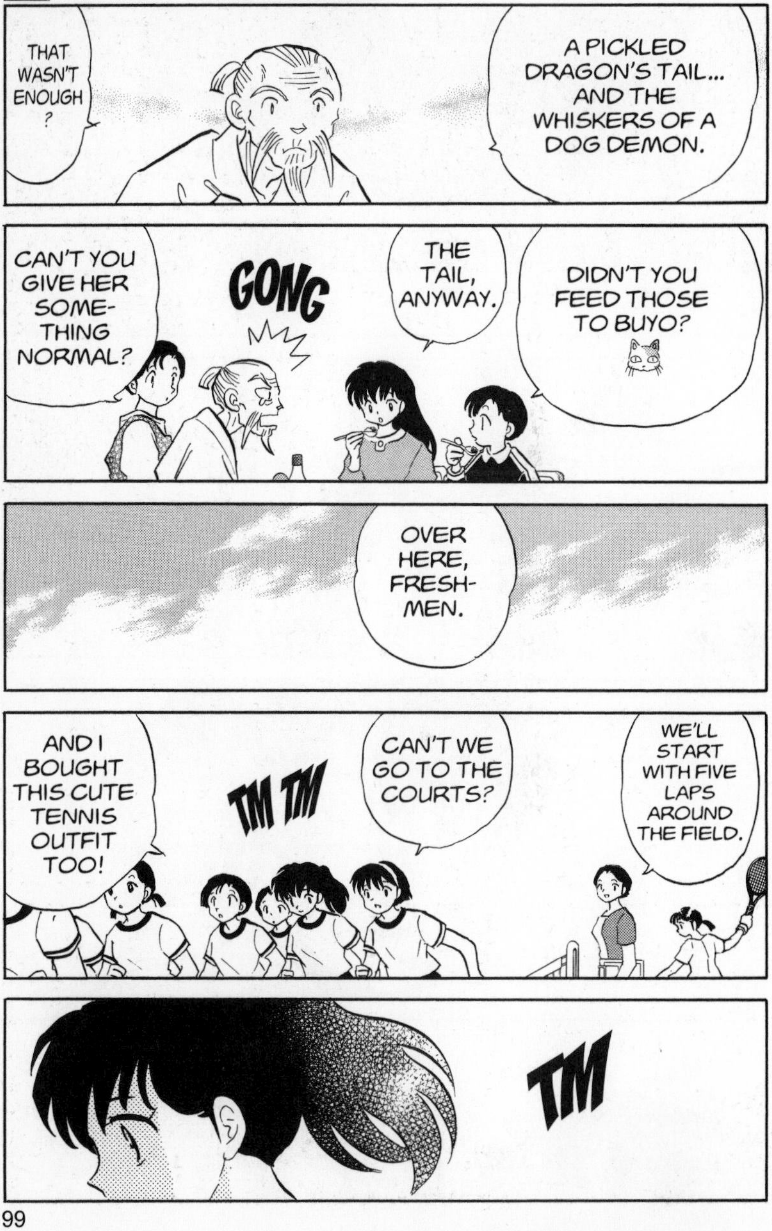
A PICKLED DRAGON'S TAIL... AND THE WHISKERS OF A DOG DEMON.
THAT WASN'T ENOUGH ?
DIDN'T YOU FEED THOSE TO BUYO?
THE TAIL, ANYWAY.
GONG
CAN'T YOU GIVE HER SOME-THING NORMAL?
OVER HERE, FRESH-MEN.
WE'LL START WITH FIVE LAPS AROUND THE FIELD.
CAN'T WE GO TO THE COURTS?
TM TM
AND I BOUGHT THIS CUTE TENNIS OUTFIT TOO!
TM

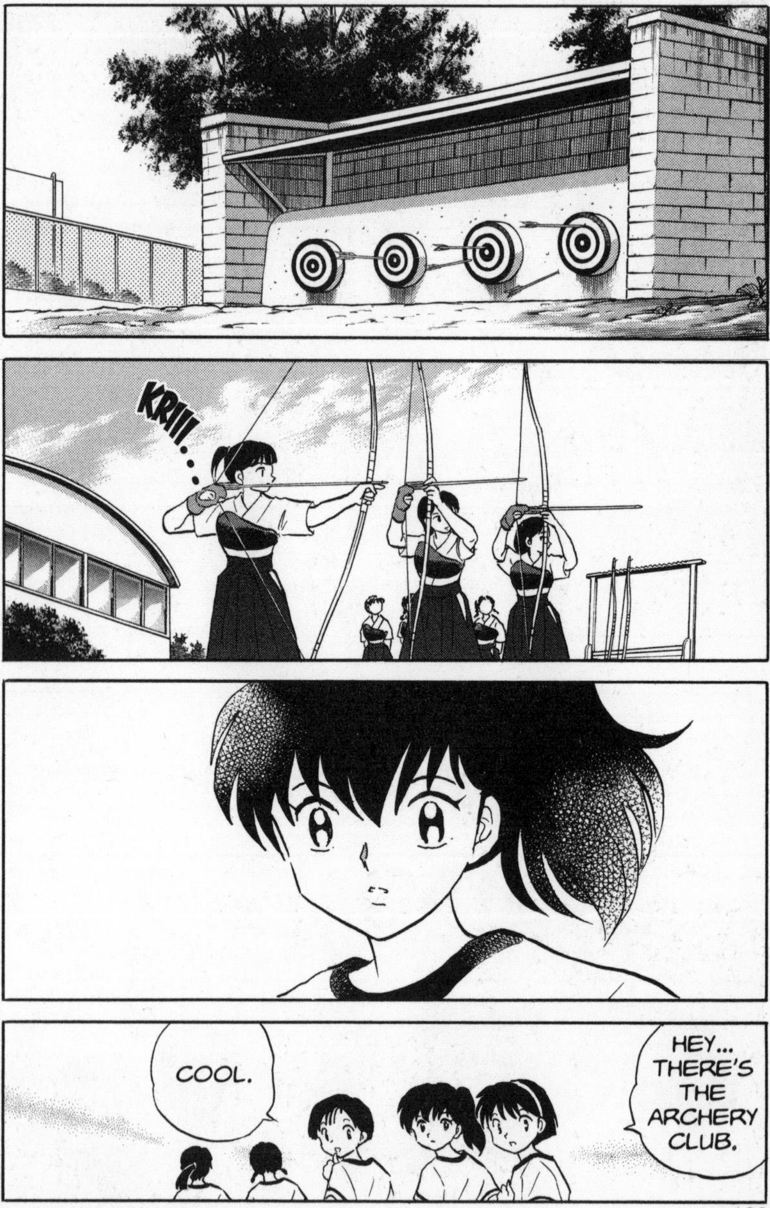
KRIII...
HEY... THERE'S THE ARCHERY CLUB.
COOL.

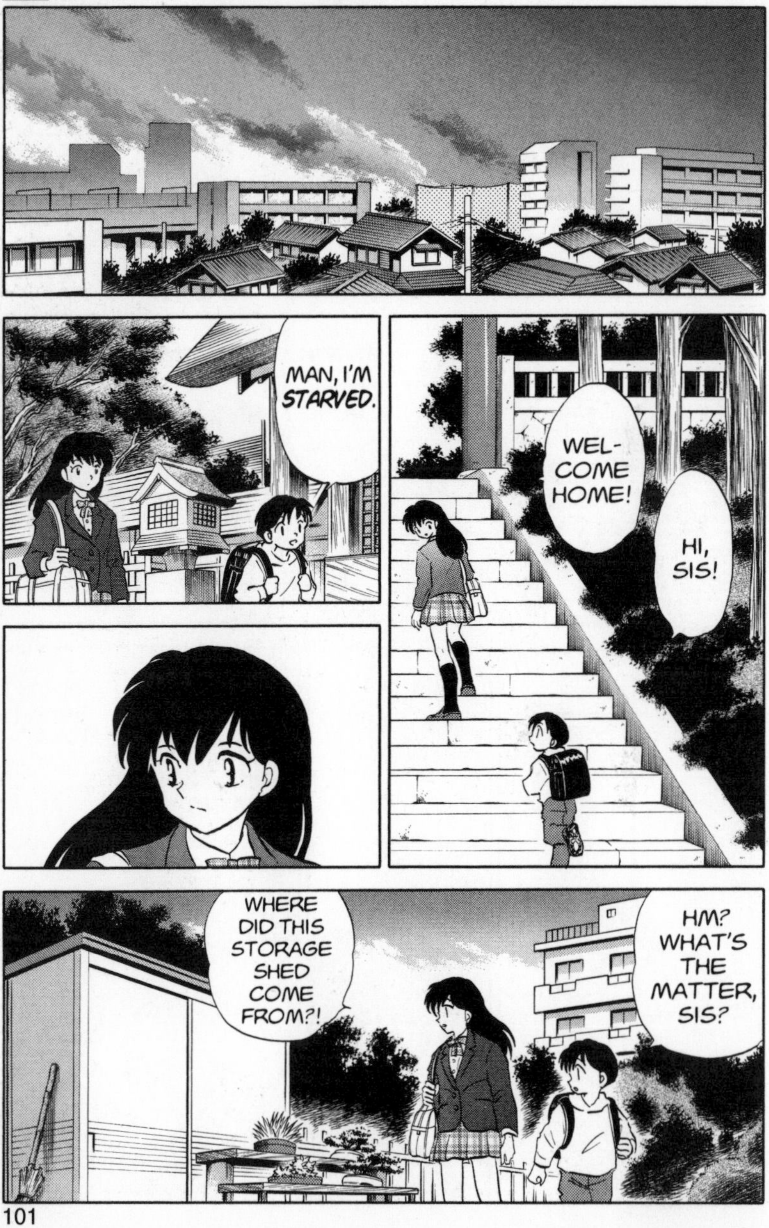
WEL-COME HOME!
HI, SIS!
MAN, I'M *STARVED*.
HM? WHAT'S THE MATTER, SIS?
WHERE DID THIS STORAGE SHED COME FROM?!

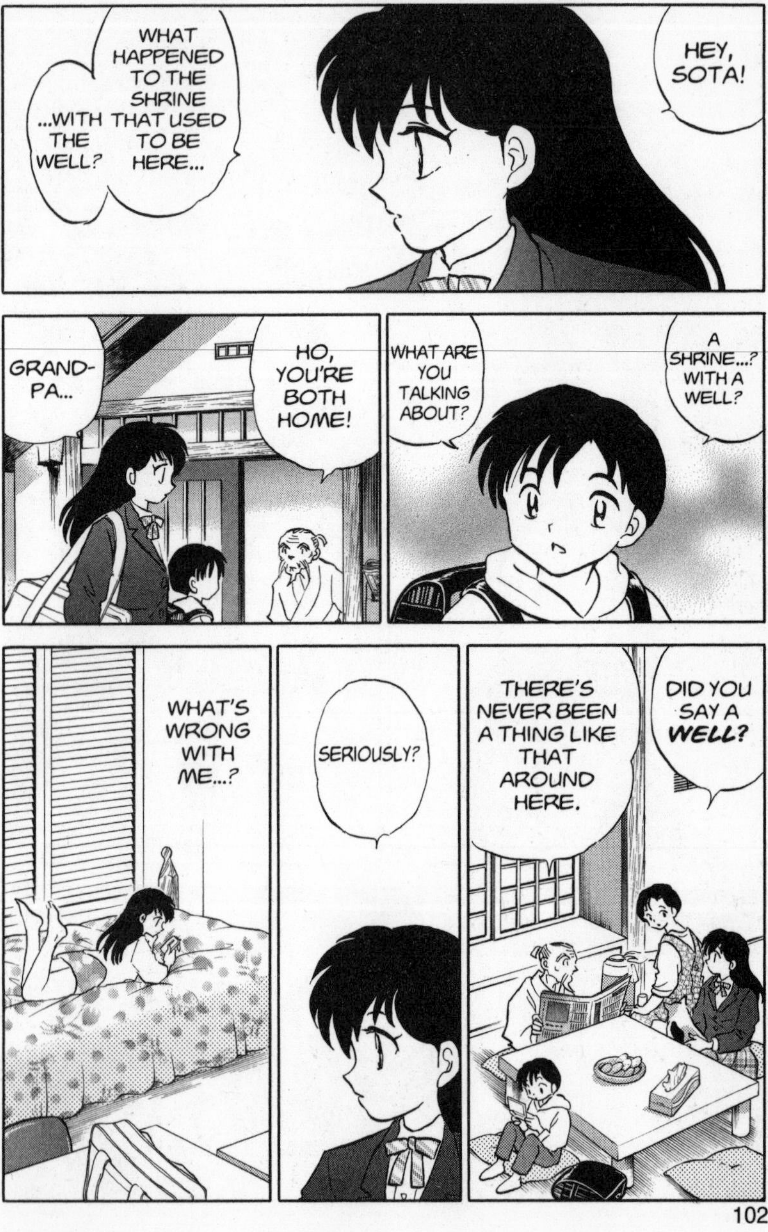
HEY, SOTA!
WHAT HAPPENED TO THE SHRINE THAT USED TO BE HERE...
...WITH THE WELL?
A SHRINE...? WITH A WELL?
WHAT ARE YOU TALKING ABOUT?
HO, YOU'RE BOTH HOME!
GRAND-PA...
DID YOU SAY A ***WELL?***
THERE'S NEVER BEEN A THING LIKE THAT AROUND HERE.
SERIOUSLY?
WHAT'S WRONG WITH ME...?

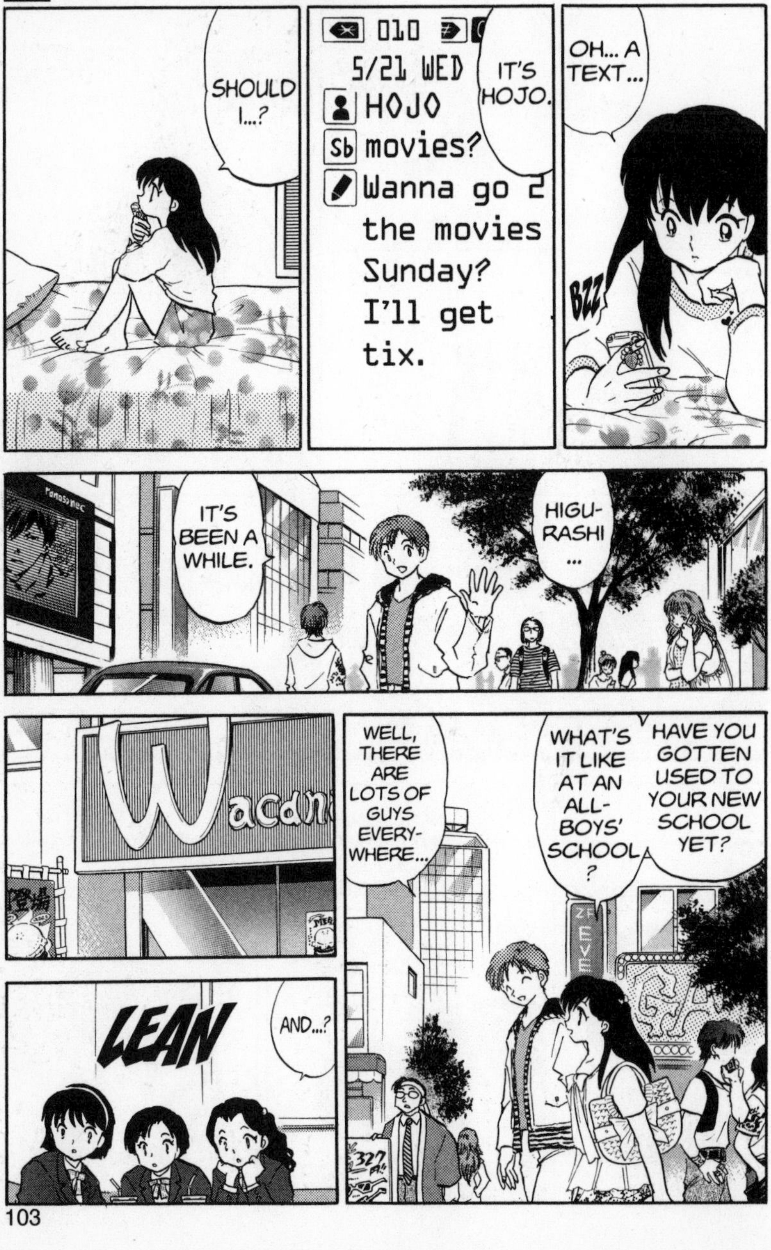
OH... A TEXT...
BZZ
IT'S HOJO.
010
5/21 WED
HOJO
movies?
Wanna go 2 the movies Sunday? I'll get tix.
SHOULD I...?
HIGU-RASHI ...
IT'S BEEN A WHILE.
HAVE YOU GOTTEN USED TO YOUR NEW SCHOOL YET?
WHAT'S IT LIKE AT AN ALL-BOYS' SCHOOL?
WELL, THERE ARE LOTS OF GUYS EVERYWHERE...
LEAN
AND...?

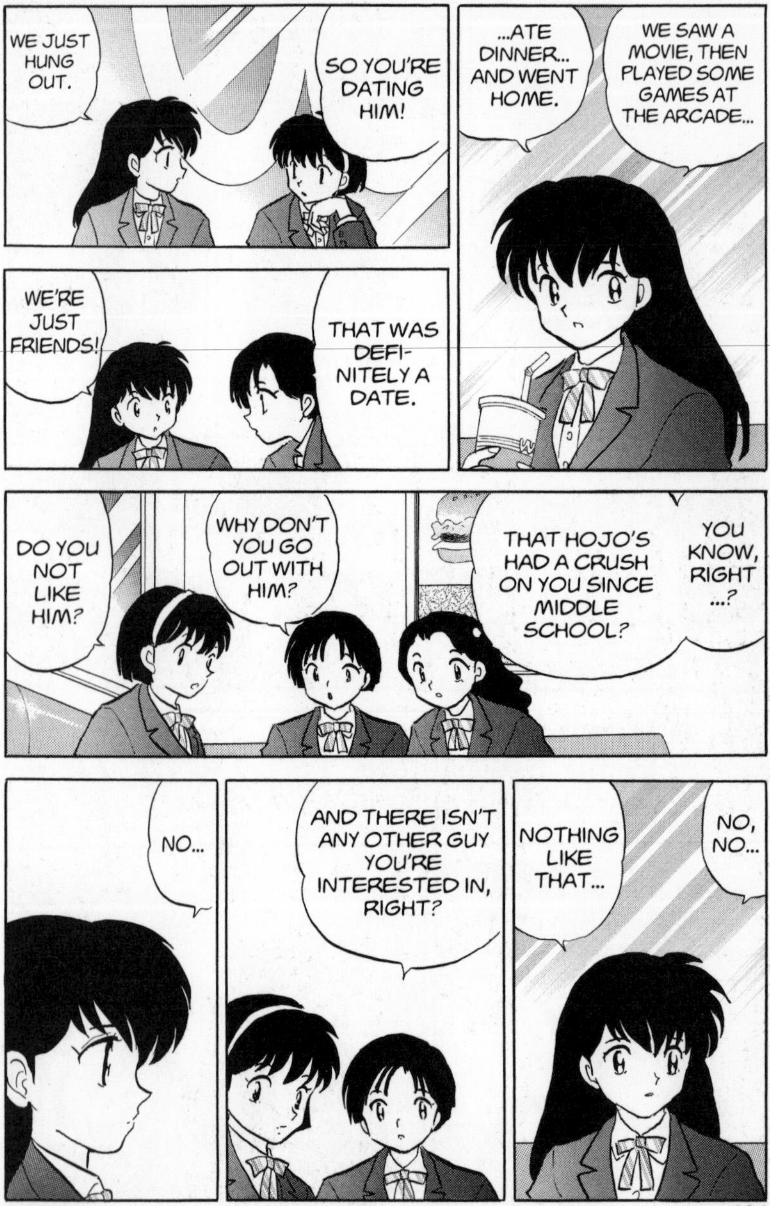
WE SAW A MOVIE, THEN PLAYED SOME GAMES AT THE ARCADE...
...ATE DINNER... AND WENT HOME.
SO YOU'RE DATING HIM!
WE JUST HUNG OUT.
THAT WAS DEFI-NITELY A DATE.
WE'RE JUST FRIENDS!
YOU KNOW, RIGHT ...?
THAT HOJO'S HAD A CRUSH ON YOU SINCE MIDDLE SCHOOL?
WHY DON'T YOU GO OUT WITH HIM?
DO YOU NOT LIKE HIM?
NO, NO...
NOTHING LIKE THAT...
AND THERE ISN'T ANY OTHER GUY YOU'RE INTERESTED IN, RIGHT?
NO...

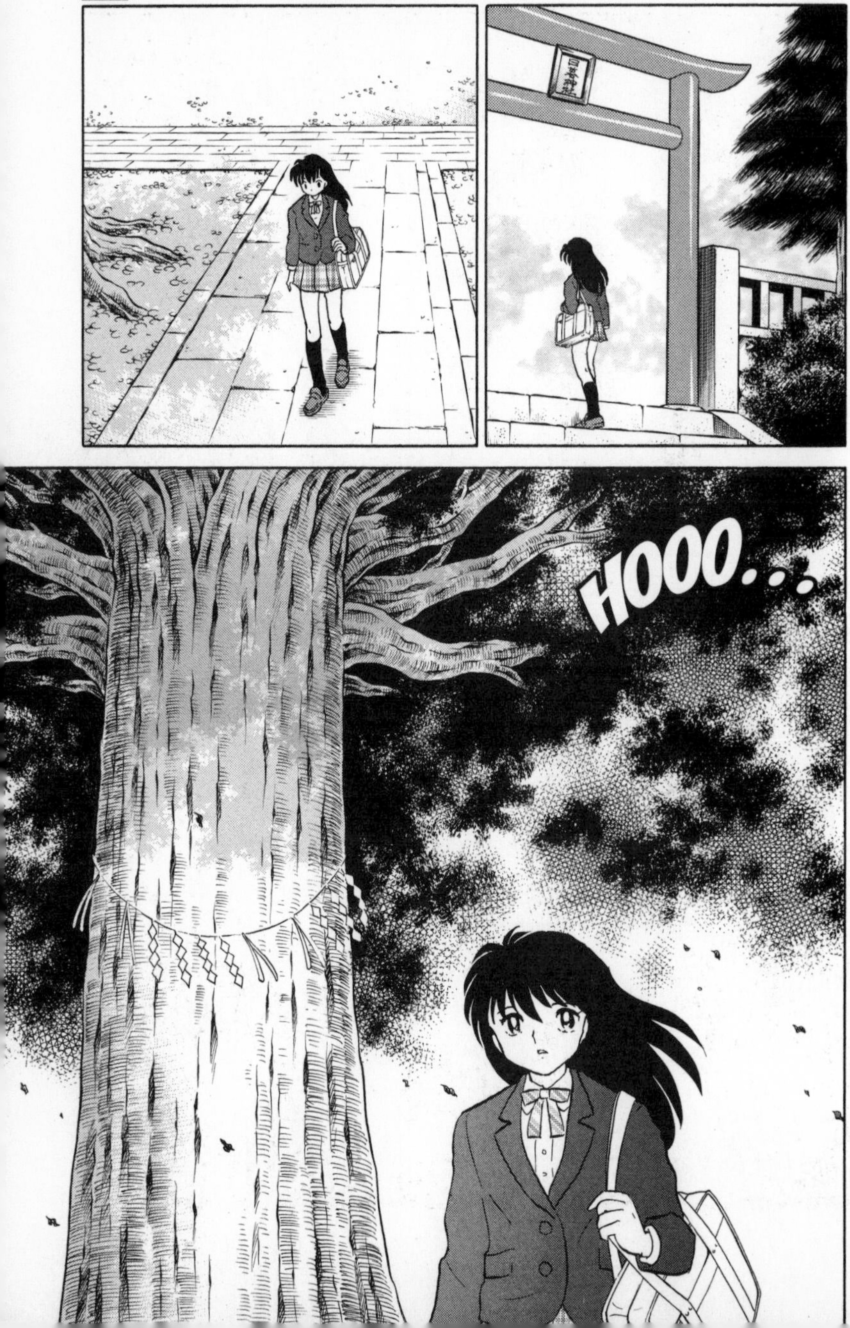
HOOO...

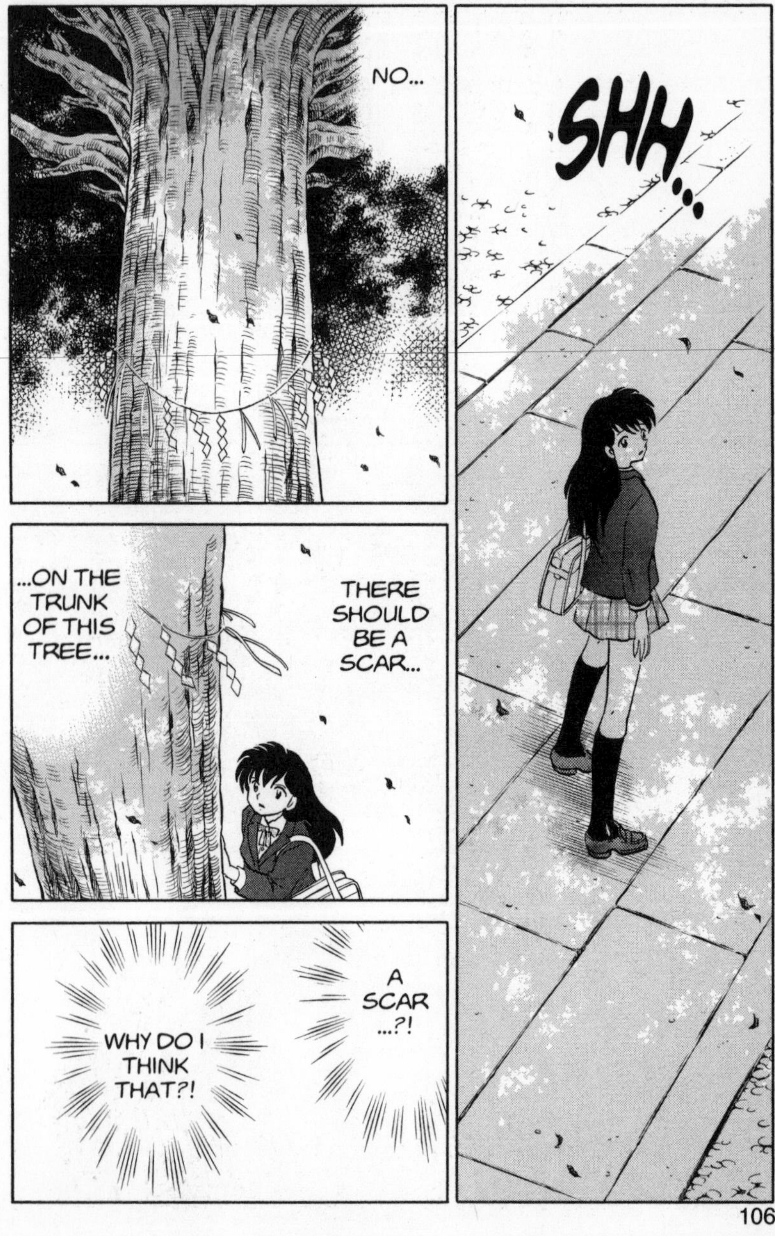
SHH...
NO...
THERE SHOULD BE A SCAR...
...ON THE TRUNK OF THIS TREE...
A SCAR ...?!
WHY DO I THINK THAT?!

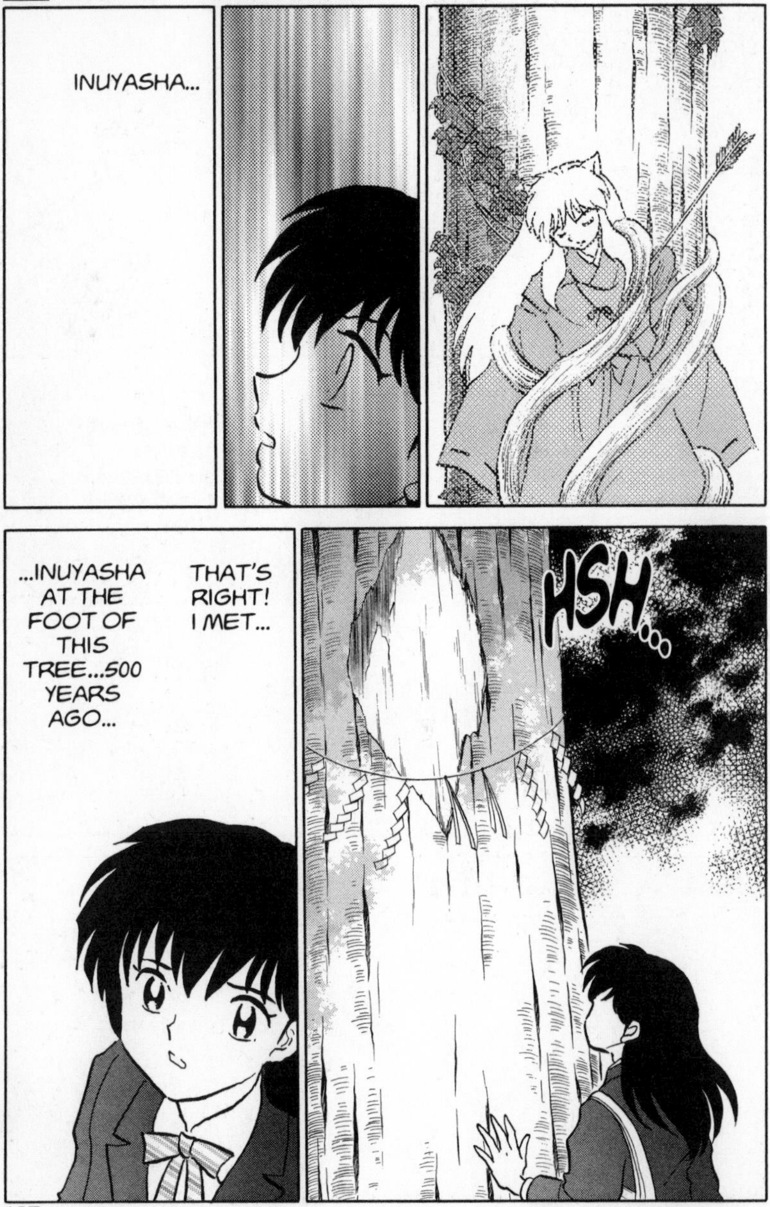
INUYASHA...
HSH...
THAT'S RIGHT! I MET...
...INUYASHA AT THE FOOT OF THIS TREE...500 YEARS AGO...

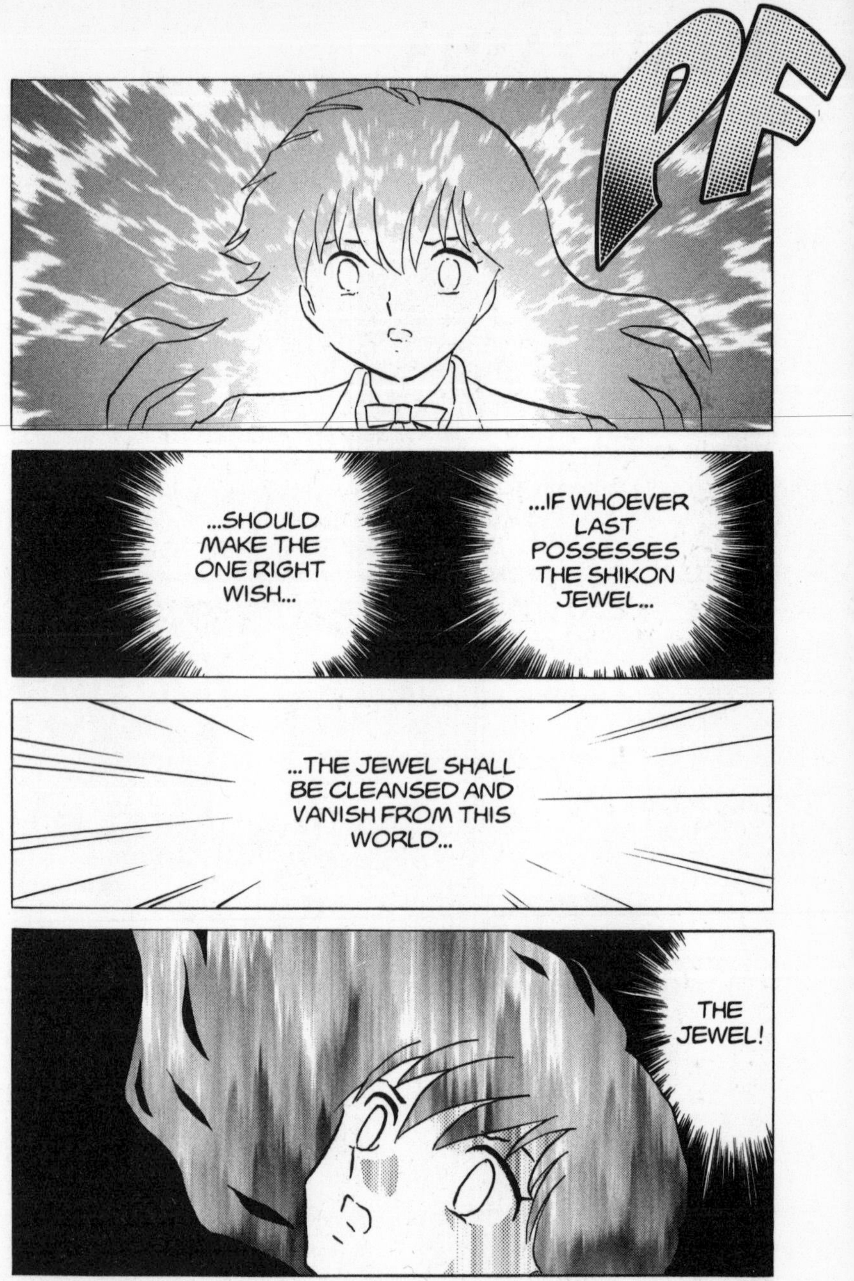
PF
...IF WHOEVER LAST POSSESSES THE SHIKON JEWEL...
...SHOULD MAKE THE ONE RIGHT WISH...
...THE JEWEL SHALL BE CLEANSED AND VANISH FROM THIS WORLD...
THE JEWEL!

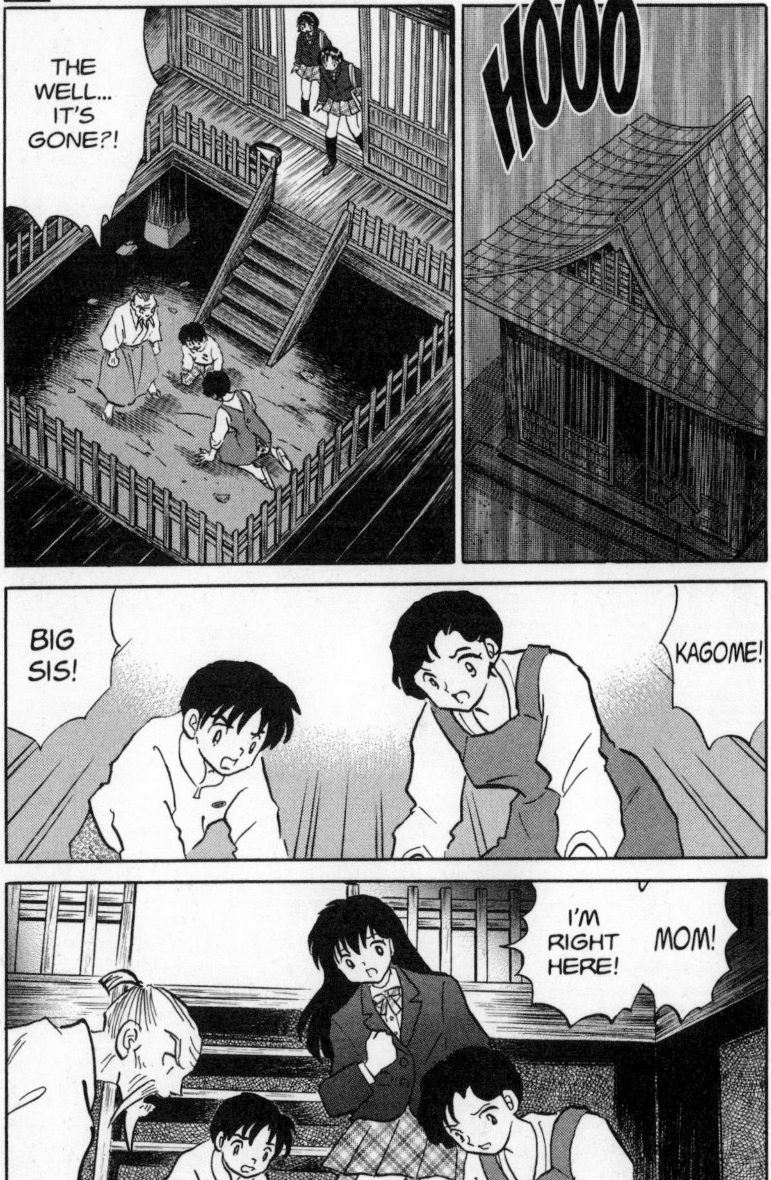
HOOO
THE WELL... IT'S GONE?!
KAGOME!
BIG SIS!
MOM!
I'M RIGHT HERE!

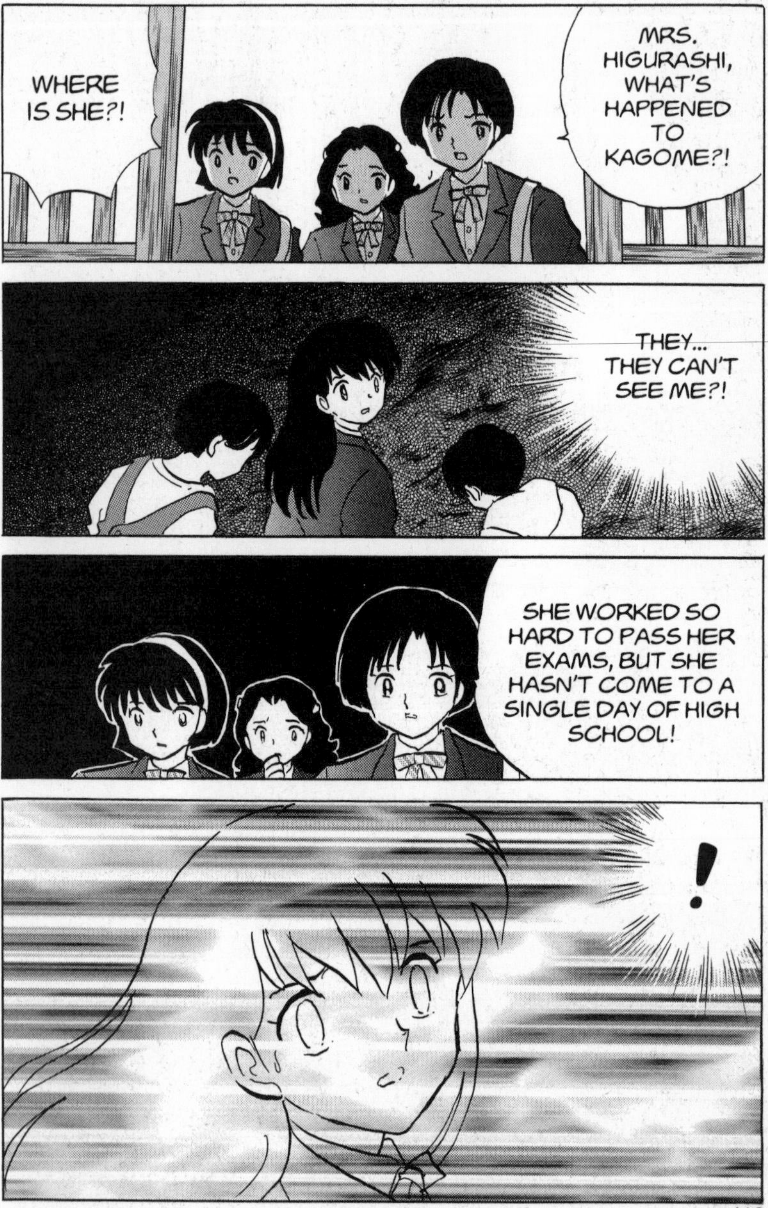
MRS. HIGURASHI, WHAT'S HAPPENED TO KAGOME?!
WHERE IS SHE?!
THEY... THEY CAN'T SEE ME?!
SHE WORKED SO HARD TO PASS HER EXAMS, BUT SHE HASN'T COME TO A SINGLE DAY OF HIGH SCHOOL!
!

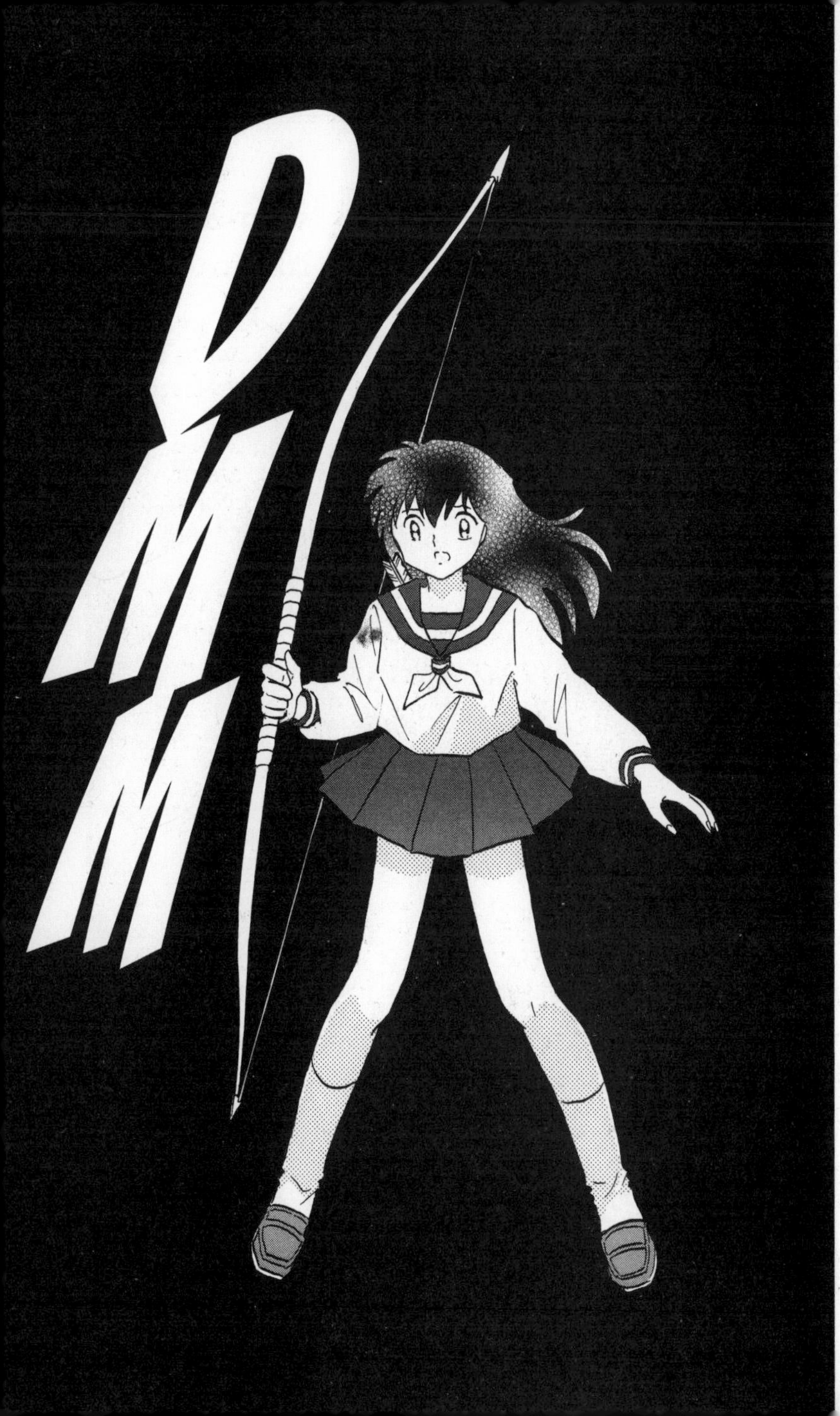
DMMM

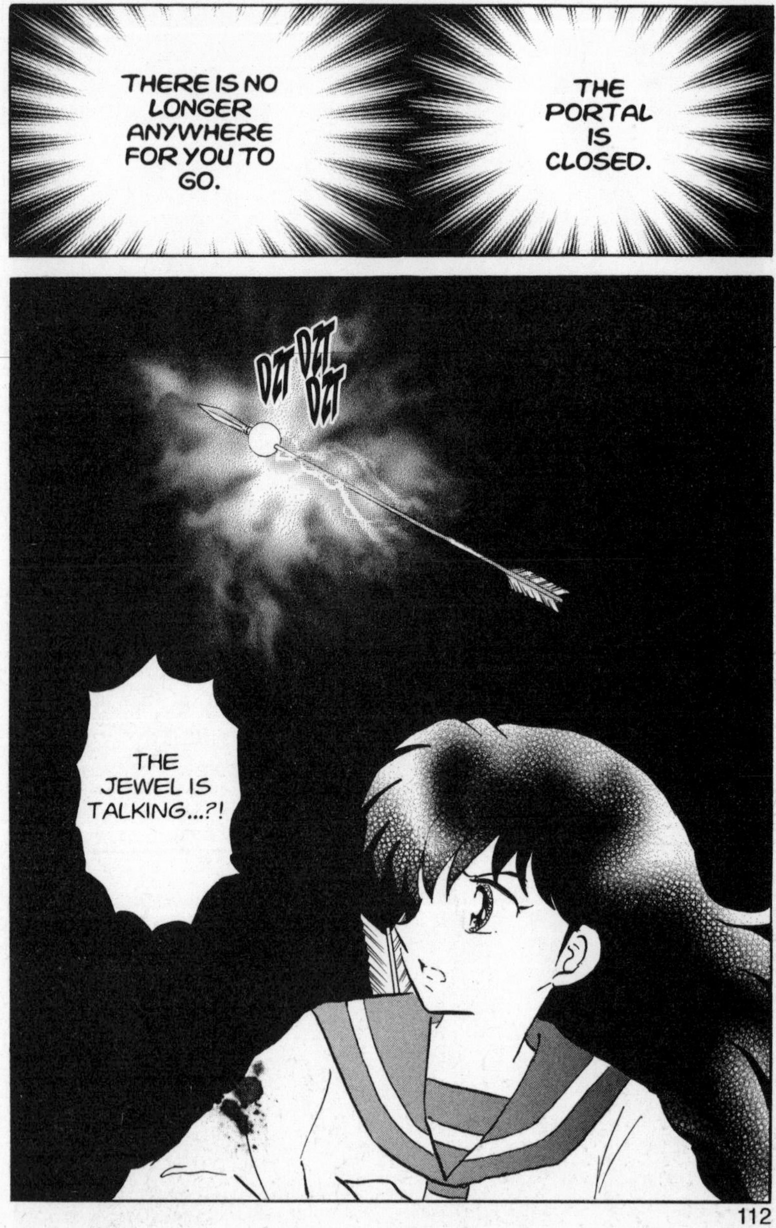
THE PORTAL IS CLOSED.
THERE IS NO LONGER ANYWHERE FOR YOU TO GO.
DZT DZT DZT
THE JEWEL IS TALKING...?!

SCROLL 7
THE DARKNESS

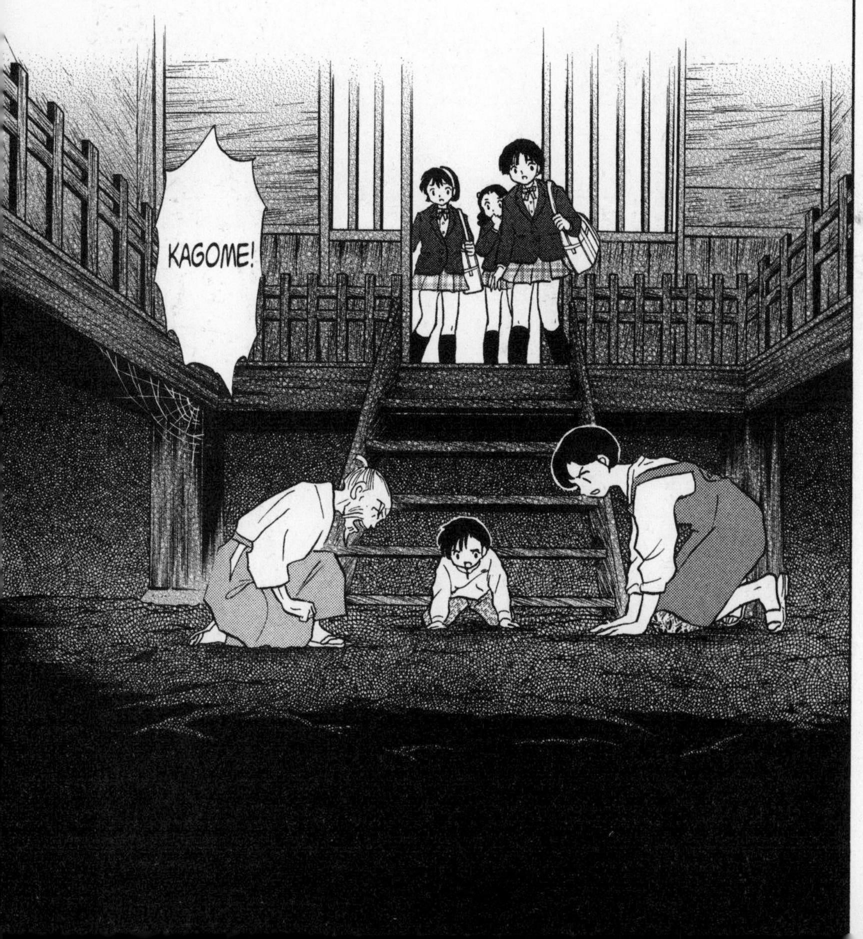

KAGOME!

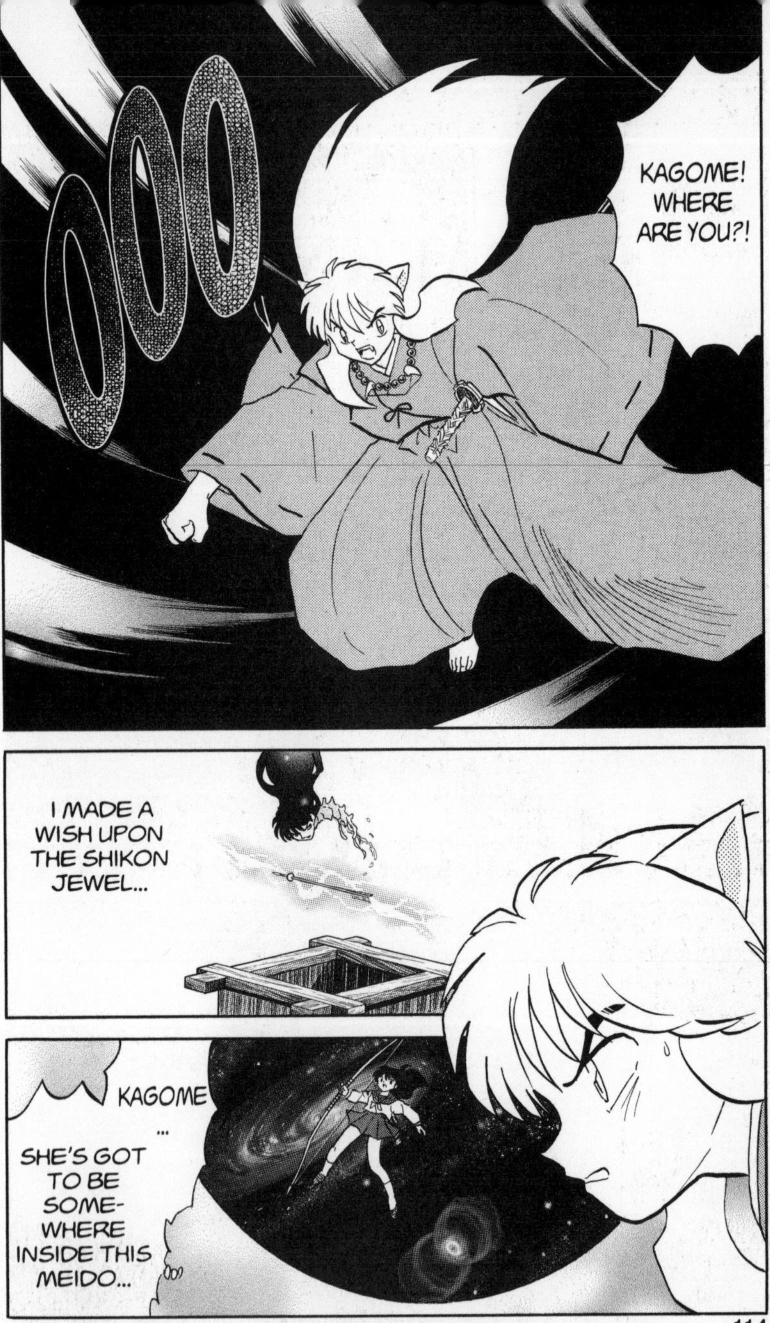
KAGOME! WHERE ARE YOU?!
I MADE A WISH UPON THE SHIKON JEWEL...
KAGOME ...
SHE'S GOT TO BE SOME-WHERE INSIDE THIS MEIDO...

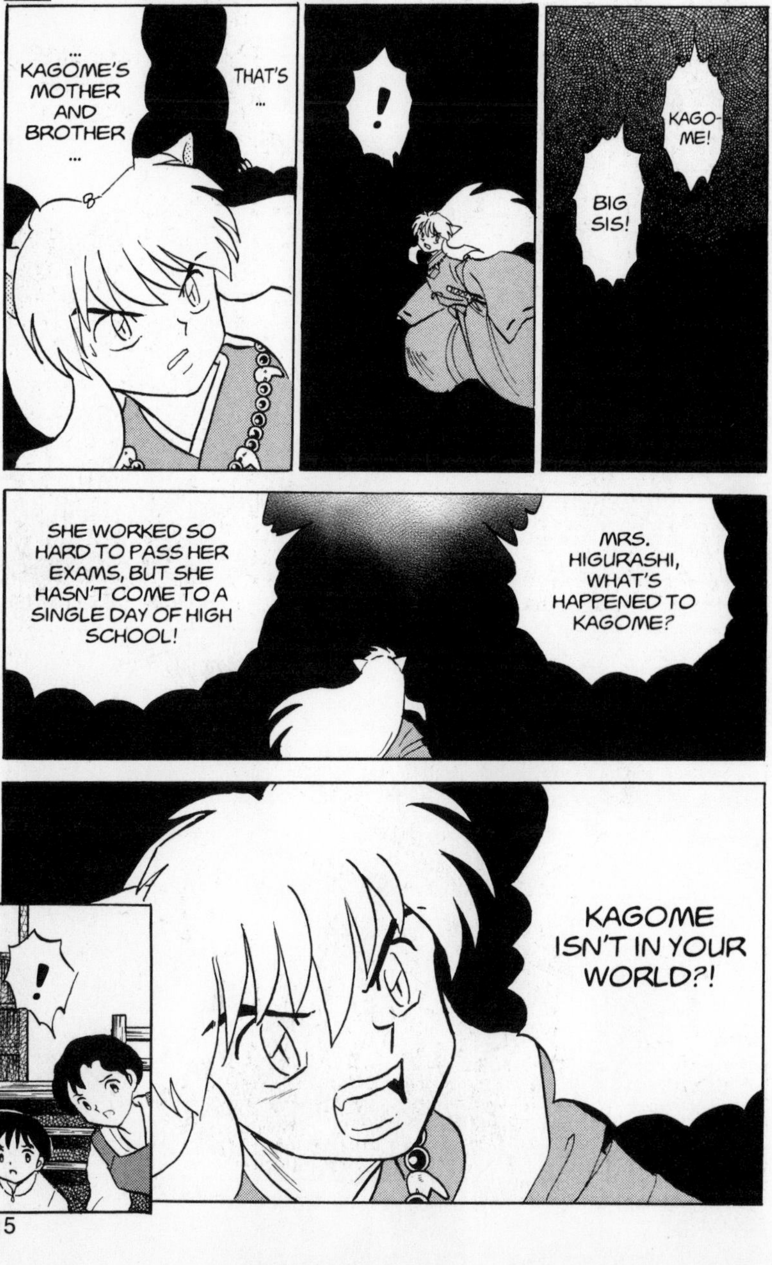
KAGO-ME!
BIG SIS!
!
THAT'S ...
... KAGOME'S MOTHER AND BROTHER ...
MRS. HIGURASHI, WHAT'S HAPPENED TO KAGOME?
SHE WORKED SO HARD TO PASS HER EXAMS, BUT SHE HASN'T COME TO A SINGLE DAY OF HIGH SCHOOL!
KAGOME ISN'T IN YOUR WORLD?!
!

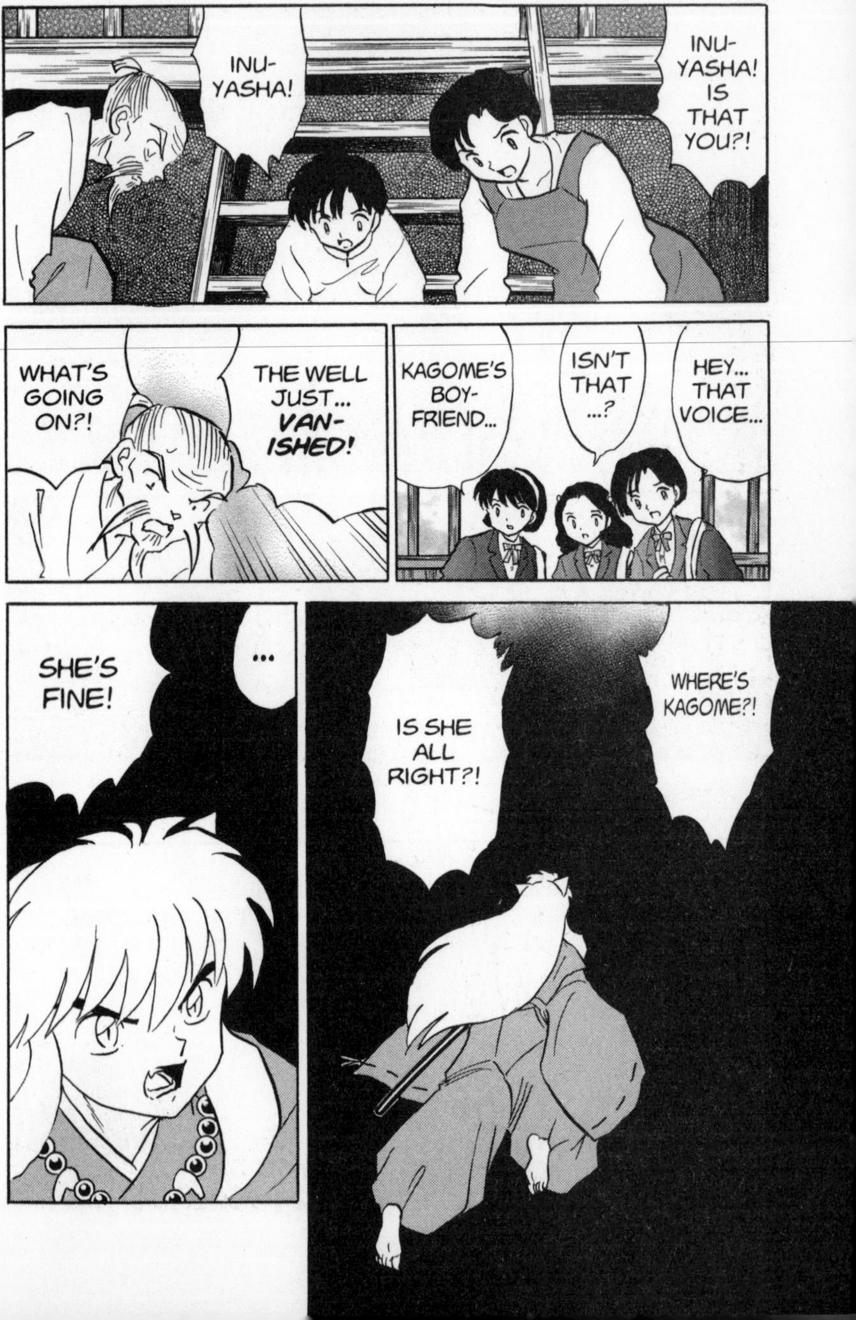
INU-YASHA! IS THAT YOU?!
INU-YASHA!
HEY... THAT VOICE...
ISN'T THAT ...?
KAGOME'S BOY-FRIEND...
THE WELL JUST... VAN-ISHED!
WHAT'S GOING ON?!
WHERE'S KAGOME?!
IS SHE ALL RIGHT?!
...
SHE'S FINE!

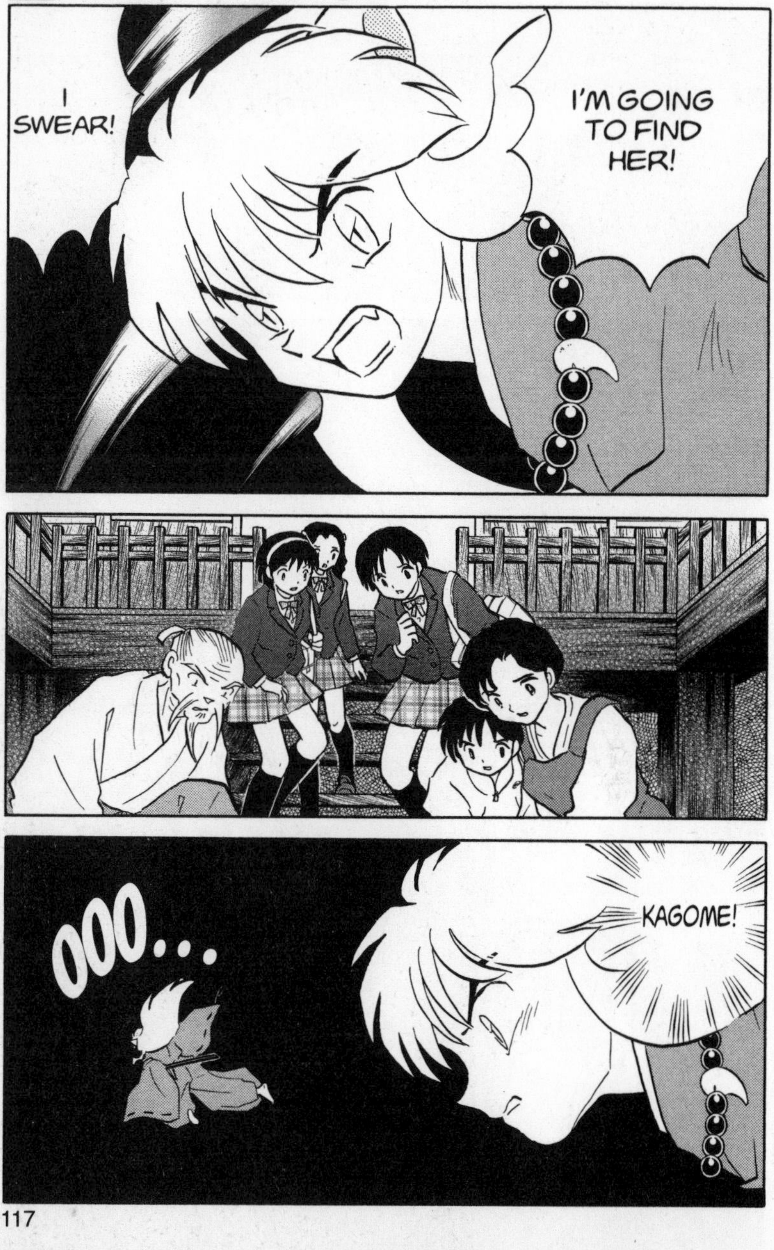
I'M GOING TO FIND HER!
I SWEAR!
KAGOME!
OOO...

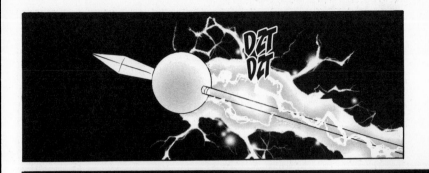

DZT
DZT

SHIKON
JEWEL...

WHERE
DID YOU
BRING
ME?!

WHERE
AM I?!

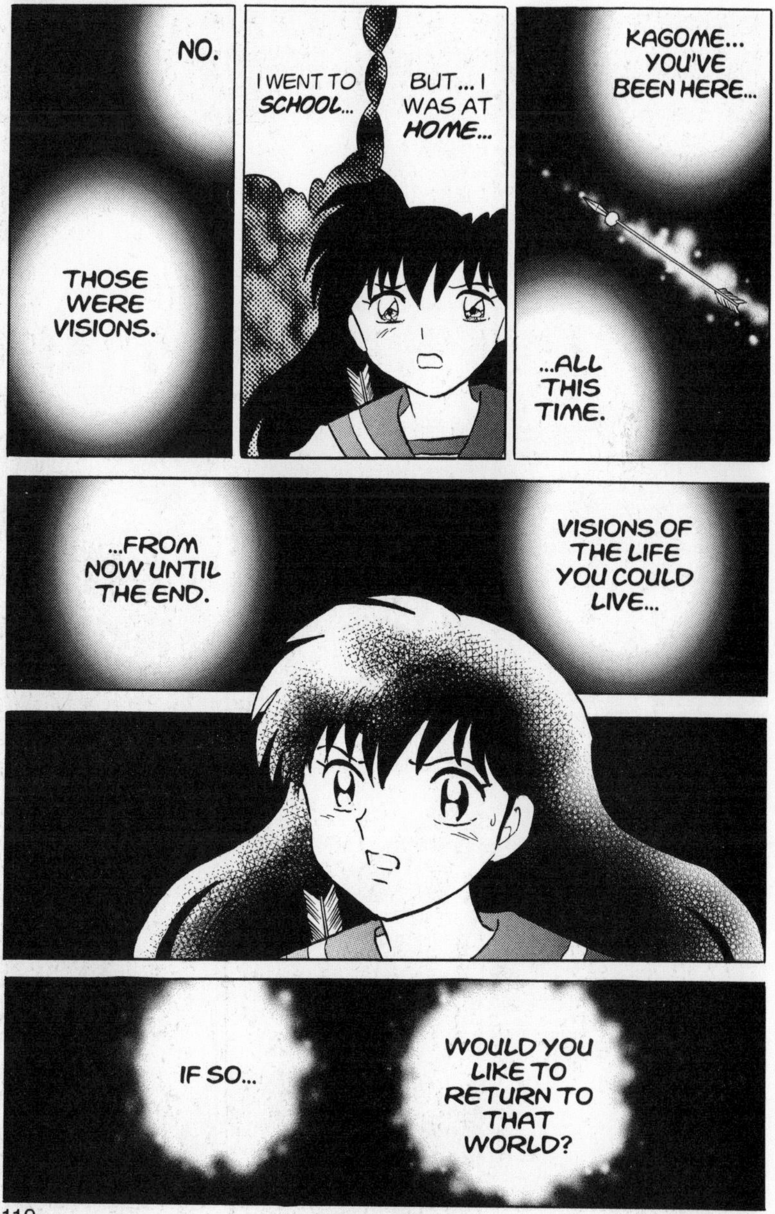
KAGOME... YOU'VE BEEN HERE...
...ALL THIS TIME.
I WENT TO SCHOOL...
BUT... I WAS AT HOME...
NO.
THOSE WERE VISIONS.
VISIONS OF THE LIFE YOU COULD LIVE...
...FROM NOW UNTIL THE END.
IF SO...
WOULD YOU LIKE TO RETURN TO THAT WORLD?

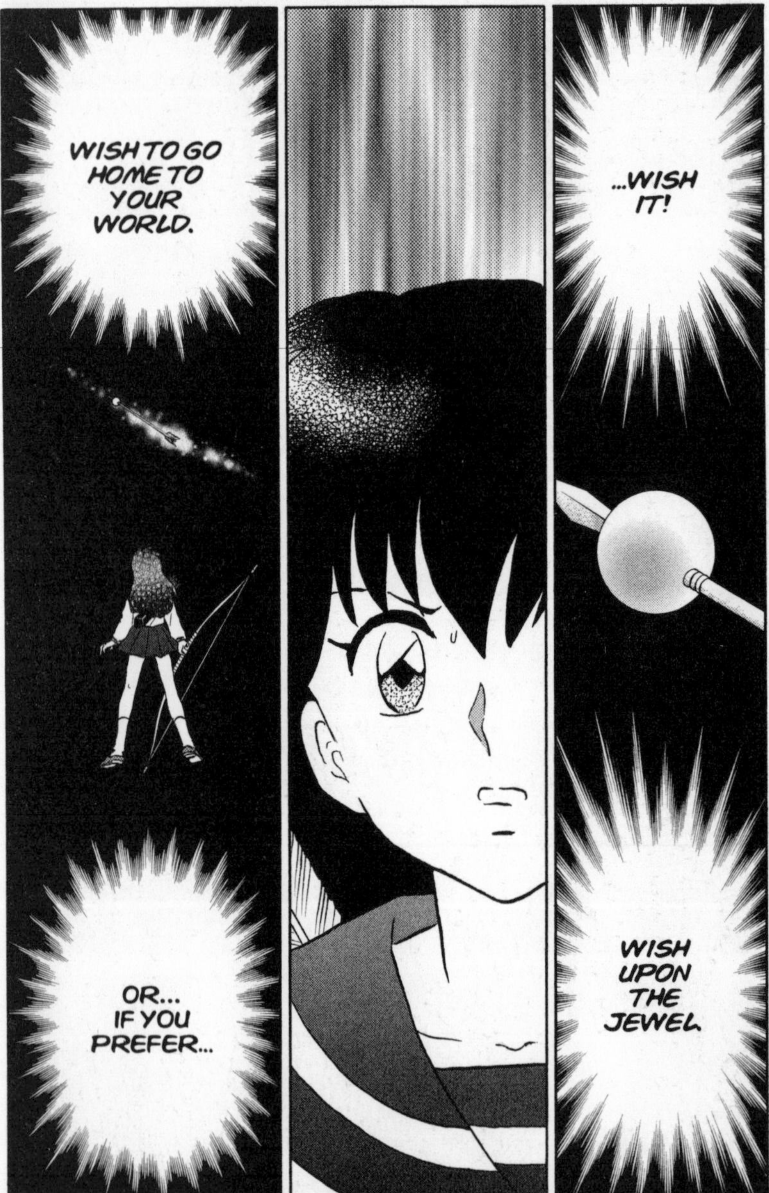
WISH TO GO HOME TO YOUR WORLD.
OR... IF YOU PREFER...
...WISH IT!
WISH UPON THE JEWEL.

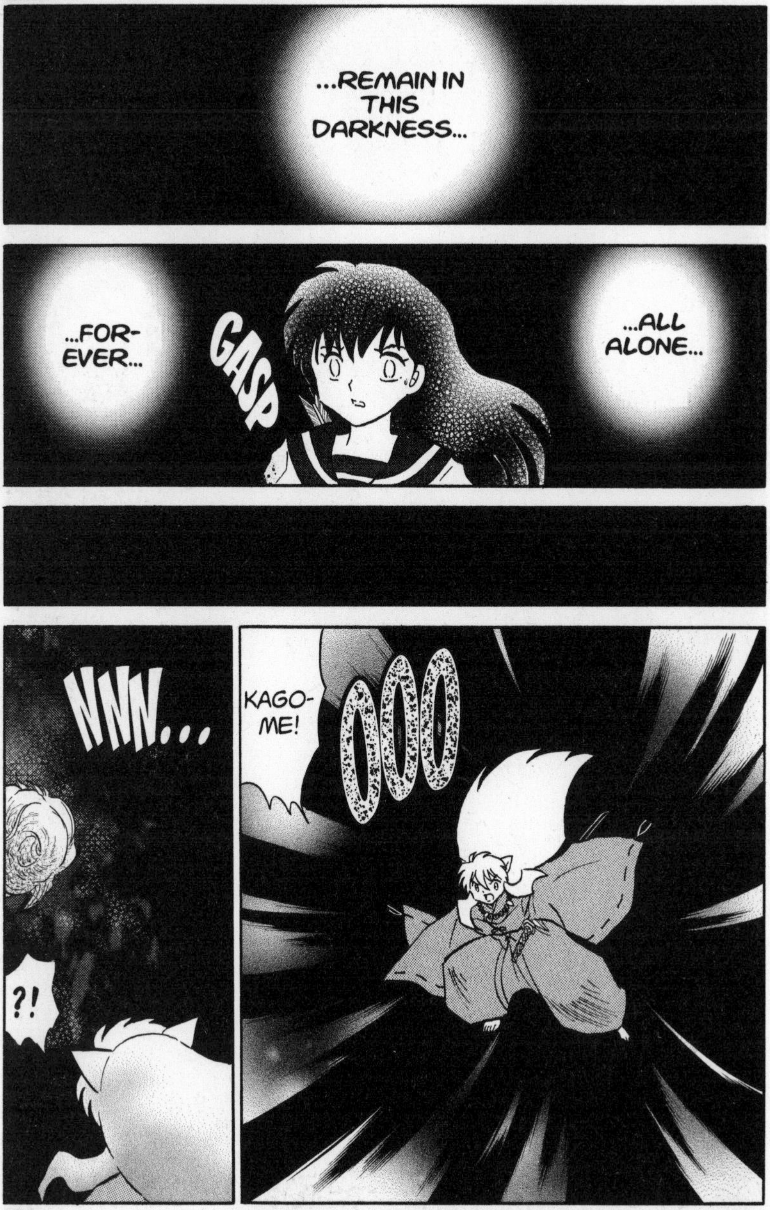
...REMAIN IN THIS DARKNESS...
...ALL ALONE...
GASP
...FOR-EVER...
KAGO-ME!
NNN...
?!

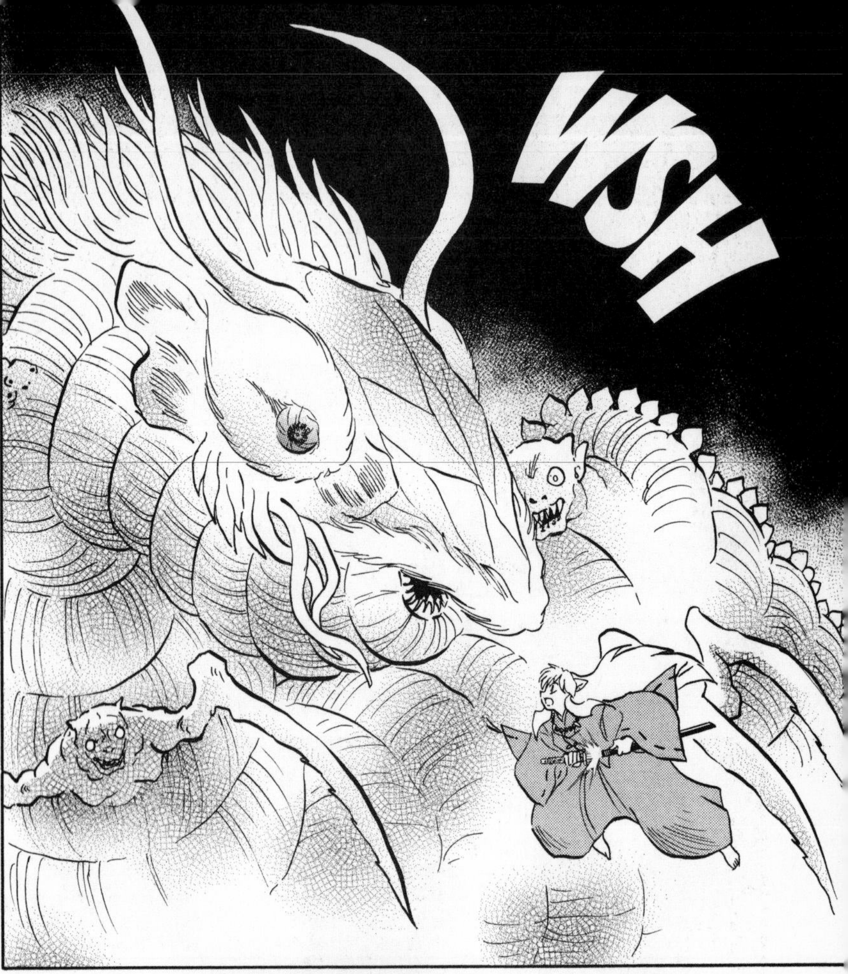
WSH
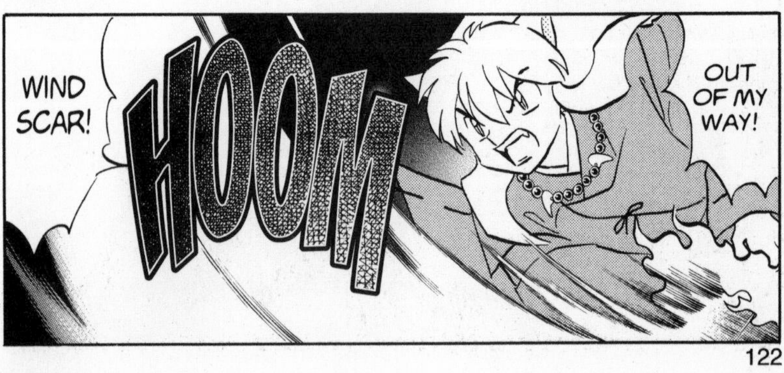
OUT OF MY WAY!
HOOM
WIND SCAR!

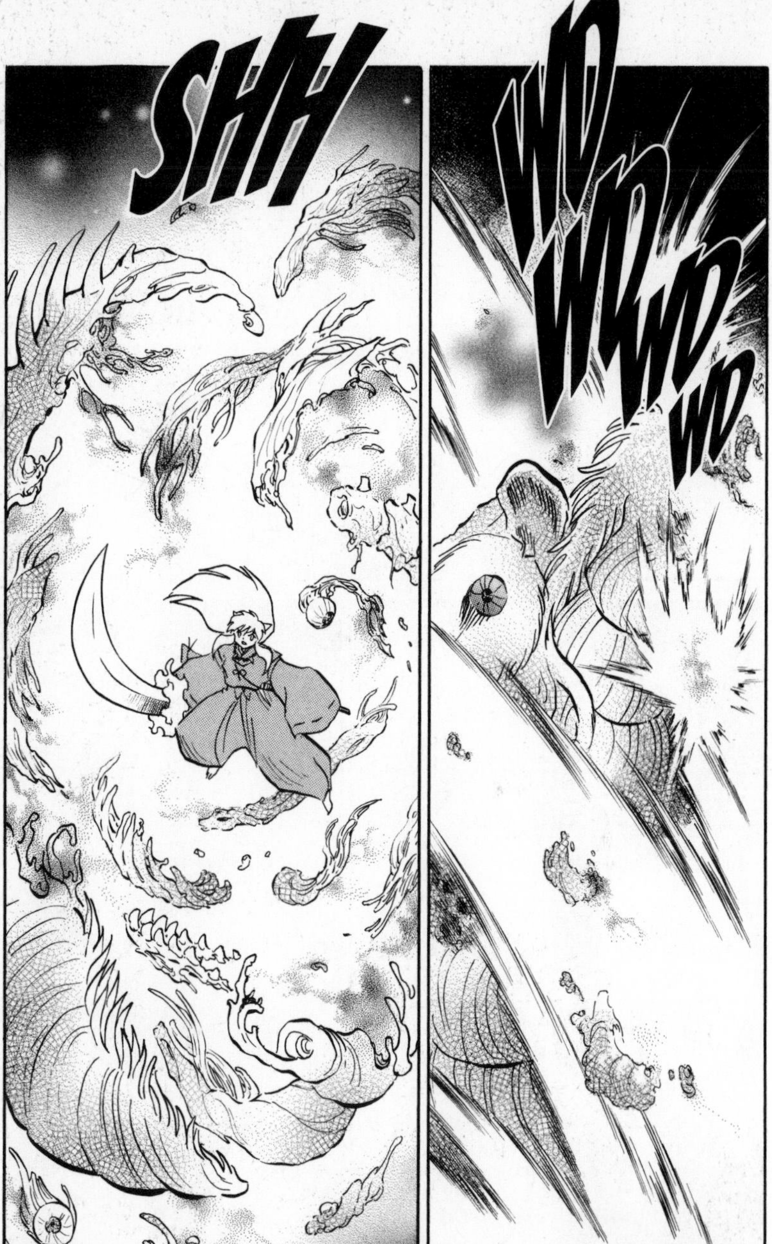
WO WO WO WO
SHH

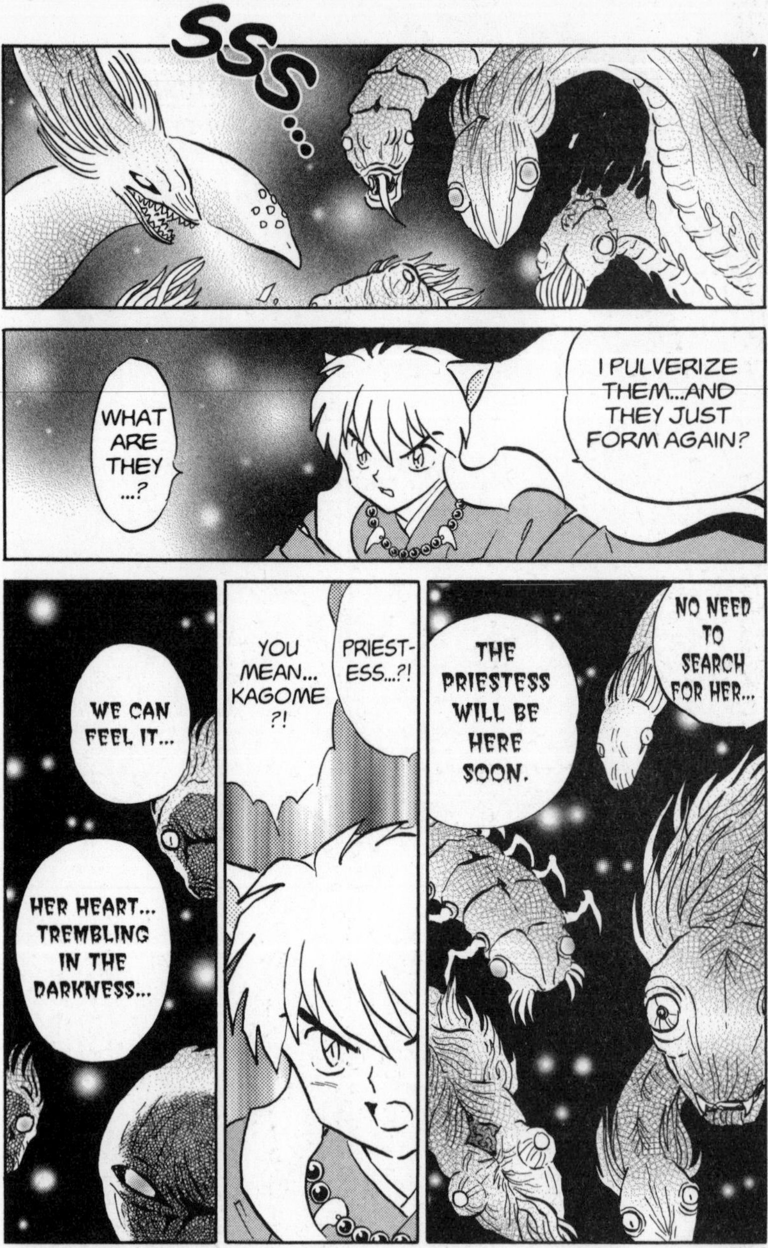
SSS...
I PULVERIZE THEM...AND THEY JUST FORM AGAIN?
WHAT ARE THEY ...?
NO NEED TO SEARCH FOR HER...
THE PRIESTESS WILL BE HERE SOON.
PRIEST-ESS...?!
YOU MEAN... KAGOME ?!
WE CAN FEEL IT...
HER HEART... TREMBLING IN THE DARKNESS...

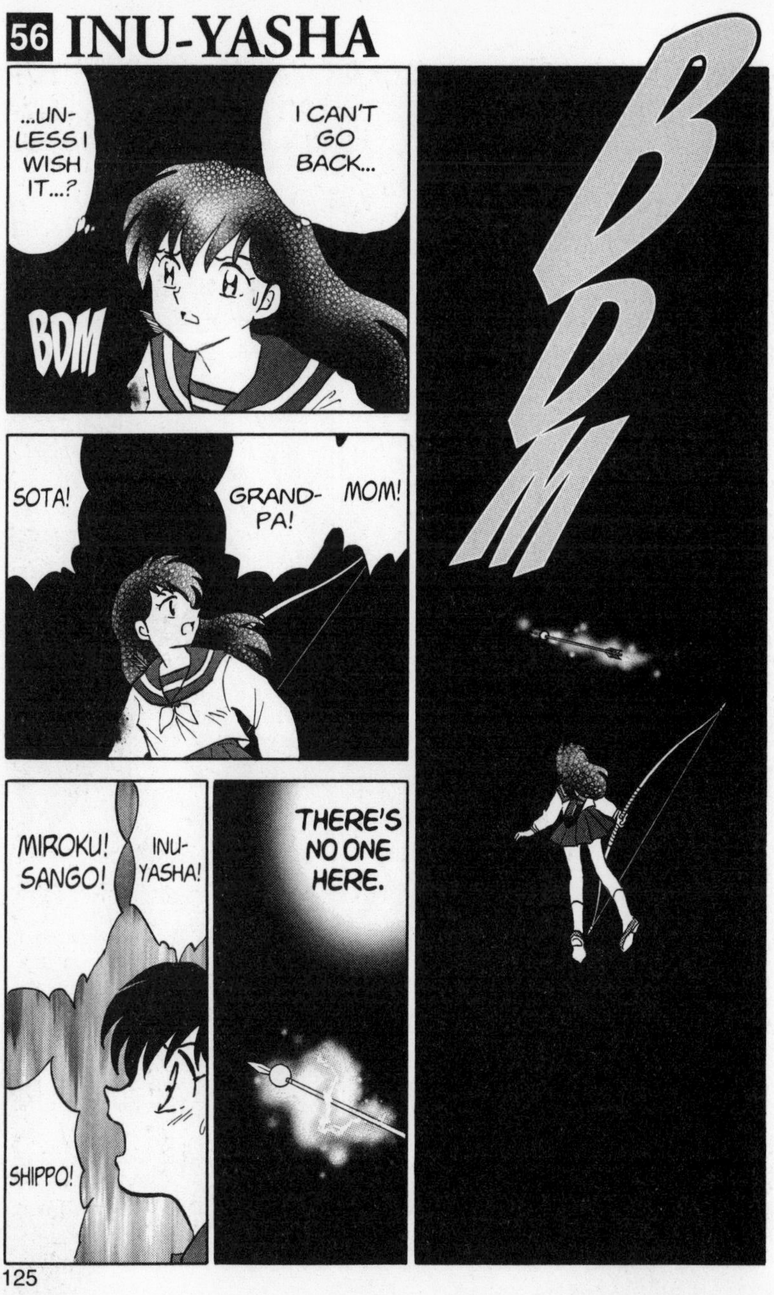
BDM
I CAN'T GO BACK...
...UN-LESS I WISH IT...?
BDM
MOM!
GRAND-PA!
SOTA!
THERE'S NO ONE HERE.
INU-YASHA!
MIROKU! SANGO!
SHIPPO!

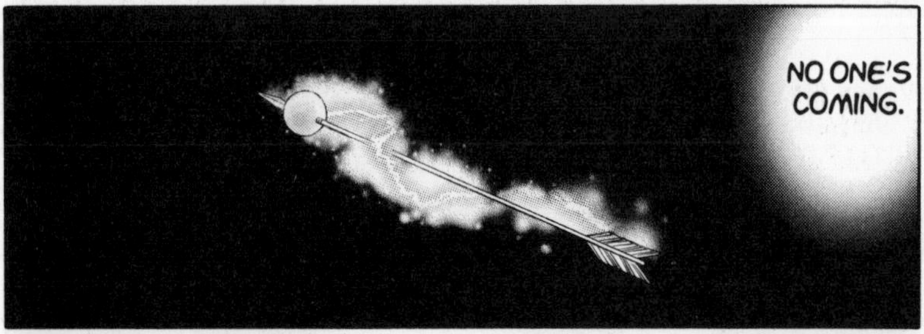
NO ONE'S COMING.
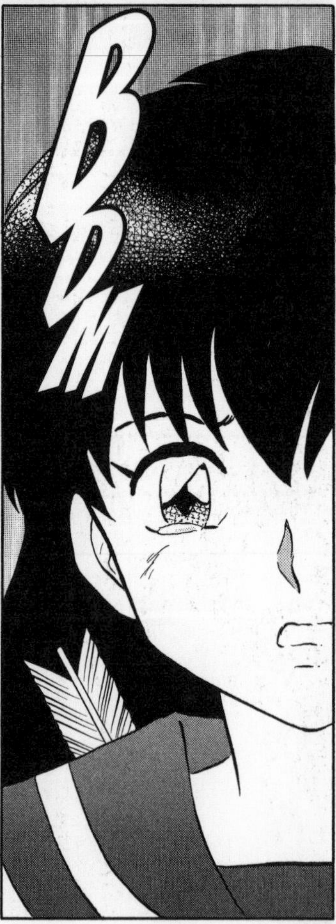
BDM
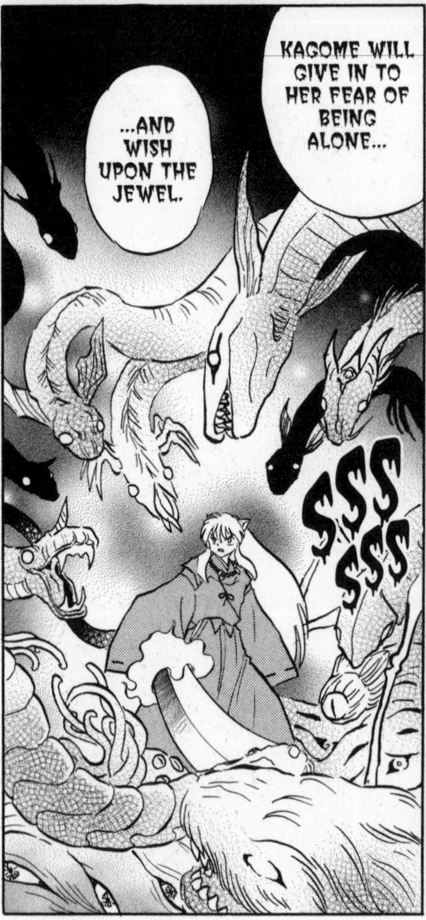
KAGOME WILL GIVE IN TO HER FEAR OF BEING ALONE...
...AND WISH UPON THE JEWEL.
SSS SSS

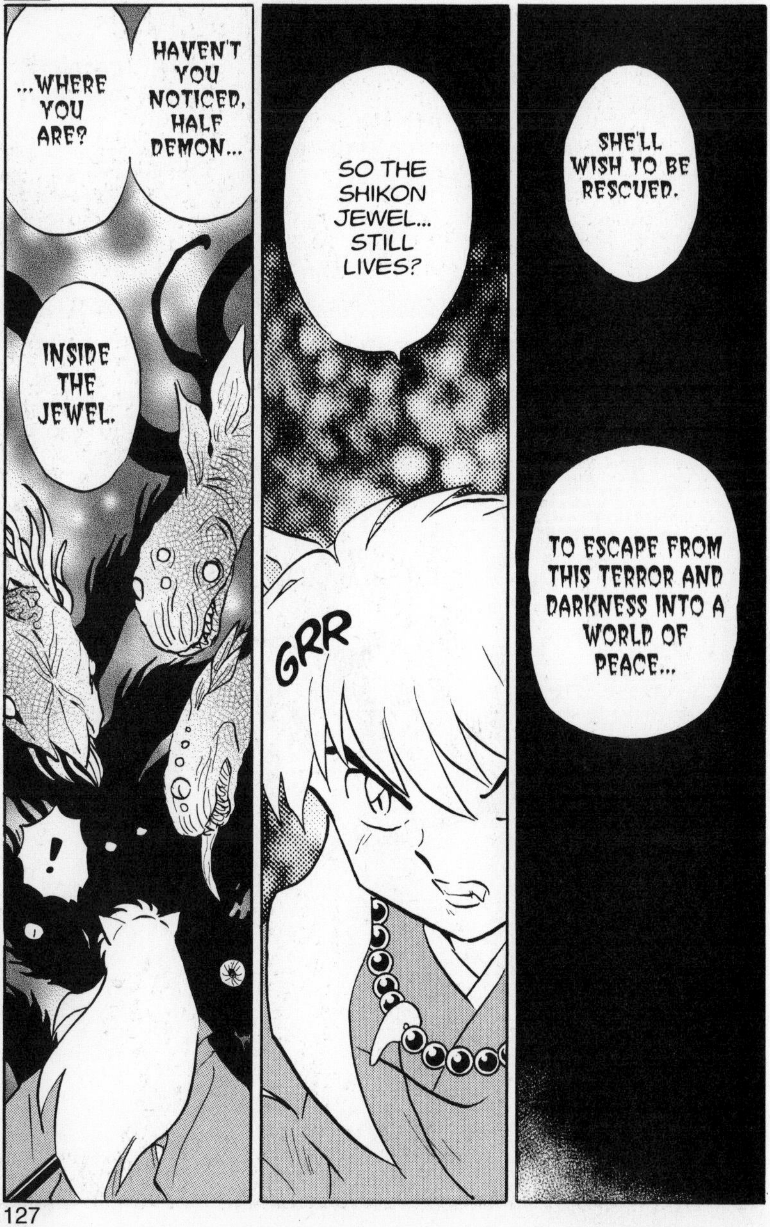
SHE'LL WISH TO BE RESCUED.
TO ESCAPE FROM THIS TERROR AND DARKNESS INTO A WORLD OF PEACE...
SO THE SHIKON JEWEL... STILL LIVES?
GRR
HAVEN'T YOU NOTICED, HALF DEMON...
...WHERE YOU ARE?
INSIDE THE JEWEL.
!

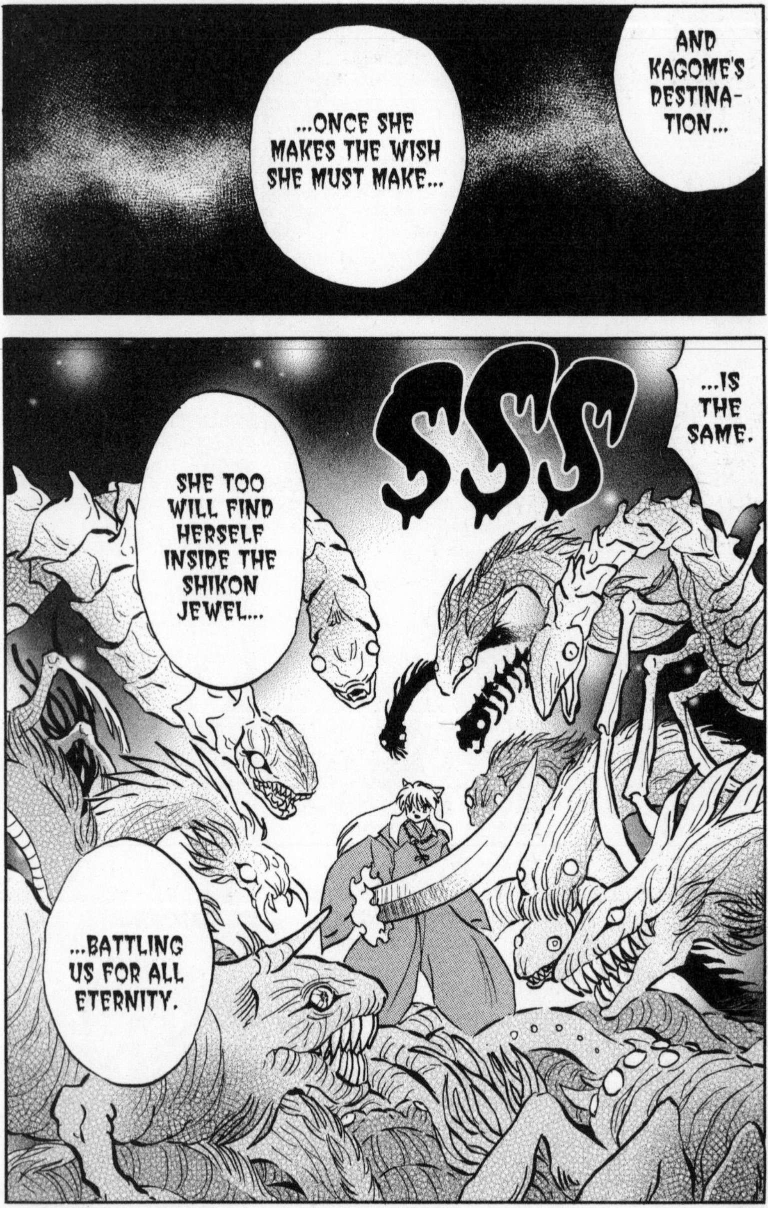
AND KAGOME'S DESTINATION...
...ONCE SHE MAKES THE WISH SHE MUST MAKE...
...IS THE SAME.
SSS
SHE TOO WILL FIND HERSELF INSIDE THE SHIKON JEWEL...
...BATTLING US FOR ALL ETERNITY.

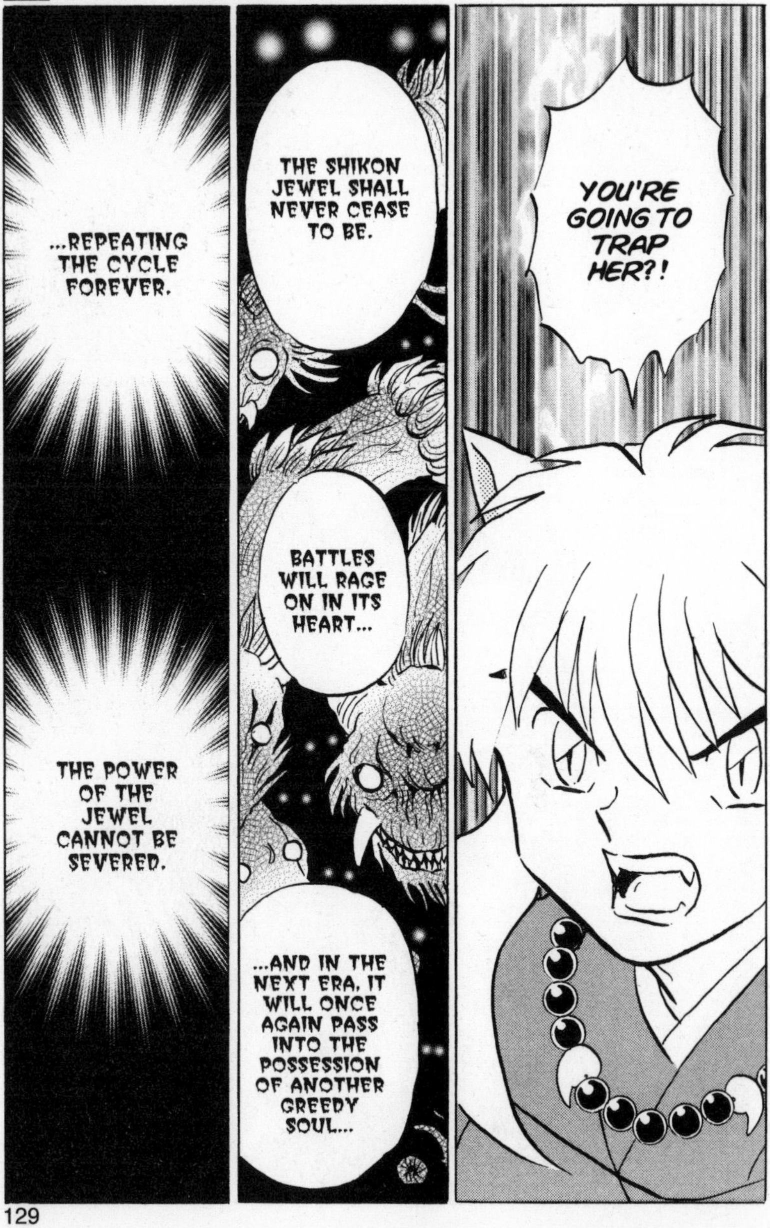
YOU'RE GOING TO TRAP HER?!
THE SHIKON JEWEL SHALL NEVER CEASE TO BE.
BATTLES WILL RAGE ON IN ITS HEART...
...AND IN THE NEXT ERA, IT WILL ONCE AGAIN PASS INTO THE POSSESSION OF ANOTHER GREEDY SOUL...
...REPEATING THE CYCLE FOREVER.
THE POWER OF THE JEWEL CANNOT BE SEVERED.

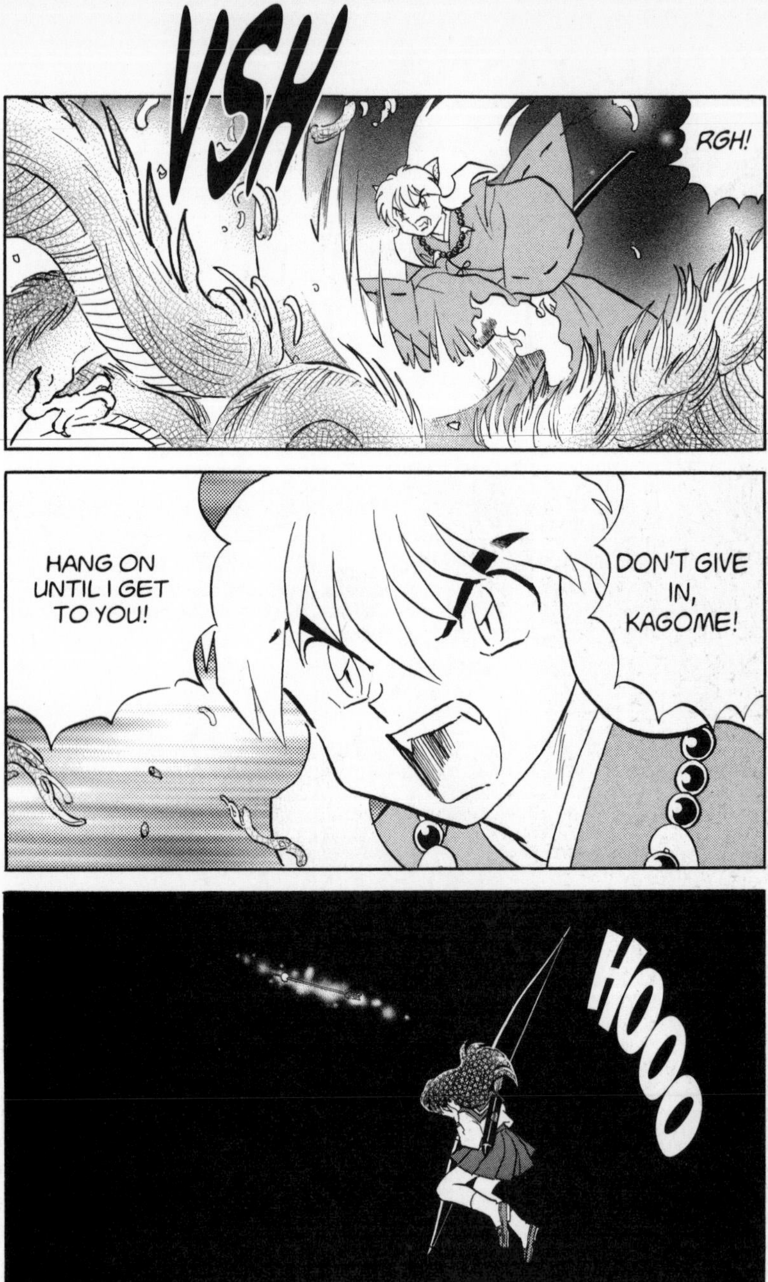
VSH
RGH!
DON'T GIVE IN, KAGOME!
HANG ON UNTIL I GET TO YOU!
HOOO

SCROLL 8

DESTINY

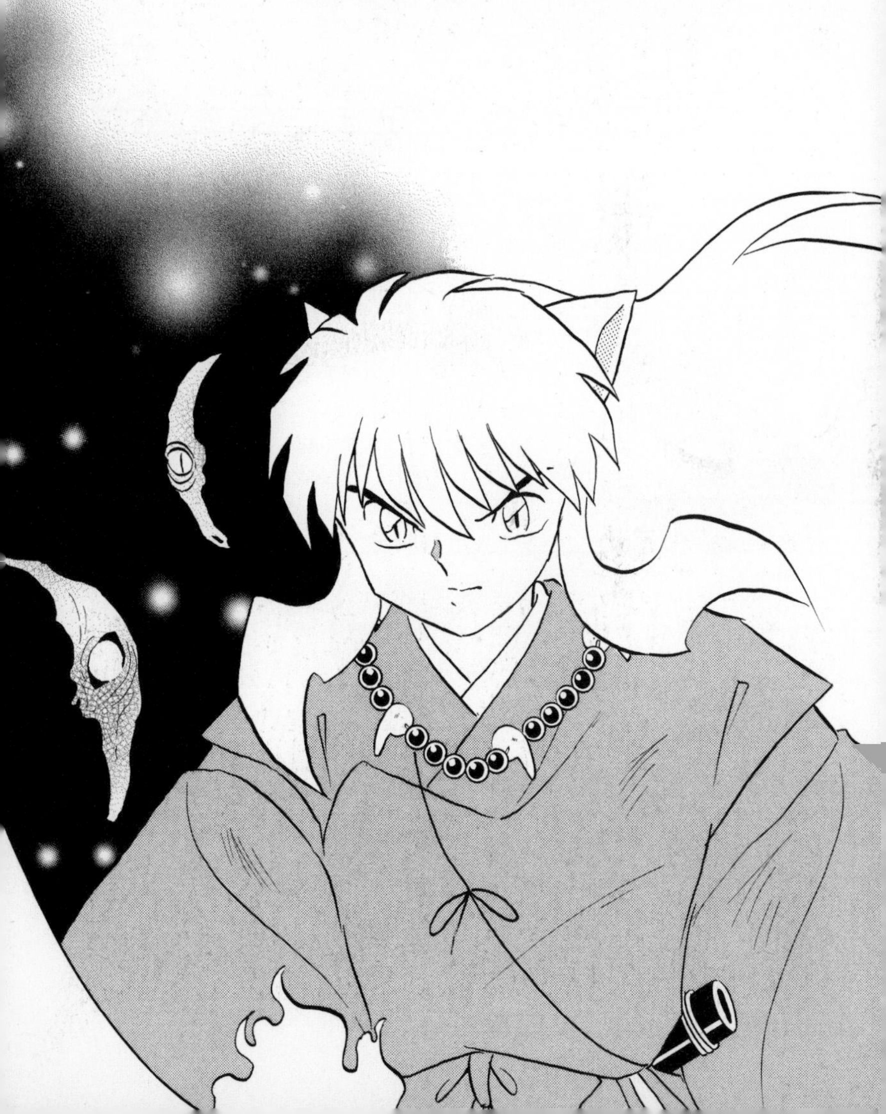

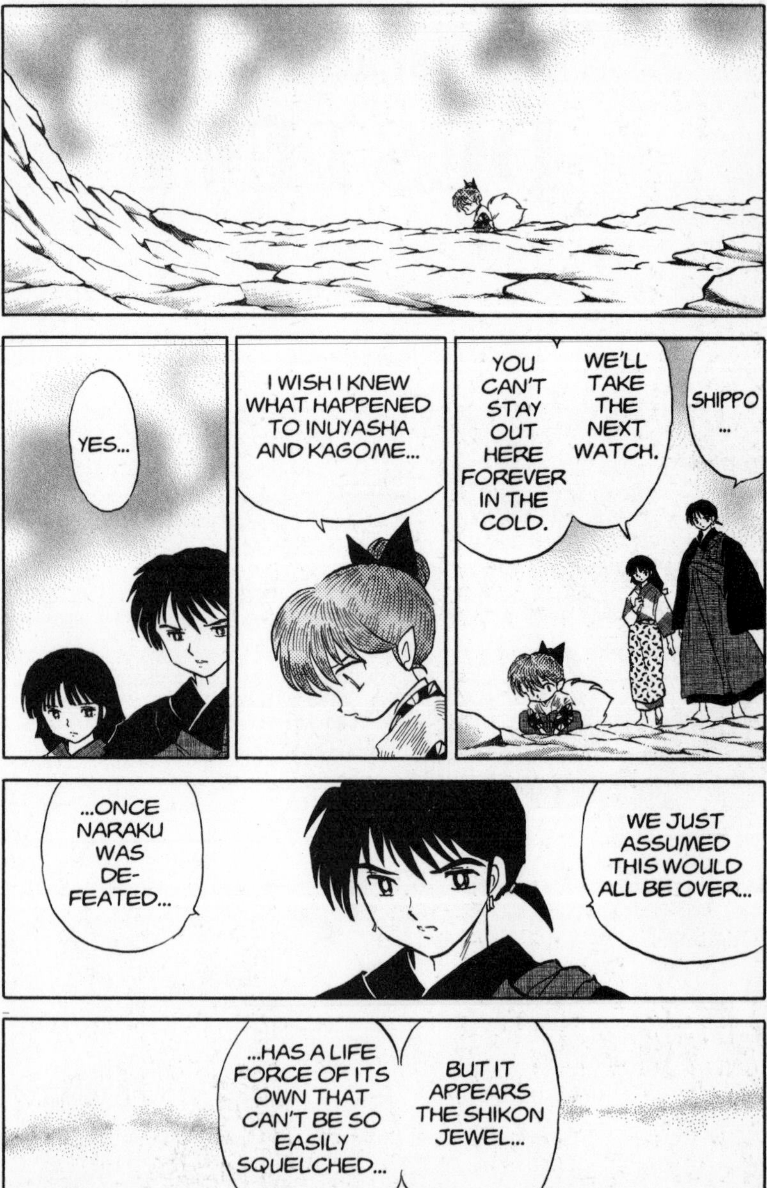
SHIPPO ...
WE'LL TAKE THE NEXT WATCH.
YOU CAN'T STAY OUT HERE FOREVER IN THE COLD.
I WISH I KNEW WHAT HAPPENED TO INUYASHA AND KAGOME...
YES...
WE JUST ASSUMED THIS WOULD ALL BE OVER...
...ONCE NARAKU WAS DE-FEATED...
BUT IT APPEARS THE SHIKON JEWEL...
...HAS A LIFE FORCE OF ITS OWN THAT CAN'T BE SO EASILY SQUELCHED...

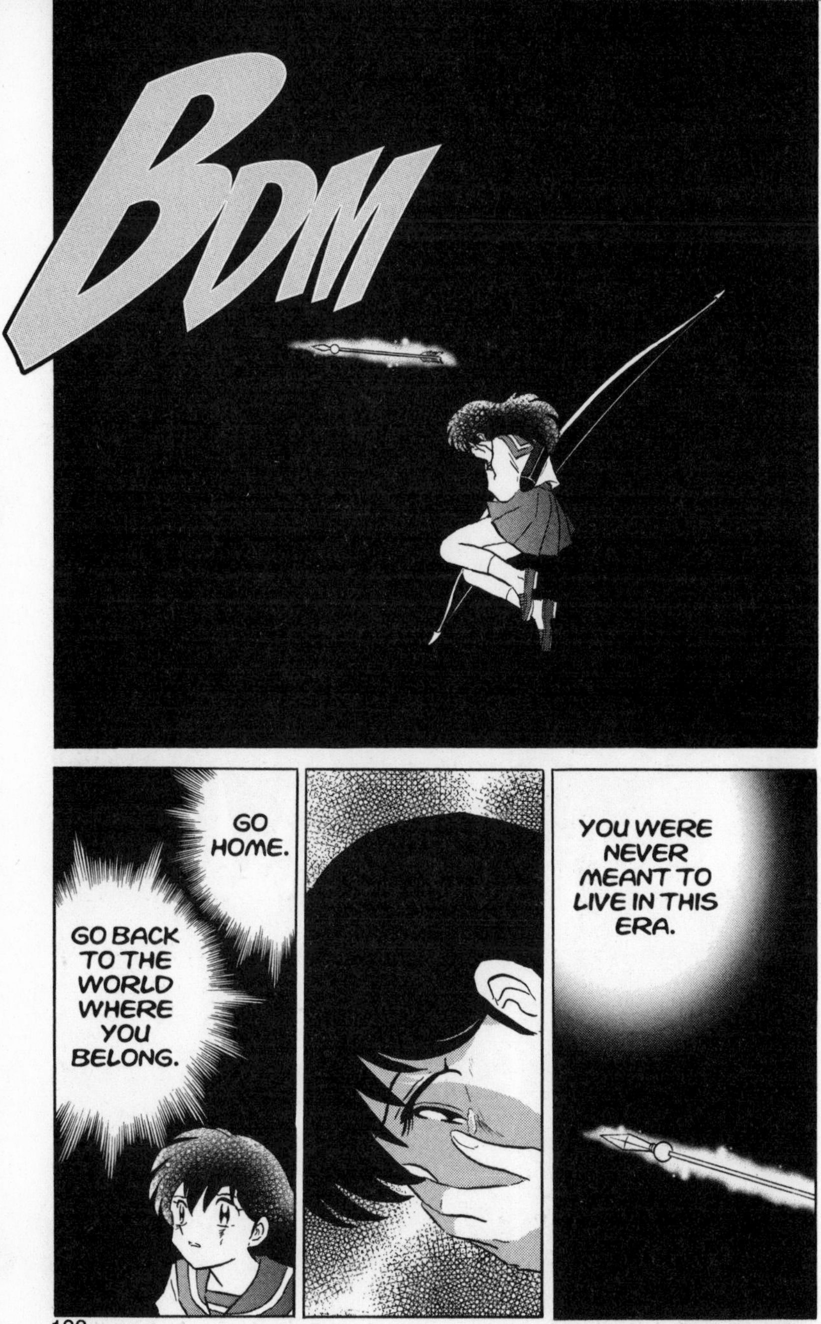
BDM
YOU WERE NEVER MEANT TO LIVE IN THIS ERA.
GO HOME.
GO BACK TO THE WORLD WHERE YOU BELONG.

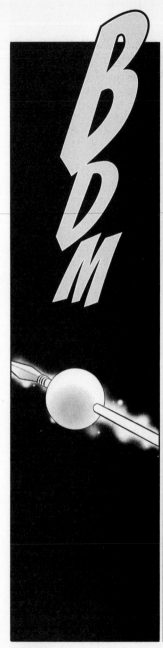

YOU MEAN I CAN GO HOME...

...IF I WISH IT?!

134

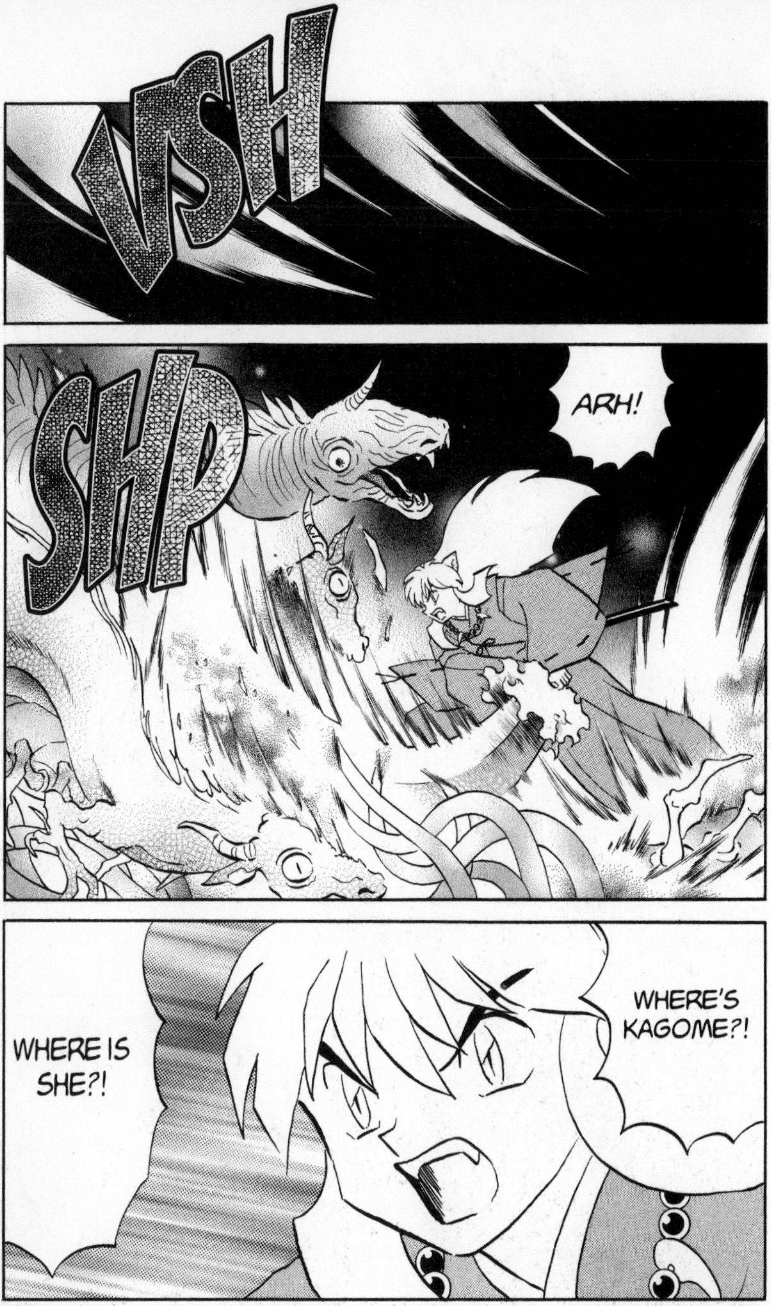
VSH
ARH!
SHP
WHERE'S KAGOME?!
WHERE IS SHE?!

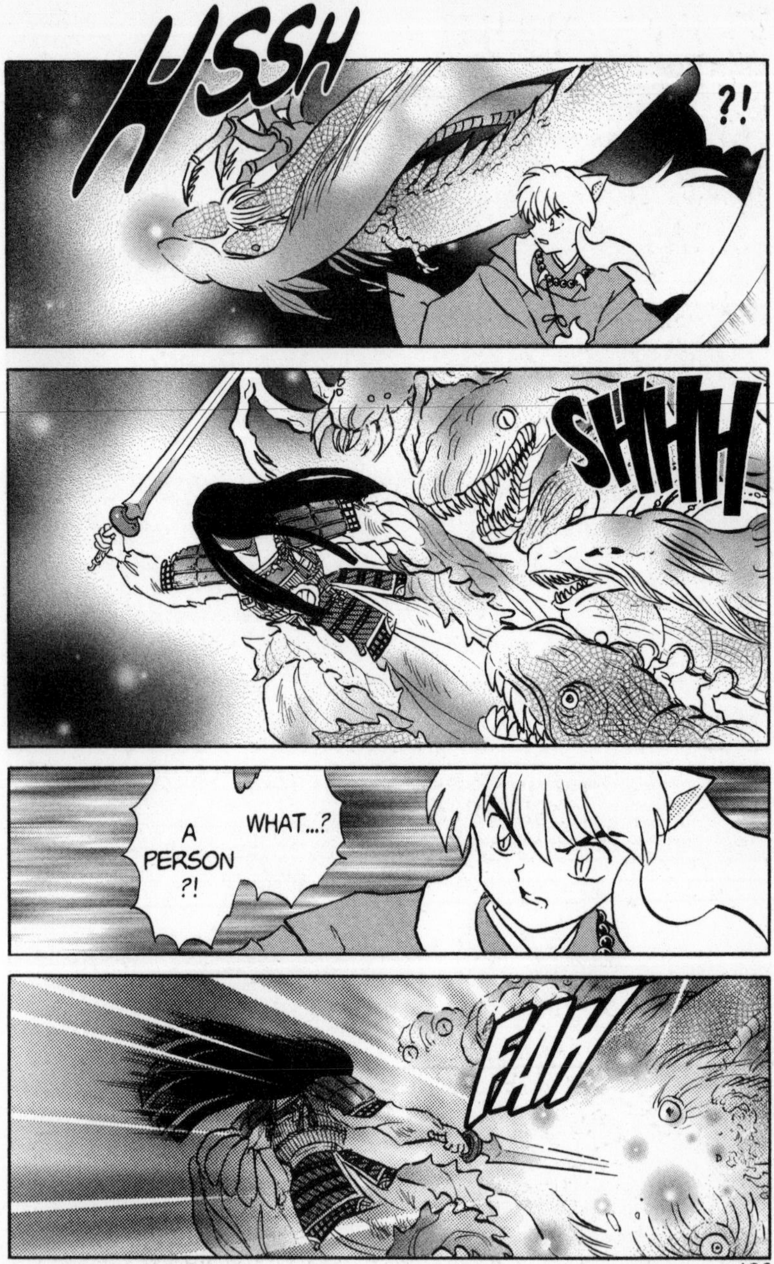
?!
HSSH
SHHH
WHAT...?
A PERSON ?!
FAH

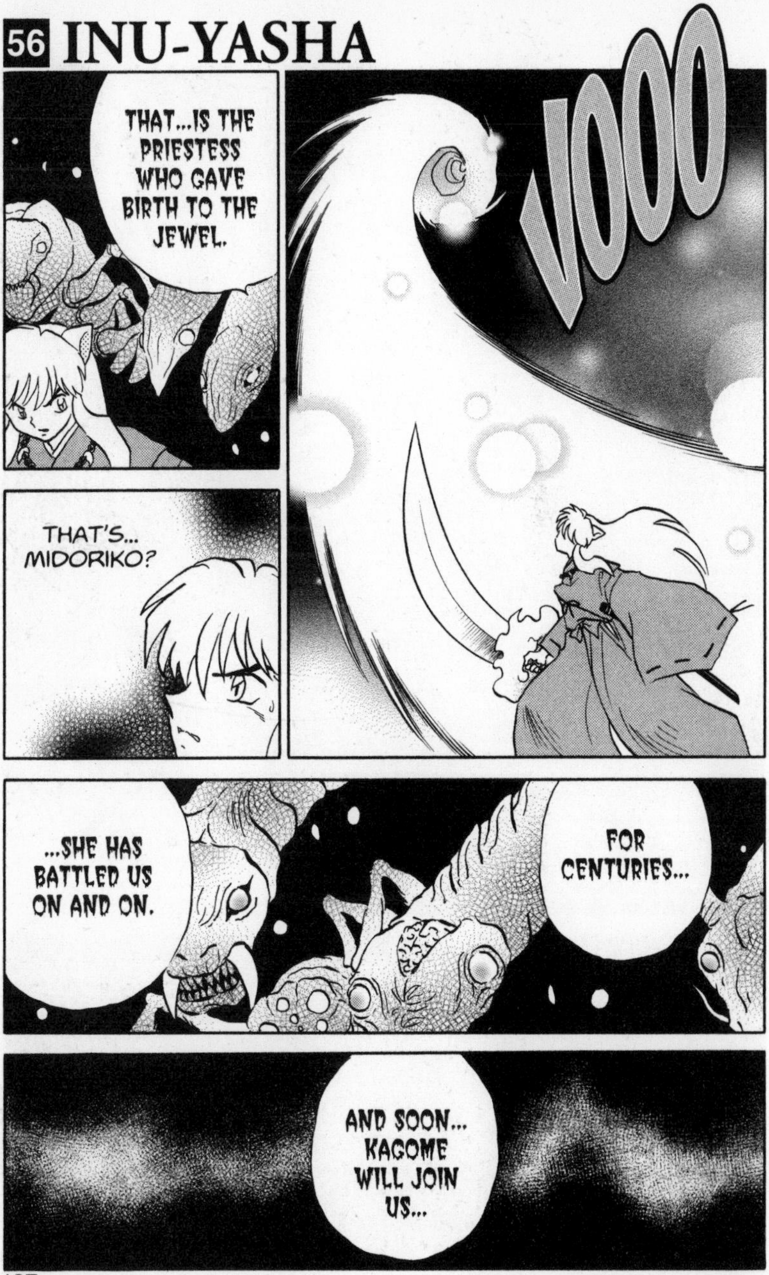
VOOO
THAT...IS THE PRIESTESS WHO GAVE BIRTH TO THE JEWEL.
THAT'S... MIDORIKO?
FOR CENTURIES...
...SHE HAS BATTLED US ON AND ON.
AND SOON... KAGOME WILL JOIN US...

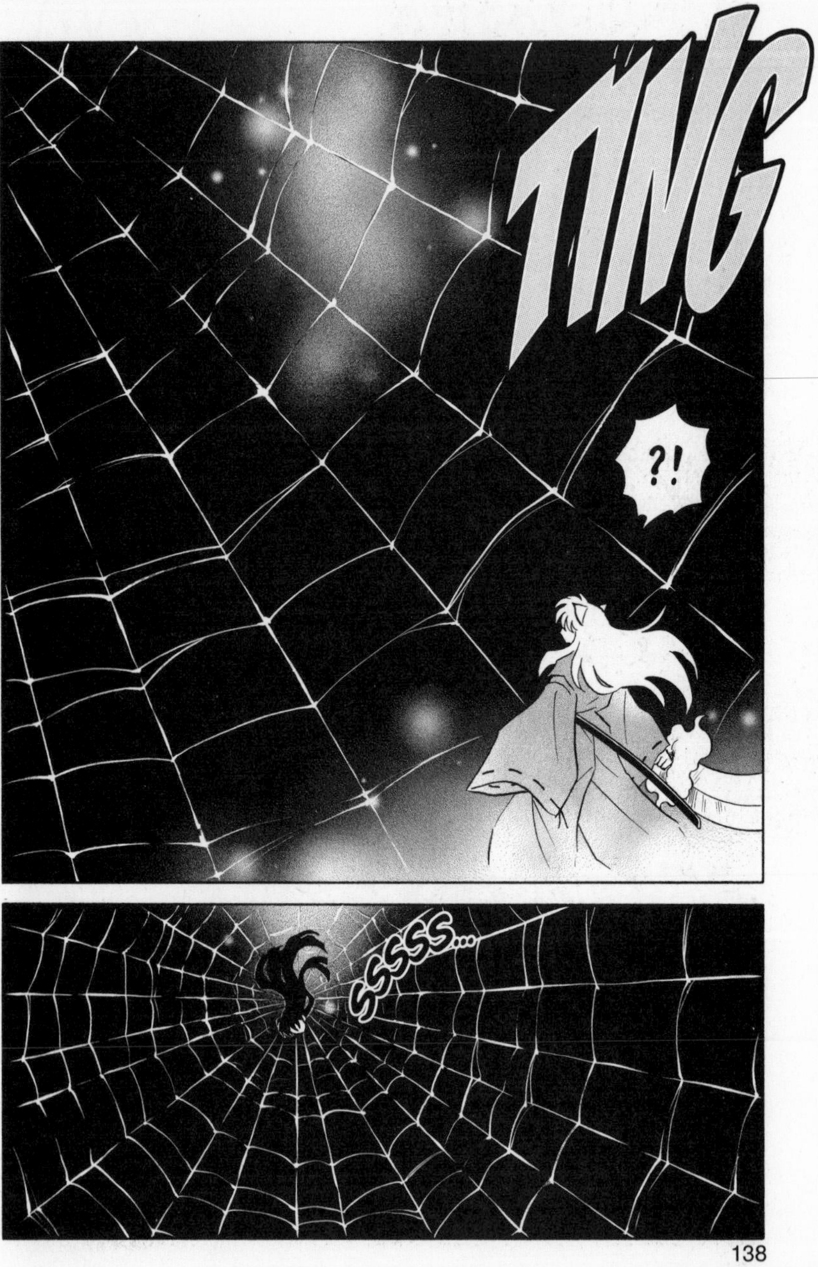
TING
?!
SSSSS...

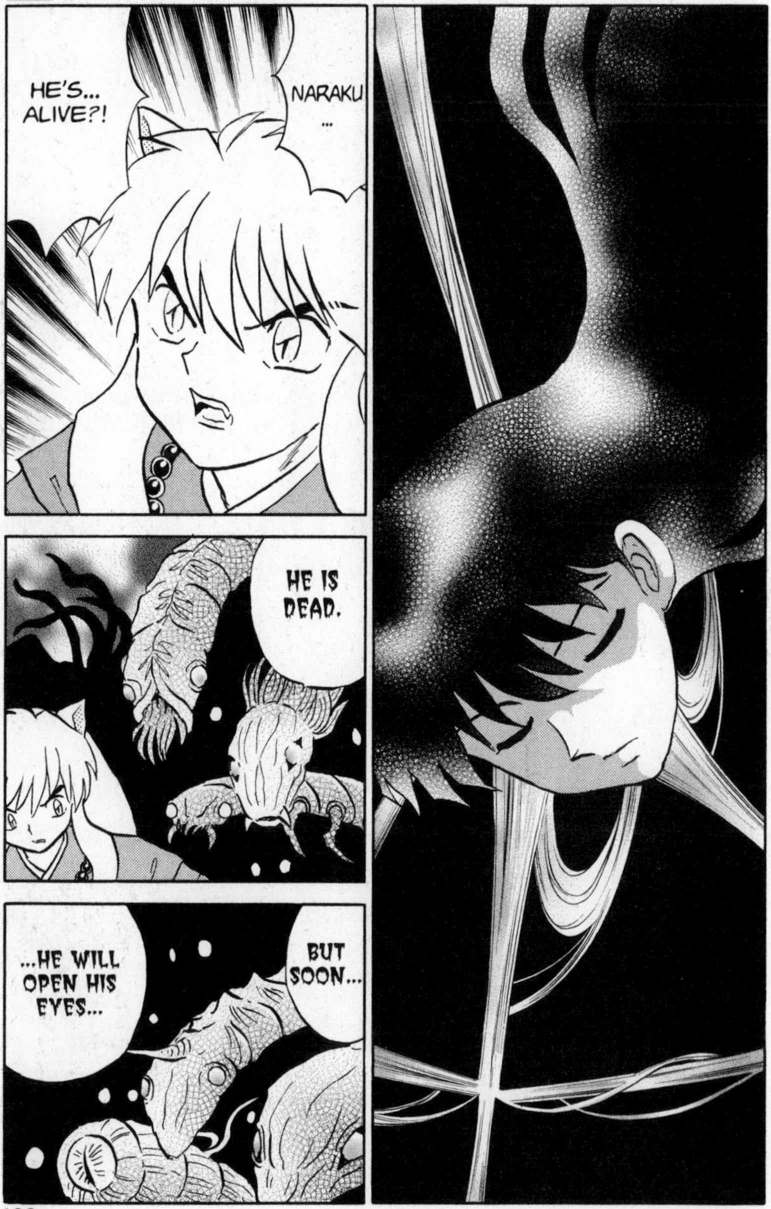
NARAKU...
HE'S... ALIVE?!
HE IS DEAD.
BUT SOON...
...HE WILL OPEN HIS EYES...

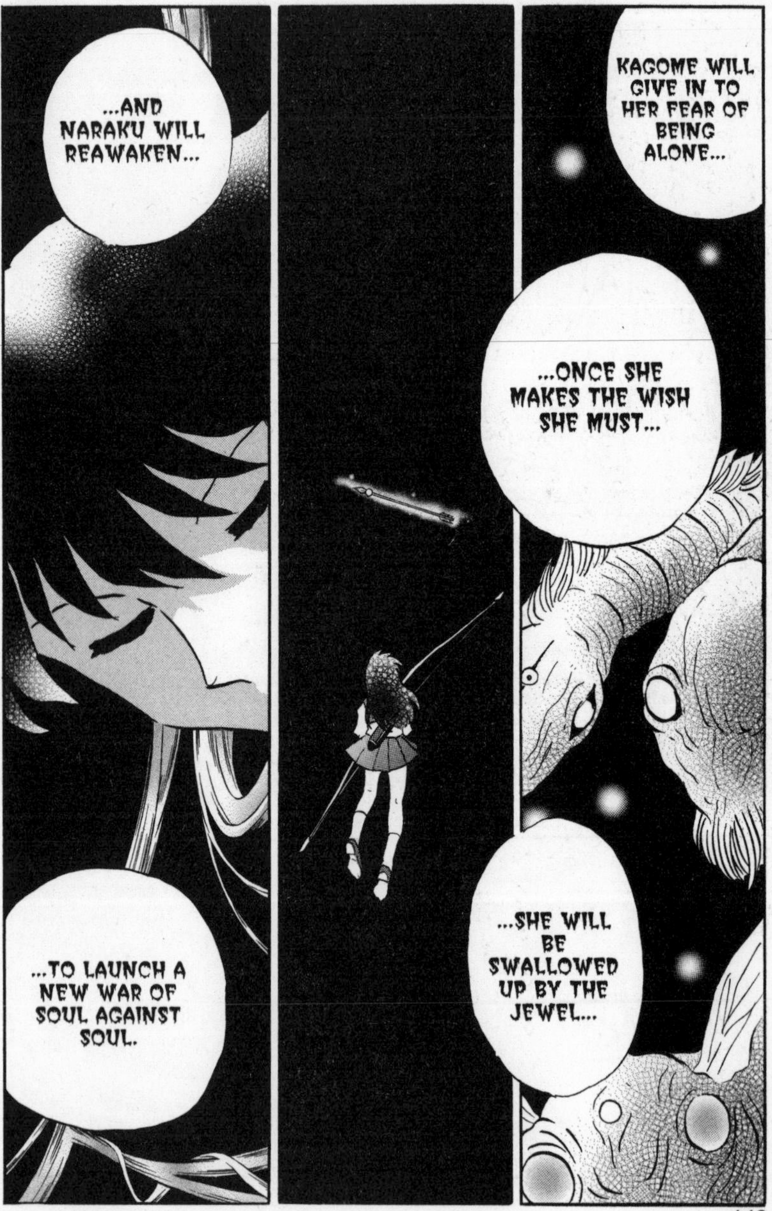
KAGOME WILL GIVE IN TO HER FEAR OF BEING ALONE...
...ONCE SHE MAKES THE WISH SHE MUST...
...SHE WILL BE SWALLOWED UP BY THE JEWEL...
...AND NARAKU WILL REAWAKEN...
...TO LAUNCH A NEW WAR OF SOUL AGAINST SOUL.

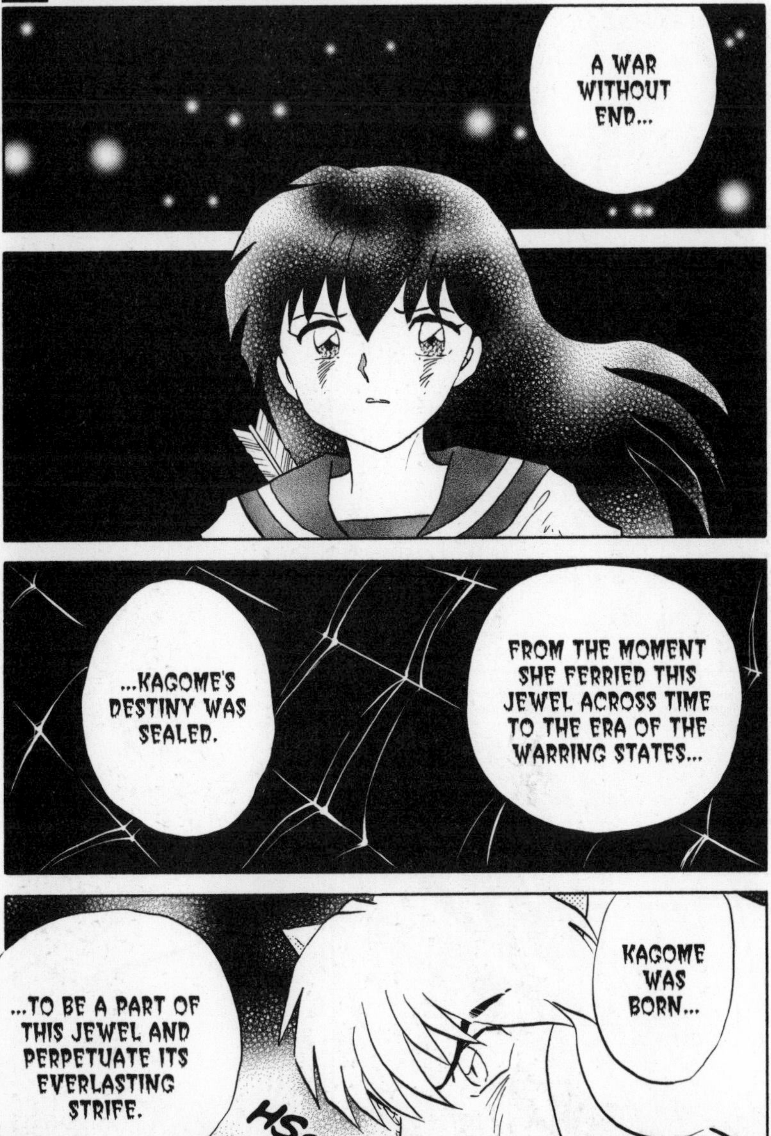
A WAR WITHOUT END...
FROM THE MOMENT SHE FERRIED THIS JEWEL ACROSS TIME TO THE ERA OF THE WARRING STATES...
...KAGOME'S DESTINY WAS SEALED.
KAGOME WAS BORN...
...TO BE A PART OF THIS JEWEL AND PERPETUATE ITS EVERLASTING STRIFE.
HSS...

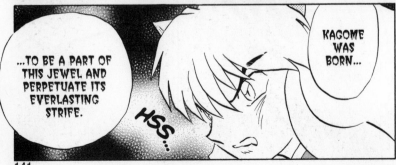

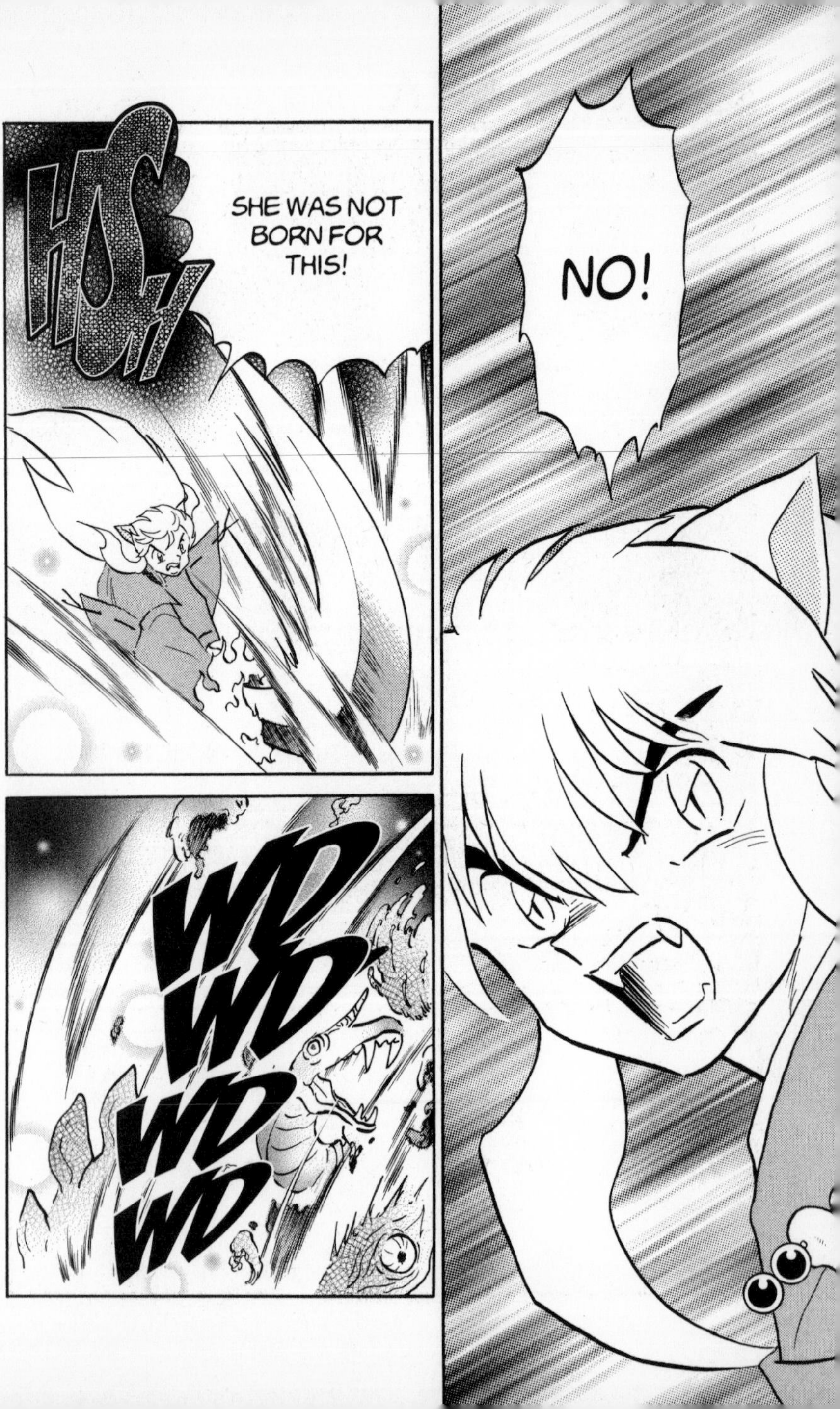
NO!
HOSH
SHE WAS NOT BORN FOR THIS!
WD WD WD WD WD

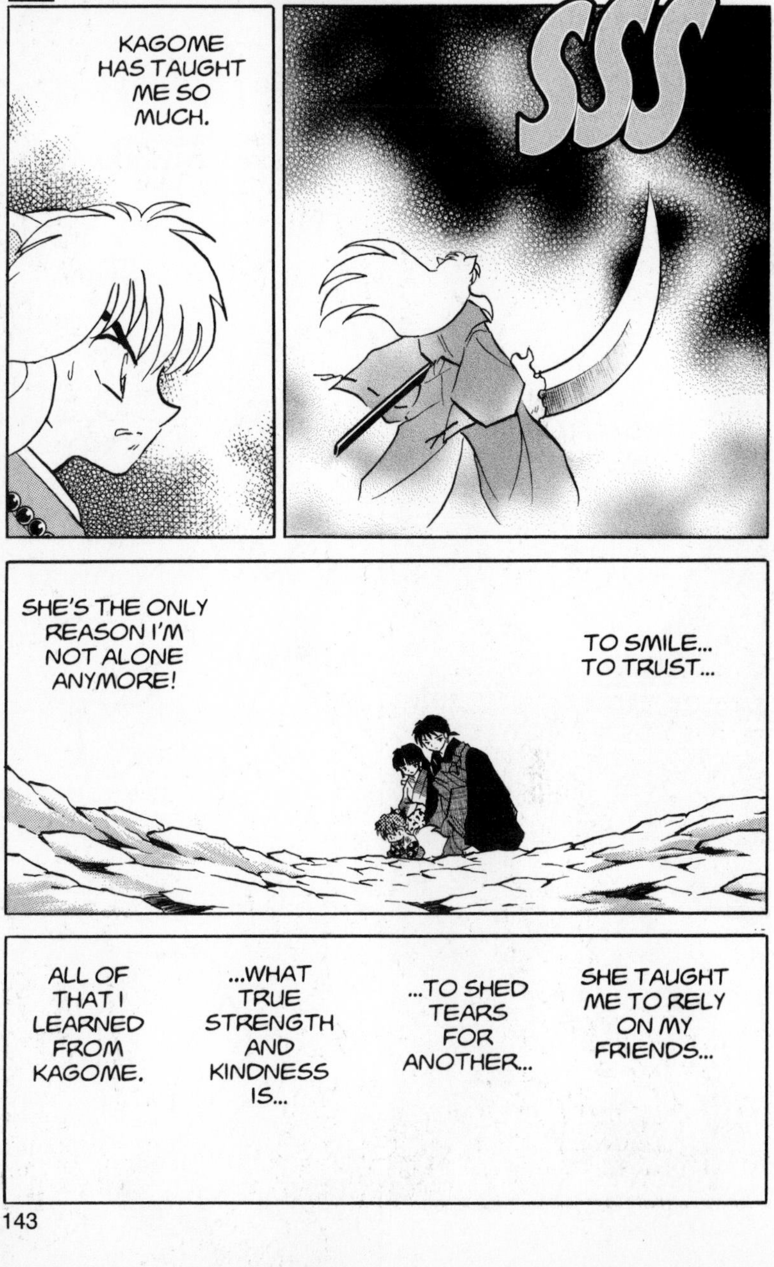
SSS
KAGOME HAS TAUGHT ME SO MUCH.
SHE'S THE ONLY REASON I'M NOT ALONE ANYMORE!
TO SMILE... TO TRUST...
SHE TAUGHT ME TO RELY ON MY FRIENDS...
...TO SHED TEARS FOR ANOTHER...
...WHAT TRUE STRENGTH AND KINDNESS IS...
ALL OF THAT I LEARNED FROM KAGOME.

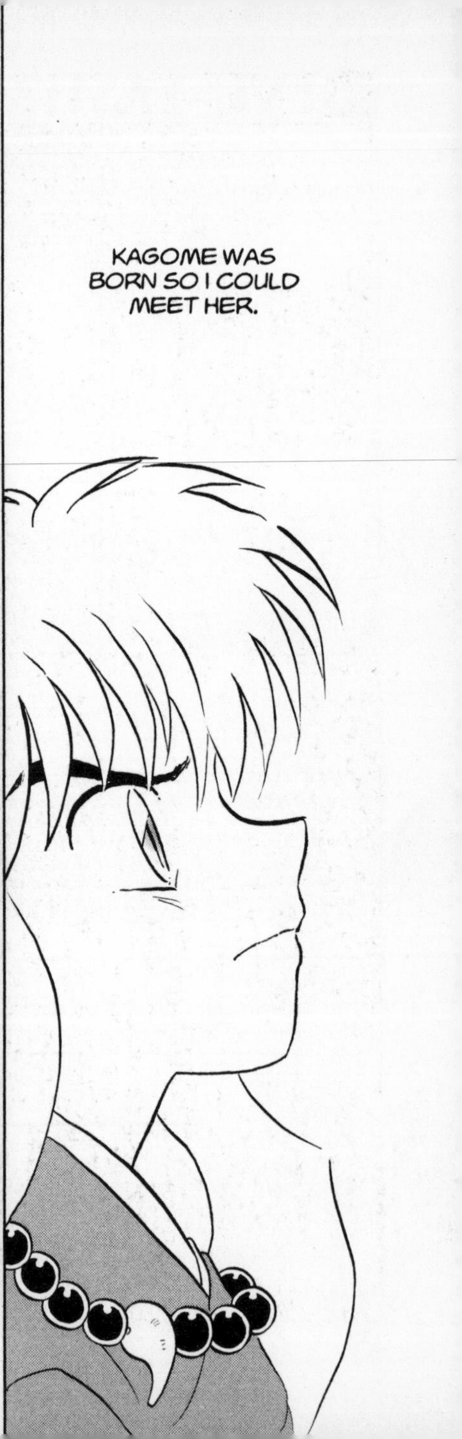
KAGOME WAS BORN SO I COULD MEET HER.

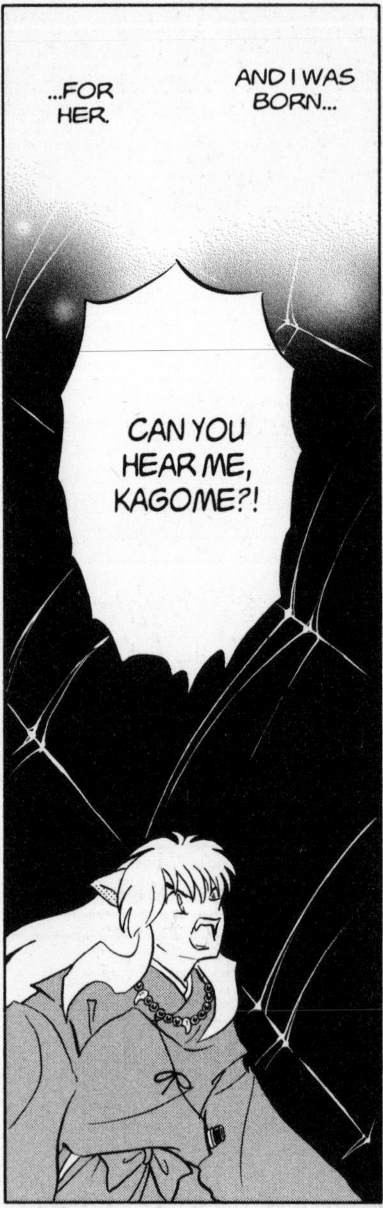
AND I WAS BORN...
...FOR HER.
CAN YOU HEAR ME, KAGOME?!

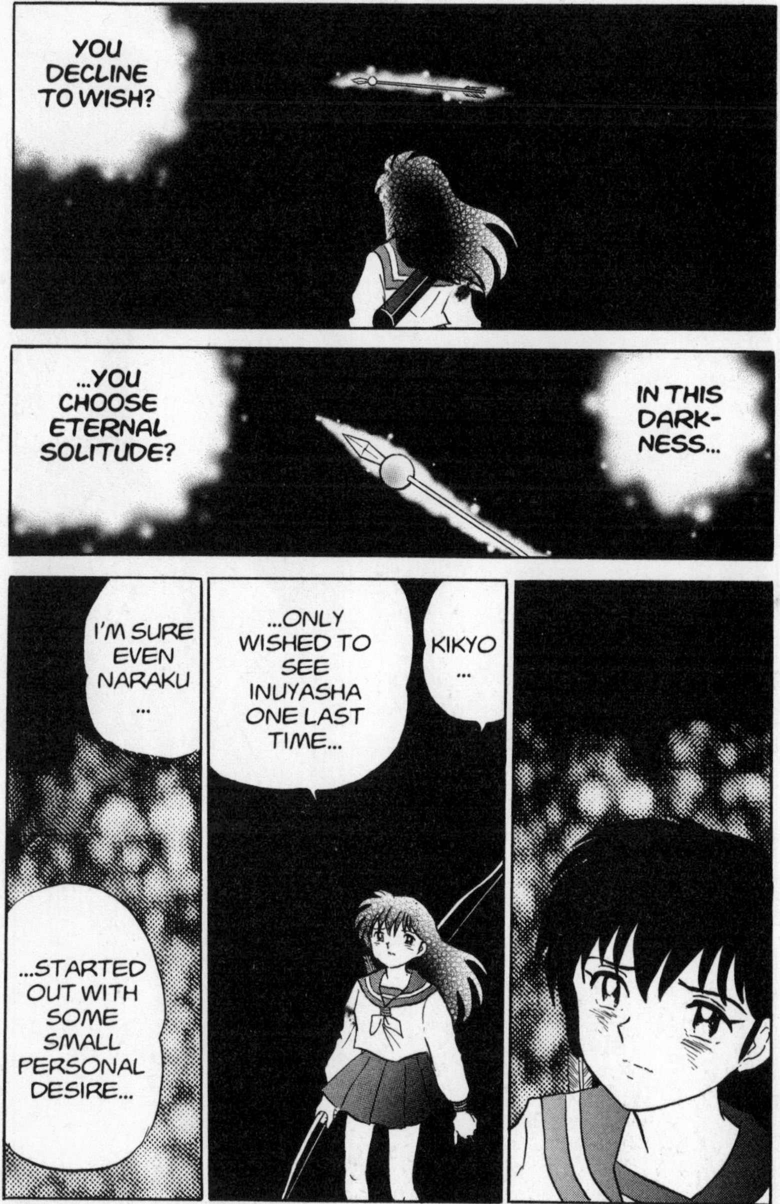
YOU DECLINE TO WISH?
IN THIS DARKNESS...
...YOU CHOOSE ETERNAL SOLITUDE?
KIKYO...
...ONLY WISHED TO SEE INUYASHA ONE LAST TIME...
I'M SURE EVEN NARAKU...
...STARTED OUT WITH SOME SMALL PERSONAL DESIRE...

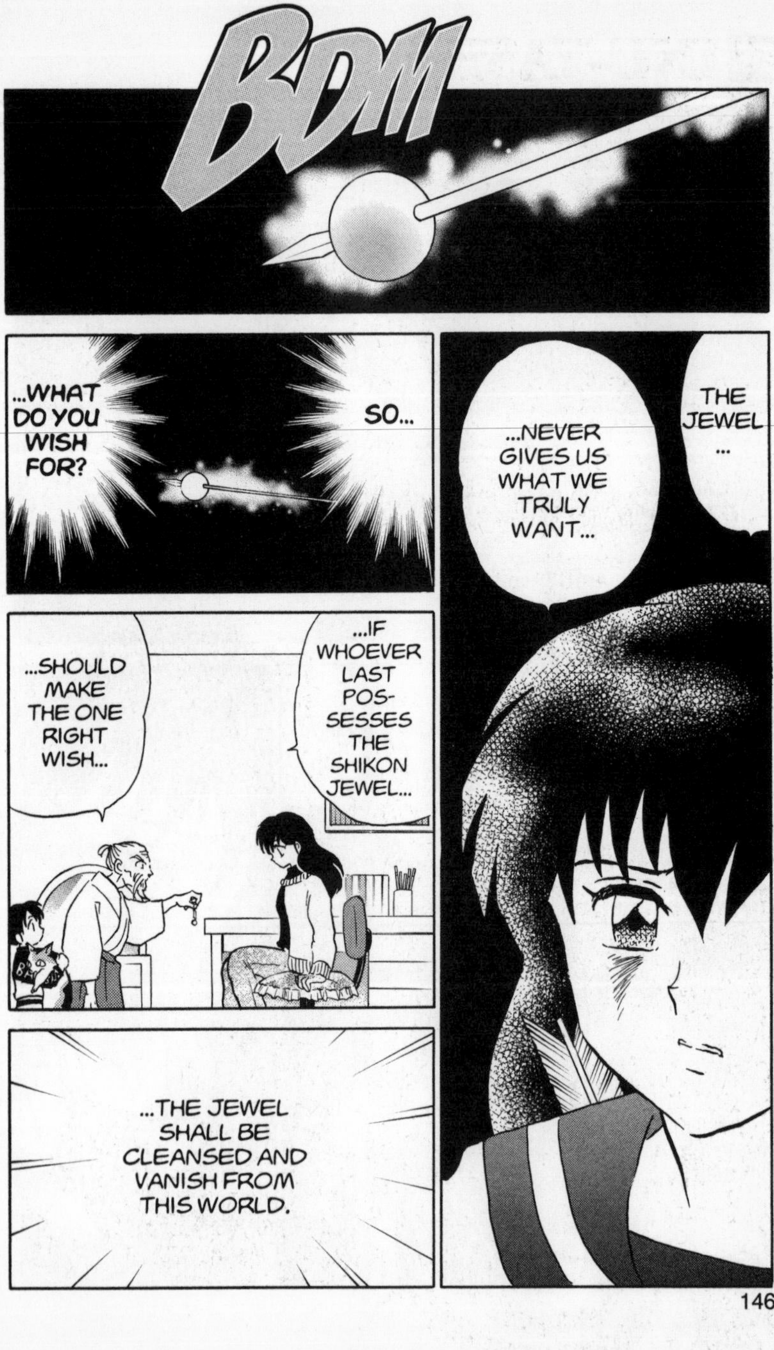
BDM
THE JEWEL...
...NEVER GIVES US WHAT WE TRULY WANT...
SO...
...WHAT DO YOU WISH FOR?
...IF WHOEVER LAST POS-SESSES THE SHIKON JEWEL...
...SHOULD MAKE THE ONE RIGHT WISH...
...THE JEWEL SHALL BE CLEANSED AND VANISH FROM THIS WORLD.

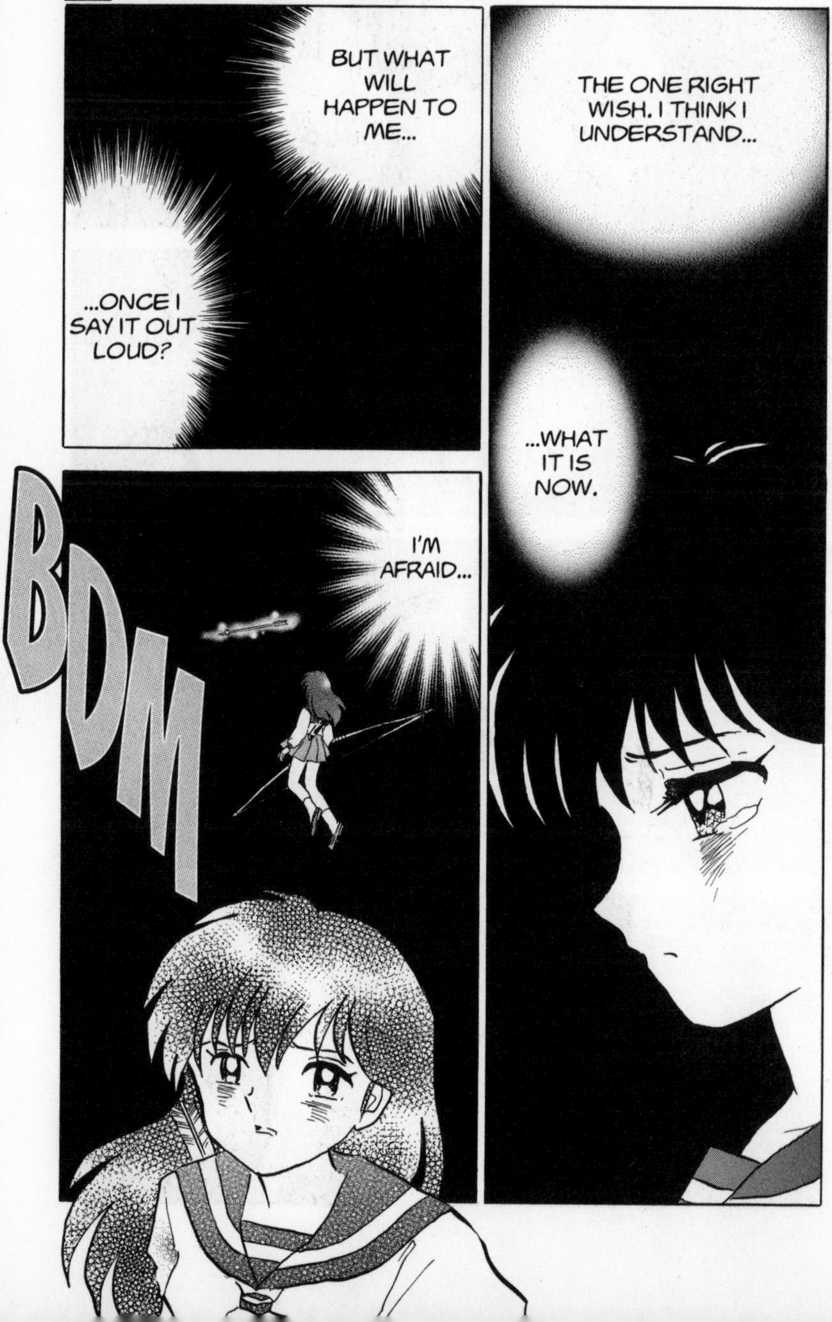
THE ONE RIGHT WISH. I THINK I UNDERSTAND...
...WHAT IT IS NOW.
BUT WHAT WILL HAPPEN TO ME...
...ONCE I SAY IT OUT LOUD?
I'M AFRAID...
BDM

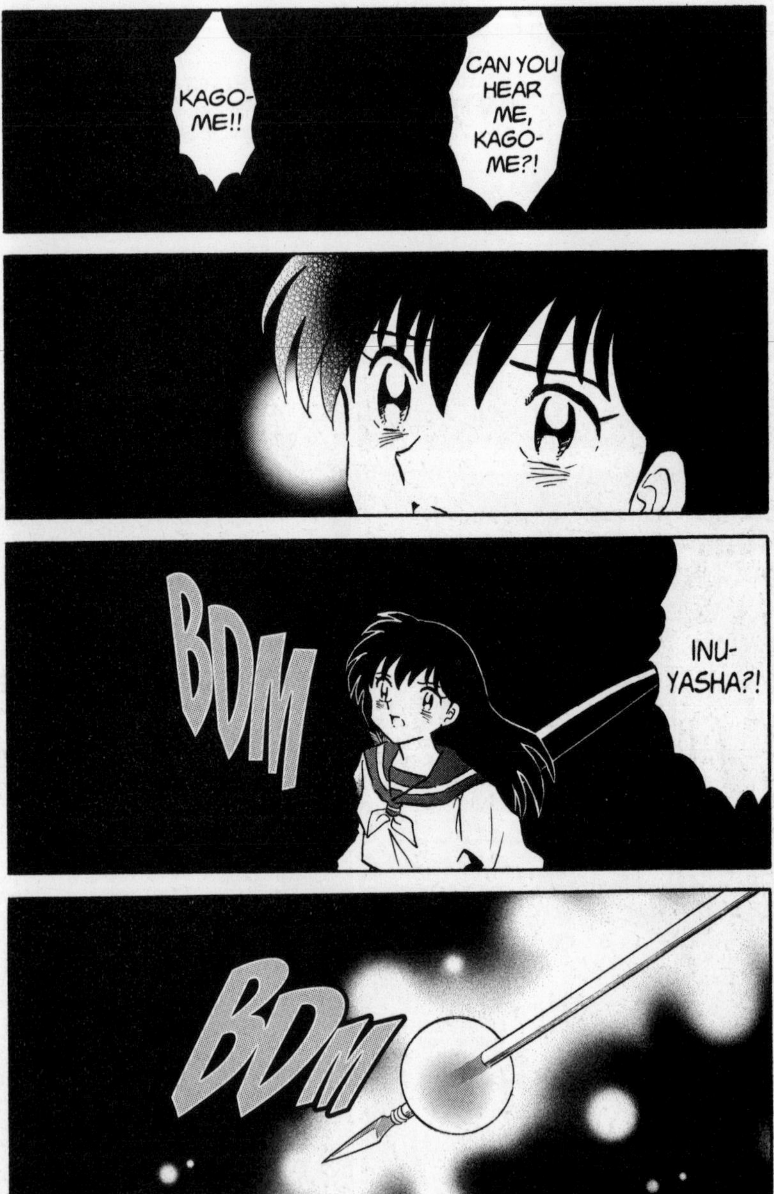
CAN YOU HEAR ME, KAGOME?!
KAGOME!!
INU-YASHA?!
BDM
BDM

SCROLL 9

I WANT TO SEE YOU

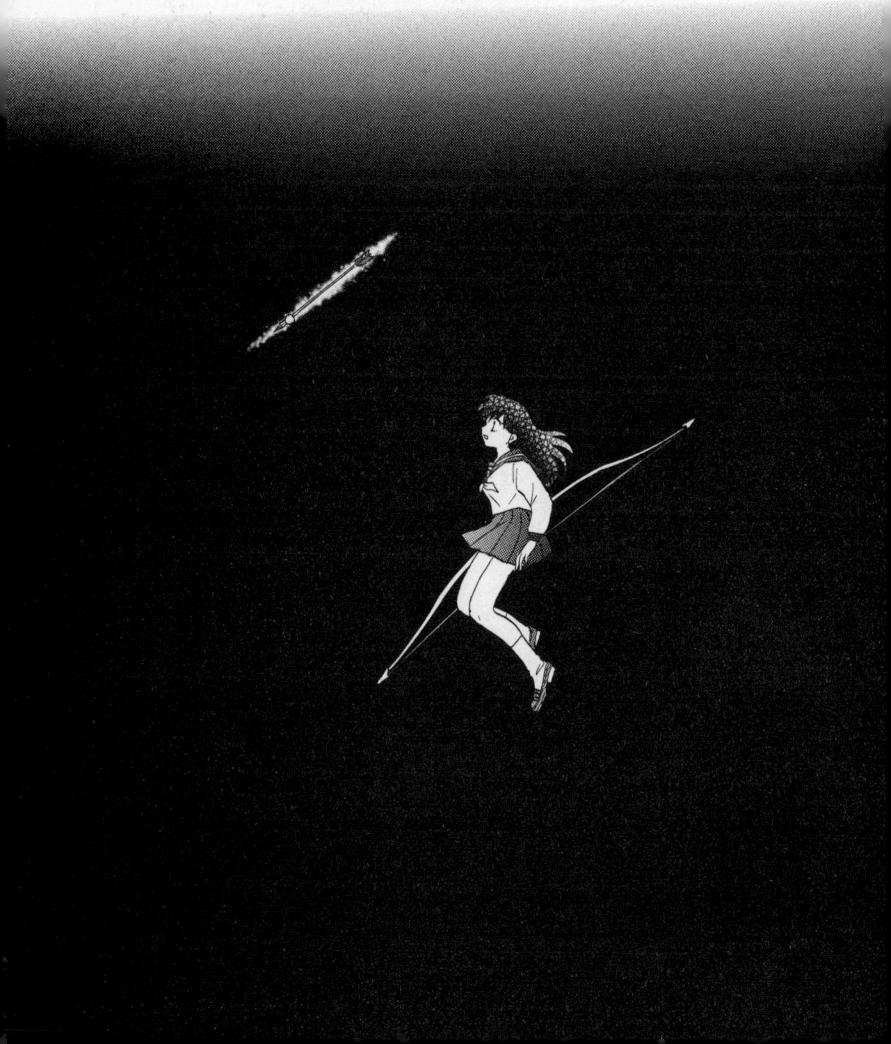

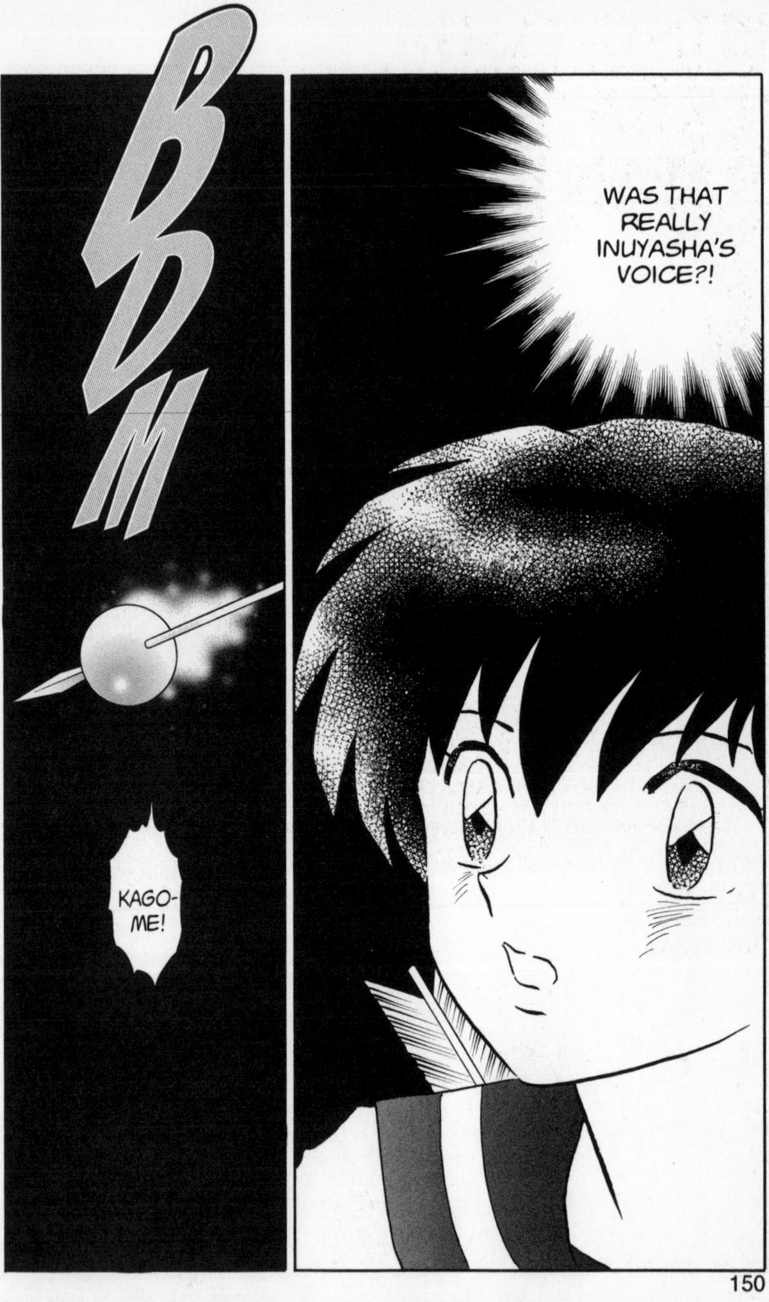
WAS THAT REALLY INUYASHA'S VOICE?!
BDM
KAGO-ME!

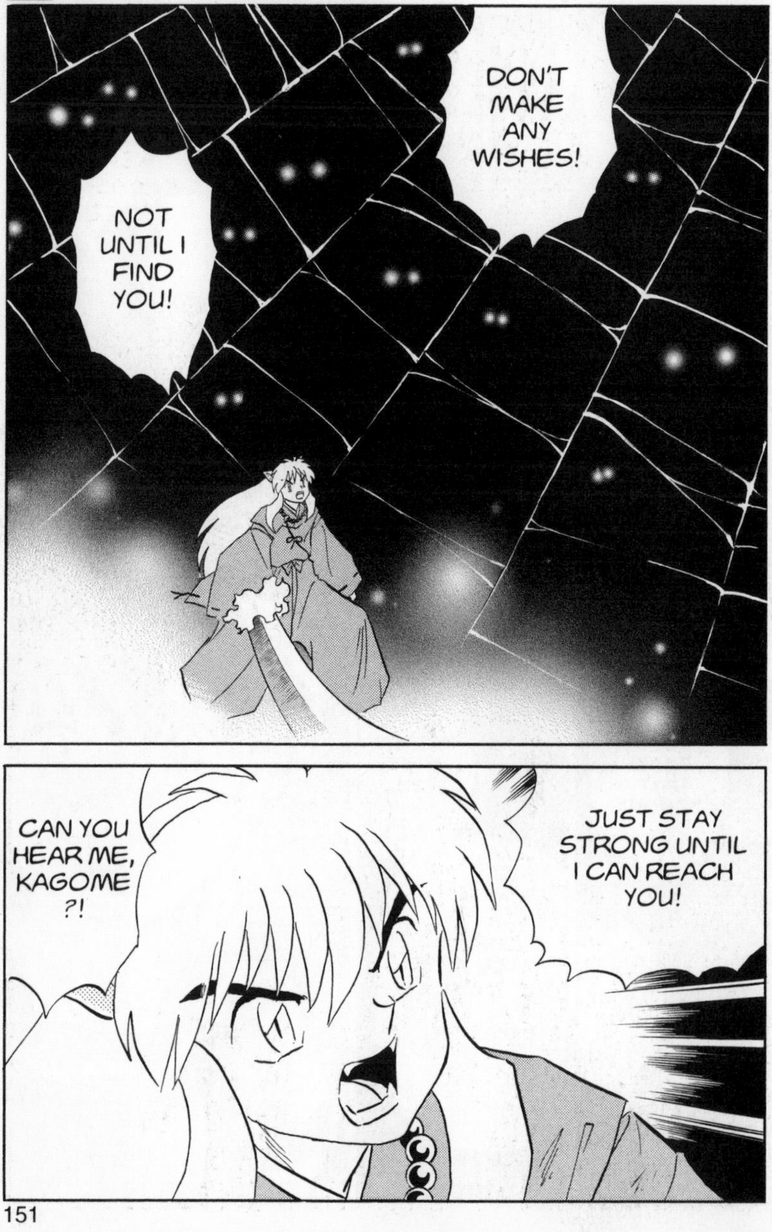
DON'T MAKE ANY WISHES!
NOT UNTIL I FIND YOU!
JUST STAY STRONG UNTIL I CAN REACH YOU!
CAN YOU HEAR ME, KAGOME ?!

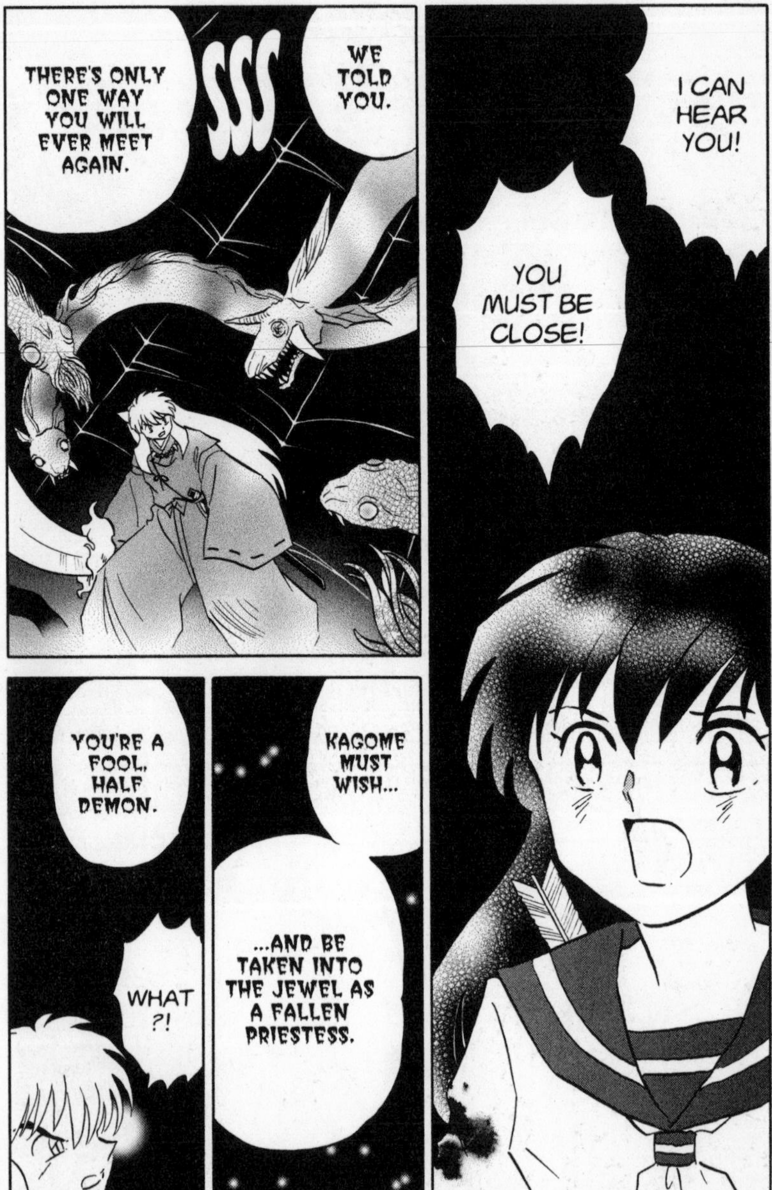
I CAN HEAR YOU!
YOU MUST BE CLOSE!
WE TOLD YOU.
SSS
THERE'S ONLY ONE WAY YOU WILL EVER MEET AGAIN.
KAGOME MUST WISH...
...AND BE TAKEN INTO THE JEWEL AS A FALLEN PRIESTESS.
YOU'RE A FOOL, HALF DEMON.
WHAT ?!

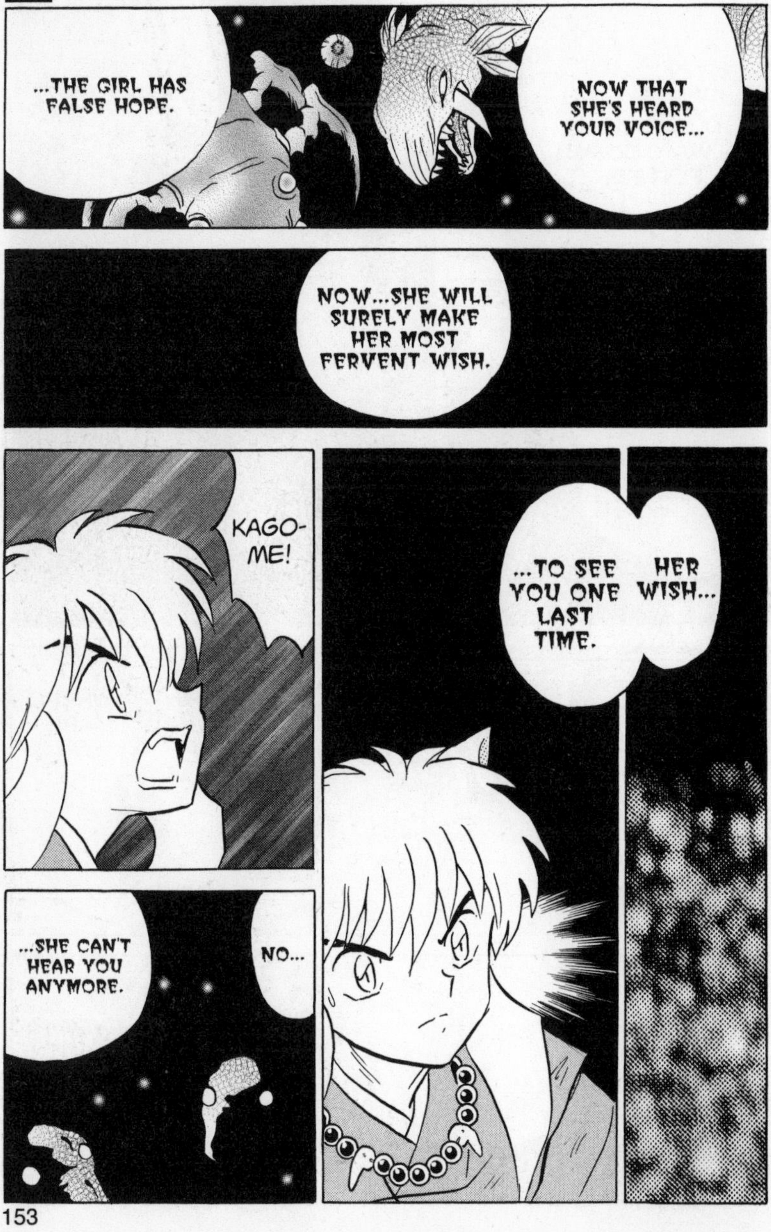
NOW THAT SHE'S HEARD YOUR VOICE...
...THE GIRL HAS FALSE HOPE.
NOW...SHE WILL SURELY MAKE HER MOST FERVENT WISH.
HER WISH...
...TO SEE YOU ONE LAST TIME.
KAGO-ME!
NO...
...SHE CAN'T HEAR YOU ANYMORE.

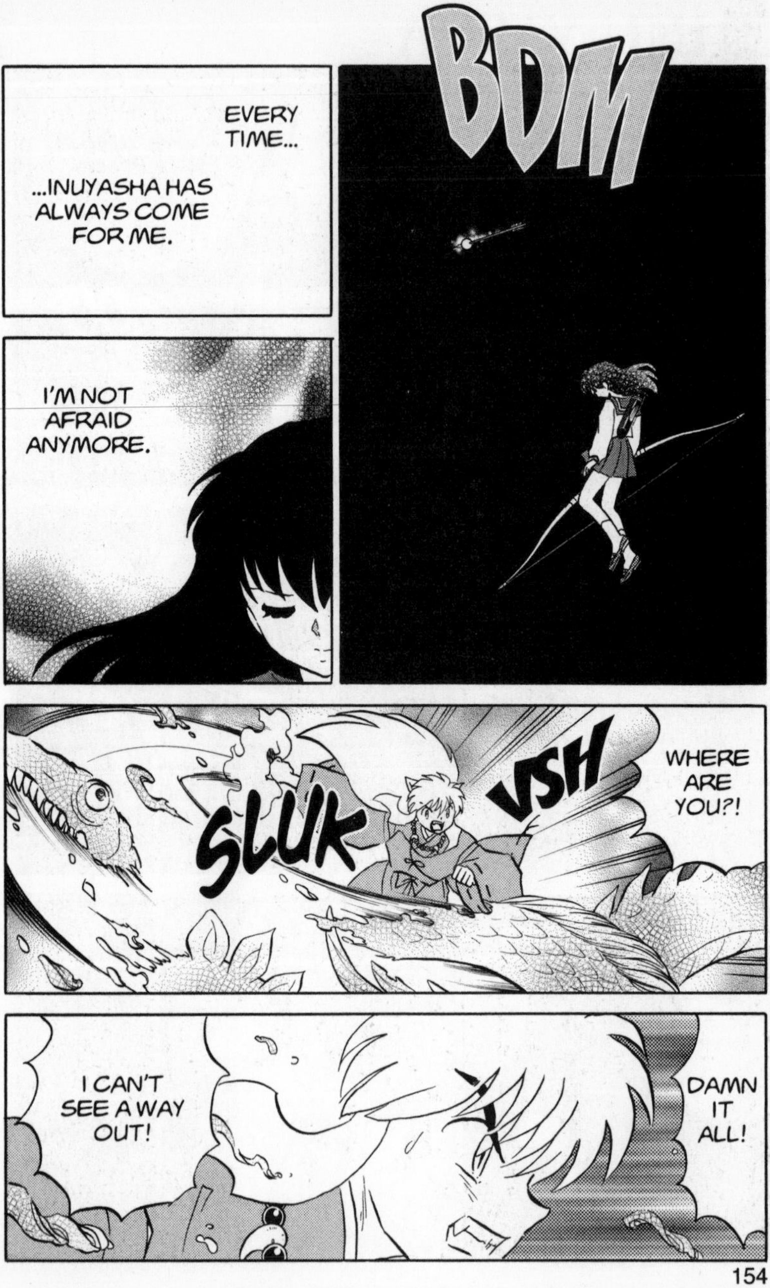
BDM
EVERY TIME...
...INUYASHA HAS ALWAYS COME FOR ME.
I'M NOT AFRAID ANYMORE.
WHERE ARE YOU?!
VSH
SLUK
DAMN IT ALL!
I CAN'T SEE A WAY OUT!

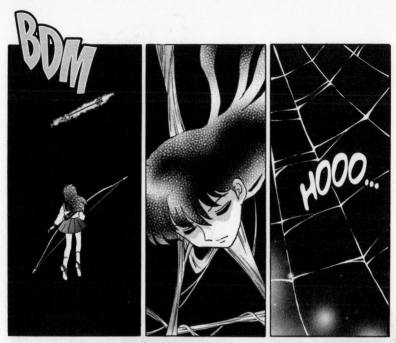

HOOO...

DO YOU WISH TO SEE INUYASHA?

BDM

...

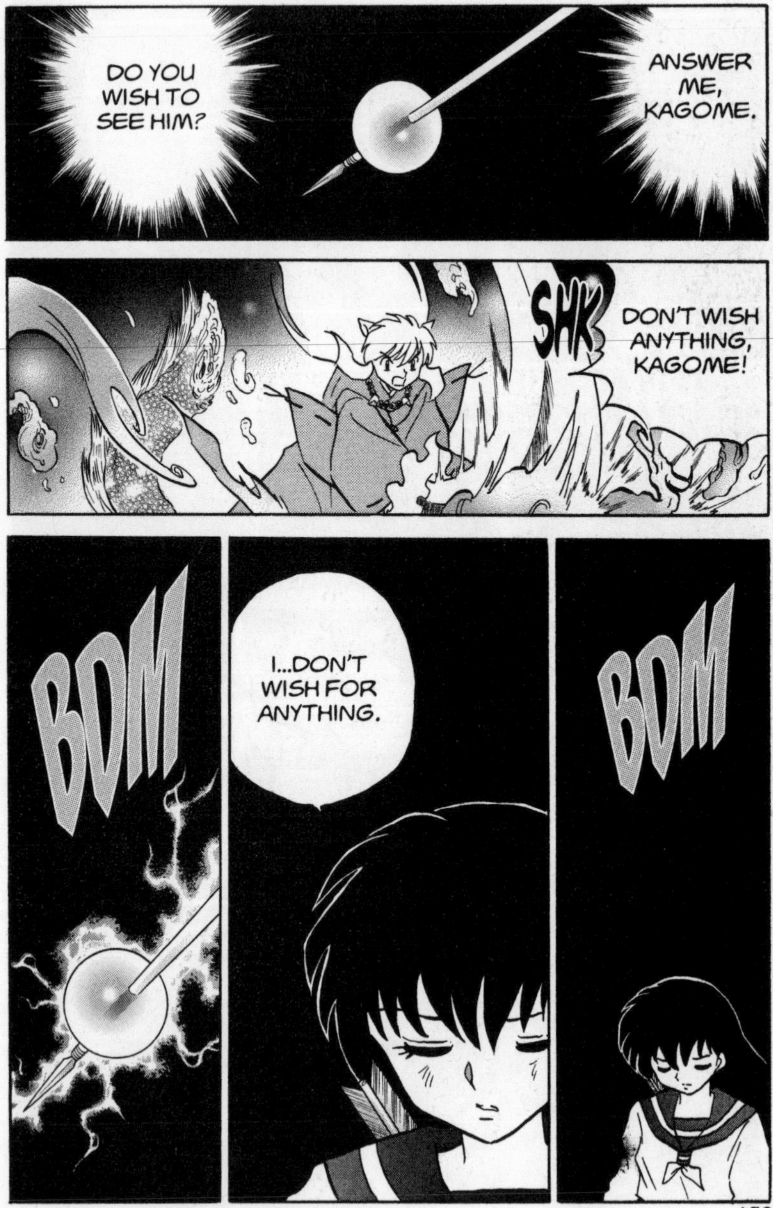
ANSWER ME, KAGOME.
DO YOU WISH TO SEE HIM?
SHK
DON'T WISH ANYTHING, KAGOME!
BOM
I...DON'T WISH FOR ANYTHING.
BOM

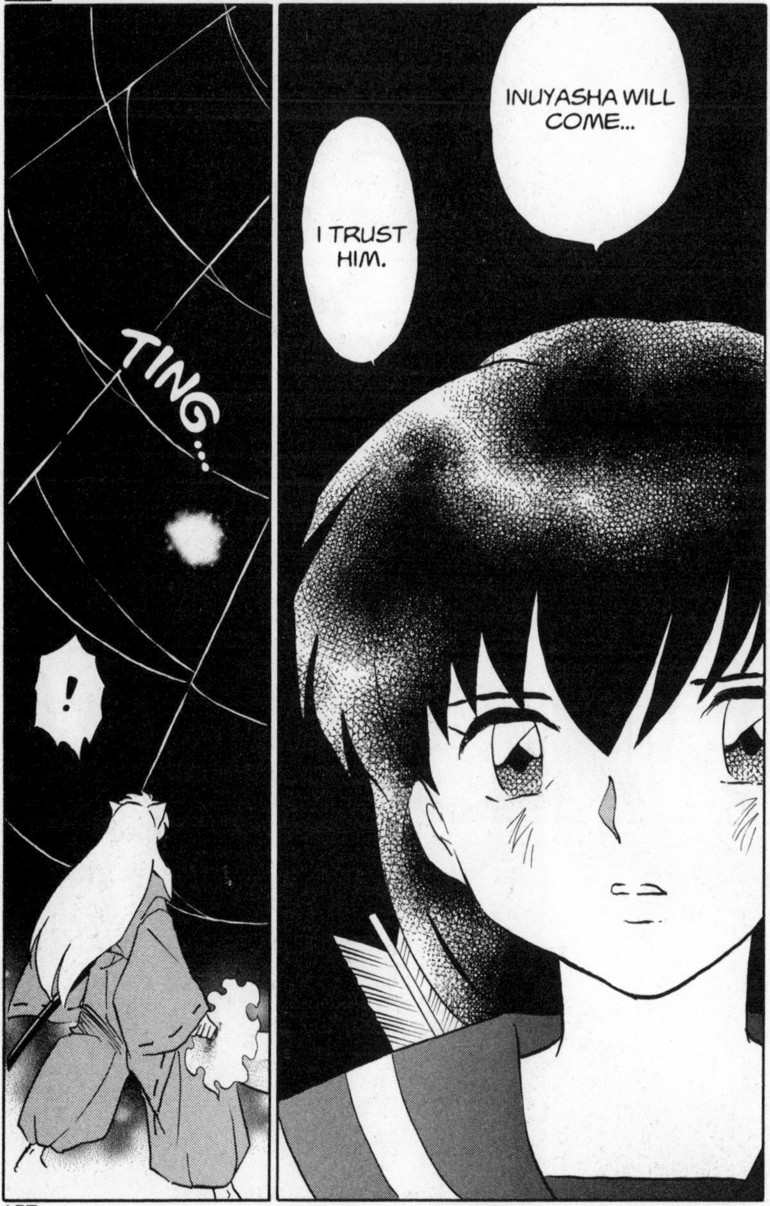
INUYASHA WILL COME...
I TRUST HIM.
TING...
!

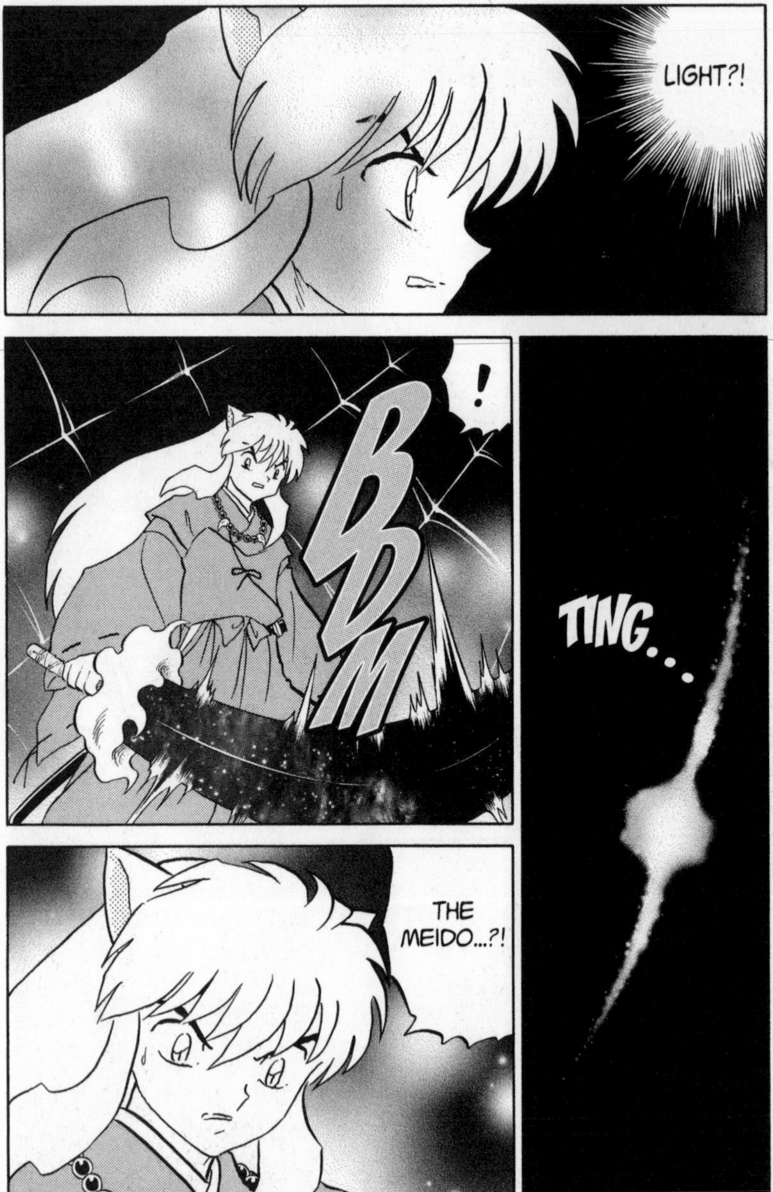
LIGHT?!
TING...
!
BOOM
THE MEIDO...?!

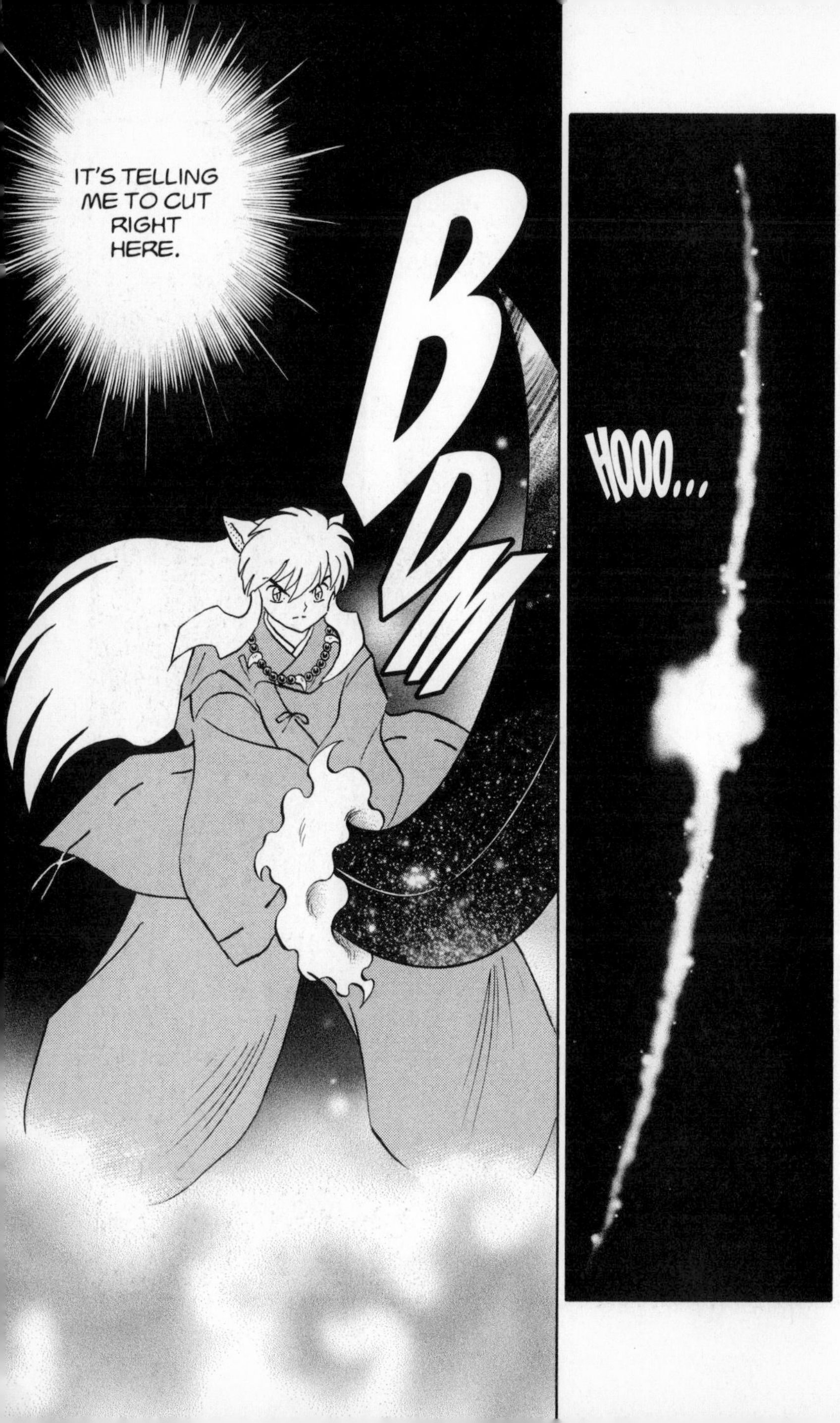
HOOO...
BDM
IT'S TELLING ME TO CUT RIGHT HERE.

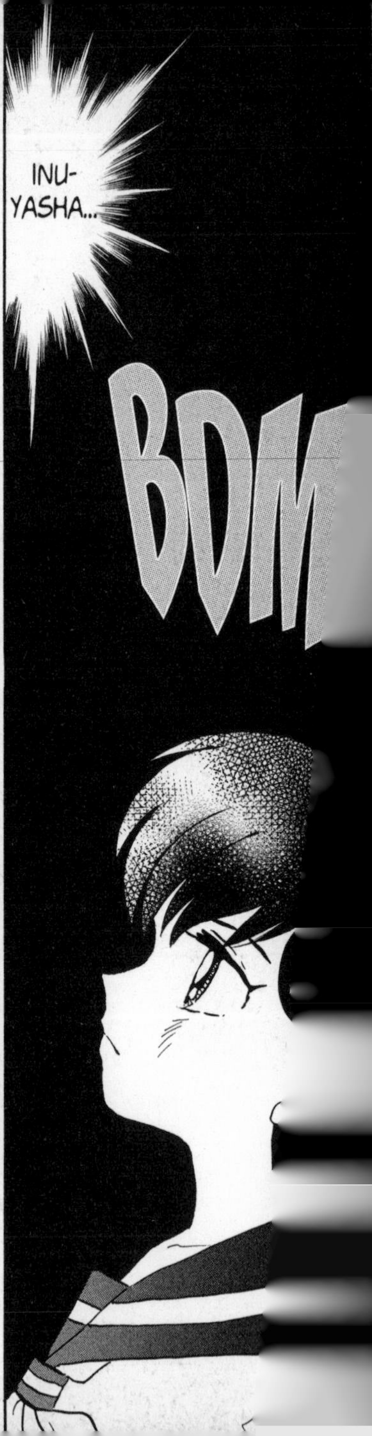
INU-
YASHA...
BOM
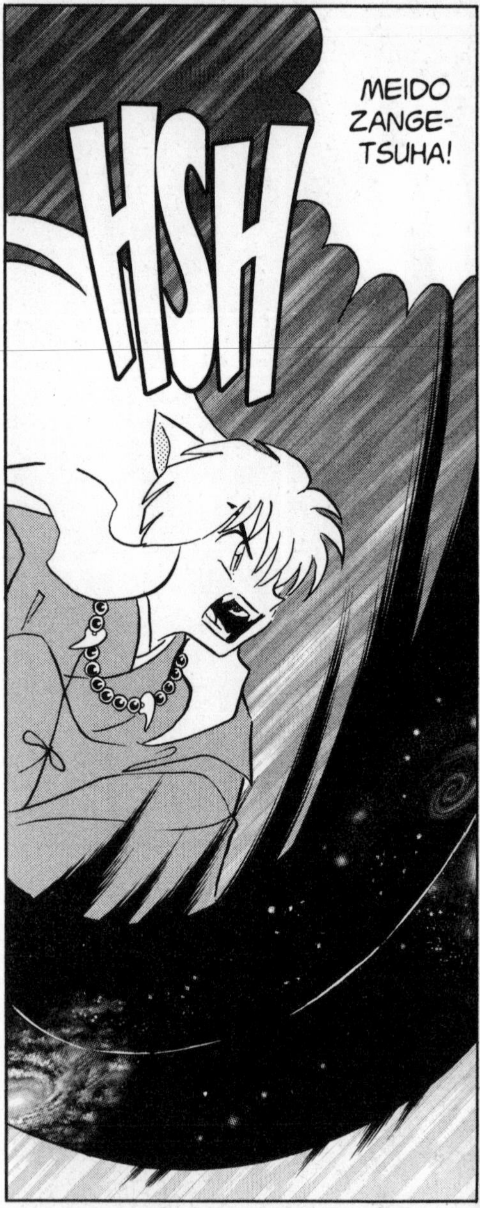
MEIDO
ZANGE-
TSUHA!
HSH

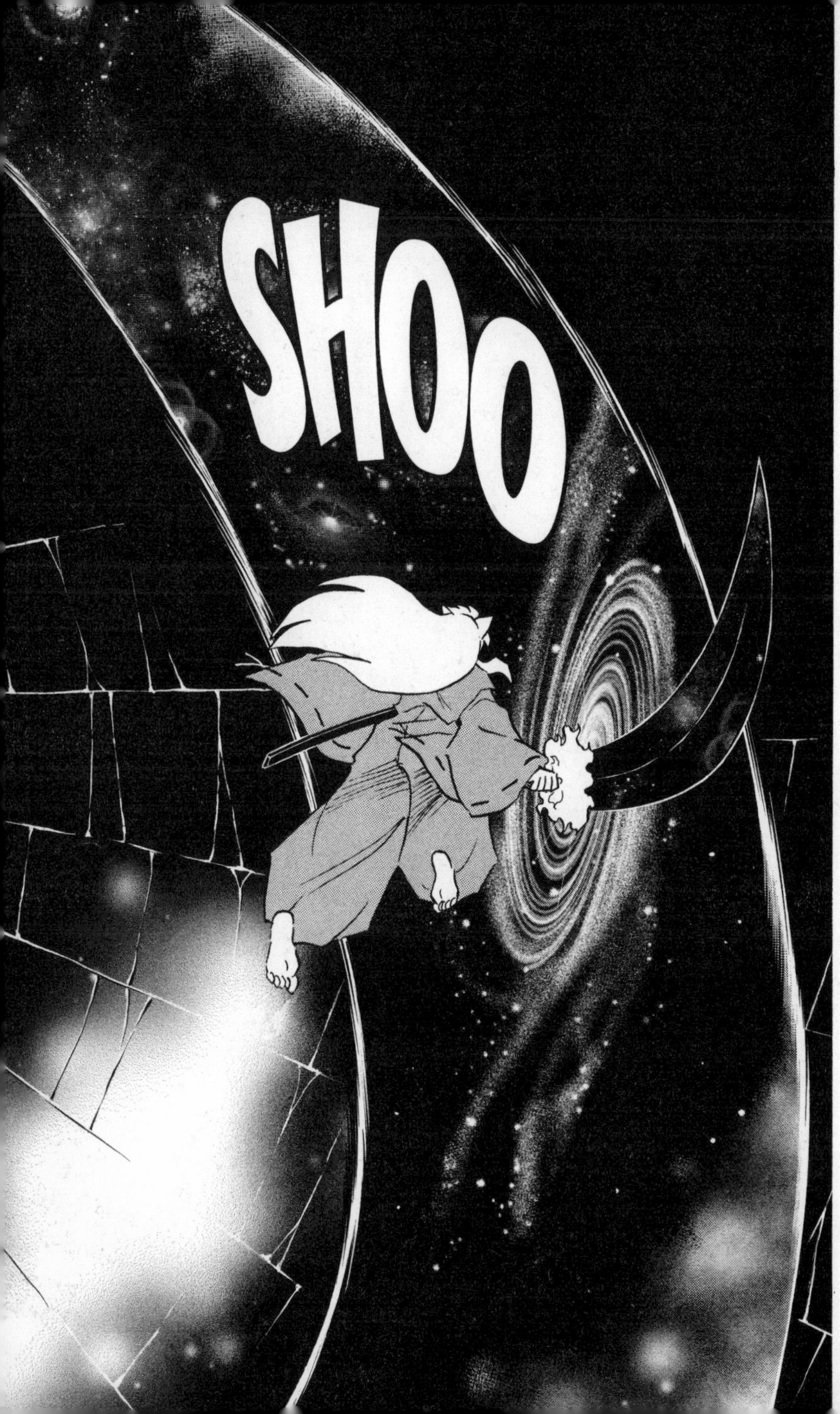
SHOO

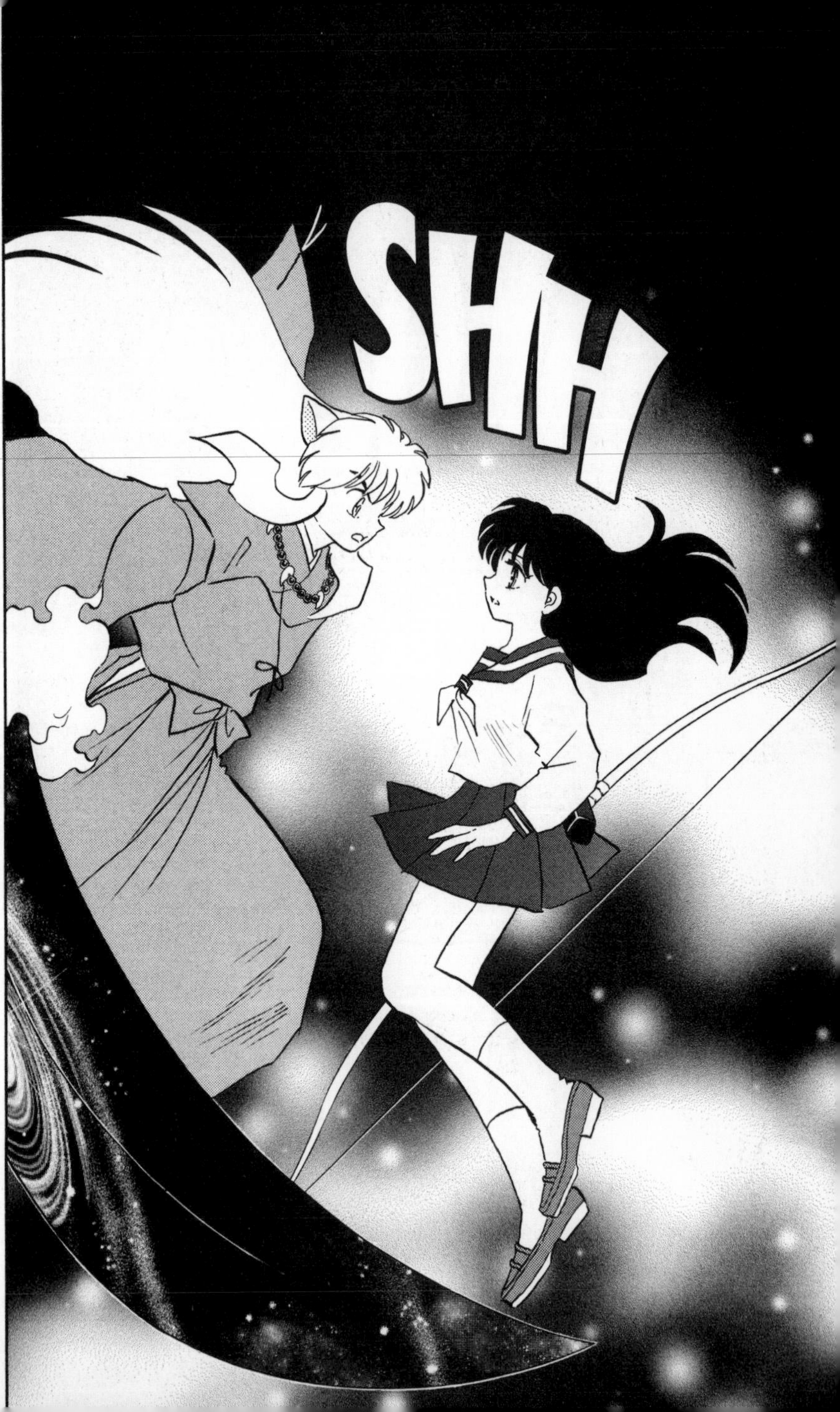
SHH

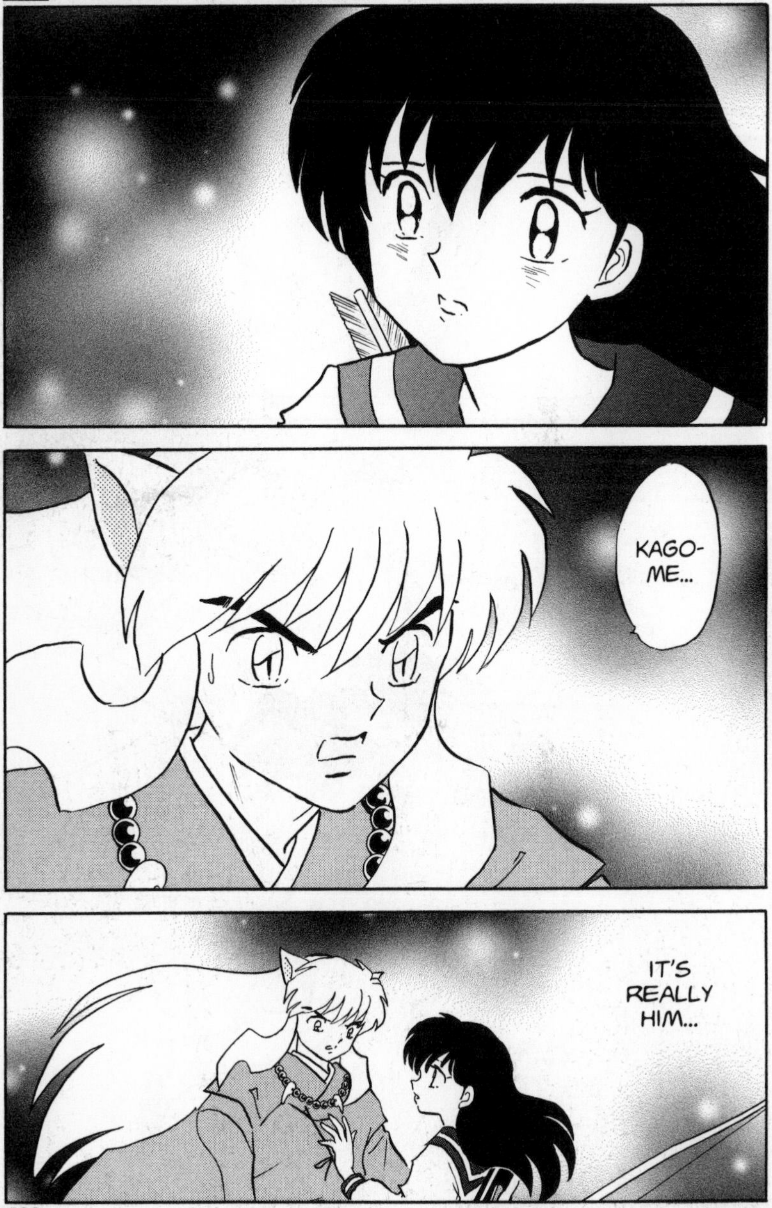
KAGO-
ME...
IT'S
REALLY
HIM...

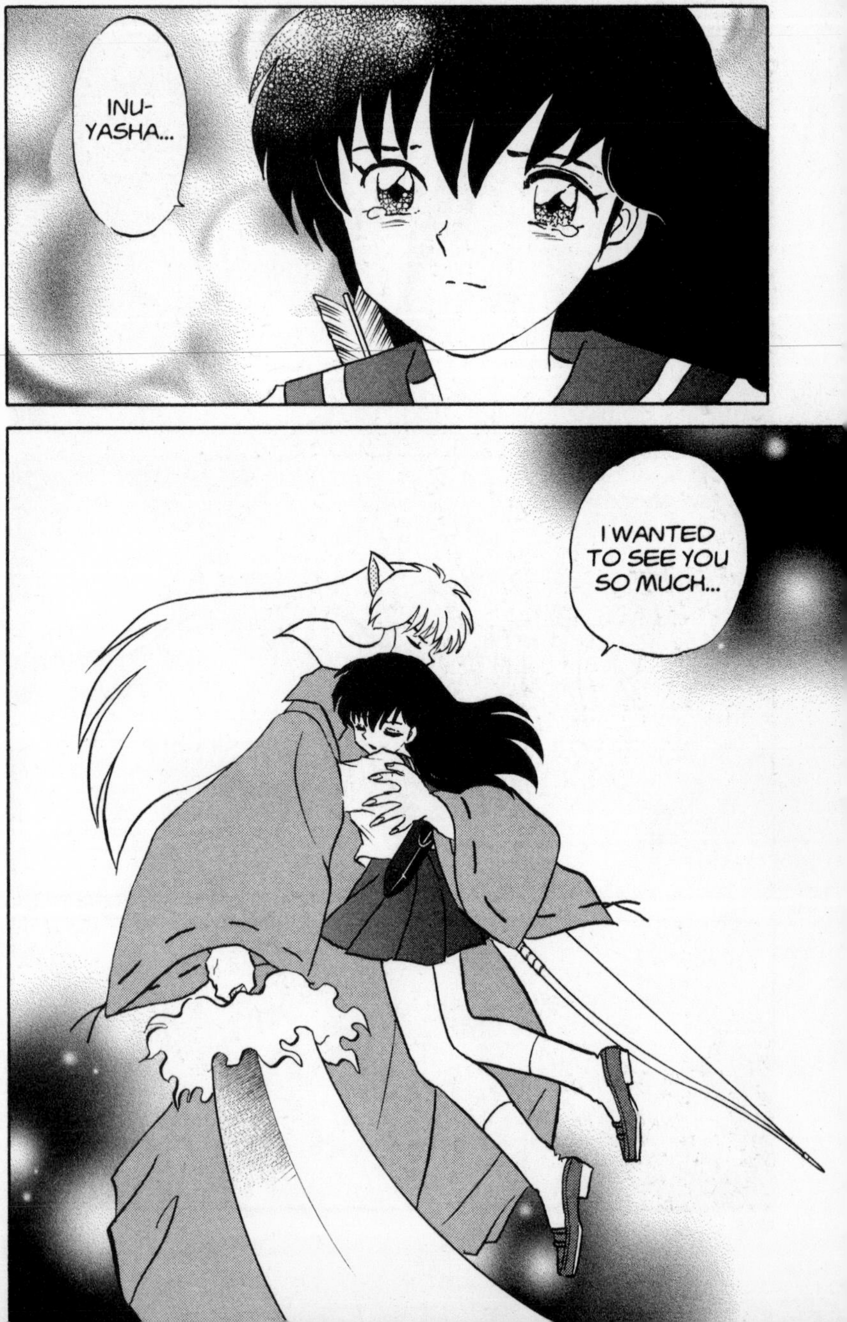
INU-
YASHA...
I WANTED TO SEE YOU SO MUCH...

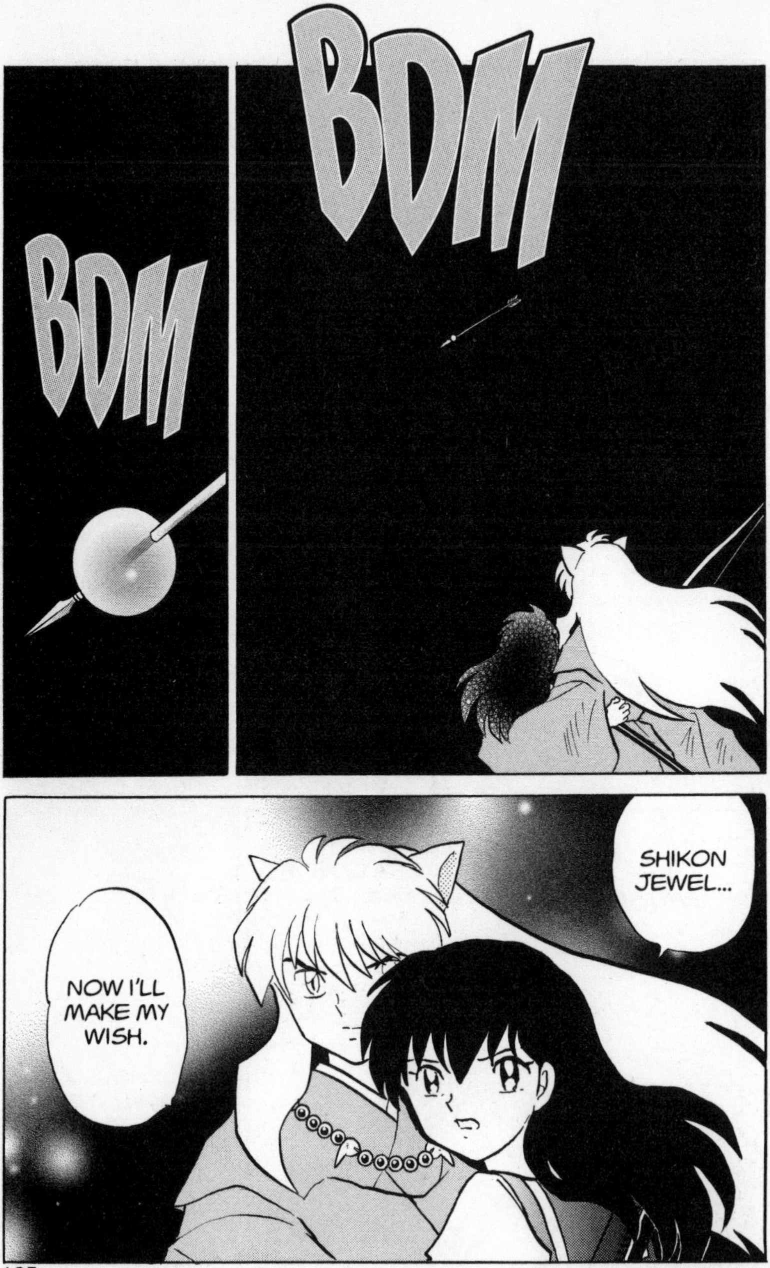
BDM
BDM
SHIKON JEWEL...
NOW I'LL MAKE MY WISH.

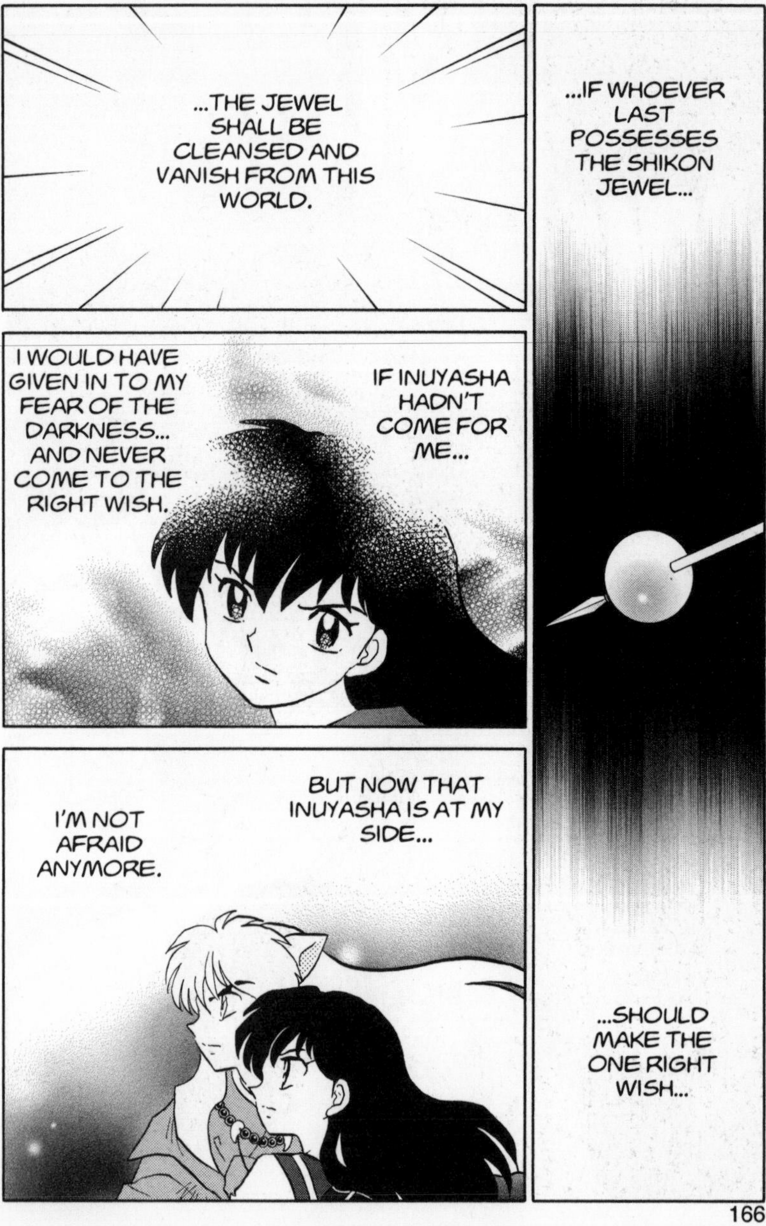
...IF WHOEVER LAST POSSESSES THE SHIKON JEWEL...
...SHOULD MAKE THE ONE RIGHT WISH...
...THE JEWEL SHALL BE CLEANSED AND VANISH FROM THIS WORLD.
IF INUYASHA HADN'T COME FOR ME...
I WOULD HAVE GIVEN IN TO MY FEAR OF THE DARKNESS... AND NEVER COME TO THE RIGHT WISH.
BUT NOW THAT INUYASHA IS AT MY SIDE...
I'M NOT AFRAID ANYMORE.

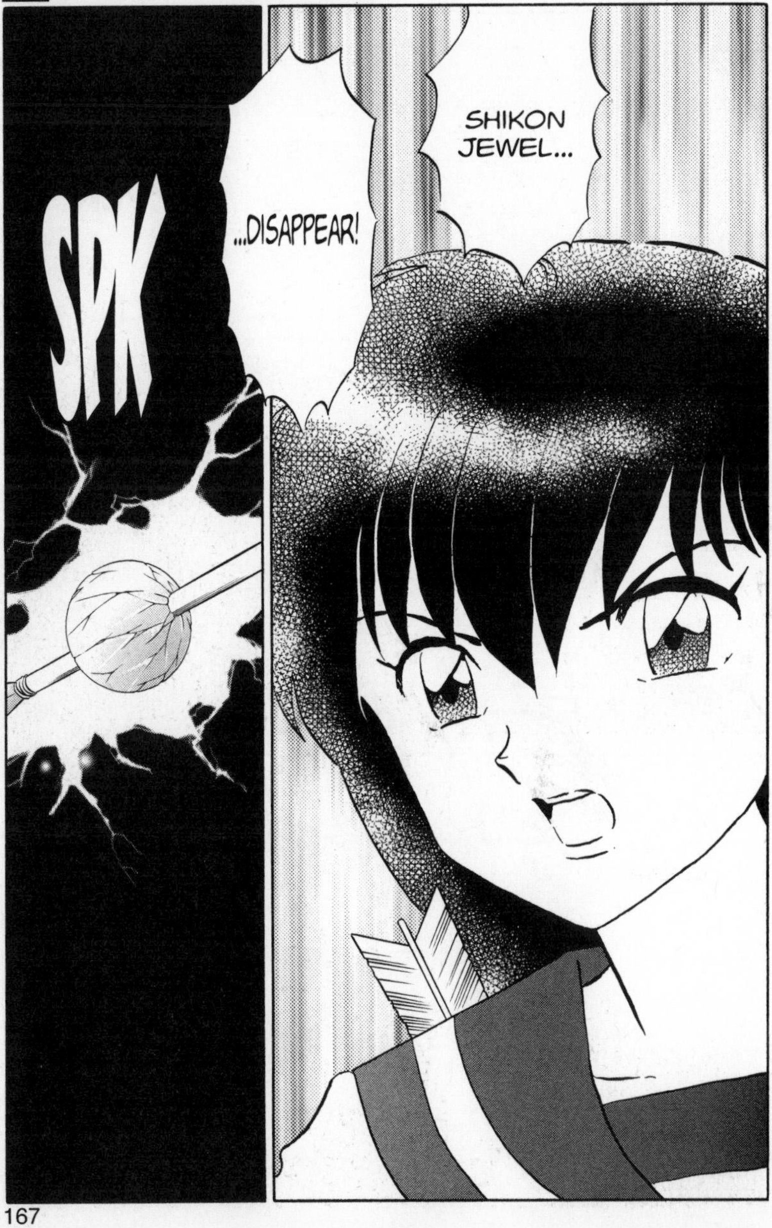
SHIKON JEWEL...
...DISAPPEAR!
SPK

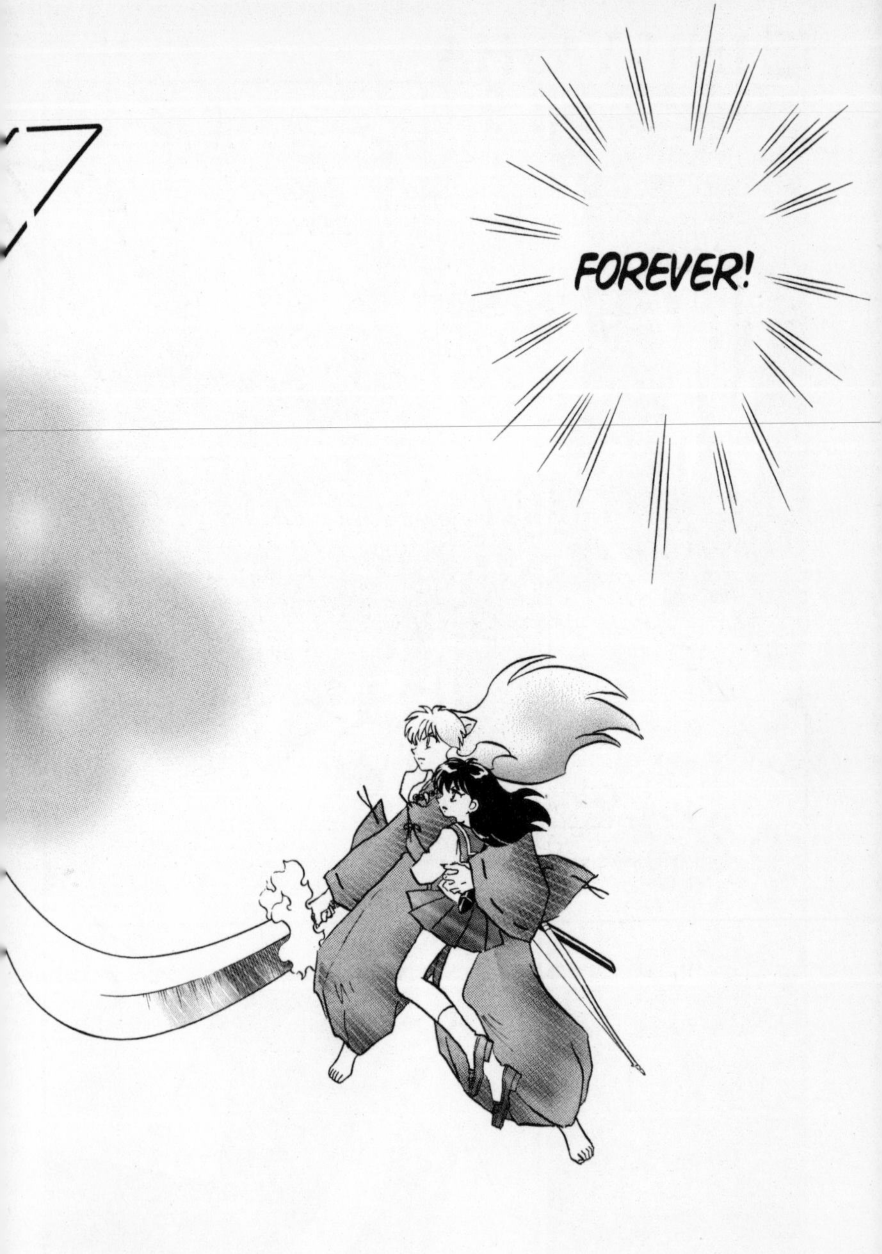
FOREVER!

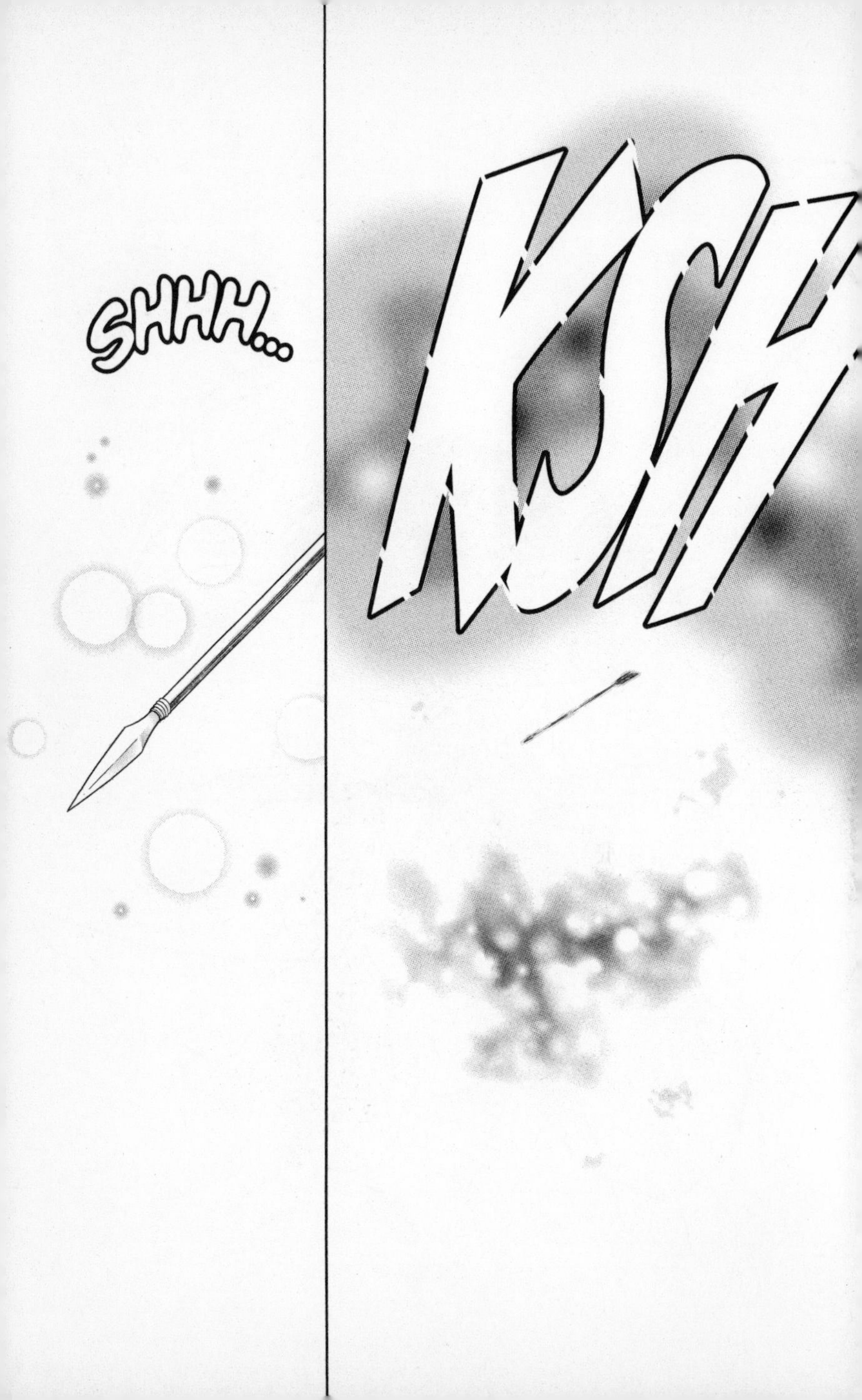
KSH
SHHH...

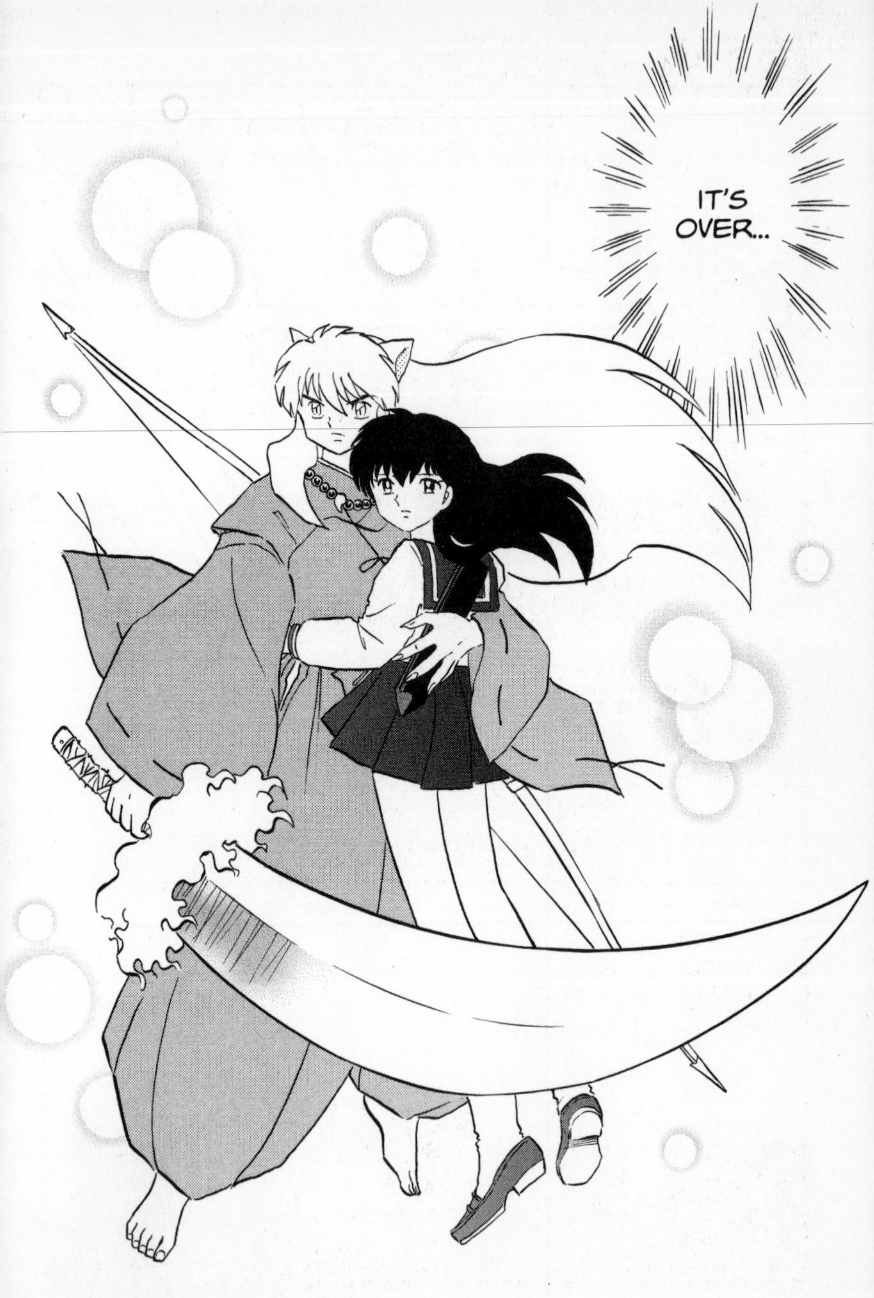
IT'S OVER...

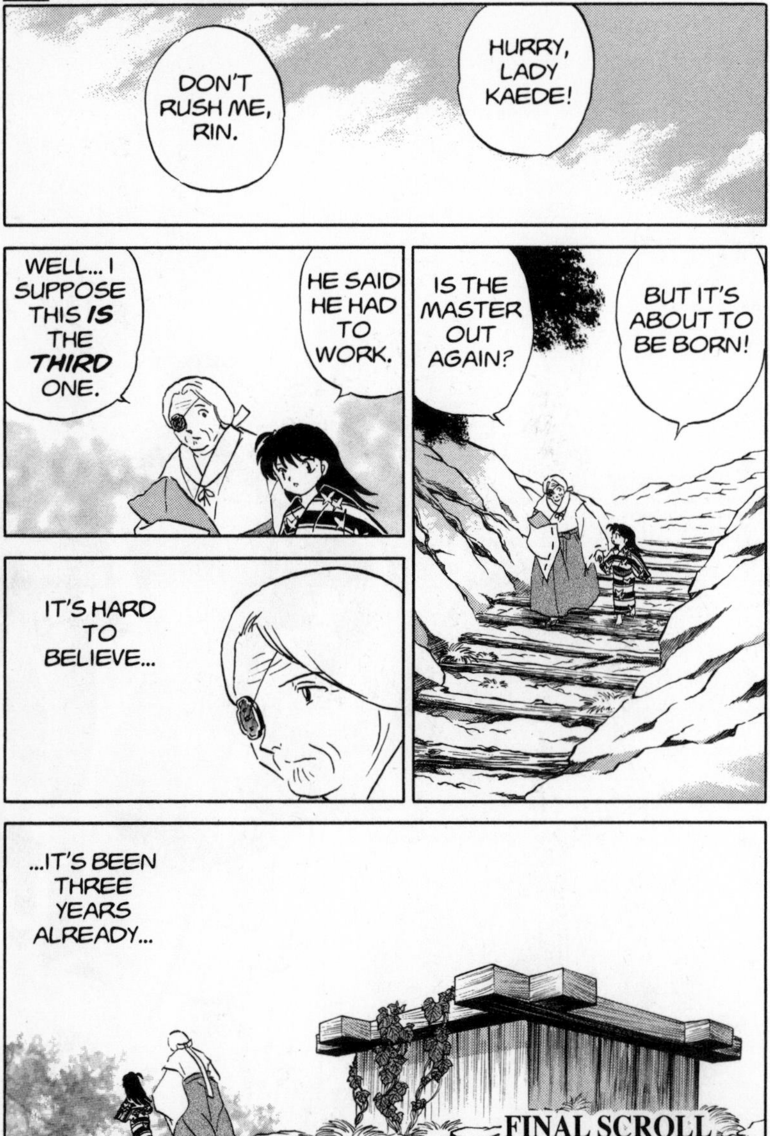
HURRY, LADY KAEDE!
DON'T RUSH ME, RIN.
BUT IT'S ABOUT TO BE BORN!
IS THE MASTER OUT AGAIN?
HE SAID HE HAD TO WORK.
WELL... I SUPPOSE THIS *IS* THE *THIRD* ONE.
IT'S HARD TO BELIEVE...
...IT'S BEEN THREE YEARS ALREADY...

FINAL SCROLL TOMORROW

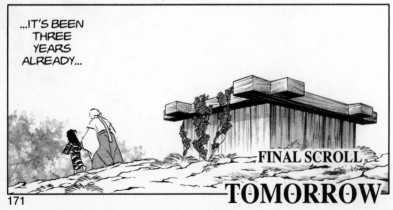

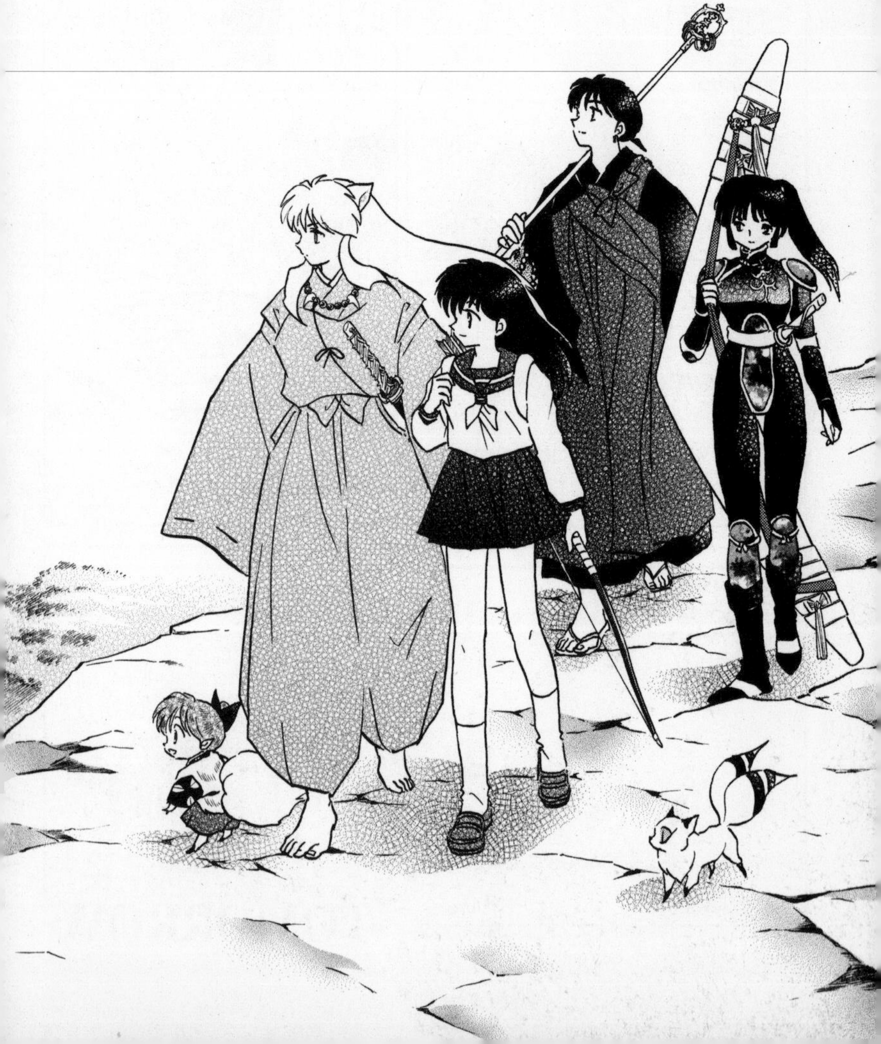

FINAL SCROLL
TOMORROW

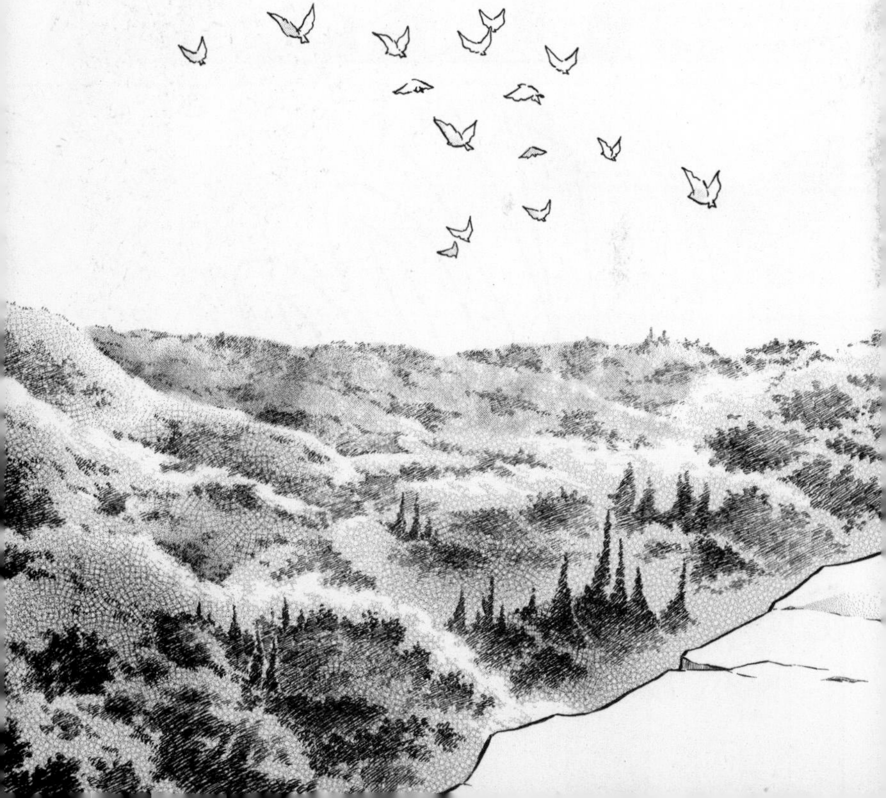

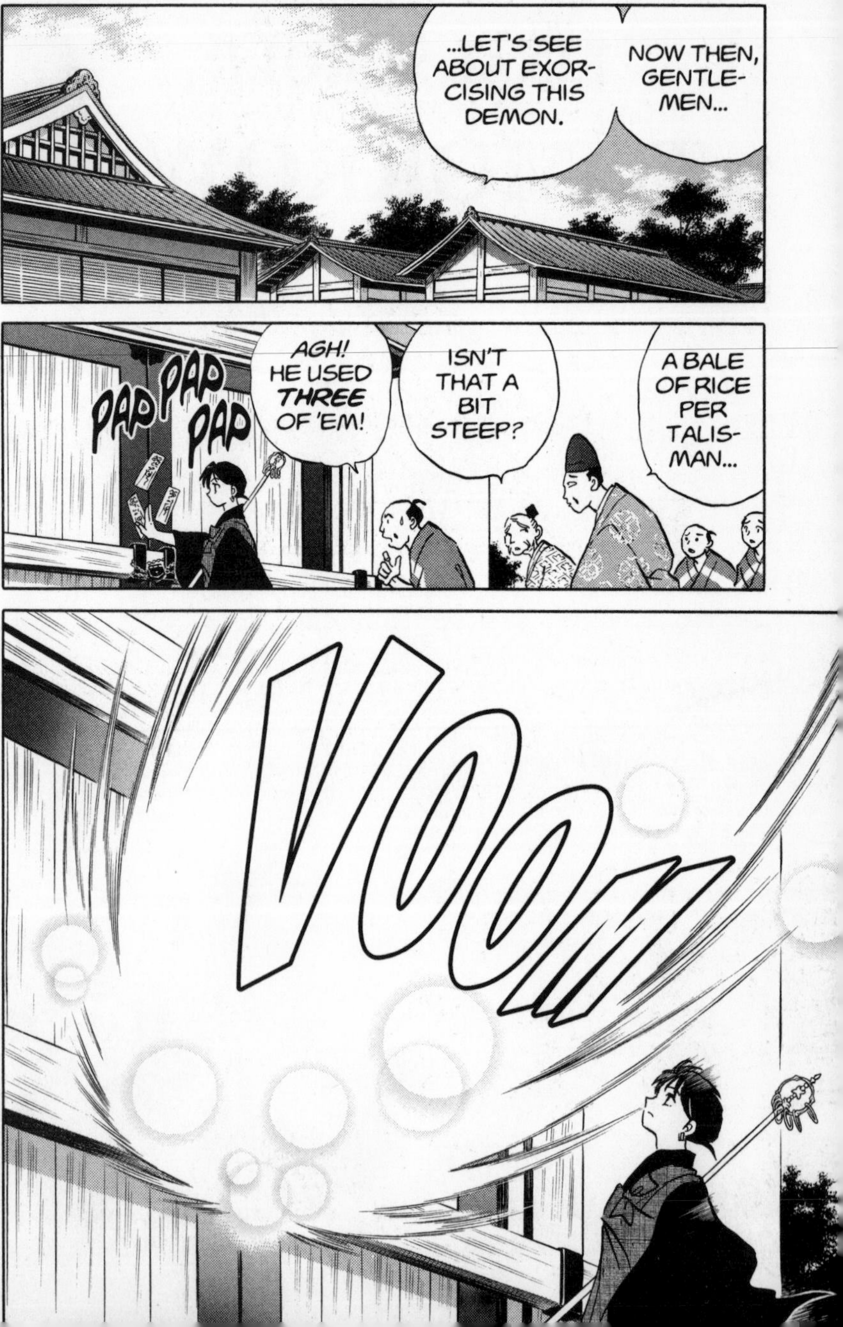
NOW THEN, GENTLEMEN...
...LET'S SEE ABOUT EXORCISING THIS DEMON.
A BALE OF RICE PER TALISMAN...
ISN'T THAT A BIT STEEP?
AGH! HE USED *THREE* OF 'EM!
PAP PAP PAP
VOOM

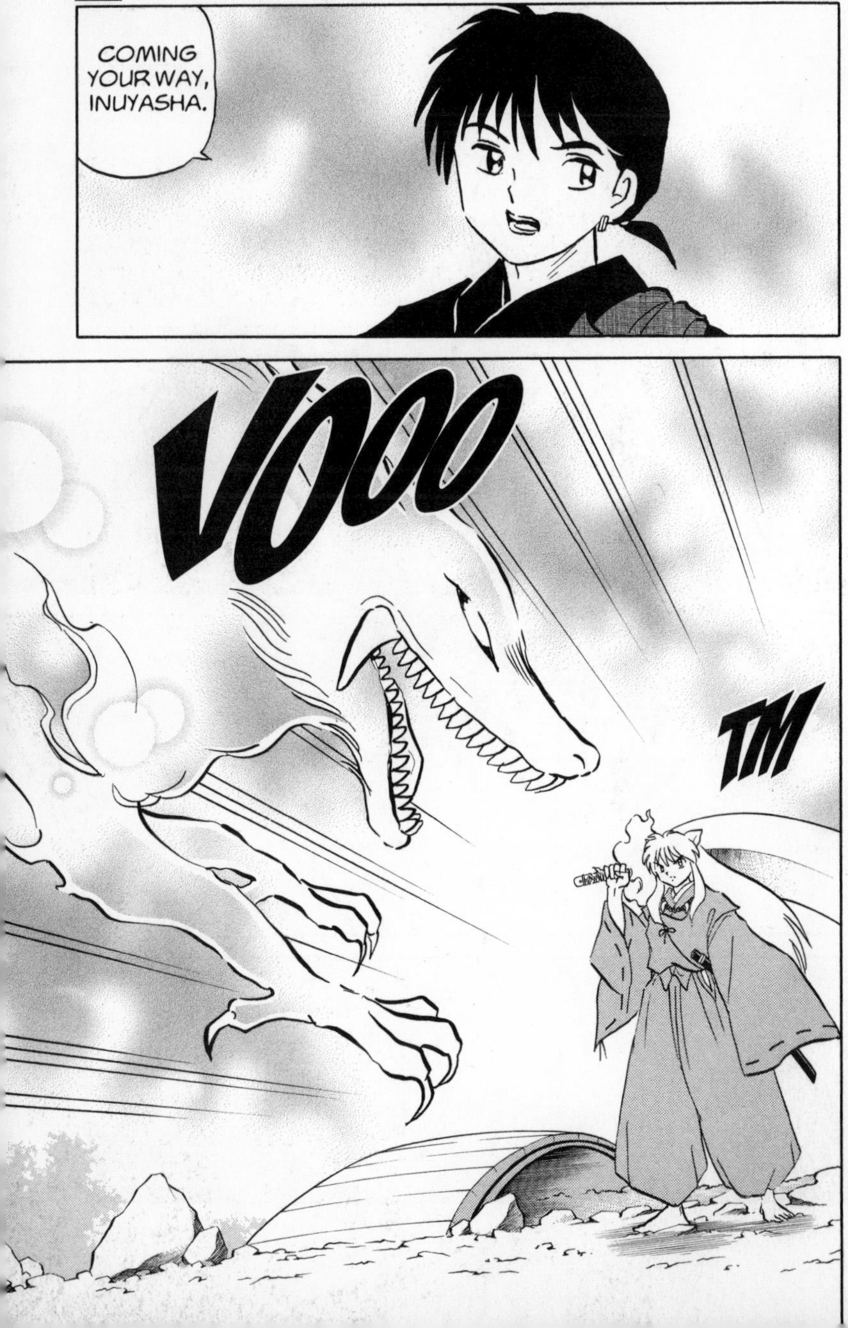
COMING YOUR WAY, INUYASHA.
VOOO
TM

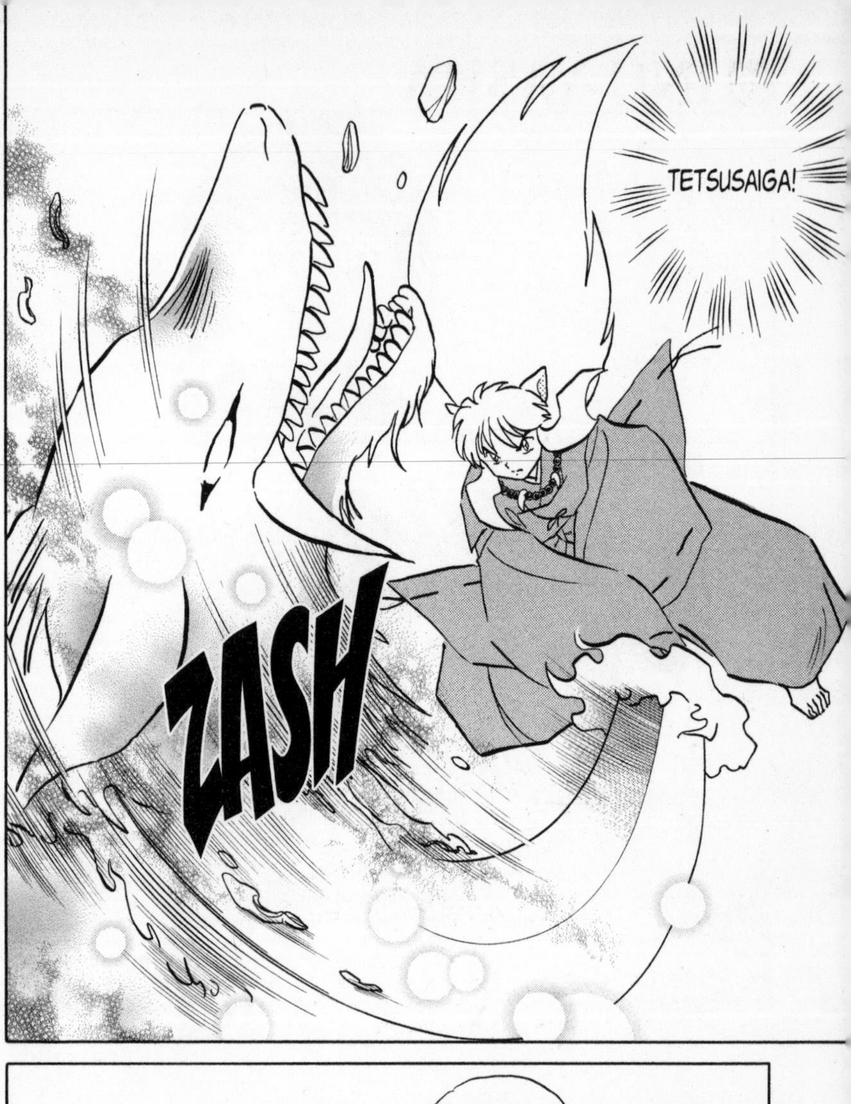
TETSUSAIGA!
ZASH
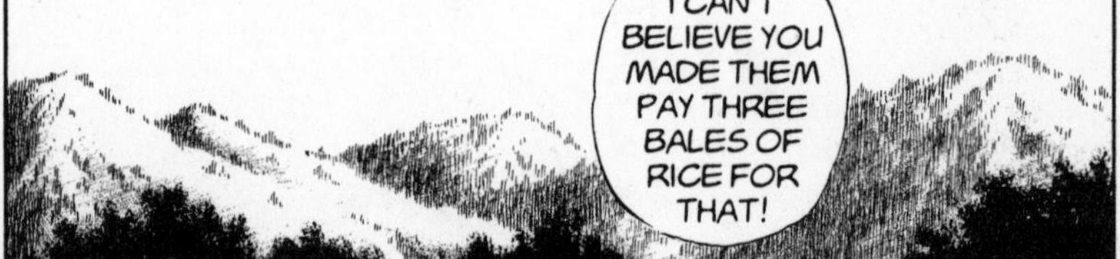
I CAN'T BELIEVE YOU MADE THEM PAY THREE BALES OF RICE FOR THAT!

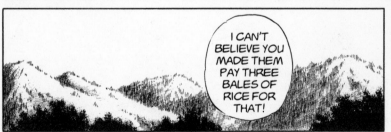

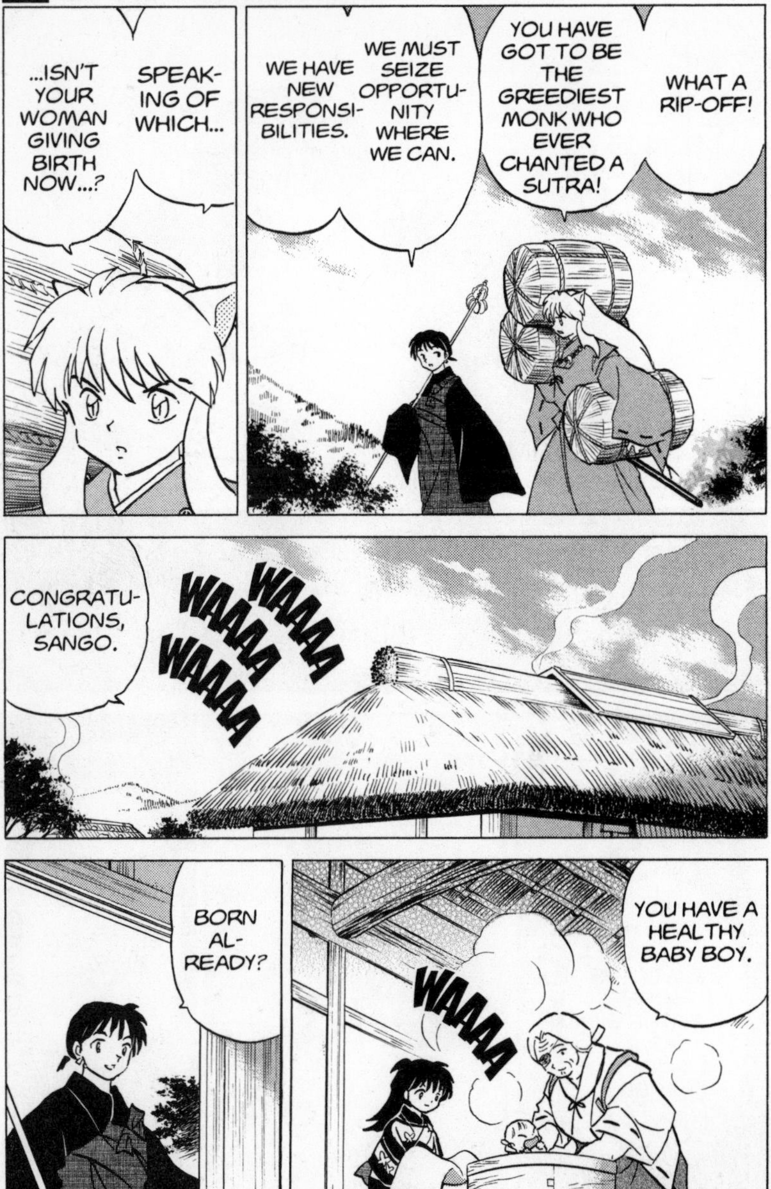
WHAT A RIP-OFF!
YOU HAVE GOT TO BE THE GREEDIEST MONK WHO EVER CHANTED A SUTRA!
WE MUST SEIZE OPPORTUNITY WHERE WE CAN.
WE HAVE NEW RESPONSIBILITIES.
SPEAKING OF WHICH...
...ISN'T YOUR WOMAN GIVING BIRTH NOW...?
WAAAA
WAAAA
WAAAA
WAAAA
CONGRATULATIONS, SANGO.
YOU HAVE A HEALTHY BABY BOY.
WAAAA
BORN ALREADY?

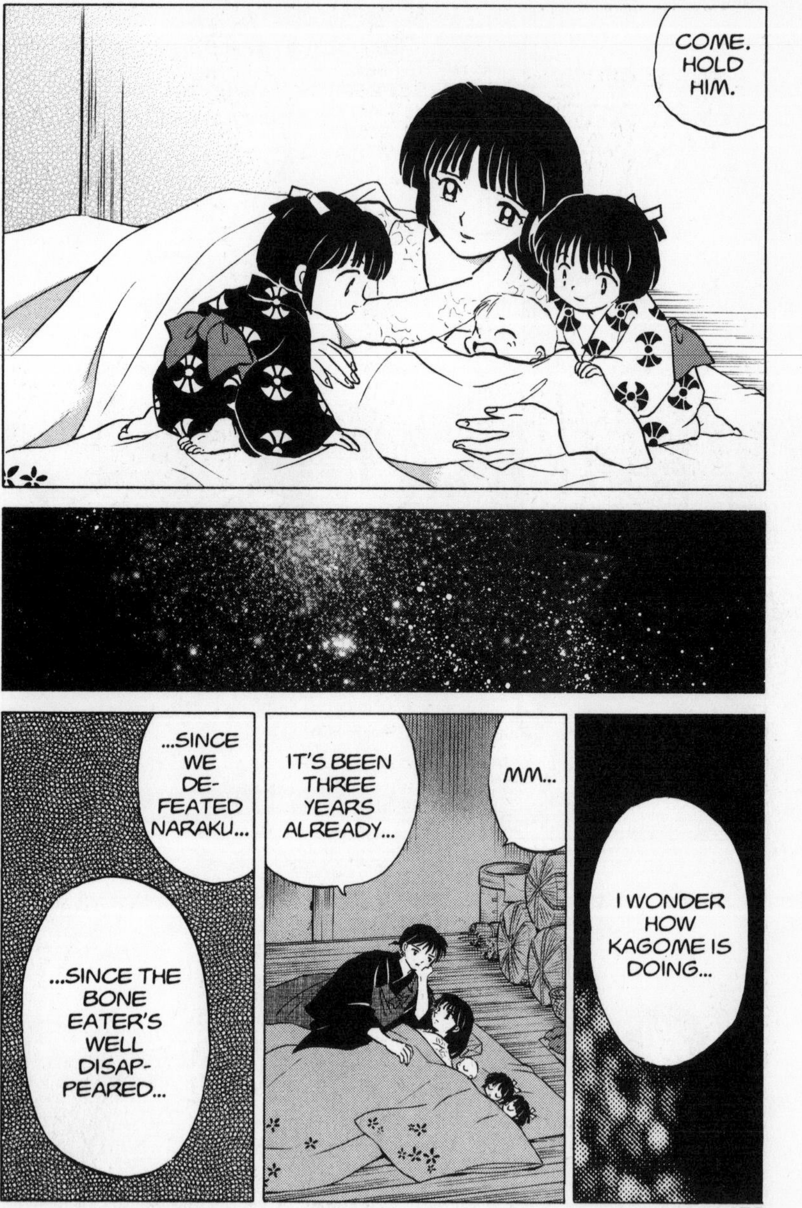
COME. HOLD HIM.
I WONDER HOW KAGOME IS DOING...
MM...
IT'S BEEN THREE YEARS ALREADY...
...SINCE WE DE-FEATED NARAKU...
...SINCE THE BONE EATER'S WELL DISAP-PEARED...

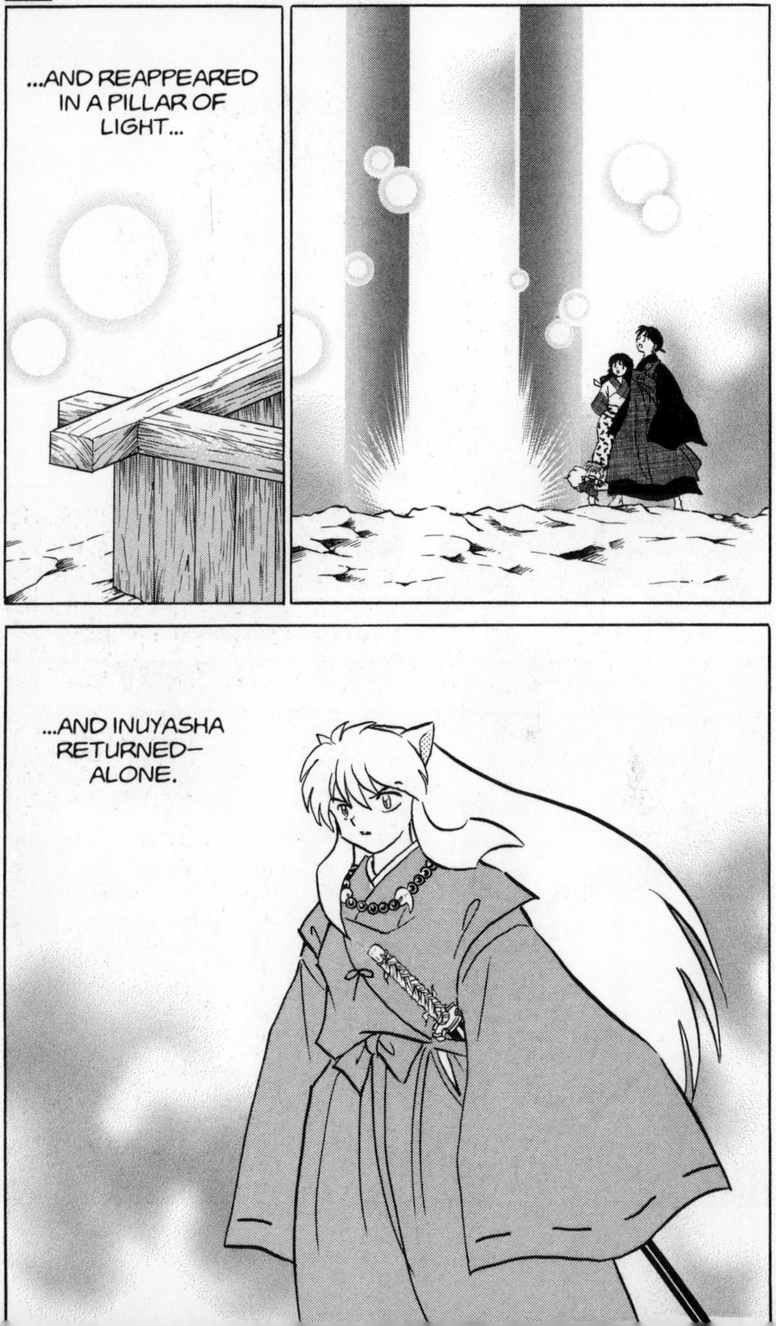
...AND REAPPEARED IN A PILLAR OF LIGHT...
...AND INUYASHA RETURNED—ALONE.

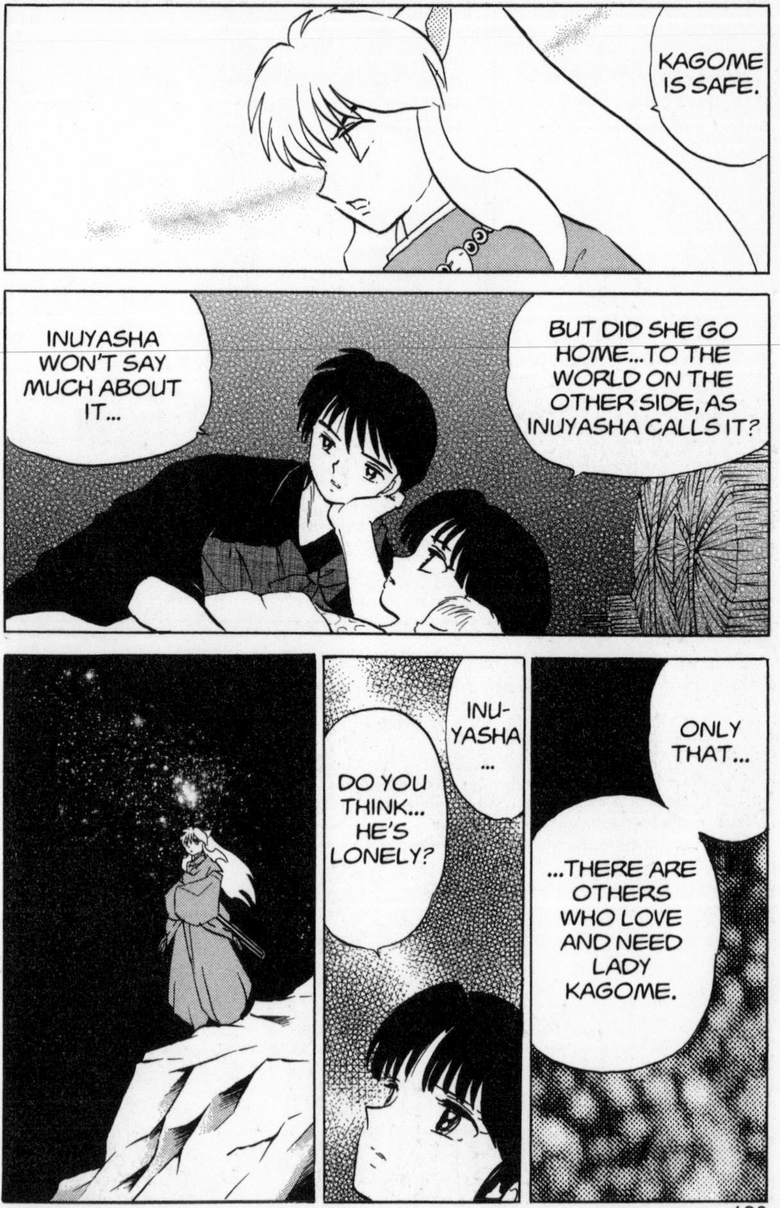
KAGOME IS SAFE.
BUT DID SHE GO HOME...TO THE WORLD ON THE OTHER SIDE, AS INUYASHA CALLS IT?
INUYASHA WON'T SAY MUCH ABOUT IT...
ONLY THAT...
...THERE ARE OTHERS WHO LOVE AND NEED LADY KAGOME.
INU-YASHA ...
DO YOU THINK... HE'S LONELY?

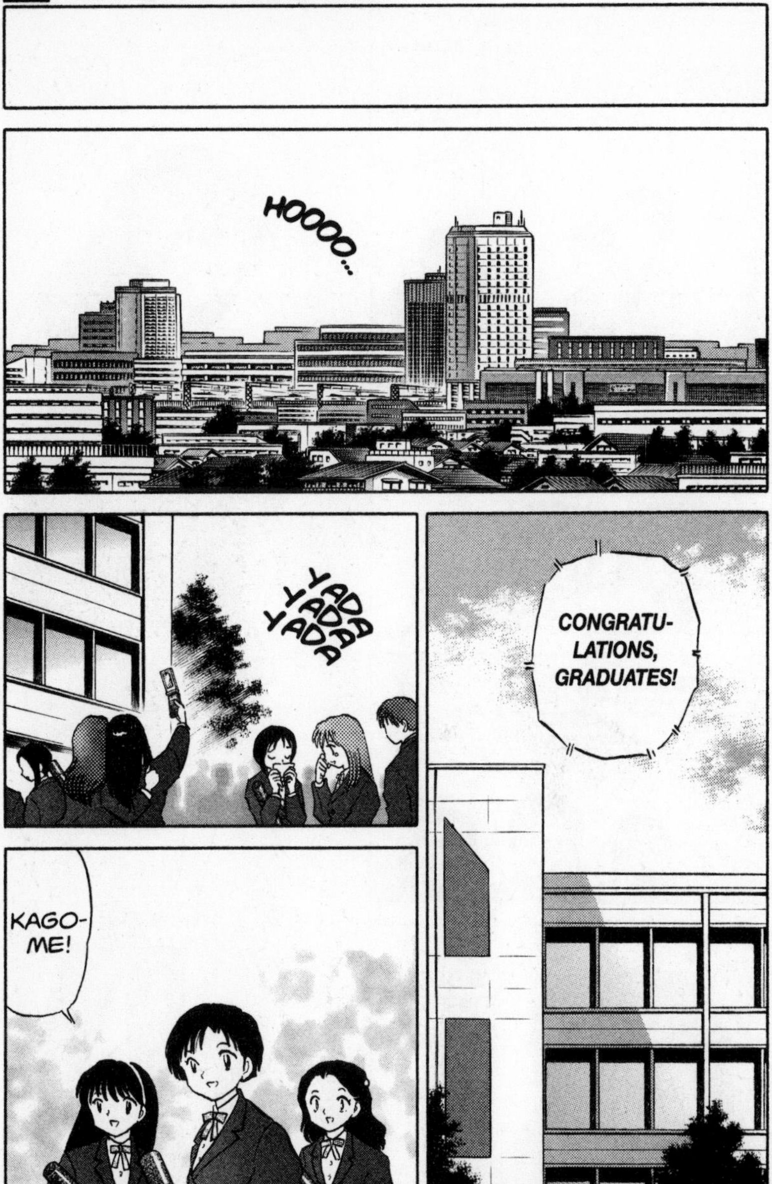
HOOOO...
CONGRATU-LATIONS, GRADUATES!
YADA YADA YADA
KAGO-ME!

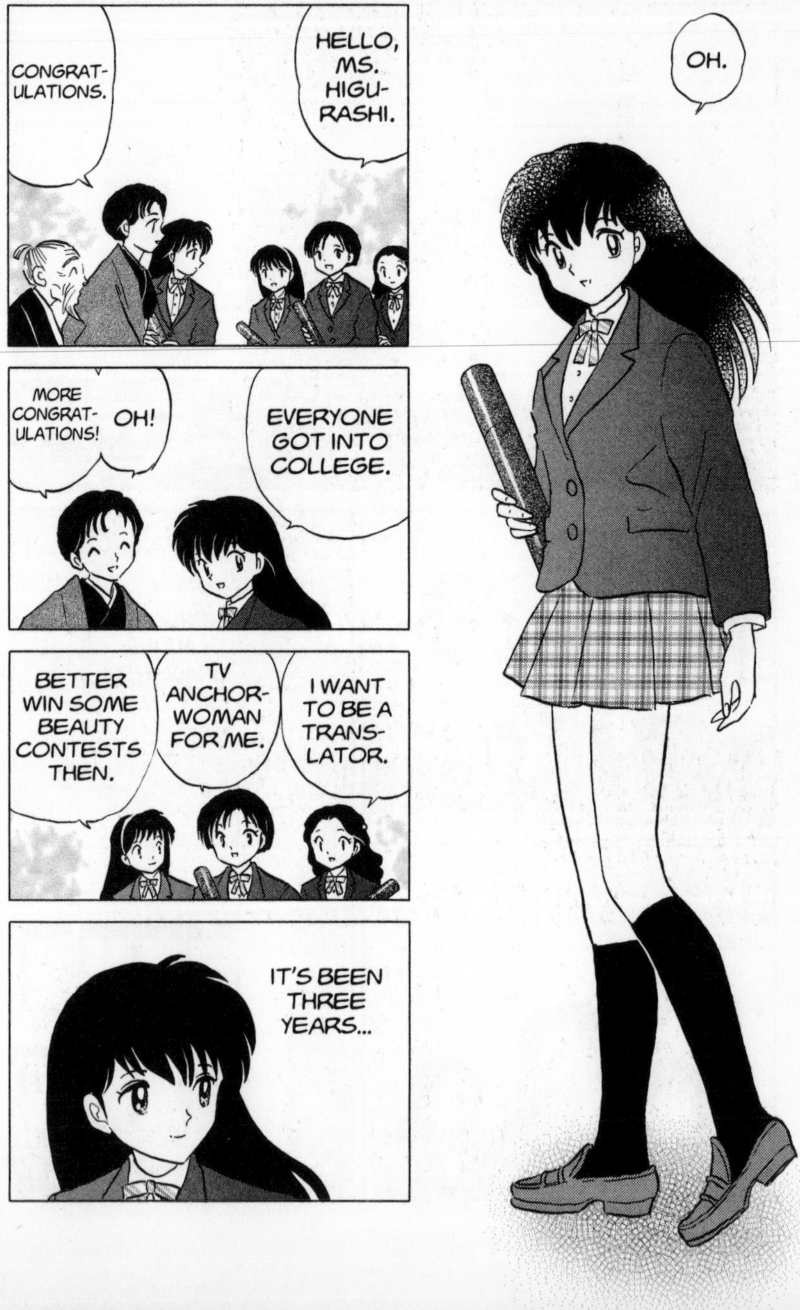
OH.
HELLO, MS. HIGURASHI.
CONGRATULATIONS.
EVERYONE GOT INTO COLLEGE.
OH!
MORE CONGRATULATIONS!
I WANT TO BE A TRANSLATOR.
TV ANCHORWOMAN FOR ME.
BETTER WIN SOME BEAUTY CONTESTS THEN.
IT'S BEEN THREE YEARS...

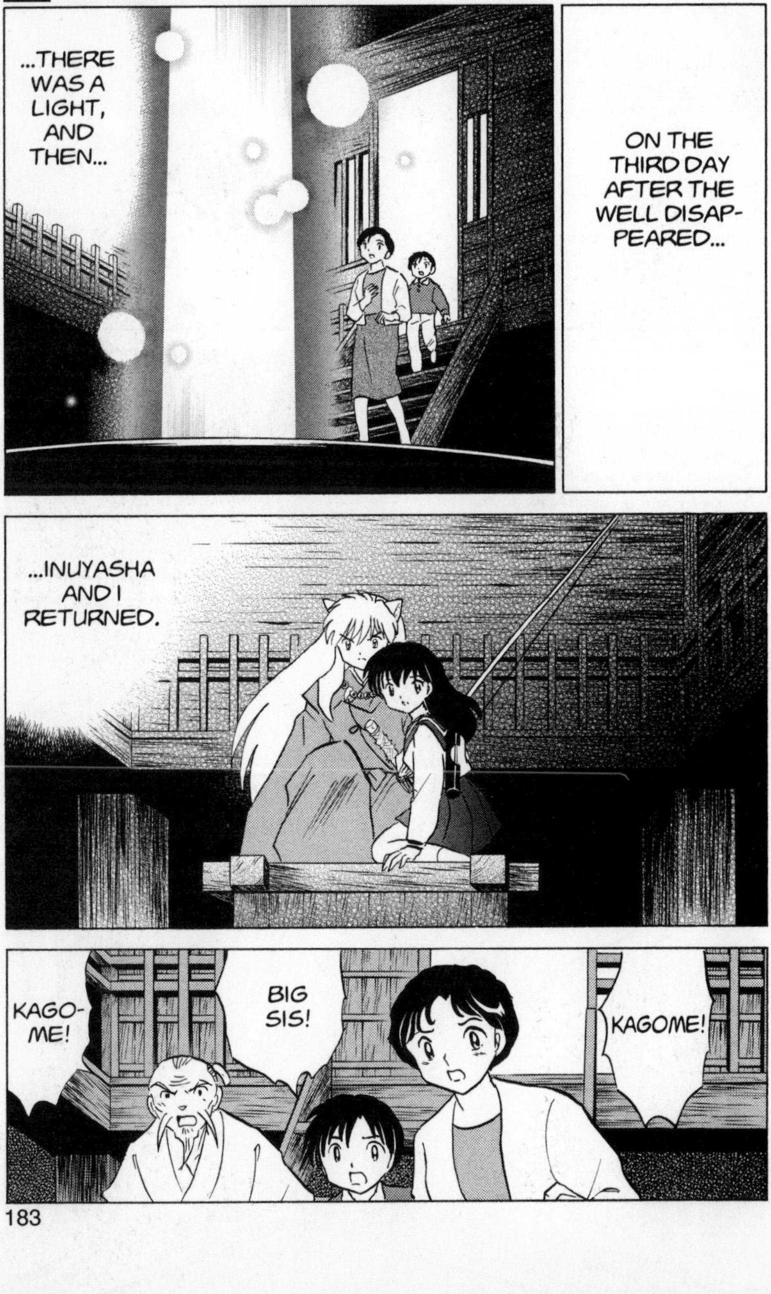
ON THE THIRD DAY AFTER THE WELL DISAP-PEARED...
...THERE WAS A LIGHT, AND THEN...
...INUYASHA AND I RETURNED.
KAGOME!
BIG SIS!
KAGO-ME!

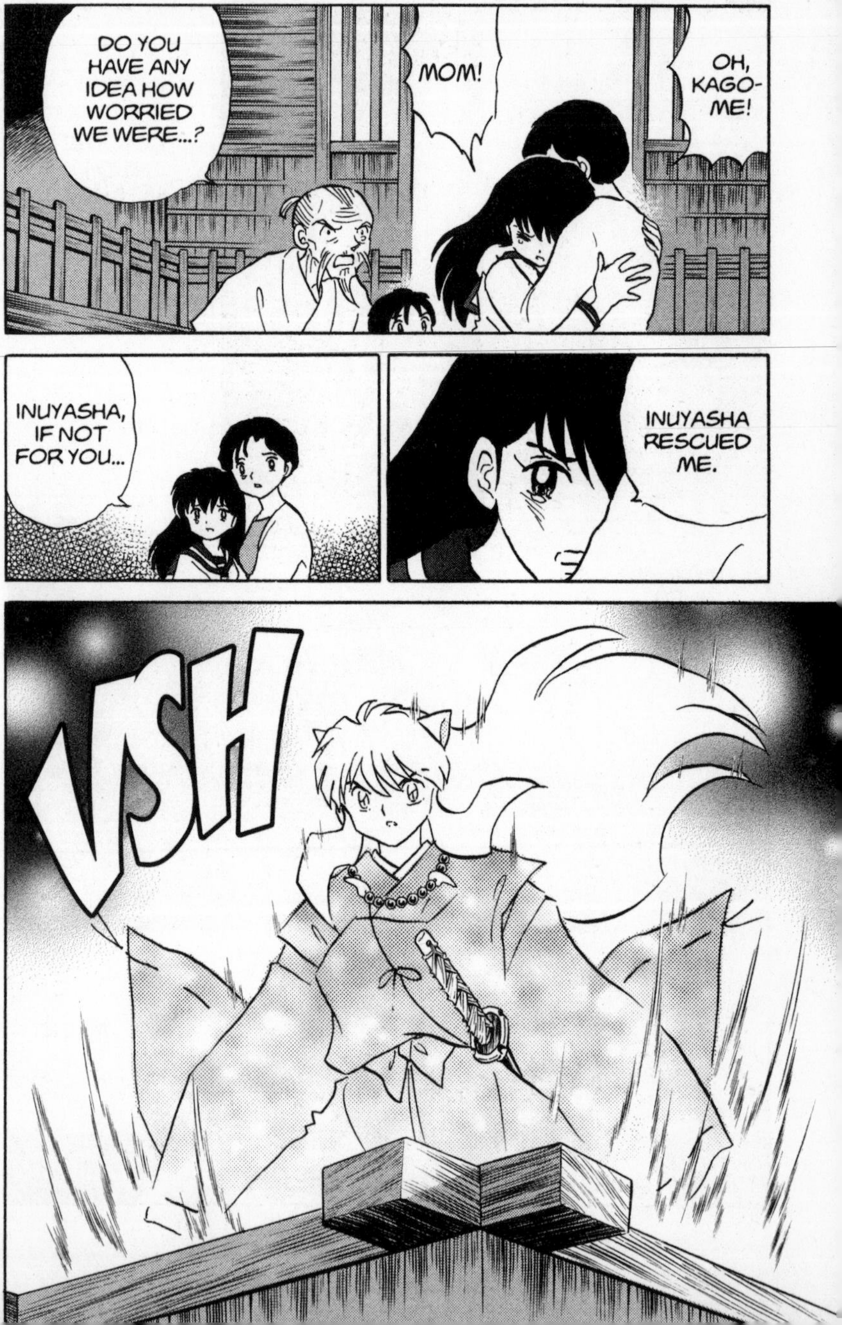
OH, KAGO-ME!
MOM!
DO YOU HAVE ANY IDEA HOW WORRIED WE WERE...?
INUYASHA RESCUED ME.
INUYASHA, IF NOT FOR YOU...
VSH

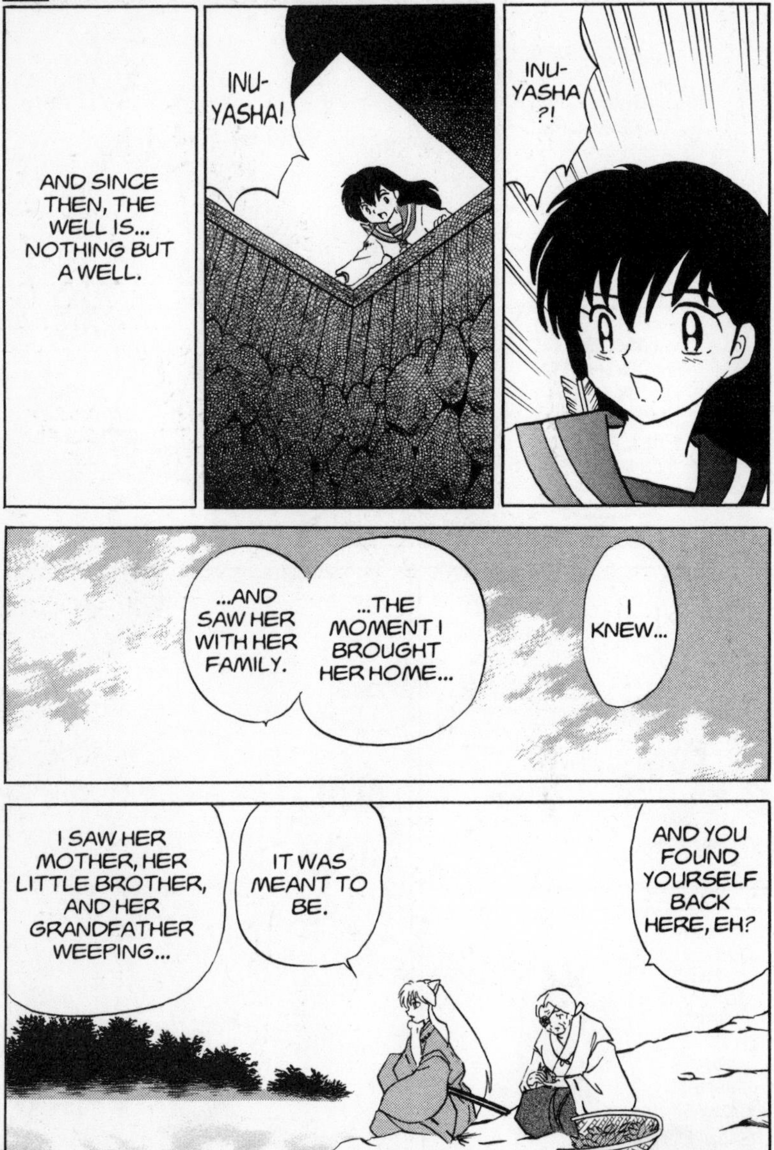
INU-YASHA?!
INU-YASHA!
AND SINCE THEN, THE WELL IS... NOTHING BUT A WELL.
I KNEW...
...THE MOMENT I BROUGHT HER HOME...
...AND SAW HER WITH HER FAMILY.
AND YOU FOUND YOURSELF BACK HERE, EH?
IT WAS MEANT TO BE.
I SAW HER MOTHER, HER LITTLE BROTHER, AND HER GRANDFATHER WEEPING...

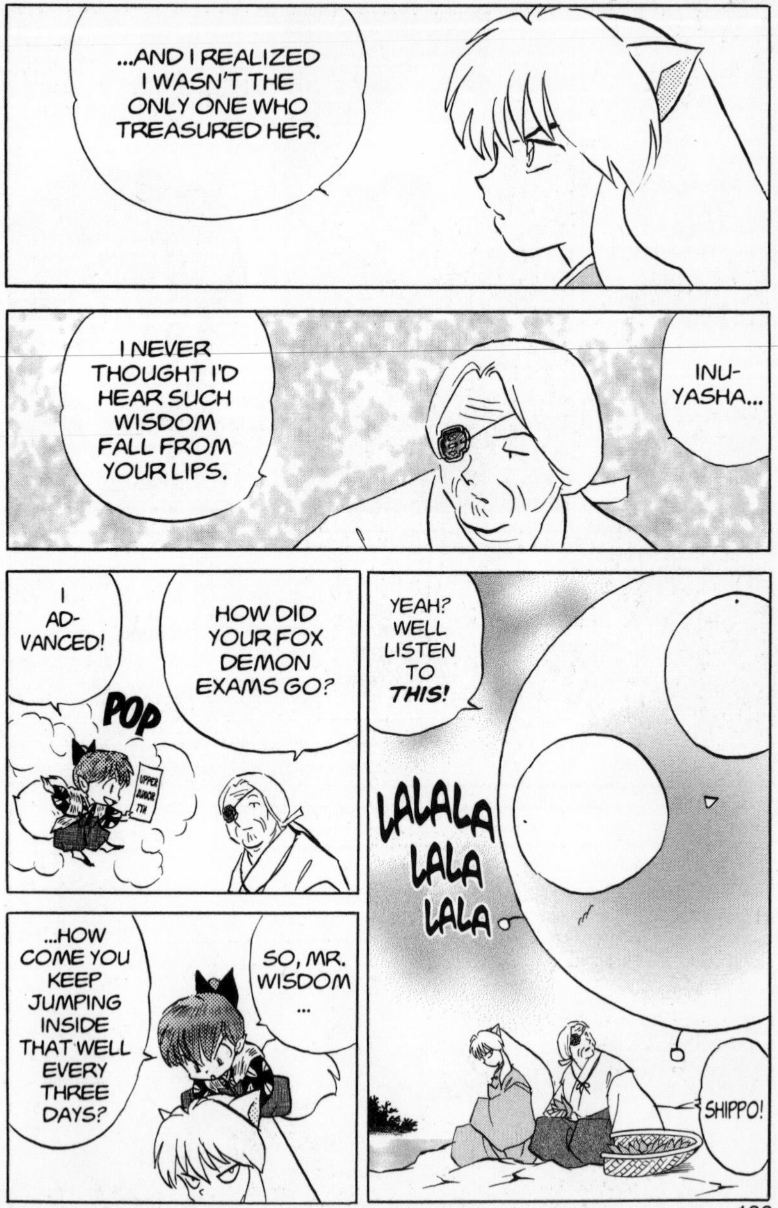
...AND I REALIZED I WASN'T THE ONLY ONE WHO TREASURED HER.
INU-YASHA...
I NEVER THOUGHT I'D HEAR SUCH WISDOM FALL FROM YOUR LIPS.
YEAH? WELL LISTEN TO THIS!
LALALA LALA LALA
SHIPPO!
HOW DID YOUR FOX DEMON EXAMS GO?
I ADVANCED!
POP
UPPER JUNIOR 7TH
SO, MR. WISDOM...
...HOW COME YOU KEEP JUMPING INSIDE THAT WELL EVERY THREE DAYS?

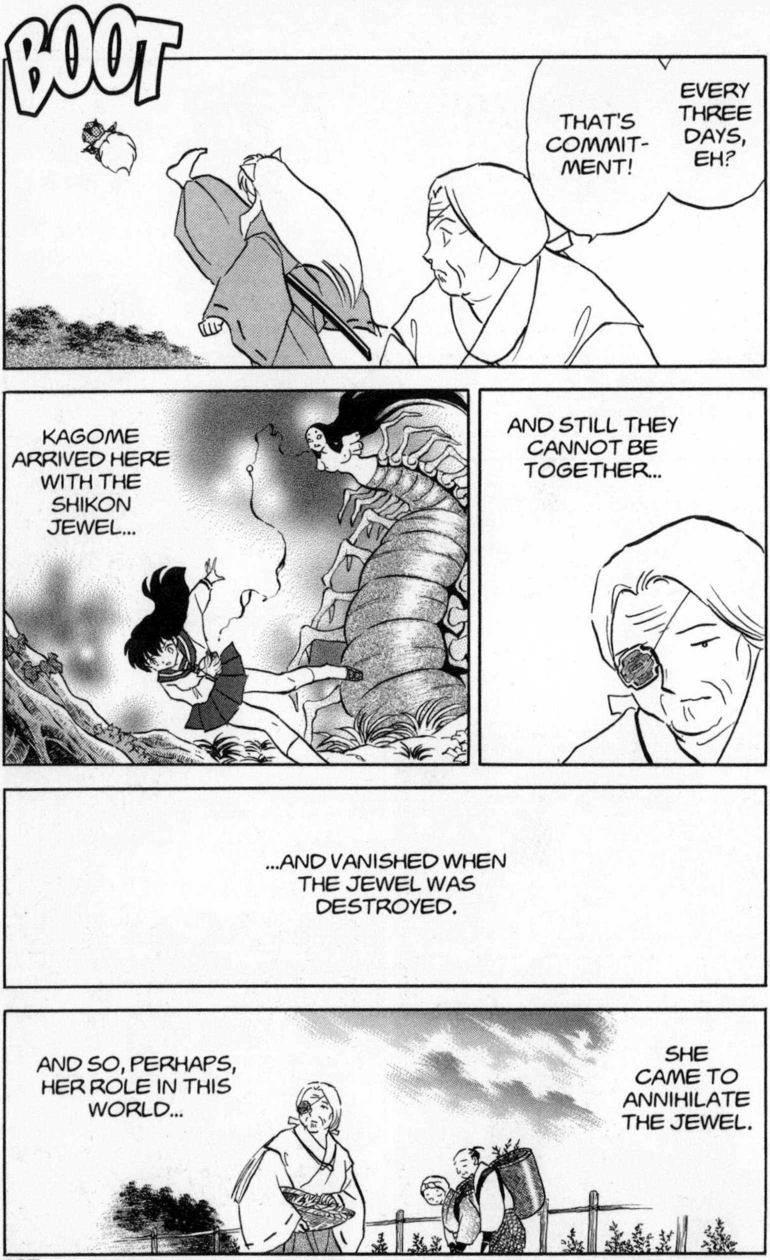
BOOT
EVERY THREE DAYS, EH?
THAT'S COMMIT-MENT!
AND STILL THEY CANNOT BE TOGETHER...
KAGOME ARRIVED HERE WITH THE SHIKON JEWEL...
...AND VANISHED WHEN THE JEWEL WAS DESTROYED.
SHE CAME TO ANNIHILATE THE JEWEL.
AND SO, PERHAPS, HER ROLE IN THIS WORLD...

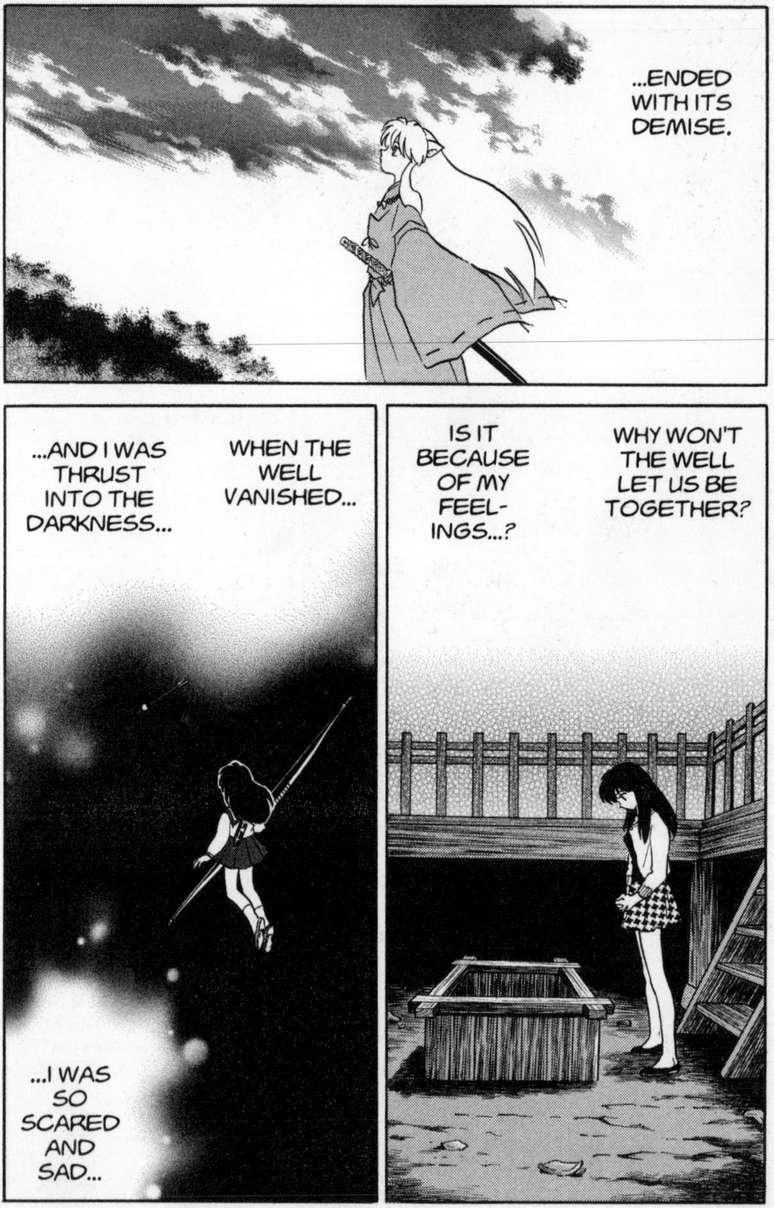
...ENDED WITH ITS DEMISE.
WHY WON'T THE WELL LET US BE TOGETHER?
IS IT BECAUSE OF MY FEEL- INGS...?
WHEN THE WELL VANISHED...
...AND I WAS THRUST INTO THE DARKNESS...
...I WAS SO SCARED AND SAD...

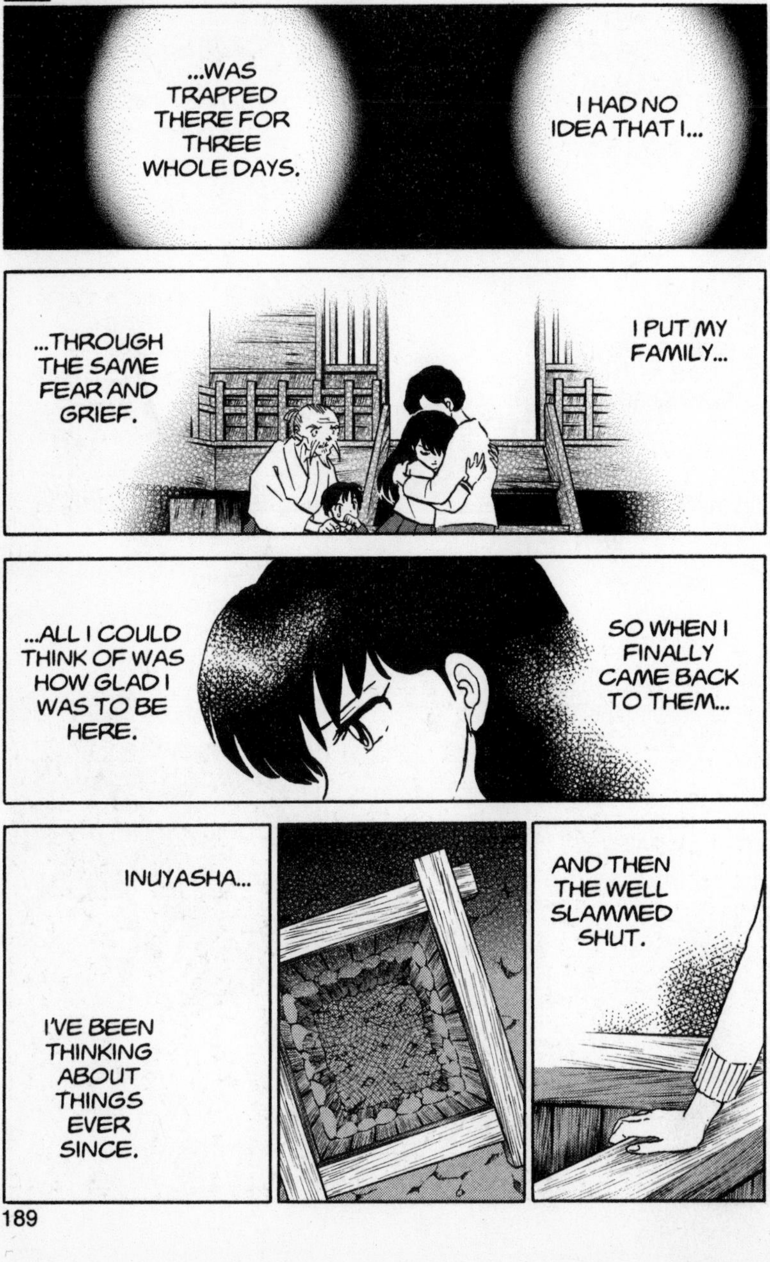
I HAD NO IDEA THAT I...
...WAS TRAPPED THERE FOR THREE WHOLE DAYS.
I PUT MY FAMILY...
...THROUGH THE SAME FEAR AND GRIEF.
SO WHEN I FINALLY CAME BACK TO THEM...
...ALL I COULD THINK OF WAS HOW GLAD I WAS TO BE HERE.
AND THEN THE WELL SLAMMED SHUT.
INUYASHA...
I'VE BEEN THINKING ABOUT THINGS EVER SINCE.

THE REASON I WAS TRANSPORTED TO YOUR ERA...

...MUST BE THE SAME REASON THE WELL CLOSED AFTER THE SHIKON JEWEL VANISHED.

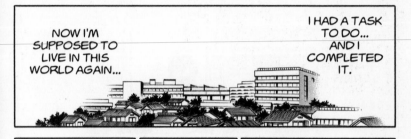

I HAD A TASK TO DO... AND I COMPLETED IT.

NOW I'M SUPPOSED TO LIVE IN THIS WORLD AGAIN...

...THIS WORLD WITHOUT... YOU.

BUT, INUYASHA...

I WANT TO SEE YOU AGAIN.

190

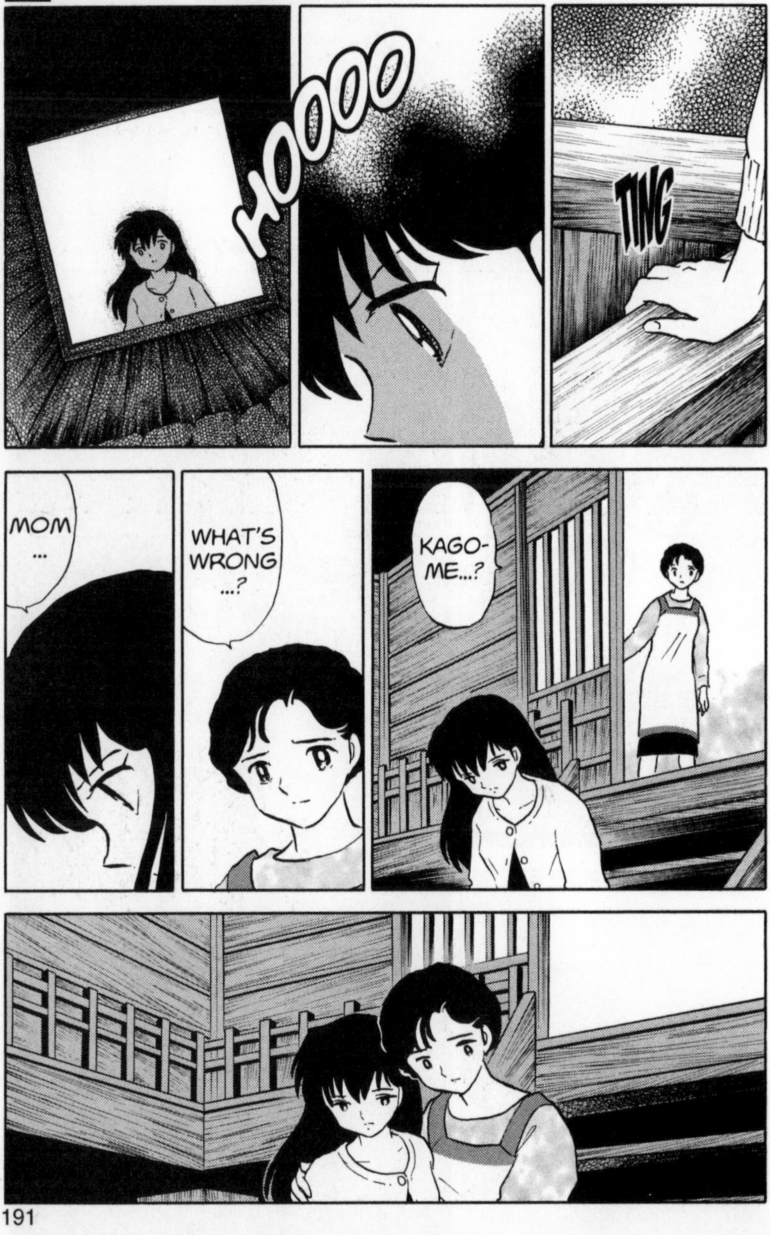
TING
HOOOO
KAGO-ME...?
WHAT'S WRONG ...?
MOM ...

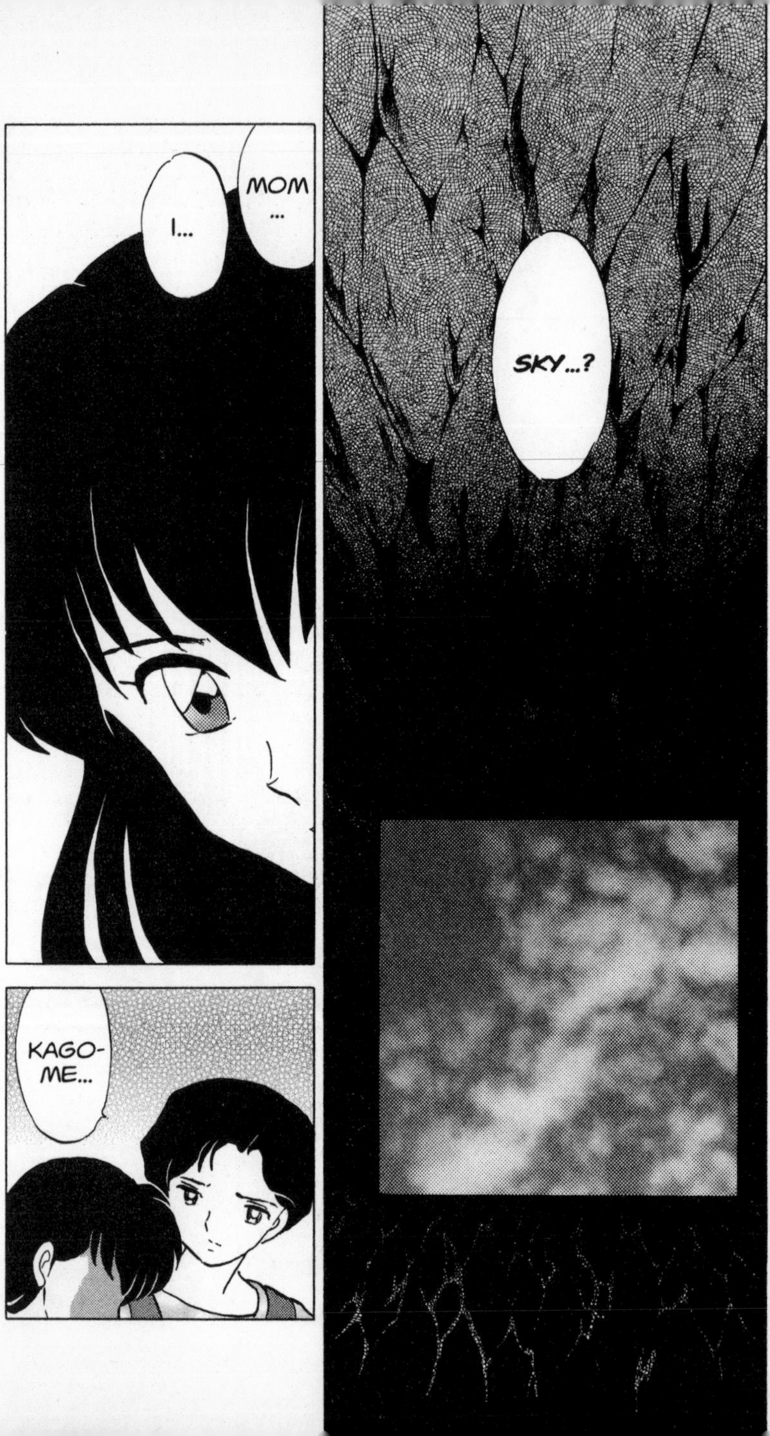
SKY...?
MOM ...
I...
KAGO-ME...

DOGGIE!
DOGGIE!
DOGGIE!
YOU'RE A TOY NOW.
COULD SOMEONE DO SOMETHING ABOUT THESE TWINS?
JERK
YANK
REMEMBER NOT TO PULL HIS EARS.
I'M SO SORRY, INU-YASHA.
HSH...
!

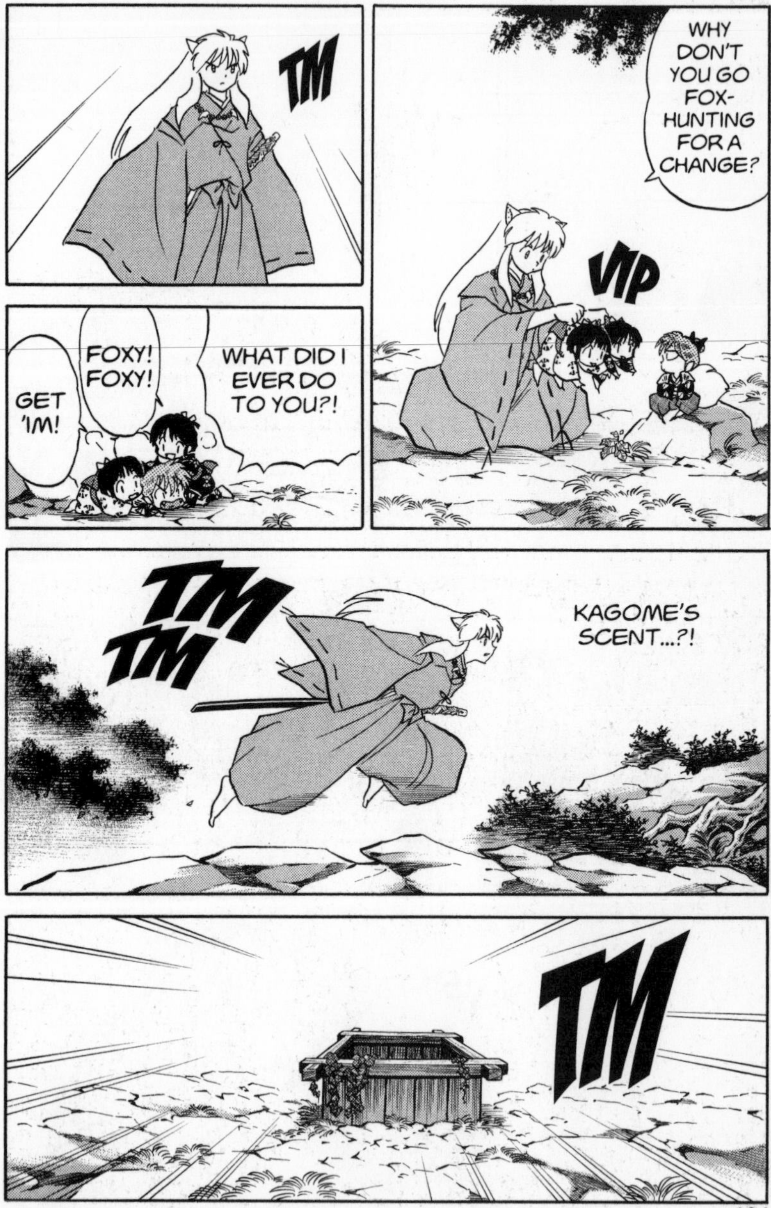
WHY DON'T YOU GO FOX-HUNTING FOR A CHANGE?
VIP
TM
WHAT DID I EVER DO TO YOU?!
FOXY! FOXY!
GET 'IM!
KAGOME'S SCENT...?!
TM TM
TM

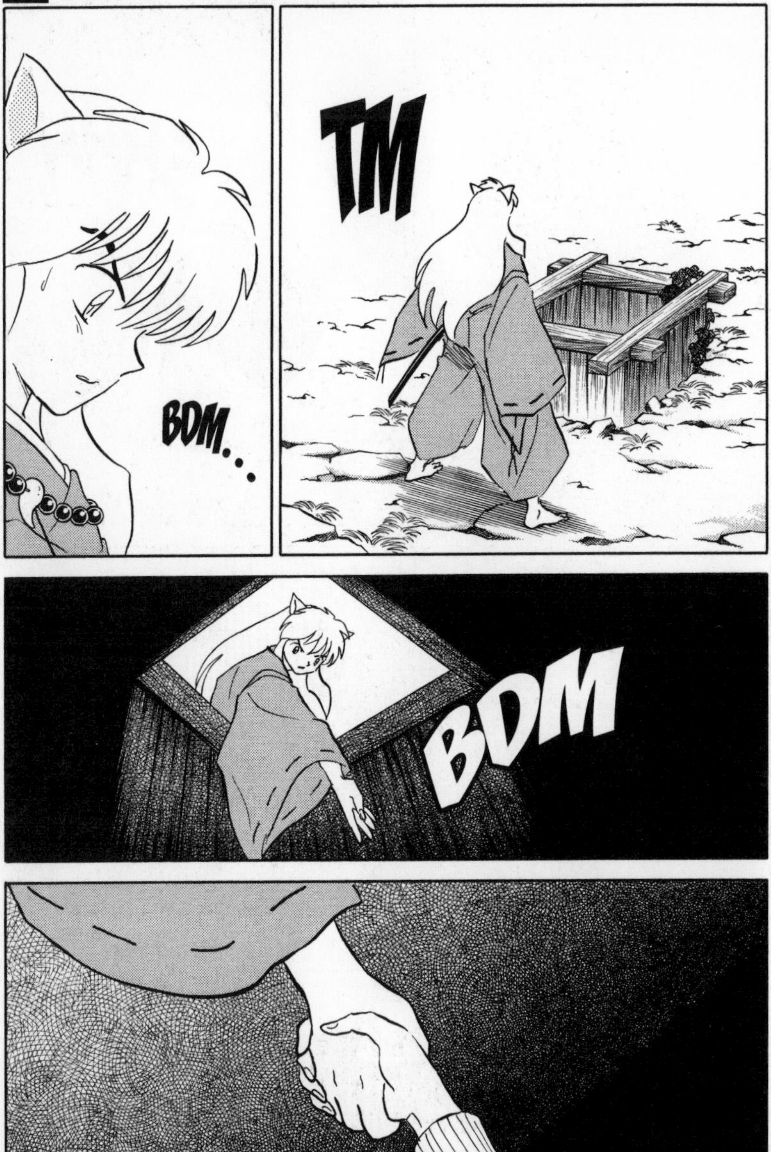
TM
BDM...
BDM

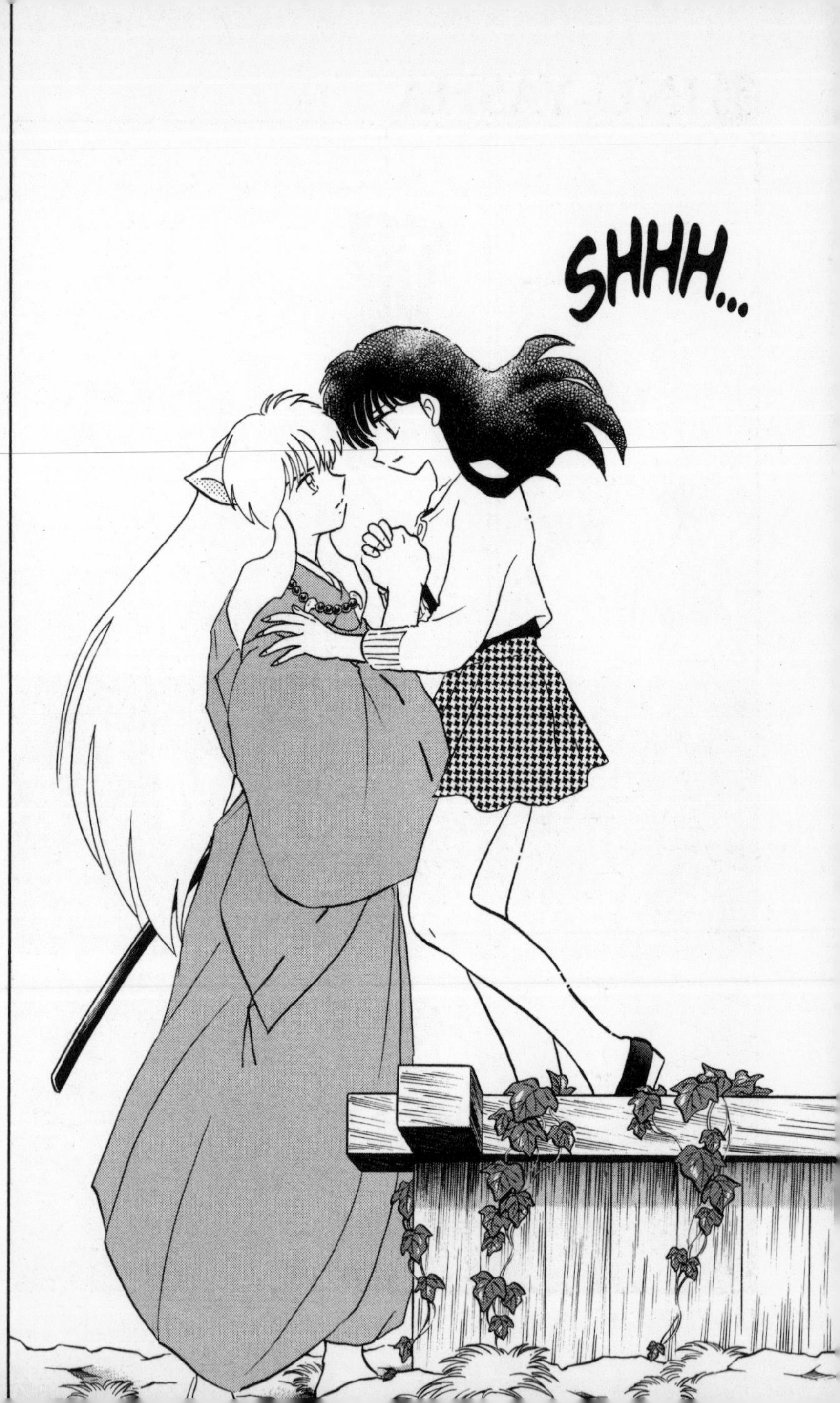
SHHH...

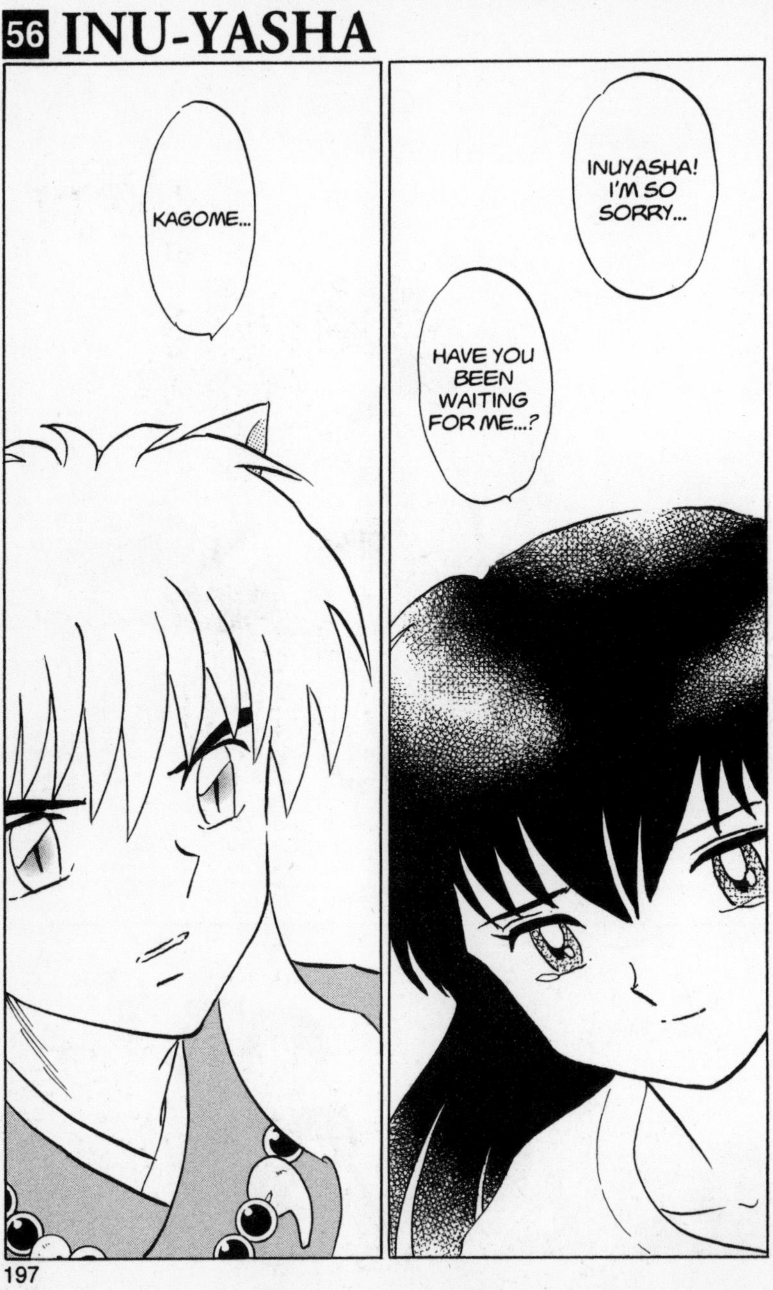
INUYASHA! I'M SO SORRY...
HAVE YOU BEEN WAITING FOR ME...?
KAGOME...

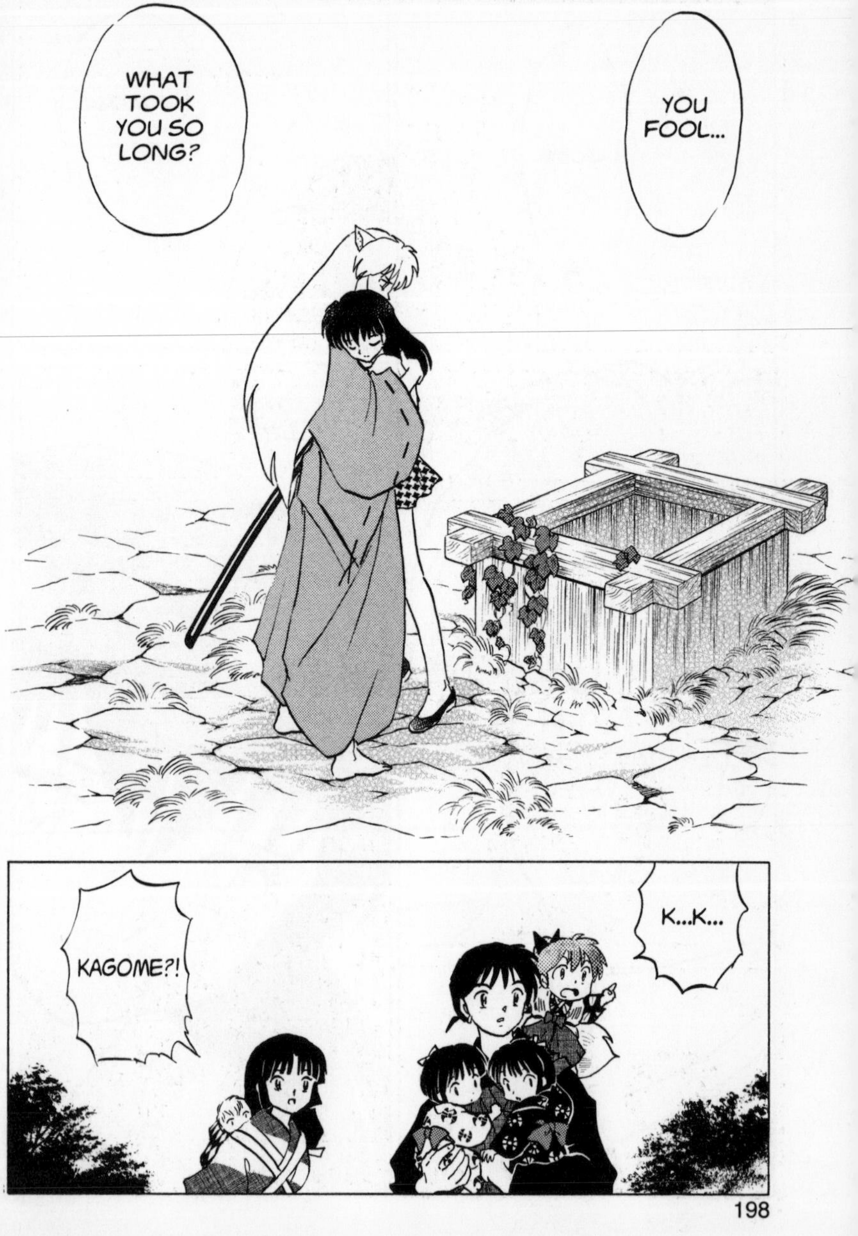
YOU FOOL...
WHAT TOOK YOU SO LONG?
K...K...
KAGOME?!

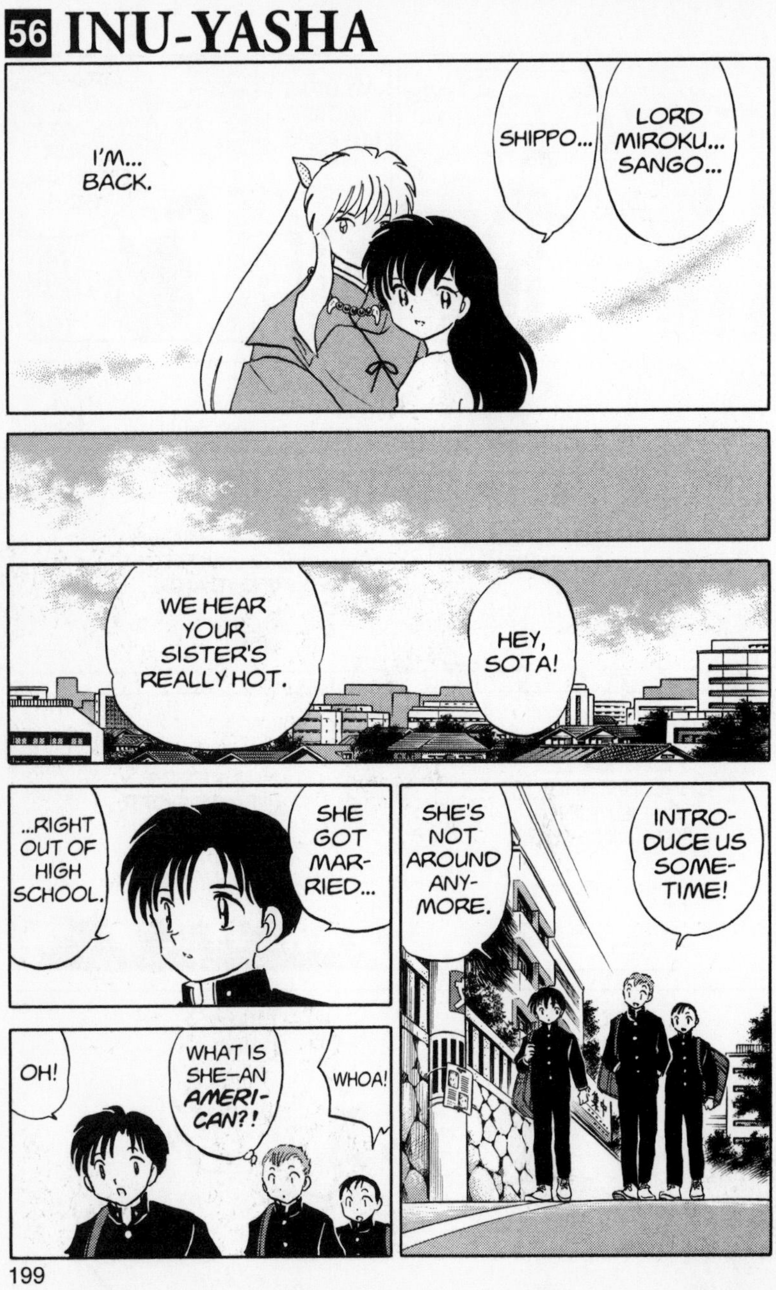
LORD MIROKU... SANGO...
SHIPPO...
I'M... BACK.
HEY, SOTA!
WE HEAR YOUR SISTER'S REALLY HOT.
INTRO-DUCE US SOME-TIME!
SHE'S NOT AROUND ANY-MORE.
SHE GOT MAR-RIED...
...RIGHT OUT OF HIGH SCHOOL.
WHOA!
WHAT IS SHE—AN *AMERI-CAN?!*
OH!

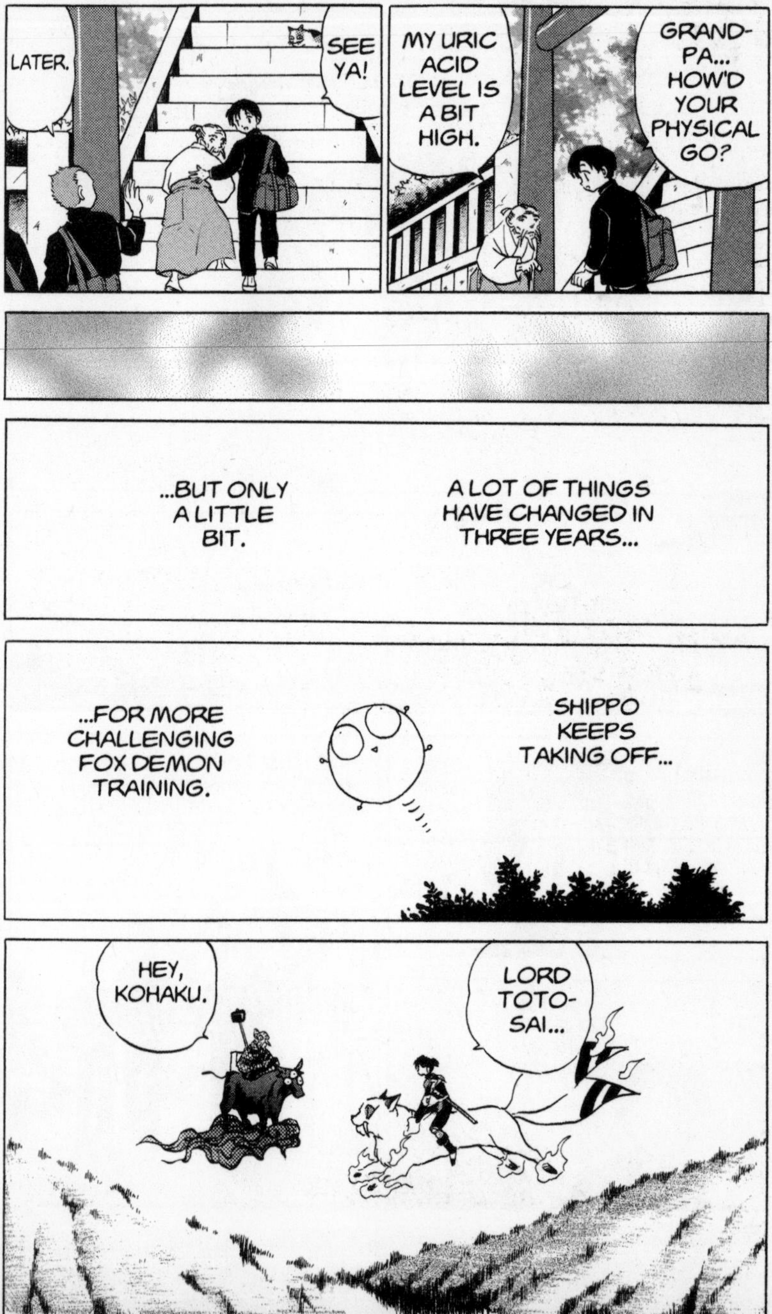
GRAND-PA... HOW'D YOUR PHYSICAL GO?
MY URIC ACID LEVEL IS A BIT HIGH.
SEE YA!
LATER.
A LOT OF THINGS HAVE CHANGED IN THREE YEARS...
...BUT ONLY A LITTLE BIT.
SHIPPO KEEPS TAKING OFF...
...FOR MORE CHALLENGING FOX DEMON TRAINING.
LORD TOTO-SAI...
HEY, KOHAKU.

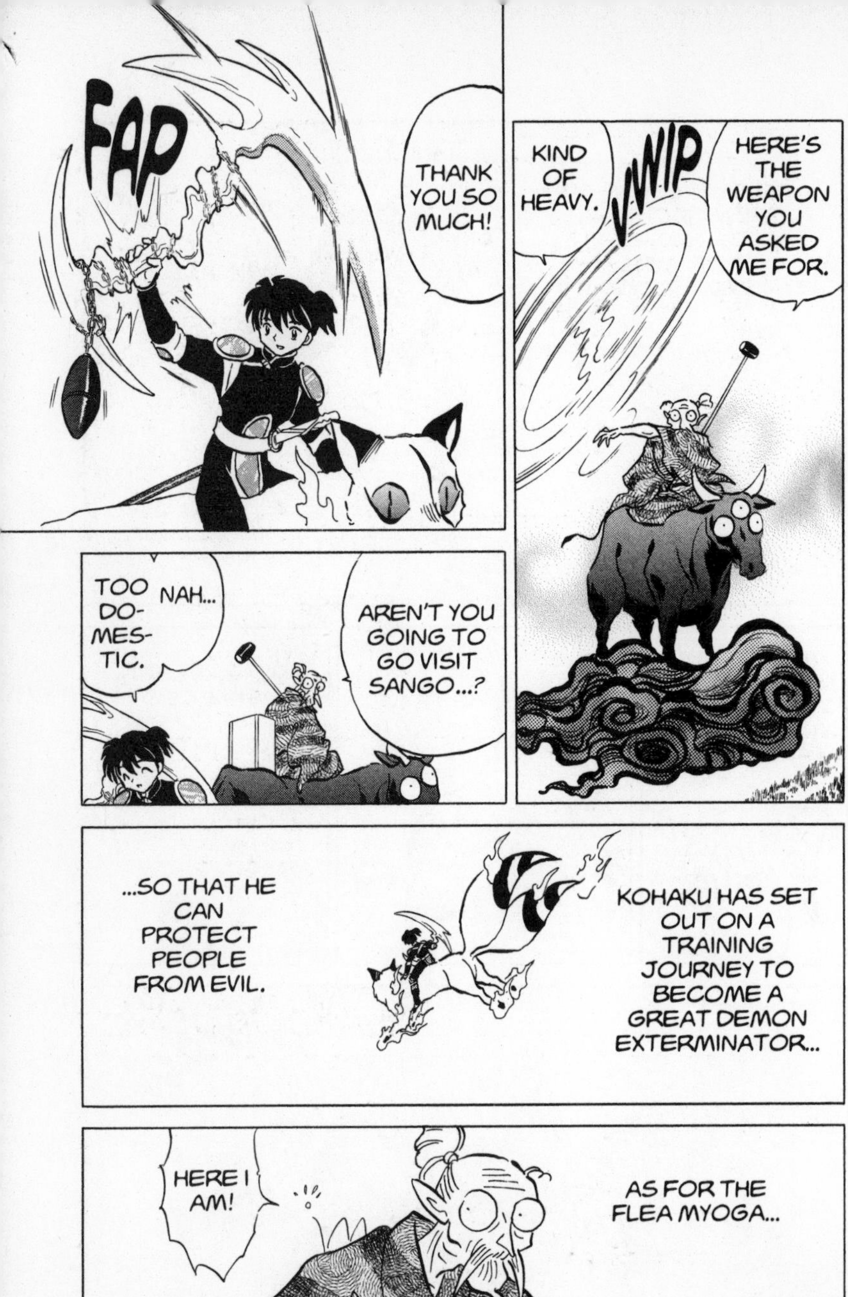
HERE'S THE WEAPON YOU ASKED ME FOR.
VWIP
KIND OF HEAVY.
FAP
THANK YOU SO MUCH!
AREN'T YOU GOING TO GO VISIT SANGO...?
NAH...
TOO DOMESTIC.
KOHAKU HAS SET OUT ON A TRAINING JOURNEY TO BECOME A GREAT DEMON EXTERMINATOR...
...SO THAT HE CAN PROTECT PEOPLE FROM EVIL.
AS FOR THE FLEA MYOGA...
HERE I AM!

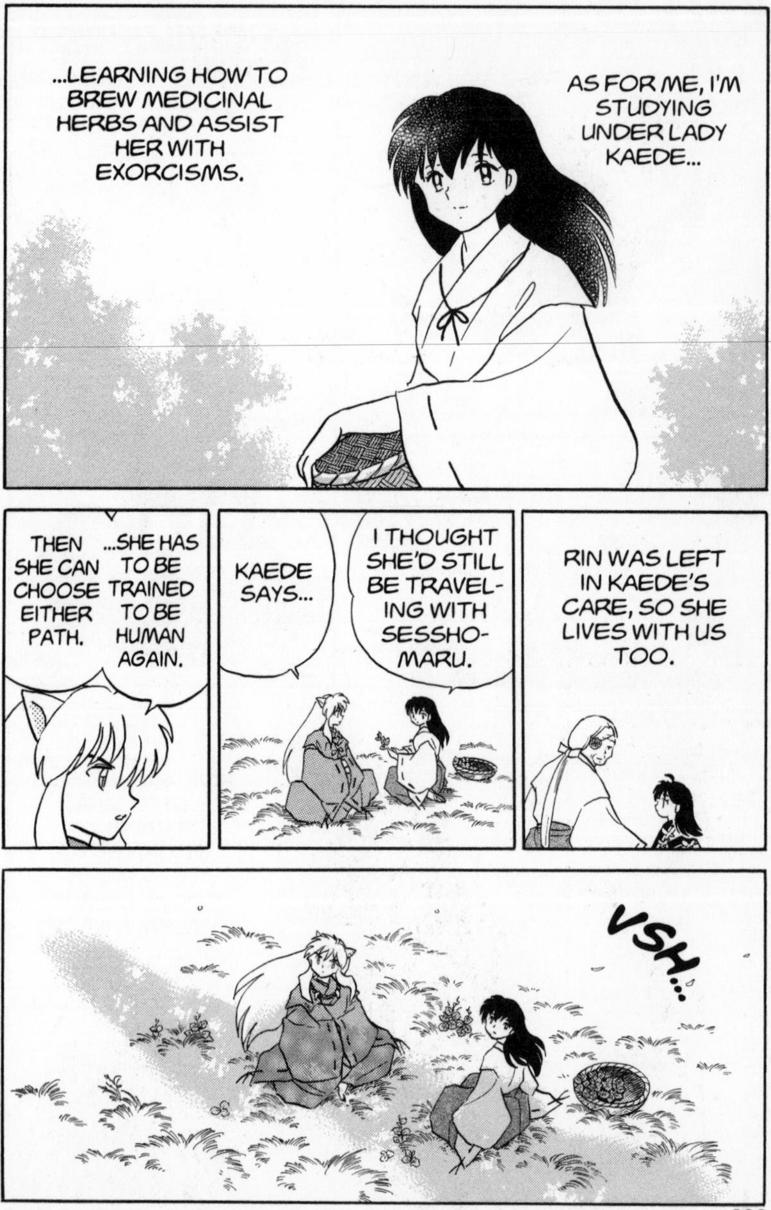
AS FOR ME, I'M STUDYING UNDER LADY KAEDE...
...LEARNING HOW TO BREW MEDICINAL HERBS AND ASSIST HER WITH EXORCISMS.
RIN WAS LEFT IN KAEDE'S CARE, SO SHE LIVES WITH US TOO.
I THOUGHT SHE'D STILL BE TRAVEL-ING WITH SESSHO-MARU.
KAEDE SAYS...
...SHE HAS TO BE TRAINED TO BE HUMAN AGAIN.
THEN SHE CAN CHOOSE EITHER PATH.
VSH...

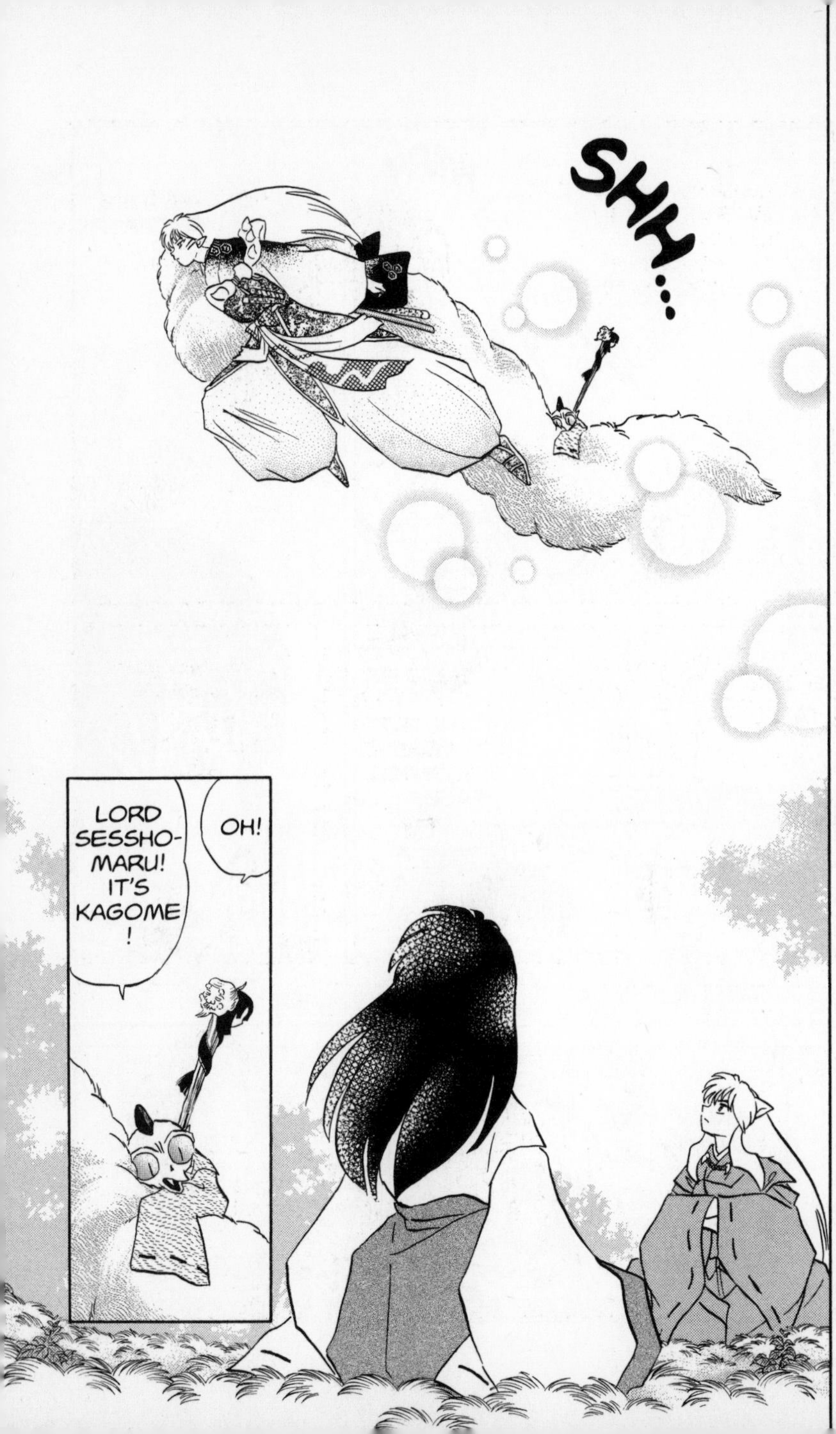
SHH...
OH!
LORD SESSHO-MARU! IT'S KAGOME!

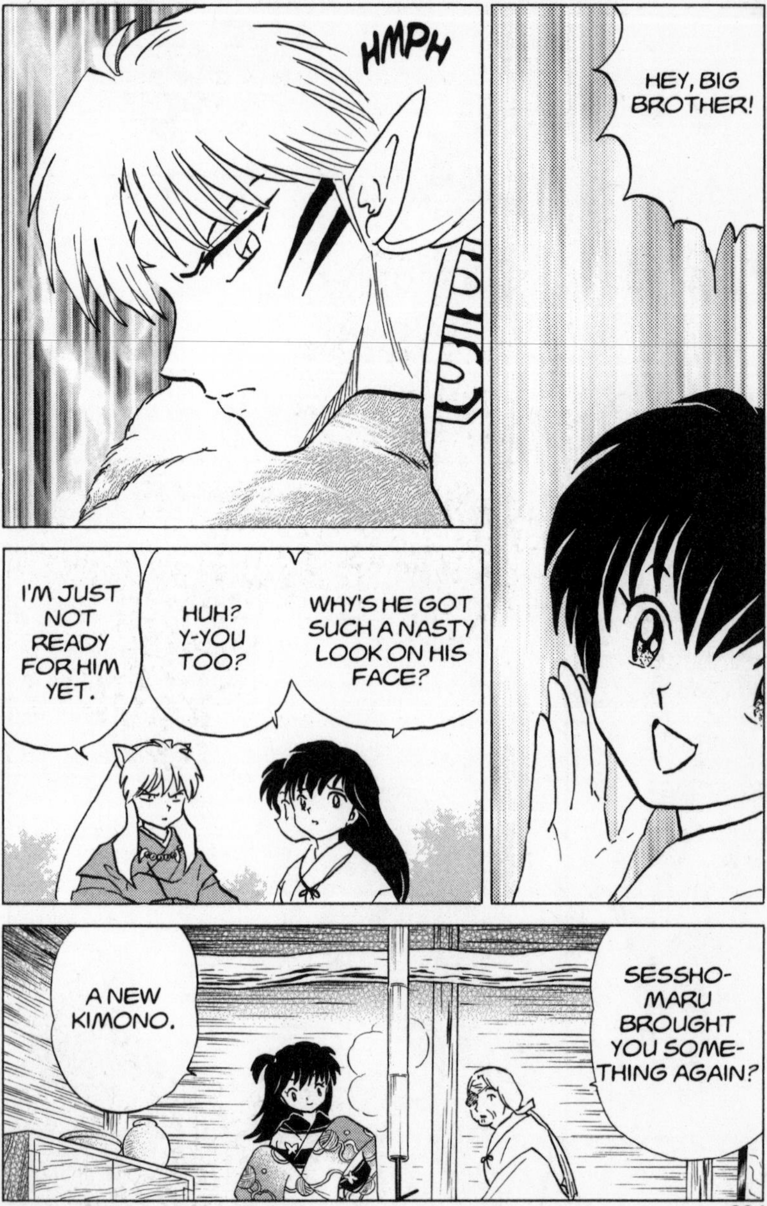
HEY, BIG BROTHER!
HMPH
WHY'S HE GOT SUCH A NASTY LOOK ON HIS FACE?
HUH? Y-YOU TOO?
I'M JUST NOT READY FOR HIM YET.
SESSHO-MARU BROUGHT YOU SOME-THING AGAIN?
A NEW KIMONO.

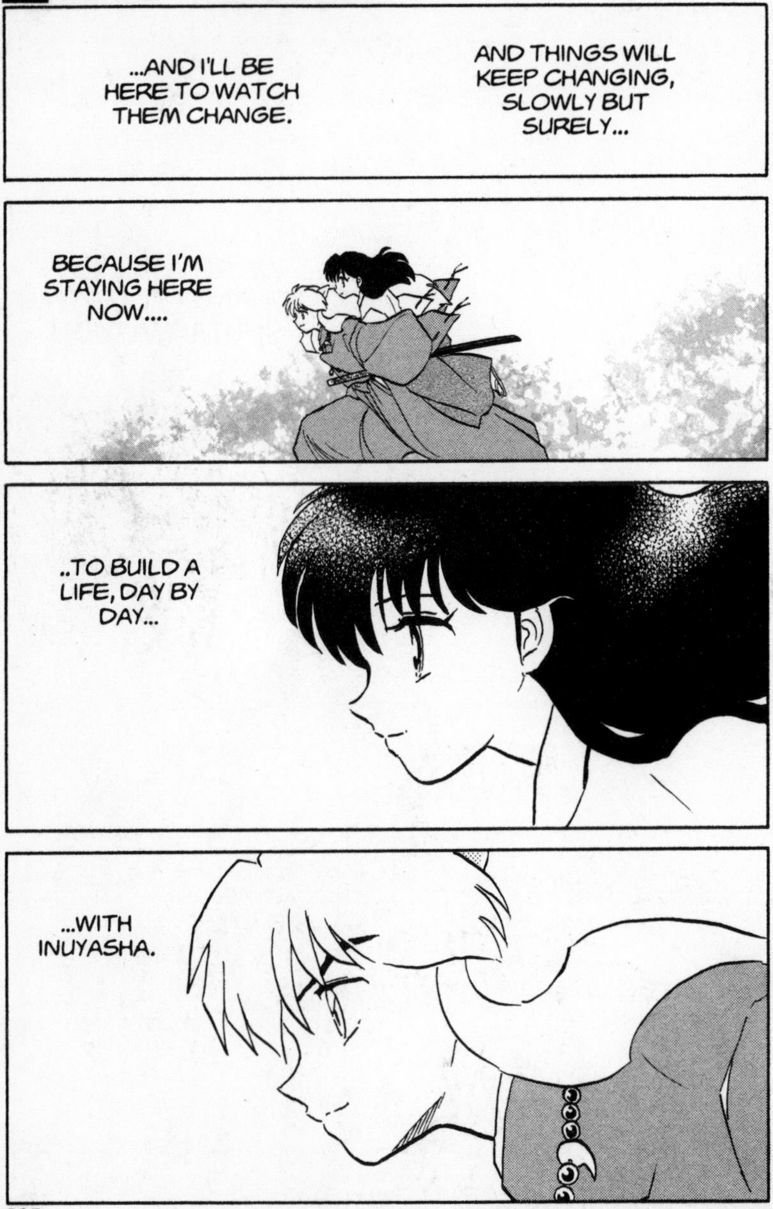
AND THINGS WILL KEEP CHANGING, SLOWLY BUT SURELY...
...AND I'LL BE HERE TO WATCH THEM CHANGE.
BECAUSE I'M STAYING HERE NOW....
..TO BUILD A LIFE, DAY BY DAY...
...WITH INUYASHA.

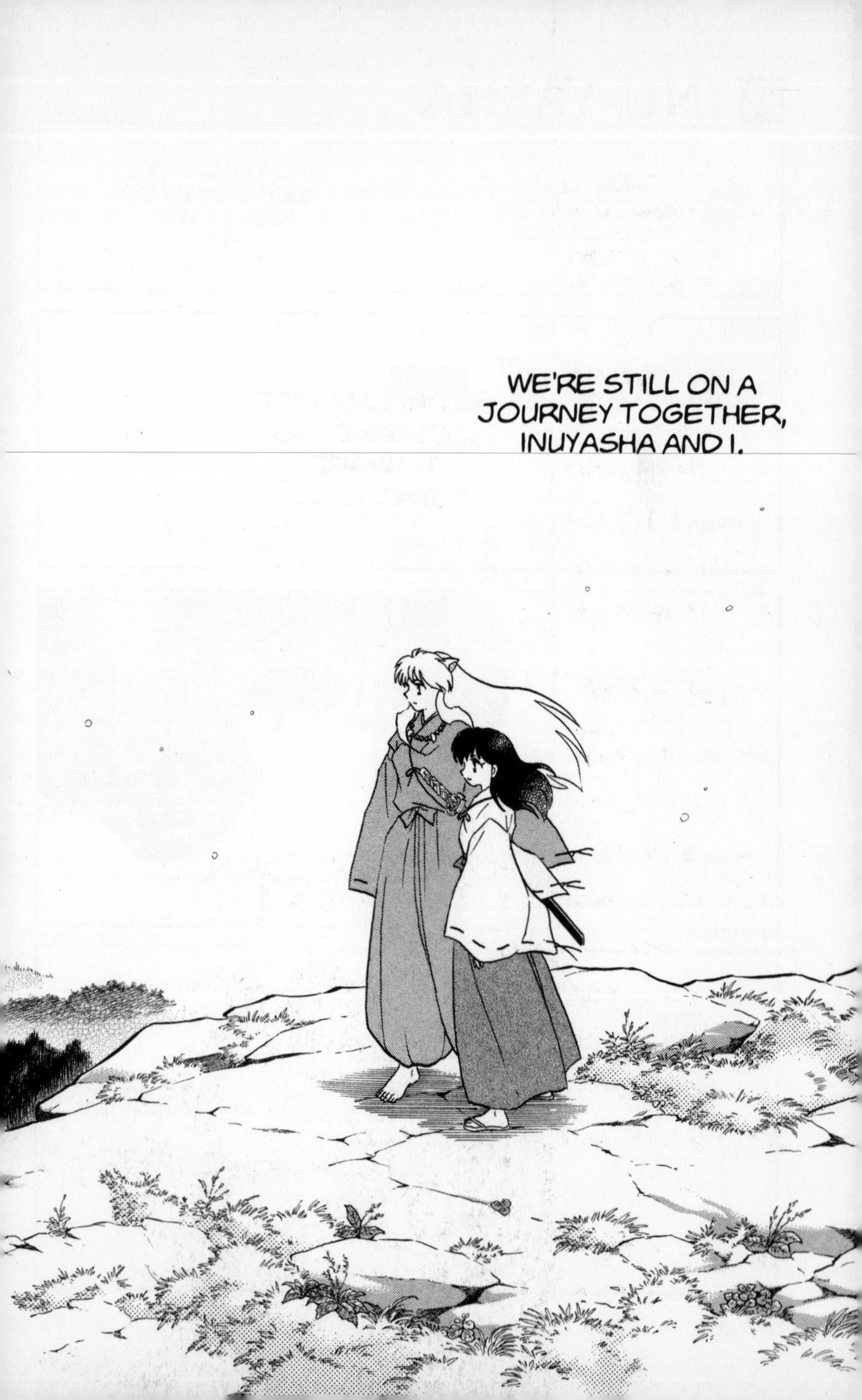
WE'RE STILL ON A
JOURNEY TOGETHER,
INUYASHA AND I.

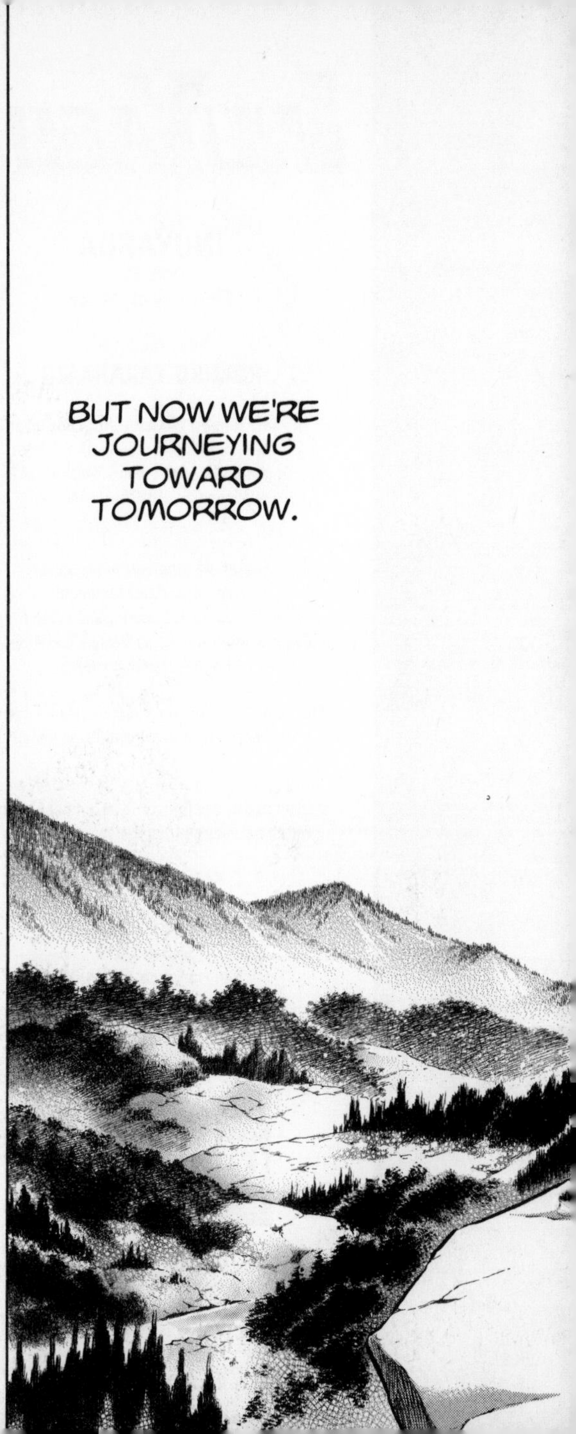
BUT NOW WE'RE JOURNEYING TOWARD TOMORROW.

ACKNOWLEDGEMENTS:

PRODUCTION ASSISTANCE

KEIKO KOBAYASHI

TAKAKO GOTO

KIYOKO KAWANO

RIE KAWANO

TOMOMI ADACHI

HIROKO TANAKA

MOEKO FUJII

NAOKO OSAKA

EDITORIAL STAFF

TOSHIYUKI SENOU

MASAKI NAWATA

KAZUTO YOSHIDA

MASANAO MURAKAMI

TAKASHI KUMAGAI

SYUHOU KONDO

YOSUKE IZUKA

SHUNSUKE MOTEKI

INUYASHA
THE END

INUYASHA

INUYASHA
VOL. 56
Shonen Sunday Edition

Story and Art by
RUMIKO TAKAHASHI

Original Japanese edition "INUYASHA"
published by SHOGAKUKAN Inc.

English Adaptation/Gerard Jones
Translation/Mari Morimoto
Touch-up Art & Lettering/Bill Schuch
Cover & Interior Graphic Design/Yuki Ameda
Editor/Annette Roman

Printed in the U.S.A.

Published by VIZ Media, LLC
P.O. Box 77010
San Francisco, CA 94107

10 9 8 7 6 5 4 3 2 1
First printing, January 2011

RATED T+ FOR OLDER TEEN
PARENTAL ADVISORY
INUYASHA is rated T+ for Older Teen and is recommended for ages 16 and up. This volume contains violence.
ratings.viz.com

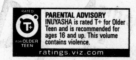

www.viz.com WWW.SHONENSUNDAY.COM